CULTURE
OF STONE

Number Two:
*Texas A&M
University
Anthropology
Series*

Culture
of Stone

Sacred and Profane Uses of Stone among the Dani

O. W. "BUD" HAMPTON

TEXAS A&M UNIVERSITY PRESS
College Station

The paper used in this book meets
the minimum requirements of the American
National Standard for Permanence of Paper
for Printed Library Materials, z39.48-1984.
Binding materials have been chosen for durability.

∞

Library of Congress Cataloging-in-Publication Data

Hampton, O. W., 1928–
  Culture of stone : sacred and profane uses of stone among the Dani
/ O. W. "Bud" Hampton.
    p.   cm. — (Texas A&M University anthropology series ; no. 2)
  Includes bibliographical references and index.
  ISBN 0-89096-870-5
  1. Dani (New Guinea people)—Implements.   2. Dani (New
Guinea people)—Industries.   3. Dani (New Guinea people)—
Religion.   4. Sacred stones—Indonesia—Irian Jaya.   5. Stone
implements—Indonesia—Irian Jaya.   6. Irian Jaya (Indonesia)—
Social life and customs.   I. Title.   II. Series.
DU744.35.D32H35   1999
306'.089'9912—dc21   98-49894
                                                                          CIP

Contents

Illustrations

Tables

The words of the language, as they are written or spoken, do not seem to play any role in my mechanism of thought. The physical entities which seem to serve as elements in thought are certain signs and more or less clear images which can be "voluntarily" reproduced or combined.

—ALBERT EINSTEIN

A Visual Preview of the Culture

1. This Yali man in his twilight years has lived most of his lifetime with tools of stone, wood, bone, and bamboo. He has never known basketry or pottery and will likely die with that same stage of knowledge. He was, in his younger years, a warrior and has battle scars to talk about but now says that he is too old to kill anyone.

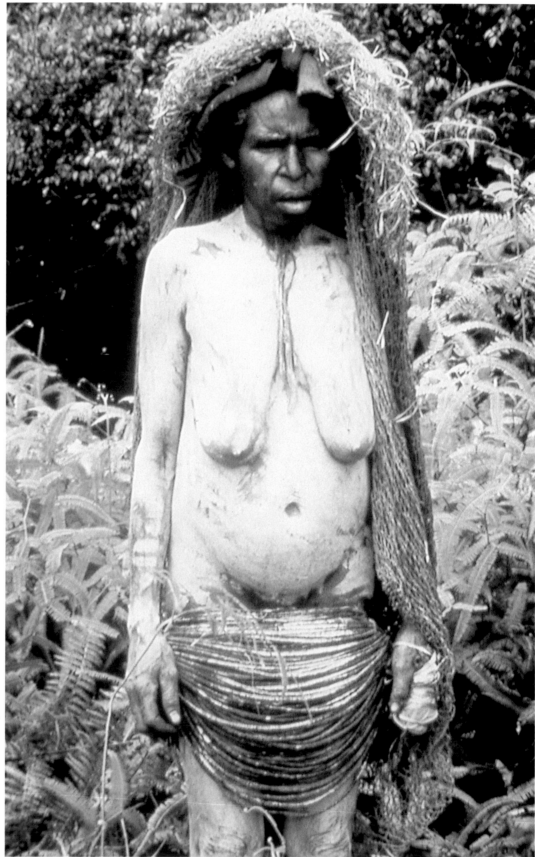

2. At this Dani woman's side hangs her hand, which has been wrapped in banana leaves. One or more joints of a finger or fingers have been chopped off as a sacrifice at a funeral to the ghost of the deceased and to ghosts in general. She has mudded her body with white clay and blotched her face with sooty pig grease. Her utilitarian carrying nets are draped over her head so that the grass in them will hide her from malevolent ghosts while she is in this particularly vulnerable state. From her neck hangs several simple fiber string necklaces, each of which has been ritually infused with supernatural power to protect her vulnerable throat from the entrance of ghosts and her body from harm. She is the epitome of Dani sadness seen after a funeral. At any time a scattering about the cultural landscape of these living female mud-colored symbols of death, grief, and ghost placation are a visual attestation to death in the Highlands.

3. *Often while others are going about their daily routines, the quarrymen and toolmakers are at the quarry sites working with a spirit of camaraderie as they cooperate in team efforts, amid much friendly advice-giving, shouts of joy at accomplishment, and coordinated help to one another.*

4. Fire is used as a quarrying technique as fathers seated on the quarry floor teach their five- to ten-year-old sons to knap and shape rough blade blanks.

5. Numerous kinds and styles of stone tools and symbolic stones are produced at several manufacturing centers from which they travel afar to ultimate users. This particular tool, held by a Yali man, traveled across at least one language boundary from the manufacturing site to get to its ultimate user.

6. *An adult female's hand with ritually sacrificed finger joints makes an unusual cosmetic container for the red juice of the jue fruit, as the woman daubs her face to reportedly protect it from the heat of the noonday sun.*

7. In the upper photograph, a raised cabinet is festooned with sacralized ferns; the area below adorned with religious objects and icons. The standing puluen at the base of the fern-covered cabinet door is an empowered sacred stone with a go-between function between the world of the seen and the world of the unseen. In the fern-covered raised cabinet, very special sacred stones are maintained that furnish the material props for a complex belief system and which exude awesome supernatural power. The smoked and pig grease–rubbed pig mandibles are mementos from sacrificial ceremonies at which pigs were the bloody sacrifice. The mandibles serve as icons for all who see them.

8. *Stored to the right of the sacred cabinet shown in plate 7 is a horizontally hung, specially treated container (top photo) with its contents of seven anointed and touching human mandibles (bottom photo). The maintenance and ritual use of these mandibles makes a revealing statement about the evolutionary uses of human relics for religious purposes and even about the creation of god-power itself.*

Through most of prehistoric time, since the first appearance of stone tools about 2.5 million years ago, stone (rock that has been altered by other than geologic processes) has been the most pervasively preserved artifact with which archaeologists define prehistory. This book was written to present the dynamics of a complete, cultural inventory of stone tools and symbolic stones and its relevance as a *system* at a geographically specific location and particular evolutionary cultural stage, before the use of metals had permeated the system. I happened upon a scene in the Highlands of Irian Jaya that may have relevance to our understanding and interpretation of a part of that prehistory. I hope the book will be of interest not only to academic scholars but also to inquisitive and reflective readers of the general public. It is based on fieldwork that was conducted over a twelve-year period (seventeen field trips, about nineteen months) from May of 1982 through the summer of 1993. The "work" is an outgrowth of my doctoral dissertation (1997) at Texas A&M University but is not a publication of that document.

Of the diverse academic scholars for whom the book was written, it was formatted primarily to assist archaeologists in meeting their *greatest* continuing challenge of inferring the correct behavior for time and place that was associated with static stone artifacts and their spatial arrangements as present at archaeological sites. The ultimate solution to the challenge would, of course, be to step into a time machine for transportation back into the prehistoric, *observe what was really going on*, return to the present and write up ethnographies. Since we cannot enjoy that experience of observing the statics of the archaeological objects with the associated dynamics of simultaneous behavior in the prehistory, archaeologists *must* develop their ideas for assemblage identification and

associated behavioral inferences from recorded history or the study of present-day behavior.

The sources for the application by archaeologists of the principle of the present as a key to the past are written histories, ethnographies written by anthropologists, experimental archaeology, and ethnoarchaeology. Ethnoarchaeology is the study of behavior associated with material goods in present-day cultural situations to answer archaeological questions about the past, with archaeologists, not anthropologists, planning and doing the ethnographic fieldwork. Ethnoarchaeology is now a proper subdiscipline under the broad umbrella of anthropology. Louis Binford, the most visible proponent and spokesperson for the scientific movement "New Archaeology" felt so strongly about the ethnoarchaeological approach in his studies of stone tools in the central desert of Australia that he stated of his own work that, "If understood in great detail, it would give us a kind of Rosetta Stone: a way of "translating" the static material stone tools found on an archaeological site into the vibrant life of a group of people who in fact left them there" (Binford 1983:24). However, since human culture has an almost infinite capacity for diversity, perhaps there are few models with archetypal application of the type that Binford suggested. Functionalists might contest my cautionary comment. Notwithstanding, I posit, and most archaeologists would agree, that to enhance the reliability of inferences made about past behavior from behaviors associated with material goods observed in the present, we must pay *careful* attention to constructs of the *multiple contexts* in which material goods occur—both those in the present and those in the past of our present-past research method.

This book was written with the foregoing in mind. As an ethnography, it focuses on the stone artifact and the ways that stone goods related to structure and event and as active media in the construction of meaning and of cultural systems. In one sense the book is an archaeological anthropology written to contribute to the efforts of archaeologists writing anthropological archaeologies.

In the introductory chapter, the various evolutionary, cultural, and environmental contexts in which material goods occur are presented. The chapter was written to first provide an overview of the setting (evolutionary, cultural, and environmental) in which the stones were manufactured and used; then to be an accessible ready reference for any reader to glean details of "context" to suit individual interests and projects. I continue to believe that details are the stuff of which the most valuable ethnographies for archaeologists are made. Following Christopher Hawkes' (1954) "ladder of reliability," where those domains of knowledge are reliable and secure, we have no problem, but as is true in more cases than not, our ability to improve the reliability of our inferences about past behavior is strictly dependent upon our ability to both recognize and understand the controlling contexts that were at play with the static artifacts of the archaeological record and that are at play in the present dynamic situation from which the behavioral models are derived. To be able to stretch and infer more complex, far-reaching behavior from our present-past methodology, we must be able to expand and tighten contextual controls by identifying the objects at play within as many controlling contexts as possible. Many— perhaps most—of the disagreements between archaeologists about their interpretations stem from misunderstandings of contextual controls.

Subsequent to chapter 1, descriptions of the static stone objects are presented, just as they might be described were they found at archaeological sites, followed by associated behavioral data, concepts, and ideas to help archaeologists analyze their own work and with which to create inferences of behavior for their own applications. The complete cycle of the quarrying, manufacture, trade, and uses of stones is presented, not only of the profane but of the sacred. Specific questions that confront archaeologists every day are addressed: What stimulated production? Who owns quarries and has the rights to quarry stones? What is the role of women in quarrying and production of stone tools? How are tool and symbolic stones manufactured? How long does it take to make a particular tool? Who establishes the value of different kinds of finished tools? How do processed stone goods get from the quarries to users? What kinds of trade mechanisms are at work. Do stone trade networks function across language, political, and religious boundaries? Does the distribution of stone tools correlate with language boundaries? Within production and user systems, are there predictable relations between profane utilitarian tool blades and sacred symbolic stones and sacred tools? To approach this last question, the cultural flow of stones from the profane to the sacred is presented. The creation of sacred objects is explicitly explained and visually shown. This behavior may have archetypal application to our understanding of certain assemblages that are present in the archaeological record.

I visualize the mechanism of application of my work by others to be one of a thought process rather than, perhaps, the more often used fitting and measuring of behavioral models into and against archaeological data. This is not to say that the latter will not or should not be done.

When I first entered the Grand Valley of the Baliem at Wamena (May 1982; fig. P.1), I had no preconceived idea that sixteen years later a book such as this one would be one of the results. On that first trip I walked out from Wamena with a small group of anthropologically interested expatriates who lived in Indonesia to spend a week moving about the area of the warring fields of the traditional ritual wars that had been so dramatically brought to worldwide attention by the classical anthropological film *Dead Birds* (Gardner 1963) and the books *Under the Mountain Wall* (Matthiessen 1962), *Gardens of War: Life and Death in New Guinea Stone Age* (Gardner and Heider 1968), and *The Dugum Dani: A Papaun Culture in the Highlands of West New Guinea* (Heider 1970).

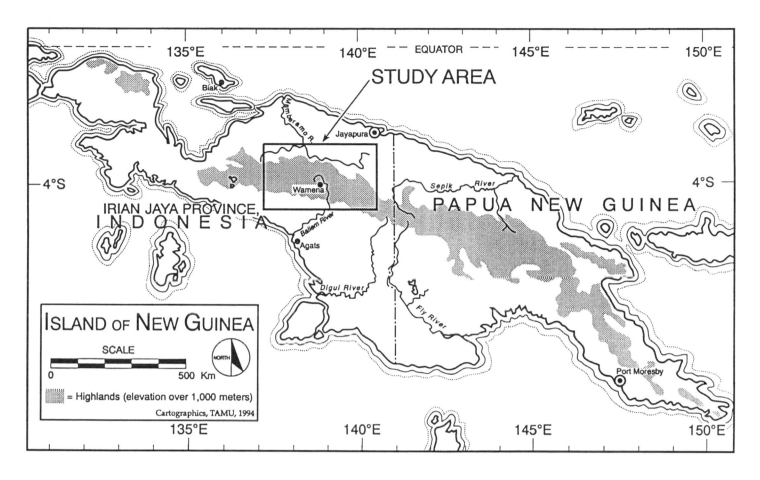

Fig. P.1. *The study area within the province of Irian Jaya, Indonesia*

Those early workers (Robert Gardner in Gardner and Heider 1968:xv; Karl Heider 1991:25, 57; and Denise O'Brien, 1966:31) had defined the Dani of the ritual warfare epoch as being at a "Neolithic Stone Age" cultural stage of evolution. I wanted to identify and locate yet-living individuals who had been photographed by the Harvard-Peabody Expedition to determine the feasibility of commencing to record those peoples' social and mental journeys (longitudinal studies) of acculturation from the documented Stone Age baseline into the prevailing Indonesian society. On that first trip, Sjamsuarni Sjam, a self-made explorer-anthropologist from the island of Sumatra, Indonesia, and one of the few people who had ever lived for a period of time with the Dugum Dani, led us to meet Wali (alt. name Um'ue) and Pua. Wali was the Highlander who had the courage to step forward as a young leader from his traditional group on a day in February of 1961 and accept Robert Gardner and the entire Harvard-Peabody New Guinea Expedition for

the duration of their work (Gardner and Heider 1968:6–7; and Heider 1991:5–7). (Wali went on to become Karl Heider's primary informant for his doctoral ethnography as reported in the book *Dugum Dani* [Heider 1970:x, 87] and then an important informant of mine.) Pua was the swineherd young boy featured in the film *Dead Birds* and documented with photographs by Matthiessen (1962: Tukum, photographs 71, 72, 73, 74) and Gardner and Heider (1968:20, 65). On subsequent trips I met others who had been photographed by the Harvard-Peabody group, including the powerful warrior and leader Gutelu (alt. spelling Kurelu); Hanomuak, who remains a close friend and confidant of Wali's; Siba, a nephew of Wali's; Limo; Husuk; Yeke; Asuk; Keaklkelk; Alorao; and wives and children of some of these men. The players could be identified. As far as they were concerned, longitudinal studies seemed feasible.

But during my early visits outside the environs of Wamena to more remote Highlands areas, I discovered that it *was* still possible to observe and live with people who utilized a stone tool technology and who relied on traditional products for their daily lives. Scattered pockets of unaffected contemporary "Stone Age" people merged almost imperceptibly with neighbors who were in various stages of acculturation (including the uses of steel axes, machetes, and shovels) into an Indonesian society. Some of the Highlanders remained among the most isolated people in the world, protected from more accessible, but still often little-known neighbors and modern outsiders by a harsh terrain. Remnant cultural facets of the Stone Age could be seen everywhere, in varying degrees of change, relative to scattered different times of first-contact (mostly mid-1900s) with modern outsiders, but more to scattered points of influence from government and outsider missionary activity. (For a history of first-contact and research by others see Hampton 1997:9–14.)

The possibility for a broad-based, holistic ethnography, with detailed attention paid to behavior associated with traditional cultural artifacts was indeed provocative. Time was of the essence. The opportunity to learn from even isolated pockets of aboriginals in their natural ecological setting was diminishing rapidly. In one sense, I felt, as Robert Gardner (in Gardner and Heider 1968), like a conservator of a passing age who could and should document all that was possible. I quickly expanded my own field-work horizons to use a descriptive, cultural holistic approach in a broad-based, material-behavior-oriented ethnography, which would pay attention to detail, stress visual anthropology with the medium of colored slide photography, and use sound recordings. Behavior associated with all kinds of material goods—not just stone tools and symbolic stones—was documented. Details of acculturation were pointedly observed and recorded. Most of the longitudinal observations, as originally planned, however, will have to be the subject of other venues, as the focus of this book is on the role of stone goods in the Highlands at that fragile moment of a people, as Margaret Mead said (in Gardner and Heider

1968:ix), "trembling on the edge of change" before their Stone Age culture becomes extinct.

Methods

Field techniques included still photography (over 20,000 slides), sound recordings, personal observations, and the use of informants in formal as well as informal situations. From the outset I knew that I wanted to use a holistic descriptive approach (Malinowski 1922:xvi), pay attention to detail (Boasian "detailism"), and stress visual anthropology with the medium of colored slide photography. Data were gathered by being at times an unobtrusive observer and at other times a participant. Besides living with and interviewing the indigenous people in their ecological settings, I conducted other interviews with my own teams of indigenous helpers put together over the years, and Indonesian government officials, including the provincial governor, foreign and Irianese Christian missionaries, and colleagues who have worked elsewhere in Irian Jaya. From time to time, questionnaires were used to guide discussions.

Each field season I went back to areas where the Highlanders already knew me and also explored new territory. Wamena was logistically the hub (fig. P.1). This approach worked well. As the people became familiar with me from repeated visits, some came to accept my presence matter-of-factly during their many activities. Also, each year I was able to recheck data and ask expanded, more complicated questions of the same people, which lead to the accumulation of reasonably in-depth knowledge and helped build a solid base of information. I was learning from those people who were beginning to understand what I was trying to do as well as from people whom I had never seen before.

As I extended my research into new geographical areas, I followed a simple but time-consuming format: (1) spread the word of my regional presence by local couriers to community leaders in advance of my local arrival; (2) call on local headmen before questioning or photographing; (3) present a thoughtful but simple and inexpensive gift to the headman of each hamlet in which I desired to stay; and

(4) be willing to spend the time to visit, be concerned with local problems, become known to the people, and, most importantly, move at the headman's pace. I made it a practice to always carry my camera, show it, talk about it, and let those interested look through the viewfinder. Usually the headman, his council of advisers, and various relatives and close friends would become quite interested in me and what I was doing. The headman and some of his council, as the controllers of information, usually became my most-used informants in each area. I always obtained permission from a headman well in advance of talking to local women. Through the added process of being careful to keep the men informed, I was able to work in natural situations with women as primary informants.

I would validate information with follow-up queries with more than one independent informant. Often I would attempt verification of data from people with different political and geographic perspectives. Reliable informants could, in this way, usually be identified. In one sense I used data published by anthropologists who had done mostly doctoral research at different locations in the Highlands as "informant information" (Broekhuijse [1967], Heider [1970], Koch [1967], Larson [1987], O'Brien [1969], Peters [1975], Pospisil to the west outside of my research area [1956]) (Hampton 1997:12–14). I felt that this research by trained professional anthropologists gave me geographically scattered points of grounded information, against which to check my field-derived data and from which to add to my base of working information. I evaluated the validity of the other researchers' data just as I did that from indigenous informants. None of these previous researchers had focused on aspects of stone tool technology. (You should be appraised, however, of recent references to stone tools in the Highlands from work that was mostly done when my field work was nearing completion and which did not play a role in my research: Clark [1991], Ligabue [1991], Toth, Clark, and Ligabue [1992], and Petrequin and Petrequin [1988].)

To get from area to area, Mission Aviation Fellowship small aircraft were chartered to fly me and two or three of my Irianese team of assistants to remote landing strips at missionary outposts. From those outposts, I trekked through areas of interest to reach specific isolated habitation centers to do holistic work and sometimes to explore for caves and rock quarries and to analyze hypothetical trade routes.

Logistics were rarely simple as we often had to arrange for porters who spoke different languages and to trade off porters as we passed from one territory into the next, where the indigenous people were sometimes unfriendly to outside porters. Much preplanning was involved. Always there were unforeseen circumstances.

During the entire Irian Jaya project, I sometimes worked alone but sometimes with my own teams of indigenous helpers plus one Indonesian logistics person who had been born and raised on another island of the Indonesian archipelago. For me, it took aloneness and concentration to catch perceived interactions between the *seen* entities and the numerous *unseen* entities (ghosts and spirits) of the Highlands cultural systems, and to plan ahead and keep up with the work on a daily basis.

Communication Problems

During the course of the project I traversed across or conducted research within twelve different adjacent-living language groups within the overall study area. From east to west, these groups consist of the Una, Kimyal (two dialects), Yali (three dialects), Hupla, Silimo, Dani (three dialects), Walak, Western Dani, Nduga, Wano, Duvle, and Damal. By Western standards, these are not easy languages to learn. My problem was twofold: (1) How to develop word lists and at least some degree of proficiency in the indigenous languages, and (2) How to develop teams of indigenous co-workers who could move about safely within this maze of languages and be able to communicate satisfactorily to help me get the job done. Overall success of the project hung in the balance.

Communication with my teams of helpers in Irian Jaya and the indigenous people whom we encountered was the single most difficult and continuing problem of the entire project.

Other difficulties, such as contending with local political situations, sometimes health and accident problems, or interesting terrain situations, focused my attention only from time to time. The drama and difficulty of those kinds of problems were soon forgotten; but not so the problem of verbal communication, which was continuous. With elapsed time, nighttime work, and study done while away from the Highlands with missionary linguists, my word lists and a degree of understanding of the languages grew.

Rudy Willem (Indonesian) of Sentani annually put together a team of five to seven Irianese assistants, some of whom could communicate not only in their own local language but, with varying degrees of ability, also in one or more other indigenous languages or dialects as well as Bahasa Indonesian. This team was the core that helped with local translations when I was among the Dani and Western Dani. In areas away from Dani and Western Dani language influence, other Irianese of multilanguage ability who were acceptable to us, and we to them, had to be procured. In such situations our porters also usually had to be changed because of rivalry between different language groups.

Many headmen did not want certain of my team members around during private discussions and would designate who, if any, of my people could be present at private or "secret" conversations. When none were welcome, I was sometimes dependent on the headmen to provide local young people with bilingual language ability to assist.

Many of my primary informants, including Wali (alt. name Um'ue) Wilil, Hanomuak, Kusa, and Pua of the Dugum Dani Neighborhood (mid–Grand Valley dialect of Dani), always thought that I was completely conversant in their language. They would individually come to me with information that they thought of great importance or just something that they wanted to pass on or talk about and speak as if I were understanding *every* word. Unfortunately I was not. Even under the best circumstances of communication, I would often feel disposed to check the same material with another source or again at a later date with the same informant. Such conversations might even be repeated over a time span of three years. Repetition led to clarity and greater elucidation, as well as to the laborious correction of field notes because either I, an informant, or sometimes a translator had misunderstood part of a conversation. Because aural comprehension exceeds speaking ability, I was sometimes able to catch mistakes of fact being made by my translators.

This project would not have been completed without the assistance of *many* people. Their diverse backgrounds make a strong statement about the importance of a multi-disciplinary effort in an endeavor such as this one.

I express my thanks to President Suharto and the Indonesian government for allowing me to live as an expatriate resident of Indonesia (1981–84) and then for allowing me to return on an annual basis for field seasons of cultural observations and still photography. I wish to thank Governor Hindom of the Indonesian province of Irian Jaya, his successor, and the Heads of Army and Police for their early and continued cooperation. After I moved from Indonesia, it was, at times, arduous, and sometimes not possible, to obtain police papers *(surat jalan)* to allow my presence in certain remote areas of the Highlands, but I was able to continue to work with this inconvenience and complete the project.

I acknowledge special thanks to Sjamsuarni Sjam (deceased), the female, self-made explorer-anthropologist who first introduced me to the Grand Valley of the Baliem. Sjam and I shared a fascination and mutual efforts in trying to "get inside" the mind-set of the indigenous inhabitants of remote areas in both Borneo and Irian Jaya. I was *much* saddened by Sjam's untimely death in 1993 of stomach cancer and will miss exploring the contemporary "Stone Age" mind-set with her.

Without reservation I would like to forthrightly acknowledge the Highlanders of Irian Jaya who had the patience to deal with my inquisitiveness and invasion of their private and social lives. I cannot thank them enough.

For linguistic and other informational support and for personal friendliness, I would like to acknowledge and thank specific Christian missionaries in Irian Jaya: (1) of the Christian Missionary Alliance (CMA)—Tom Bozeman (deceased), Myron Bromley (Ph.D. anthropology, linguistics), Helen Ellenberger, Nina Fowler, Don and Alice Gibbons, Ted and Judith Heglund, Gordon Larson (Ph.D. anthropology), Jim and Carol McDonald, Eddy Susanto, and Pat Worsley; (2) of the Unevangelized Fields Mission (UFM)—Leon Dillenger, James Larkin, and Char Murdock (details, Hampton 1997:v, vi).

I acknowledge the Mission Aviation Fellowship (MFA) for furnishing flights in their small Cessna aircraft to those scattered, small landing strips that afforded me access to many remote areas. I especially thank pilot Rick Willems for safely negotiating his plane on my behalf in and out of some particularly tricky spots.

I thank many on the staff of the Summer Institute of Linguistics (SIL) for their generous time in helping me with local languages, especially Dick and Margaret Kroneman (of SIL), and also the Netherlands Reformation Church for allowing me to use the church's guest facility at Langda while I was conducting research there.

My sincere appreciation is expressed to Dr. E. V. Vriend, the Dutch medical surgeon at the Indonesian hospital in Wamena, for many of his insights about the Dani and Western Dani. Also, I thank Dr. Tigor Ceribon and staff members at the Wamena hospital for receiving me on an annual basis to discuss in a relaxed fashion various matters relating to the health and life expectancy of the indigenous people.

Year after year Rudy Willem of Sentani was able to handle logistics and get me into locales of my choice. I want to acknowledge this assistance and thank Rudy for his continuing help. Our local Highlands Papuan Dani and Western Dani team of Winoco, Libarek, Obet, Elly, Mathius, Julius, and others, and in the latter two years, the Melanesian, Hengke, from the lowlands Lake Sentani area have patiently listened to my same questions, repeated year after year, and still responded directly or in translation chores with others without irritation and who joined me willingly to transport loads of gear into some unusual situations. Some of these men suffered injuries from falls and illnesses on my behalf, and they have my everlasting gratitude. The times of appreciated assistance from other Highlands people for short periods of time are too numerous to itemize.

I thank Frederick W. Lange, curator of anthropology, University of Colorado Museum, for his helpful review (in 1986) of the results of my field work for the period May 1982 through March 1984 (while I was residing in Indonesia) and for his comments in preparation for further field studies. Fred kindly continued to offer helpful comments through the period of active field work (1993). I acknowledge and thank Peter W. Van Arsdale (cultural and applied anthropologist, Denver University and Colorado Mental Health Department) for his enthusiasm and consultation regarding my annual field work for the period 1988–93, and for his detailed helpful editorial comments on the resultant dissertation (1993–97). Peter had completed his doctoral dissertation at the University of Colorado after living with the Asmat, in the adjoining south lowlands to my Highlands study area in the early 1970s. During that period, Peter made first-contact with a band of indigenous lowland personnel. Before the field season of 1987, Peter perceptively alerted me to a key article on stone as a cultural factor in the Highlands by his deceased acquaintance, a geographer R. D. Mitton (1972). Mitton's article led to my on-the-ground research regarding stone patterns (as seen from the air) as potential archaeological sites.

I thank Vaughn W. Bryant, Jr., palynologist, paleoethnobotanist and department head of anthropology, Texas A&M University, for continually and patiently listening and commenting on my reviews of annual field work and for encouraging my longitudinal and comprehensive approach (1988–97). I thank Thomas R. Hester, director of the Texas Archaeological Research Laboratory, University of Texas, Austin, for likewise being an encouraging listener

to annual results of field work from 1990 and always sharing with me articles pertinent to my work. Tom first started pushing for publication of my field reports in 1991. I acknowledge and thank Harry J. Shafer, professor of anthropology (specialty, archaeology), Texas A&M University, for his enthusiasm and support from late 1991. Toward the end of the project, in the spring of 1992 (before that year's annual field work), Harry Shafer and Tom Hester spent a good deal of collaborative effort formulating, from an archaeologist's perspective, a list of questions of interest to Shafer and Hester regarding the manufacture, trade, and uses of stone tools. I presumed they felt that my data would furnish ethnographically derived alternatives—a testing ground, if you will—for behavioral inferences (and theory) of the observed archaeological record.

In the fall of 1993 my doctoral advisory committee was formed at Texas A&M University, with Vaughn Bryant and Harry Shafer as co-chairs. Full membership finally grew to include Vaughn M. Bryant, Jr., Thomas R. Hester, Marvin Rowe (professor of chemistry, Texas A&M University), Harry J. Shafer, D. Gentry Steele (professor of anthropology, physical anthropologist, and zoarchaeologist Texas A&M University), and Peter W. Van Arsdale. I thank the entire committee for their support.

Professor James L. Munoz, Ph.D. Geology, University of Colorado; R. Jeffrey Swope, Ph.D. candidate in geology (1992–94); and Elizabeth Medlin, graduate student in geology (1992–94) at the University of Colorado, are thanked and acknowledged for their petrographic analyses of various tool blades, symbolic stones, and rock quarry material. I have relied heavily on their data for rock and mineral identification. Renald N. Guillemette, Ph.D. associate research scientist at Texas A&M University department of geology electron microprobe laboratory is thanked for his mineralogical and rock analyses of the Langda-Sela knives and for comparative analyses of knives collected from different locales in the eastern part of the research area. Dr. Thomas T. Tieh, professor of geology at Texas A&M University, is acknowledged for additional consultation on rock mineralogy within the research area. Dr. R. R. Berg, (a longtime friend) professor emeritus, geology, Texas A&M University, is thanked for facilitating the mineralogic work at Texas A&M University.

I want to acknowledge John E. Dockall and William A. Dickens, graduate students at Texas A&M University, for their ready help with my lithics research. Being with both of these students was not only a real pleasure but a valuable learning experience. John Dockall has been awarded a Ph.D. in archaeology, and Bill Dickens is on a trajection toward a Ph.D.

W. C. Smith of cartographics in the geography department at Texas A&M is acknowledged for his excellent work in transposing my map figures and some of my sketches into computer graphic format. I thank Helen C. Dewolf at Texas A&M University for her expert assistance in helping me with illustrations and sharing with my wife, Fleur Hampton, techniques of artifact illustration. I thank Fleur and Debbie O. Hutchinson for their talented work with both the stone tool and symbolic stone pen and ink illustrations. R. Paul Firnhaber is acknowledged for his consultation and assistance with studio photography.

I want to thank several people who read and commented so helpfully on the manuscript: Richard Gould, Brown University, USA; Brian Hayden, Simon Fraser University, Canada; Payson Sheets, University of Colorado, Boulder, USA; and an unidentified reader of the original, rather lengthy manuscript. I acknowledge and thank the University of Texas Press for orienting me to the book publication process and, of course, Texas A&M University Press for their sponsorship. I cannot thank Gentry Steele and the staff of Texas A&M University Press enough for their roles in the publication of this book.

Jody E. Trenckmann is acknowledged and thanked for her work at the computer to produce the manuscript.

CULTURE

OF STONE

Anthropology's greatest and most lasting contribution to the social sciences lies in its recognition that context [interrelated conditions in which something exists or occurs] is everything in explaining variability and change in human behavior. The credibility of anthropology depends on its ability to control for the context in which various kinds of human behavior occur, and this is equally true of archaeological attempts to explain variability and change in past human behavior. It is also true that when disagreements arise in archaeological interpretation, they usually spring from different assumptions about what constitutes the relevant context: Not all archaeologists can agree on what contextual variables to control for, with the result that there may be widely divergent explanations for the same archaeological assemblages.

—RICHARD A. GOULD, *Recovering the Past*

CHAPTER 1

Setting the Stage

Evolutionary, Cultural, and Environmental Contexts

The Early Migrants

In an epic colonization that provides by far the earliest evidence for the use of watercraft by humans, the people of Southeast Asia (Sunda, fig. 1.1) became sea voyagers and made landfall by at least 40,000 ya (years ago) on the large island continent of Sahul (New Guinea, Australia, and Tasmania) at a sea level that had lowered during the late Pleistocene. Other claims of contested validity push the first landfall by humans on Sahul back to about 55,000 ya. Groube et al. (1986) gave a date of 40,000 ya for the earliest occupation in Papua New Guinea, as evidenced by several waisted axes sealed beneath volcanic ash. J. H. and G. S. Hope (1976) cite the dating of a fossil human bone in the southern Papuan Highlands to about 40,000 ya. The islands of New Britain and New Ireland in the Bismarck Archipelago to the east of New Guinea in the Solomon Archipelago, had been colonized about 35,000 ya, dispelling the early believed "fluke colonization" theory. The early settlers were believed to intentionally be using watercraft to travel over water from

visible island to visible island. The first settlers were hunter-gatherers who apparently brought with them from southeasternmost Asia typical Middle Paleolithic flake tool assemblages.

For a worldwide cultural perspective I point out that the early colonization of Australia–New Guinea is but one of several "cultural explosions" that occurred around the world at different places and times between 60,000 and 30,000 years ago. This was the time when the first complex technology, art, and religion appeared at least somewhere in the world. It was well after the last spurt of brain size enlargement between 500,000 and 200,000 years ago. A second pulse of cultural explosions occurred worldwide about 10,000 to 4,000 years ago when hunter-gatherers made the transition to sedentary lifestyles and began to plant crops and domesticate animals. Both of these dramatic transformations of human behavior are exclusively associated with *Homo sapiens sapiens*, who entered the worldwide scene 100,000 years ago.

Stephen Mithen in a provocative book entitled *The Prehistory of the Mind* (1996) argues

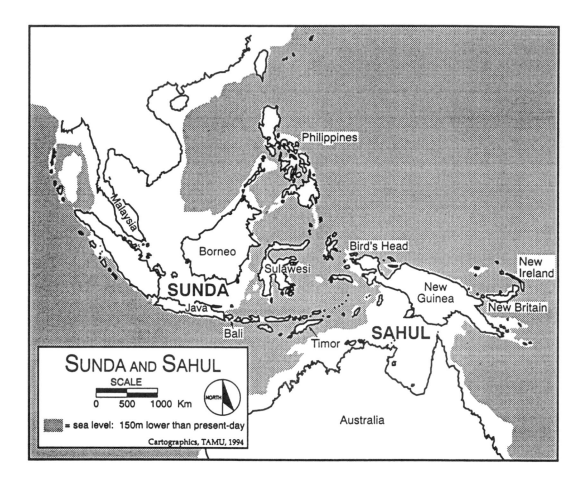

Fig. 1.1. Sunda and Sahul

that the concept of the mind consisting of modules of general intelligence, social intelligence, natural intelligence, technological intelligence, and linguistics intelligence provides the cognitive context in which the cultural complexities of the "cultural explosions" and cultural life thereafter evolved. Mithen further argues that this collection of evolved specialized intelligences and finally their interconnected manipulation within the minds of *Home sapiens sapiens* caused the cultural explosions.

From Foraging to Horticulture and the Neolithic

Archaeologists working in montane eastern Papua New Guinea after World War II at Kosipe, Yuku, Kuk, Huon, and in the vicinity of Mt. Hagen documented the transition from a Middle- and Upper-Paleolithic flaked tool kit to an evolved Neolithic ground stone tool kit

during the period from ca. 40,000 ya to ca. 9,000 ya (fig. 1.2) (Hampton 1997:22–23 from: Bulmer [1976:129–31]; Chappell [1966]; Groube [1989:294–95]; Hope [1982]; Powell [1982]; [White et al. 1970]). It would appear that the less efficient tools for clearing large forested areas and for making boards were replaced with functionally improved indigenous implements for these purposes. Jack Golson (1989:678–87) argued that evidence for agricultural management water control ditch systems was evident at Kuk swamp as early as 9,000 ya. By about 5,000 ya, the montane forest of Papua New Guinea had been extensively cleared of trees (Powell 1982), and pig husbandry had begun. It was thought that taro was the main staple crop during the early stages of Highlands horticulture until the sweet potato replaced it in importance as recently as 1,000 to 300 ya. The latter date is more generally acceptable to most anthropologists. Whatever the date of the introduction of the sweet potato, it is significant as the starting point for a population explosion in the Highlands. Because of greater crop yields in shorter periods of time with less labor and growth at cooler, higher elevations, the sweet potato replaced taro as the primary staple food crop. Although taro had been domesticated for 5,000–9,000 years before sweet potatoes were available, this crop had limited the Highlanders in population densities and in the elevations they could occupy. Now big men with leadership aspirations could strive for higher levels of influence by manipulating the female labor force to produce more sweet potatoes with which they could raise more pigs, with which the big man could manipulate politics, economics, and religious groups toward their own self-serving ends. This arrival of a seemingly simple commodity, the sweet potato, accounts for and dates, in general terms, the proliferation of stone goods and other material objects with which we define in material terms Highlanders' cultural systems.

Today, the staple crops of Highlands' horti-culture are primarily the sweet potato, along with lesser amounts of yams, taro, *Pandanus* nut, sugarcane, leafy greens, and edible grass stems. The taro, *Pandanus* nut, and some yams are native to New Guinea. The wild ancestors of the New Guinea types of bananas, sugarcane, leafy vegetables, and edible grass stems are New Guinea species. Since there are no Highlands' crops derived unequivocally from Asia, it is generally acknowledged that horticulture arose indigenously in the New Guinea Highlands.

By the times of first-contact in different areas with a more modern outside world (1900s, Hampton 1997:9–12), the Highlanders of Irian Jaya had become engineers and builders, experienced horticulturists who practiced pig husbandry and, at least in the Grand Valley of the Baliem, warriors who practiced incessant warfare. The people had laced the Highlands with suspension bridges, fences, well-constructed buildings in compounds and open clusters, irrigation and drainage ditches, and tuber gardens that would be highly productive. Relative

Fig. 1.2. Archaeological sites in Papua New Guinea

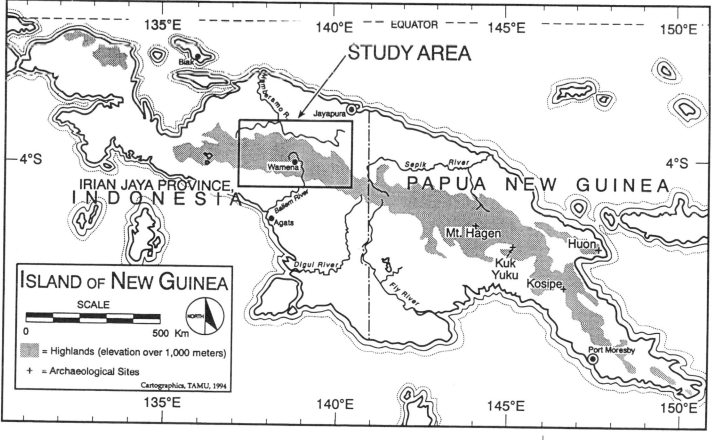

to genetic population structure in Oceania, Cavalli-Sforza et al. stated:

> Australia and New Guinea are of unique interest in having been at first European contact, at economic stages of development that had been replaced thousands of years ago in other parts of the world. Although Australians were, in a way, contemporary examples of Paleolithic hunter-gatherers, New Guineans had been through a Neolithic revolution but had not yet reached the age of metals. They represented (and still do, in part of the island) [remote locales in the Highlands of Irian Jaya] modern examples of Neolithic horticulturists. (1994:351)

Neolithic Defined and the Rest of the World

The term *Neolithic* does not define a precise time period during the evolution of humankind with an associated specific set of cultural traits and a single set of identifying material goods. Instead, it defines a period of transition between the Upper Paleolithic-Mesolithic (generally characterized by hunter-gatherers utilizing flaked stone tools, and sometimes including copper tools) and one of the metal ages (copper, bronze, or iron) with more evolved sets of cultural characteristics and material goods.

The term has created serious debate among archaeologists as its meaning has shifted through time. Initially the word meant "new Stone Age," the age of the polished axe, and referred to a technological development and a chronological phase (Tilley 1996:70). Then the actuality of pottery production was linked with the term, another technological innovation, followed by the term's association in the literature with agriculture and a mixed farming economy. New sets of social relations and ideas for organizing social labor are now becoming related to the term, with relationships being expressed through the symbolism of pottery, for example, and in Europe with monuments. Various conceptions of what is meant by the term Neolithic have an effect on the ways we understand the "transition" between the Paleolithic

and Neolithic at different locales throughout the world. This is as would be expected—not an unusual encumbrance but one to be understood, as there is no one archaeological expression for the term Neolithic and no single Neolithic lifestyle. We must be able to account for the variances of the Neolithic to be able to correctly apply the Highlands Irian Jaya cultural context to prehistoric situations. Because of the imbedded use of the term in archaeological thinking, application, and communication in the literature, I use the term. Whatever we call that period of cultural evolution and its material manifests between the Paleolithic and the age of metals, we must correctly identify "contexts" for our past-present-past research method to work for us to its fullest potential.

The Mousterian/Middle Paleolithic had its beginning 125,000 ya and ended 40,000 ya. Klein (1989:293) stated that the various Mousterian/Middle Paleolithic industrial sequences almost certainly ended at different times, depending on the place: Africa and the Near East before 40,000 to 35,000 ya, western Europe 35,000 ya, and, in central and eastern Europe, between 40,000 and 35,000 ya. Artifact assemblages throughout this time period were predominantly stone; usually no wood or bone. Assemblages included flakes, some unretouched with damaged edges, showing that they, too, were "tools," and other basic tool types such as scrapers, points, and denticulates (Bordes 1961).

Major changes in the cultural artifact record occur in the Upper Paleolithic from 40,000 to 10,000 ya. Whereas prior to that time, lithic typology had changed by increments of tens of thousands of years, during the Upper Paleolithic more advanced and variable forms of flaked and chipped lithics began to appear. During the period from approximately 34,000 to 21,000 ya, bone points and awls were present (Klein 1989:360). In a time scale shown by Klein (1989:354), the Upper Paleolithic (sometimes referred to as late Paleolithic) came to a close 12,000 ya, heralding a time of European cultural stratigraphy called Neolithic by some and Mesolithic by others. As pointed out above, I use the term Neolithic.

Childe, in a European-oriented book entitled *What Happened in History* said:

There is no "neolithic culture," but a limitless multitude of plants cultivated or of animals bred, by a different balance between cultivation and stock-breeding, by divergences in the location of settlements, in the plan and construction of houses, the shape and material of axes and other tools, the form and decoration of the pots, and by still greater disparities in burial sites, fashions in amulets, and styles of art. *Each culture represents an approximate adaptation to a specific environment with an ideology more or less adequate thereto.* The diversity results from a multiplicity of minor discoveries or inventions, at first purely local and conditioned by geological or climatic or botanical peculiarities, or from arbitrary, i.e., unexplained, idiosyncrasies. (1969:70, my emphasis)

As a part of the New Studies in Archaeology series, Bradley and Edmonds, in a book titled *Interpreting the Axe Trade: Production and Exchange in Neolithic Britain,* point out, "The middle phase of the Stone Age, the Mesolithic, has come to characterize the activities of hunter-gatherers, and the Neolithic those of the earliest farmers at the same time. The Neolithic has also been defined in terms of its material culture, for it saw the first widespread use of polished stone tools and pottery" (1993:18).

In a relative early work, *Man Makes Himself,* Childe described the ground stone tool that was once thought to herald the advent of "Neolithic":

At the time when the neolithic revolution makes itself manifest, when cultivation first becomes perceptible, North Africa and hither Asia were still enjoying a higher rainfall than today; trees still grew in regions now treeless. At the same time, in Europe, forests had replaced the tundras and steppes of the Ice Age. Man was obliged to deal with timber. The response to this stimulus was the creation of the "polished stone celt" (axe or adze), which to the older archaeologists was the distinctive mark of "neolithic times." The implement is a large slice or pebble of fine-grained stone, one end of which has been ground down to form a sharp cutting edge. It was hafted into the end of a stick or an antler to form an axe or an adze. (1963:75)

In James Mellaart's book, the *Neolithic of the Near East,* he says:

Even before the beginning of the Holocene, c. 8000 B.C. some of these groups had started to experiment with the planting of crops—the first steps toward agriculture, and the domestication of some animals. The Neolithic, i.e., the period of early farming, had begun. Over the next millennium the new techniques spread far and wide along new trade routes, and by c. 7000 B.C. (6000 B.C. in radiocarbon terms) Neolithic communities were established from southwestern Europe to the desert edge of Central Asia, and from the Caucasus to southern Palestine. The next two millennia saw the consolidation of the Neolithic, further expansion into Europe and the rise of metallurgy in the highlands area of the Near East, but its most characteristic product was painted pottery, in which was expressed a sense of individuality, artistry and abstraction lacking among many of the earlier, purely artificial household assemblages. (1975:9)

Throughout Asia and the Far East many Neolithic sites, just as in Europe and the Near East, are described as containing pottery (Nelson 1990). Wen-ming Yan (1992:113) stated the Chinese Neolithic period can be traced back to 11,000 ya. At Zengpiyan, Yan noted that pig bones have been discovered and that the rearing of pigs would have required the support of agriculture.

Rather than reacting to the environment, during the Neolithic, humankind had come to manage the environment and become a producer. Significant sociopolitical and socioreligious changes occurred. In timbered areas, where cropland replaced virgin forest on a grand scale (and related to the kinds of rock materials available), this is the time in cultural "systems" change that was marked by the advent of large quantities of ground stone versus a preponderance of flaked stone tools. During scattered local variations of the Neolithic cultural stage, humankind expressed the ability to transform radically different physical environments into agricultural systems. This evolutionary adaptation of humans in different physical environments manifests itself with an archaeological trail of different kinds of artifacts that are strongly related to the physical environments in which the cultural systems evolved.

To help us (archaeologists) get at a frame of reference, a hypothetical classification of societies, against which to test our ideas, the American anthropologist Elman Service (from Renfrew and Bahn 1996:166–70) developed a fourfold classification: (1) band (mobile hunter-gatherers), (2) segmentary society (settled farmers and pastoralists), (3) chiefdom (central accumulation and redistribution with some craft specialization), and (4) state (centralized bureaucracy with tribute based taxation and laws). Archaeological and modern examples of Elman's (1971:167) fourfold classification are: (1) band—all Paleolithic societies, including paleo-Indians; modern examples—Eskimo, Kalahari Bushman, Australian Aborigines; (2) segmentary society—all early farmers (Neolithic/Archaic; modern examples—Pueblos of Southwest United States, New Guinea Highlanders, and Nuer and Dinka in East Africa; (3) chiefdom—many early metalworking and formative societies, Mississippian of United States, smaller African kingdoms; modern examples—Northwest Coast Indians, United States, eighteenth-century Polynesian chiefdoms in Tonga, Tahiti, Hawaii; and (4) state—all ancient civilizations, such as, in Mesoamerica, Peru, Near East, India, and China, Greece, and Rome; modern examples—all modern states. This format furnishes a helpful template with which a reader can quickly relate the Irian Jaya Highlanders (number 2 in Service's classification but in transition to becoming chiefdoms) into a worldwide view of prehistoric and historic societies.

The People

Language Groups and Linguistic Boundaries

The island of New Guinea (both highlands and lowlands) has the highest concentration of languages in the world: about 1,000 of a worldwide 6,000, all condensed into an area only slightly larger than the state of Texas in the United States. In the Highlands, the different language groups are fragmented into multiple micropopulations of about 500 to a maximum of 130,000 people by the rugged terrain of alternating steep-sided ridges and narrow canyons, covered by dense rain forest. These micropopulations are politically fragmented in Irian Jaya into hundreds of compounds and hamlets that fight as fiercely with one another as with speakers of other languages. Jared Diamond, biologist and author, felt that, when on biological explorations in Papua New Guinea with teams of New Guineans as field assistants, excellent progress was three miles a day, even when traveling over existing trails. He stated that "Most highlanders in traditional New Guinea never went more than 10 miles from home in the course of their lives" (1997:306). In Irian Jaya, I talked with numerous people who had never journeyed *even that far* from home base in their lifetimes.

In the area of research covered by this book, including the Wano rock quarry of Yeineri on the west, to and around the Una operated rock quarries on the east, Silzer and Clouse (1991:25–30) itemized eighteen language groups, some with multiple dialects (fig. 1.3) (see Hampton 1997:79–81 for detail). The linguistic classification below from Silzer and Clouse shows the populations for all of the eighteen language groups with the exception of the Duvle and Damal. The population figures are approximate, but should always at least indicate relative population sizes between groups:

    I. Trans-New Guinea Phylum
      1. Great Dani Family
        C. Dani-Kwerba Stock
          a. Dani Sub-Family
            i. Western Dani (129,000)

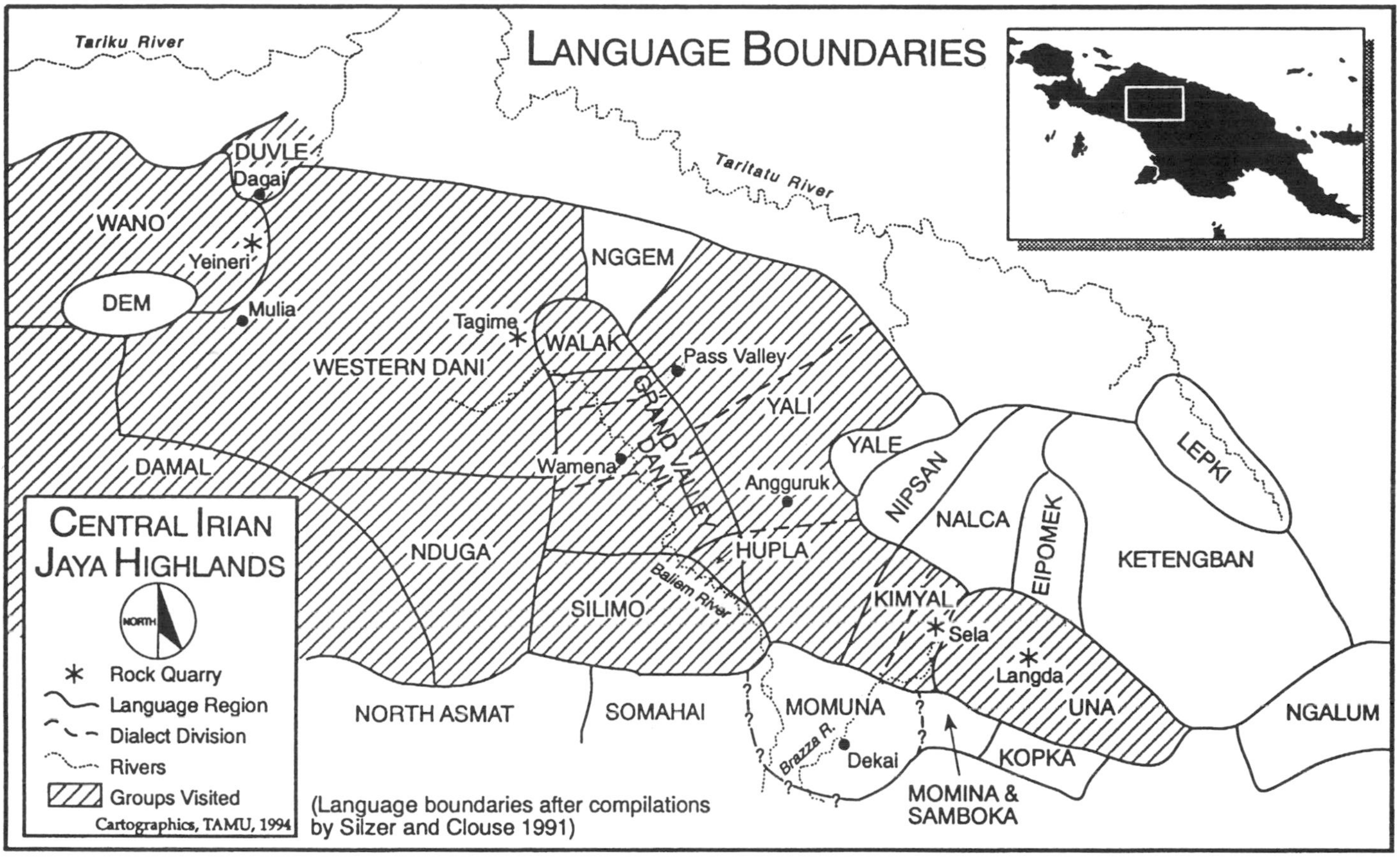

Tariku River
LANGUAGE BOUNDARIES
Taritatu River
DUVLE
Dagai
WANO
Yeineri
DEM
Mulia
NGGEM
Tagime
WALAK
WESTERN DANI
Pass Valley
YALI
GRAND VALLEY DANI
DAMAL
YALE
NIPSAN
Wamena
Angguruk
NALCA
EIPOMEK
KETENGBAN
LEPKI
CENTRAL IRIAN JAYA HIGHLANDS
NORTH
NDUGA
HUPLA
Baliem River
SILIMO
KIMYAL
Sela
Langda
Rock Quarry
Language Region
Dialect Division
Rivers
Groups Visited
Cartographics, TAMU, 1994
NORTH ASMAT
SOMAHAI
MOMUNA
UNA
NGALUM
Brazza R.
Dekai
KOPKA
(Language boundaries after compilations by Silzer and Clouse 1991)
MOMINA & SAMBOKA

Fig. 1.3. Language groups within the Irian Jaya study area

ii. Grand Valley Dani (100,000)
  a. Upper GVD Dialect
  b. Mid GVD Dialect
  c. Lower GVD Dialect
iii. Hupla (3,000)
iv. Walak (3,000)
v. Nggem (3,000)

b. Adjoining the Dani Sub-Families to the east is the Ngalik-Nguda Sub-Family consisting of
  i. Yali (30,000)
    a. Angguruk Dialect
    b. Ninia Dialect
    c. Pass Valley Dialect
  ii. Silimo (5,000)
  iii. Nduga (10,000)

c. Wano-Sub-Family-Level Isolate (3,000–3,500)

R. Mek Sub-Phylum-Level Family
  1. Western Group
    a. Yale (2,300)
    b. Nipsan (1,500–5,000)
    c. Nalca (9,000)
    d. Kimyal (6,500)
      i. Korupun Dialect
      ii. Sela Dialect
    e. Una (4,600)
    f. Eipomek (3,000)
  2. Eastern Group
    a. Ketengban (11,000)

W. Dem Stock-Level Isolate (1,000)

Of the groups listed above within the study area, my work in the field was primarily with the Wano, Western Dani, Grand Valley Dani, Yali, Kimyal, and Una; although in searching for rock quarries and following hypothetical trade routes, I spent time with the Duvle and trekked across parts of the Damal, Nduga, Walak, Silimo, and Hupla territories. Most of my time in the field was spent with the Dani and Western Dani. Among the Dani speakers, as O'Brien says, "there is a tremendous range of dialect diversity" (1969:3). Larson (1970) noted that within the 50,000 to 70,000 Western Dani language speakers there are at least four subdialects. Bromley (1967:24–27) defined three dialects within the Grand Valley Dani language (fig. 1.1).

Physical Characteristics and Life Expectancy

Knowing or inferring correct human size is basic information when developing site population inferences, as well as the nuances of the prehistoric use of space, nutritional analyses, and the mechanics of tool use. As Binford stated, "One of the elements common to all

Fig. 1.4. A Dani weaver at work with her hand-foot loom

sites, past and present, is the physical size and structure of the humans who use them: perhaps this single fact is the key to interpreting structure" (1983:14).

All of the people of the just-defined language groups in the research area are small in stature. The Yali, Una, and others have even been referred to as pygmies, a term I believe best reserved for the people so-named in Central Africa. According to Cavalli-Sforza et al. (1994:167), the smallest pygmy tribe has an average height of 145 cm (4.75 ft) in males and 137 cm (4.50 ft) in females (Mbuti, Ituri forest in northeast Zaire), which compares to the heights of the Highlanders in Irian Jaya, which are for the Dani, on average, 155 cm (5.0 ft) for males and 145 cm (4.75 ft) for females; for the Yali 145 cm (4.75 ft) for males and 140 cm (4.6 ft) for females; and for the Una 142 cm (4.65 ft) for males and 140 cm (4.6 ft) for females. Both groups have adapted to a humid, tropical forest environment. Whether the Highlanders' small stature is an evolutionary adaptation to a humid, tropical forest environment and/or the more straightforward product of nutrition is outside the scope of this book.

Physical abilities seem normal, and the Highlanders generally appear healthy. Both men and women of the Highlands are muscular. The people exhibit excellent eye-hand-foot coordination. Men use their feet for gripping and manipulating objects and exhibit an uncanny agility in climbing steep-face rocks, cliffs, and in harvesting wood in tree tops. Quarrymen *use their feet* almost as another set of hands when breaking up rock from which they make stone tools. Dani and Western Dani women often use their feet as a functional component of a hand-foot loom when weaving head-back nets (They have no fixed looms other than their own bodies.) (fig. 1.4).

Dress and Adornment

MALE, GRAND VALLEY AND WEST. Although the men often adorn themselves with bright feathers, fur headdresses and arm cuffs, and all manner of paraphernalia to emulate colorful birds (especially for ceremonies and warfare) (figs. 1.5 and 1.6), a man's basic dress is simple:

a gourd (*holim,* pronounced horeem) to cover his penis, a bark fiber string called a *dibat* (pronounced teapot) and/or a spider web necklace, both charged with supernatural power and worn as a necklace, to protect his throat from being entered by malevolent ghosts/spirits. Often a single vegetal strand or string hanging from a waist cord over the buttocks is worn to whisk flies away and to keep marauding ghosts and spirits from entering the anus.

MALE, YALI AND EAST. Along the borders with the Walak, Grand Valley Dani, and Hupla, Yali men and boys dress similarly to their neighbors in the west, but further east into Yali territory, the men's dress is quite distinctive from all other Highlanders (fig. 1.3). Above their penis gourds, the men wear rattan hoop skirts made of meters of looped rattan (fig. 1.7). Yali males often fold parts of carrying nets over their heads, both as protection from the sun and as an aesthetically pleasing item of accepted attire. Less often, they wear the tight, handwoven string net caps that are so common in the Grand Valley and West.

Most Yali, as well as other Yali and East inhabitants, do not wear the empowered fiber string (dibat) or spider web necklaces as do their neighbors to the west.

FEMALE, GRAND VALLEY AND WEST. A women's dress serves to protect her modesty, offer a degree of protection against ghosts and spirits, and provide utilitarian carrying space. Since the most vulnerable spots for the entrance of malevolent entities from the unseen world are through a women's throat, anus, and vagina, she must protect all three openings (fig. 1.8). A woman always covers her buttocks and genitals with a brief skirt. Women's dress fashions provide quite a few choices, just as in modern Western societies. Women, except the Yali, wear six different kinds of skirts: (1) and (2) are varieties of the so-called "grass skirts," which are actually made from flattened reeds, (3) the bark fiber string skirt (fig. 1.9), (4) a combination of the "grass" and string skirt, (5) a string woven looped skirt (which looks much like the woven head-back carrying net *(nogen)*,

Fig. 1.5. Artistically decorated Dani warrior emulates an owl.

and (6) in some areas in the Grand Valley and West, the colorful orchid fiber, braided wedding skirt, which replaces all other kinds of female skirts at marriage and thenceforth in those areas identifies married women (fig. 1.10).

One or more nets hung by straps from the head and down across a woman's back and over the buttocks not only cover (at least symbolically) the lower back and buttocks but serve as a functional part of a woman's attire. A woman

Fig. 1.6. Adorned Dani warriors near Pugima carry their killing spears.

Fig. 1.7. Yali men wear rattan hoop skirts even when working gardens.

its. For details of female adornment refer to Hampton (1997:170–82).

FEMALE, YALI AND EAST. Yali women, like the men, are distinguished from all other language groups within the research area by their attire. Like all women throughout the Irian Jaya Highlands, they wear head-back carrying nets to at least symbolically cover their backs and upper buttocks, but, in addition, they wear very distinctive short flattened reed strand skirts, which I have named the "Yali brush skirts" (Hampton 1997:189) (fig. 1.12). Yali females of all ages wear these skirts, although females in other language groups within the Yali and East region do not wear this kind of skirt but instead a choice of either the longer flattened reed or fiber string skirt, as are worn in the Grand Valley and West areas.

Most Yali and other women in the Yali and East area do not wear supernaturally empowered necklaces as do the women to the west.

Traditional Concepts of Life, Health, and Healing

Karl Heider's understanding of the Dugum Dani concept of life, health, and sickness applies to all language groups within the research area.

> The Dugum Dani conceptualize health and sickness, in terms of *edai-egen,* which is more psychical than physical. Minor and sometimes major physical wounds or ailments are practically ignored until they threaten an individual's *edai-egen.* . . . The strength of an individual lies in his *edai-egen,* and the state of his physical and psychical health is indicated by the state of his *edai-egen.* . . . In one sense, the *edai-egen* is an actual physical organ, the heart. Although the Dani have little knowledge of internal human anatomy, they do know the innards of pigs in detail, consider that human organs are analogous to those of pigs, and point out the pig heart as the pig's *edai-egen.* But in humans the *edai-egen* has the broader implications of soul, seat of the personality, spirit. The term may be literally translated as "seed of singing.". . . The unfavorable condition of the *edai-egen* is caused by ghosts, and while

Fig. 1.8. Dani women attired with head-back nets, string necklaces, and wedding skirts

usually wears between one and six of these nets. In them she might carry her baby (fig. 1.11), piglets, farm produce, and other items. Although the Dani women would be much embarrassed to have their genitals, lower back, or buttocks exposed, they never give it a thought that their breasts are always bare. In the Grand Valley and West, a woman, like a man, usually wears an empowered string necklace (dibat) for protection against malevolent ghosts and spir-

Fig. 1.9. Fiber string skirts worn by both children and women

the *edai-egen* is small the individual is particularly vulnerable to further damage from the ghosts. The individual is in a weakened state, he is out of joint with the world. (Heider 1970:226–27)

I found that specific diagnoses by both the people in general and curing specialists account for adverse conditions against the *edai-egen* (or life-giving soul-matter, *akotakun*) by a multitude of causative, often not mutually exclusive

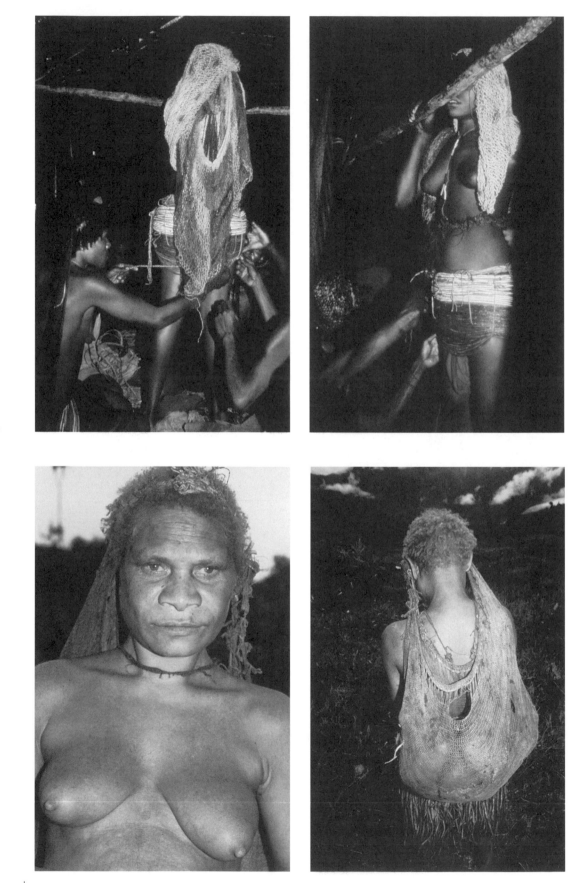

Fig. 1.10. Marriage skirt is designed onto a Dani bride.

Fig. 1.11. An albino Una woman with her baby at Langda

factors: (1) intrusion of malevolent ghosts or spirits, (2) breach of taboo, (3) soul-like (akotakun) loss, and (4) sorcery induced intrusion of potentially death dealing objects. Additionally, for certain illnesses and injuries the role of naturalistic causes is recognized and accounted for in both diagnosis and treatment. Since the medical system of the Highlanders fits the universal cause-and-treatment patterning shown to exist by Clements (1932) and Rogers (1976), it is plausible that the medical paraphernalia (artifacts) and associated treatment behavior used by the Highlanders will have valid application in our archaeological present-past research method.

Traditional Healers and Medical Practices

The traditional healers of the Highlands are part-time specialists who are adept at diagnoses and at conducting healing treatments. Some are the male sociopolitical and religious leaders of the society (big men) who have the ability to manipulate supernatural power and to go into trance. In addition, the big men can delegate the *power* to other select people (male *or* female), who then learn medical techniques and become healing specialists. These healers are medical specialists, without social and political influence. Healers (big men and specialists) with the ability to manipulate supernatural power and to go into trance I refer to as shamans; although within the Highlands' cultural systems these healers all lead normal lives with other routine responsibilities.

The patients and the shamans both feel that since injuries and diseases are caused, in one way or another, by supernatural powers, they must be treated by the manipulation and application of other supernatural powers. To effect countermeasures and cures, an endless assortment of religio-medical kits containing *power stones* and other assorted paraphernalia are used. Trancing is sometimes practiced, heat treatments often effected, and blood-letting used, plus a variety of applications of medicinal plants (Hampton 1997:96–104).

Birth to Death

Fig. 1.12. The Yali female brush skirt is worn by all ages.

Polygyny is common in all language groups within the research area. Women desire and usually raise one to three children (Hampton 1997:110–13). Polygyny was the social mechanism by which men could control the female labor force to be able to grow more sweet potatoes, with which to raise more pigs, with which to be able to manipulate with the wealth of pigs the political, economic, and religious aspects of life.

The Highlanders recognize the human life

cycle with both its positive and negative effects on individuals and the community. Their cultural response is an evolved system of rites of passage. It is not the purpose of this book to analyze the rites of passage of the indigenous Irian Jaya Highlanders, but rather to identify them within an evolutionary cultural framework for a ready reference when certain symbolic stones are being identified and the behavior surrounding their uses in the various rites discussed.

A French anthropologist, Arnold Van Gennep, undertook a detailed survey of the literature to categorize rites of passage that he regarded as "ceremonies whose essential purpose is to enable the individual to pass from one defined position to another which is equally well defined" (1960:2, 33). Van Gennep's analysis included "rites that help individuals through life crises such as birth, puberty, marriage, parenthood, advancement into a higher class, occupational specialization and death" (Haviland 1993:358). Van Gennep found it useful to divide ceremonies for all of these crises into three states he called separation, transition, and incorporation (Haviland 1993:358). For analyses of process (related ceremonies) of rites of passage, other anthropologists have generally agreed to this format, although some prefer a different tripartite nomenclature: separation, margin, and aggregation (Kottak 1991:336).

Of Van Gennep's rather comprehensive group of rites of passage, the Highlanders respond personally and as an organized systematic group to puberty (adulthood), marriage, and death with significant ritual. Birth is noted, but mostly on a personal basis. Marriage is a grand rite of passage, looked forward to and enjoyed throughout the entire Highlands area—pigs are sacrificed, feasting takes place, wealth exchanges hands, and families are united in rather complex obligatory relationships. But the most complex and important rite of passage, to the individuals and the cultural systems, is the funeral. It has several stages, over a period of years, and serves to placate the ghosts and spirits, purge grief, bind social relationships, and contribute (through wealth exchange) to a viable economy. The symbolic

display-exchange stones are extremely important facets of both marriage and death rites.

In addition to rites of passage, certain rites of intensification are also important, all of which involve the uses of different kinds of special stones. These include rituals at wartime to protect the warriors and improve the likelihood of success, rituals to stop the rain when there is too much of it, rituals to encourage good crop yields when production is off, and rituals to improve the health of a community. As Haviland defined these kinds of rituals, "These are rites that make occasions of the crisis of a group, rather than an individual" (1993:359). Although there are "rites of intensification" that can be differentiated from "rites of passage," such as those mentioned above, it is pointed out that among the Irian Jaya Highlanders, the rites of marriage and death, especially of death, are rites that also "mark the crises of a group" just as much as that of an individual.

Death, whatever the cause, initiates immediate action. The news is shouted from hamlet to hamlet and carried by messenger to distant-living kinsmen. Plans are set in motion for the first of a series of funeral rites that extend over several years. The first rite usually commences the day after a death. The immediate goals are to dispose of the body, purge the grief of kinsmen and loving friends, placate the ghost of the deceased as well as ghosts in general (always, the ghosts must be placated!), and reinforce ties of kinship. Within all of the Highlands part of the study area, bodies of the dead are disposed of by cremation. (See Hampton 1997:121, 122 for exceptions to this kind of body treatment in adjacent areas.) Although the practice of cremation is well known within cultural systems around the world today and in recent prehistory, we have little evidence as to when, where, and why the practice originated in earlier prehistoric times. The Highlanders profess to not know why they cremate or when the practice started, but I presume it commenced after the hunter-gatherer ancestors became horticulturists. Wano, Western Dani, Dani, and Yali informants stated that when they were hunting, gathering, or on trading treks a distance from their homes and a member of the party would die, they would often dispose of the corpse in rock cracks, crevices, or caves rather than cremate or transport the body home.

The fact that the Highlanders cremate may be a manifestation of the general practice of the Highlanders to clean their environment of dead and unneeded organic debris (observation by Gentry Steele as a possible reason for cremation). The Highlanders are meticulous around their habitation sites on this point, with the single exception of leaving pig scat where it naturally falls.

Because of the Highlanders' practice of cremation, only ashes and remaining small burned bone fragments make their way to ghost-spirit enclosures *(waro leget)* (Hampton 1997:121–24). There are no stone or other kinds of funerary goods that might become archaeological remainders. Some few body parts of departed influential leaders are occasionally maintained by their descendants as sacred objects. An ethnographic example of this practice is presented during the discussion of big man Gutelu's sacred ancestor stones (chapter 4). Little else is known of this practice of preserving body parts for religious purposes, and the practice cannot be quantitatively assessed.

In addition to the apparently rare custom of the preservation of body parts for religious purposes, the presence of three soot-blackened, pig-grease-rubbed mummies are known in the Grand Valley as well as scattered human skeletons in crevices, rock shelters, and caves (Hampton 1997:124–32) (figs. 1.13 and 1.14).

Belief System
According to the peoples' worldview, all space is occupied by entities in two separate but comingled worlds—the world of the seen and the world of the unseen. Living entities such as humans, animals, and plants occupy the world of the seen along with inanimate objects like rocks, earth, water, the sun, the moon, and stars. The world of the unseen is occupied by ghosts and spirits. Ghosts and spirits are everywhere, and their presence is pervasive throughout the cosmos. From the Highlanders' viewpoint, the living entities of both the seen and

the unseen worlds cohabit the same geographic place and space, creating observable behavioral complexities in people that are often not understood by an outside researcher.

In an esoteric classificatory system of ghosts and spirits, there is one general category of ghosts and two broad categories of spirits. Ghosts originate, one at a time, from the life-soul matter at the death of each human. After

Fig. 1.13. The Sompaima mummy, one of Gutelu's ancestors

Fig. 1.14. Human skulls and skeletal remains in ritual configuration

variable periods of elapsed time, the durations of which are only understood by the people, ghosts become spirits, certain of which are selected by the religious men's groups from time to time for installation into stone bodies ("spirit bones"), to become part of a group of personified *ancestral spirits* that are propitiated and manipulated during culturally endemic rituals (chapter 4). The remainder *spirits* (those not chosen to be preserved in material objects as personified ancestral spirits) lose their individual human identity with time and merge into a large ephemeral mass of spirit power, which fills the landscape. Segments of spirit power from this second category of spirits or spirit power occupy, as other-than-human spirits, both inanimate objects, such as certain rocks of the landscape and lakes, as well as animate objects, such as certain birds, animals, trees, and bamboo. The method of seeming metamorphosis from human to other-than-human spirits either would not or could not be communicated by my informants.

Both ghosts and spirits of the unseen world are feared. Ghosts are thought to be mostly malevolent and must be constantly placated, diverted, and avoided. At the birth of each ghost, with the death of a human being, placa-

tion commences immediately with a complex funerary celebration that shows the ghosts that the living humans really do care about them. Great emotional displays of grief are choreographed along with live, bloody sacrifices of appeasement. Items of wealth are ostentatiously displayed and exchanged in the ghost's honor. Efforts by humans are continuously taken to appease, pacify, and divert ghosts away from habitation sites, gardens, and places of other cultural activities. Among objects so-used are ritually empowered ghost barrier bundles and rat arches.

The ancestor worship of the Irian Jaya Highlanders is but one part, although I believe the core, of the religious aspect of a complex belief system. The people fear but respect ancestral spirits that are propitiated and manipulated in numerous rituals on behalf of all manner of social causes (chapter 4). Both live, bloody sacrifices and bloodless sacrifices are offered to ancestral spirits in a continuum of deeply rooted cultural rituals. The people also go to varying degrees of effort to pacify and avoid the multitude of other-than-human spirits that occupy the landscape. In addition, some of the Highlanders, in at least a large part of the Grand Valley and West region, conduct religious ritual to propitiate and manipulate the sun (and some, the moon) just as they do to propitiate and manipulate their own ancestral spirits (chapter 4).

Females are included in funerary rituals for deceased humans but are excluded from rituals celebrated for ancestral spirits. The ancestor worship is, in one sense, a very tangible linkage of patrilineage relations between the male elders and their male juniors. The juniors learn from observation, and finally participation, how to install their ancestors' spirits into tangible "spirit bones" and to preserve them as viable and visible entities from the spirit world of the unseen. The patrilineage-formed socio-religious *ganekhe* groups, while gathered at rituals to honor, propitiate, and manipulate their ancestors (in stone bodies), are, from an esoteric viewpoint, gatherings composed of both the living and the dead (chapter 4). Within these groups, the transmission of the knowledge and practice of the religious ritual of ancestor worship is vertical, thus, accounting in part, for the evolutionary process of religious practice. The use of icons within religious space attests to the early use of this practice predating historical religions (chapter 4).

Sacrifice

As attested to by the history of religions, a broad range of specific practices and multiple kinds of objects are used in sacrifice to supernatural beings. Sacrifices of blood offerings of human beings and animals as the gifts as well as the bloodless offerings of flowers (or of sweet fragrance from certain flowers, woods, and incense), vegetative materials from cultivators, and a multitude of inanimate objects are well documented. Practices of headhunting and cannibalism are sometimes included as variations of kinds of blood sacrifices. It is in blood sacrifices, especially where human beings are offered instead of animals, that "part-for-the-whole" sacrifices, like the offerings of human fingers, hair, or blood drawn through self-inflicted wounds are sometimes used as replacements (Eliade 1987b:546).

From a theoretical viewpoint, Eliade expressed the opinion that for "palaeo-agricul-tural peoples, what is essential is periodically to evoke the primordial event that established the present condition of humanity" ["A human blood sacrifice"] (1987a:101). It is Volhardt who Eliade credited with first demonstrating the religious meaning of cannibalism. Eliade combined his own thoughts with those of Volhardt when he said, "the killing and devouring of sows at festivals, eating the first fruits when tubers are harvested, are an eating of the divine body, exactly as it is eaten at cannibal feasts. Sacrifice of sows, headhunting, cannibalism are symbolically the same as harvesting tubers or coconuts" (1987a:182).

Within the realms of this provocative and (to this research) pertinent issue, which is elucidated above by Mircea Eliade, I would offer, but not argue in this book, my theory that within the cultural systems of the research area, the well-known practice of "ritual warfare" is but a complex variation of better-known scenarios of human sacrifice. Theoretically, if the ritual warfare process were carried to its ultimate end, the people would have sacrificed their entire population.

In addition to this theory of sacrifice by ritual warfare within the repertoire of Highlander practices, other more straightforward forms of sacrifice that were embedded in the cultural systems by the times of first-contact were cannibalism, finger and joint amputation and ear excision (part-for-the-whole), pig sacrifices, and the bloodless sacrifices of sweet potato offerings (figs. 1.15, 1.16) (Hampton 1997:136–54).

Around the world, the most common bloody sacrifice to propitiate or avert the anger of supernaturals is animals. In Irian Jaya that animal has been pigs. Pigs are used as necessary sacrifices at carefully orchestrated ritual events. The continuum of "pig ceremonies" is an important cultural binder that in one sense could be considered to give meaning to cultural life as a system. Many pigs are chosen at birth, or soon thereafter, to be raised as sacred *(wusa)* pigs to be sacrificed later to *specific* ancestral spirits; others chosen in a similar manner are raised as sacred animals to be sacrificed for other ritual purposes. Pigs so-

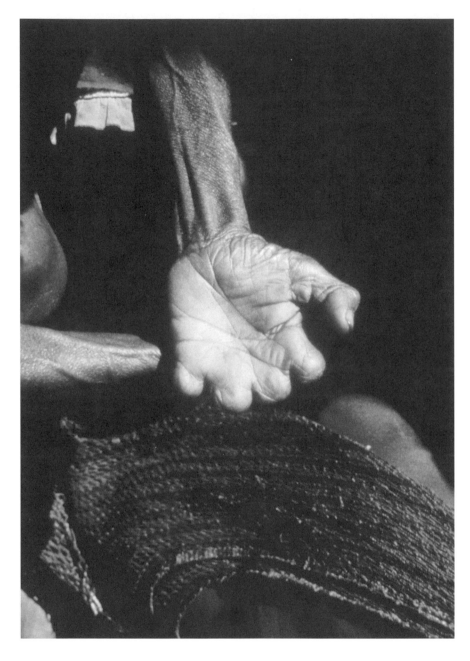

Fig. 1.15. This woman has sacrificed four fingers on one hand.

ists. Instead, in the Irian Jaya Highlands, "first fruits" are often purposefully left to rot in the gardens for the "creator spirits."

Leadership

All the leaders are men. The Highlanders' world is a "man's world" with the areawide most prevailing taboo being against women entering the men's houses or participating in many of the endless numbers of sacred rituals. The male leaders do not inherit their leadership, nor can they pass it on automatically to a son, although the eldest son of an important leader has many advantages toward being next in line. Leaders are called big men (*ab goktek* in the mid–Grand Valley Dani dialect) who rise to several hierarchical positions of influence by a combination of having skill in warfare, households with multiple wives, control of gardenland, accumulated wealth (pigs and certain durable material goods), perceived abilities (by the constituency) as religious leaders with shamanic powers, political charisma, and general cleverness. To achieve a high level of influence, a big man must acquire and maintain items of wealth, especially pigs, with which to manipulate the political and social scene. His leadership stature is not only measured by how many big pigs he owns but also by how many pigs he owes and his demonstrated ability to beneficially influence the economy by moving pigs and other items of wealth (primarily symbolic stones) within the cultural system. Relative positions of influence are thus achieved by political and economic maneuvering, religious acumen, and, ultimately, public consensus. The big men have no absolute power. Public action is initiated by leadership but confirmed by public consensus. Big men who break cultural taboos generally have to suffer adverse consequences from their constituencies.

Relative to the sociopolitical framework in the Grand Valley and West region, big men may rise to any of several measurable levels of leadership. On the lower but still an important level are the big men of the compounds, house clusters, and hamlets. The vast majority of big men on this level do not acquire power and prestige beyond these lower community levels. Other

defined as sacred are fed sweet potatoes from time to time that have been blessed at sacred rituals. In this way, the pigs themselves are participating in the sacrament while alive. When they are ultimately killed at a religious ritual, they are sacrifices *of* an empowered entity *to* a supernatural entity.

Bloodless sacrifices of sweet potatoes are a common accompaniment of pig sacrifices at a multitude of different rituals. I have not identified these as offerings of "first-fruits" as is the common practice worldwide among agricultur-

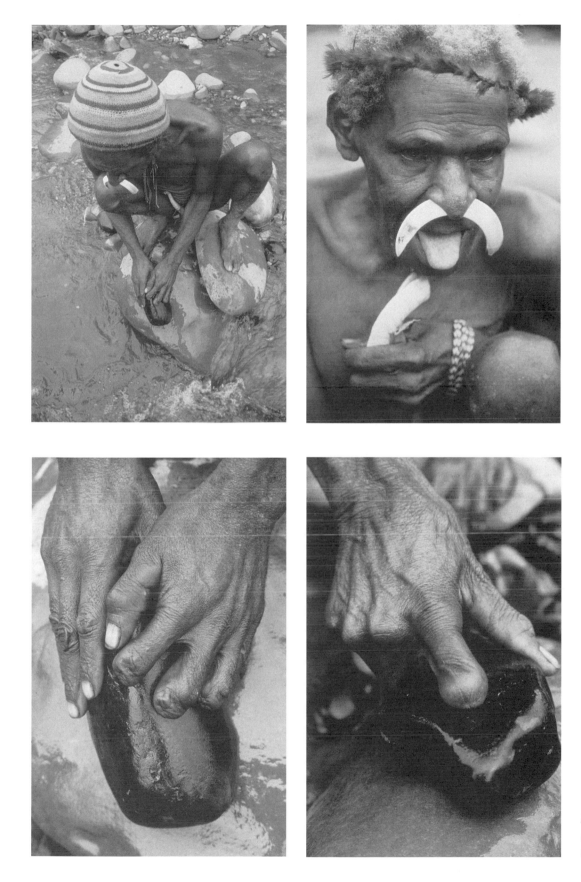

Fig. 1.16. Two Tagime quarrymen use hands with amputated finger joints.

Fig. 1.17. With a wooden paddle digging stick, a man prepares for planting.

Big men at the compound, house cluster, hamlet, confederacy, and alliance levels of influence are all shamans but with varying degrees of shamanic ability. In their shamanic roles, to their constituents, they both *have* the power (*wusahun, alt. wesahun*) and *are* the power. With this power, in addition to other sociopolitical responsibilities, the big men are also both healers and religious leaders (see "Ownership of the Stones" and "Houses for the Stones: Both Profane and Sacred Space," chapter 4). As the leaders of the men's religious *ganekhe* groups, the big men wield compelling socioreligious influence. To my knowledge this is the first such description entered into the anthropological literature of central New Guinea Highlands big men. They are indeed *religious*-political-economic leaders; not just secular-political-economic leaders.

Big men can delegate their power (wusahun) to those around them so that select individuals can carry out responsibilities with a full range of culturally desirable profane *and* sacred powers (including the uses of socially important power stones, chapter 4) to accomplish a delegated task. In both general secular and certain specific realities, the Irian Jaya Highlander men of achieved influence function much like the leaders in *some* Melanesian societies that Sahlins (1963) described as "big men" who achieved influence rather than inherited power.

Subsistence

VALLEY FLOOR AND HILLSLOPE GARDENS. With only simple wooden paddle spades and digging sticks, these horticulturists maintain complex ditched and mounded gardens on both valley floors (primarily Grand Valley) (fig. 1.17) and hillslopes. The valley floor gardens of the Grand Valley are generally the more productive (figs. 1.18 and 1.19). The Highlanders who live away from the Grand Valley cling tenaciously to the ridge crest and steep hillslope environments, which in many instances they put into production from the bottoms of narrow V-shaped valleys to ridge and mountain tops. Their horticultural practice is generally more extensive than the intensive practice of the Grand Valley. All horticultural practice

big men, of considerable political, religious, and social influence, head up the confederations, and those big men of maximal influence become the leaders of alliances (chapter 3 and Hampton 1997:189–95) while at the same time being the leaders of their communities of residence.

Fig. 1.18. Aerial view of sweet potato gardens in the Grand Valley

Fig. 1.19. Hillslope garden above the rock quarries at Langda

The mature gardens that are maintained today with only wooden tools were presumably originally cleared in prehistoric times with stone adzes and also maintained then as they are today with only wooden tools. To my knowledge no stone tool blades that might have been used as hoes or spades have ever been recovered in the Irian Jaya Highlands in modern times. Men are responsible to clear areas and prepare them for planting. With community work parties, they dig the ditches, mud the sides, and throw ditch material back into the gardens where it acts as a fertilizer (fig. 1.20). The women do most of the planting, weeding, and harvesting. Men are the architects, engineers, and builders, and women are the producers.

FOOD PLANTS. The people cultivate (or manipulate within the nearby forest) at least fifteen different kinds of plants. The staple food is the sweet potato (Hampton 1997:882–85).

BALIEM GORGE. In the upper reaches of the Baliem Gorge (fig. 1.21) at Kurima and to the south, the archaeological skeleton of the horticultural system with its interspersed habitation sites is made of stone walls, ditches lined with stone, and other stone structures rather than fences of wood and ditches of mud, as it is in the more-populated area of the Grand Valley to the northwest (Hampton 1997:205–17) (figs. 1.22 and 1.23). From an archaeological perspective, this is significant because upon abandonment of the sites, it is the stone remnants that would more likely be preserved in the archaeological record than the wooden skeleton that would soon rot and be gone, especially in the present Irian Jaya equatorial climate. What might be lost with time is evidence for the intensely practiced horticultural system at the center of the most-populated and economically wealthy area in the Irian Jaya Highlands. What would be disproportionately preserved relative to population and wealth distribution would be rock ruins of a sparsely settled area.

ANIMAL HUSBANDRY. The only domestic animals are dogs *(Canis familaris)* and pigs *(Sus*

Fig. 1.20. A work crew cleans a garden ditch and muds the walls.

follows the swidden technique. Lower food production in the more rugged terrain areas is often reflected in a poorer lifestyle and generally poorer health of those inhabitants. Gardens are either elaborately fenced with wooden slats and supportive posts, lashed with rattan or vines, or, around the fringes of the Grand Valley, and in other places where rock erratics are a hindrance to horticulture, walled with limestone cobbles and boulders that have been cleared from the gardens. The near-continuous networks of fences and walls were built to control the movement of pigs.

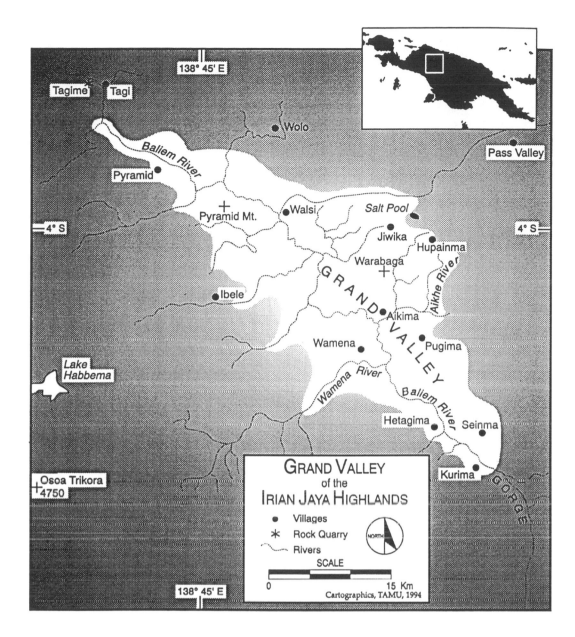

Fig. 1.21. The Grand Valley and Baliem Gorge

scrofa). The dog is eaten in some Dani areas. In most areas, the dogs' yellow buff-colored fur is much admired as men's arm cuffs, as decorations on headdresses, and to decorate objects like net purses, cowrie shell exchange bands, and funeral and bridewealth display-exchange stones. Some dogs, having a predisposed inclination, are trained and used for hunting. Although the dog is sometimes revered as having a soul-ghost like humans, it is generally relegated to a position of just *being* in the living hierarchy; whereas the pig's value is unquestioned and is generally thought to possess a soul-ghost. Indeed, pigs are both the primary

wealth item and the living entity raised to be an essential sacrificial part of a myriad of ancestor worship ceremonies, curing rituals, rites of passage, war preparation, war indemnity, and other ceremonies (Hampton 1997:218–19).

Whereas Rappaport (1984:162, 408–10), in his classical book *Pigs for Ancestors,* reached the conclusion, in a particular area of the Maring in Papua New Guinea, that the cyclical mass-killing of pigs in social rituals was a mechanism to control pig population, this same mechanism to control the size of the pig population does not apply in Irian Jaya. In the Highlands of Irian Jaya, pig movement was well controlled

Fig. 1.22. Rock-walled potato gardens

control mechanism farther to the east in Papua New Guinea. If pigs were not so valuable as wealth items and in short supply as sacrificial animals, the people would commence to eat them on a regular basis as a subsistence item. They relish the treat of eating pig meat and fat.

According to Cavalli-Sforza et al., "There are contradictory reports about the first time of entry of pigs to New Guinea: they might have been introduced by 6,000 B.P. or possibly earlier (Spriggs 1984). According to Bellwood (personal communication) a date of 2,000 B.P. would fit linguistic data better" (1994:346).

Architects, Engineers, and Builders

The Highlanders, especially those in the Grand Valley and West, are adept architects, engineers, and builders. In their living compounds they construct circular men's and women's houses, rectangular cookhouses, pig sties, small after-cremation bone enclosures (oak leget), ghost houses (wadlo leget), and fences. In the west, a basic architectural unit is a compound with one men's house, a common women's cookhouse, several women's houses, one to three pig sties, a bone enclosure, and one or two ghost houses. The entire complex is fenced or walled outwardly to keep pigs out and to offer a degree of protection against marauders. An inner fence connects the houses and pig sty or sties and provides a well protected interior courtyard as well as a fenced compound garden area located between the two fences. Minor variations in compound design occur, especially in rough terrain where it is difficult to have a centrally located fenced interior courtyard. Each compound is designed, at least in the Grand Valley, with the men's house facing the fenced-in compound entrance so the men who stay there always look out across the central open courtyard to view activities and to see who is coming and going. Correspondingly, one entering a compound looks across the open courtyard directly at the men's house.

I refer to two or more compounds joined together by a common fence, or at least adjacent to each other, as a hamlet. Grand Valley men's houses vary from two and one half to five meters in inside diameter with most being from

by the intricate networks of fences and stone walls. None of my informants knew of sweet potato shortages due to an overabundance of pigs. In fact, there never seemed to be enough pigs to saturate the need for them as the fundamental wealth item and the essential sacrificial component for the ongoing myriad of pig-killing rituals and ceremonies. Within the Grand Valley, alliance-wide leaders sometimes invoked moratoriums on pig killing so that there would be enough pigs for the cyclical "mass killings" that occur at the five-year ceremonies, the correlative Irian Jaya ceremonial that Rappaport invoked as the pig population

Fig. 1.23. Rock outlined, rectangular-shaped hillslope gardens east of Kurima

four to five meters. Houses in the Yali and East region are approximately the same size. The most powerful big men have slightly larger houses. (Details of design and construction of the men's house are discussed in "Architecture, Contents, and Spatial Relationships," chapter 4, in conjunction with religious aspects of space as it relates to sacred places, symbolic stones, and associated behavior.)

Houses and other compound buildings in the Grand Valley and West are easily distinguished from houses and buildings in the Yali and East. In the west, the roofs are thatched with grass; whereas in the east, the roofs are covered with *Pandanus* leaves or less often, with strips of bark. Another architectural difference between the two areas is community layout. In the west, interior fenced courtyards are the norm; whereas in the Yali and East (and in areas of rugged terrain in the west), interior fenced or walled courtyards are not present. The controlling factor is the rugged terrain that persistently prevails throughout the Yali and East region, where there are few locales in which such planned communities are feasible.

Possibly the most challenging engineering feats are the large suspension bridges built across rivers throughout the entire area. When Richard Archbold discovered the Grand Valley in 1938, he remarked that he was amazed at the engineering skill of the Highlanders in constructing the suspension bridges. In addition to designing and building the complex bridges that provide the only river crossings, the men are also responsible for building and maintaining temporary bridges plus the numerous single log pole bridges that furnish access across ditches within the sweet potato gardens.

The Dani watchtowers in the Grand Valley were ingenious creative constructions to allow men to view approaches to their frontiers and potato fields, thus furnishing forward lookouts for ambushes and raids. The watchtowers were always manned in the early morning hours so when an "all-clear" signal came from the lookouts, the horticulturists could then move into the gardens to perform their daily chores.

Warriors, Warfare, and Weapons

Much has been written and captured in photos about the Dani as warriors (Gardner and Heider 1969:144; Heider 1970:105; and Larson 1987:245). Berndt (1964:183) considered warfare in both Papua New Guinea and Irian Jaya to have been "chronic" and "incessant." Reports within the Dani area of the Central Highlands of Irian Jaya by Gardner and Heider (1969), Heider (1970), and Larson (1987) support this conclusion. Larson said in the Ilaga area, "every man always carried with him his bow and arrows to defend himself should he suddenly be the object of unexpected revenge, or be called upon without notice to assist members of his community in a sudden outbreak of fighting" (1987:164).

Although it is not difficult to visualize the influence that traditional warfare might have had on trade and the continuous need for rituals led by war shamans (often using sacred stones) to incite the spirits to favorable action on the warriors' behalf, the behavior of the complex system of warfare as practiced in precontact times by the Irian Jaya Highlanders could not be interpreted from its remnant artifacts of culture. The warring fields leave no boundaries or telltale markers, unlike the horticultural skeletons of rock walls, fences, and the complex of irrigation drainage ditches interwoven into a patterned mosaic with mounded gardens.

A brief description of weapons provides insight relevant to the evolution of weaponry. The use of stone materials in weaponry in the Highlands is significant by its absence. In the Grand Valley and West, the weapons of war are the long jabbing spear, shorter throwing spears (which are actually just short sharpened sticks), bows and arrows, and only on occasion, adzes. In the Yali and East region, the most common weapons are bows and arrows and adzes. The long jabbing spears are approximately 2 to 3 m long, made primarily of myrtle or laurel wood, and are the real killing weapons for warfare in the Grand Valley and West area.

The bows are approximately 1.5 m long with bowstrings made of thin strips of bamboo or sometimes rattan. Arrows are made with unfletched reed shafts and several different styles of hardwood, bamboo, and bone tips. The primary fighting arrows have barbed hardwood tips of different designs, although bamboo-tipped arrows are also often used. Whether hunting or in warfare, arrows are carried loose (or tied in a simple bundle with a string or piece of narrow rattan) in the same hand as the bow. During ritual or all-out war-

fare, arrows are fired singly by individual warriors; never in coordinated volleys.

Passive and Performing Arts

Alexander Alland defines art as "play with form producing some aesthetically successful transformation-representation" (1977:39). Marvin Harris (1980:455) says that, "To be art, as distinct from other forms of communication, the representation must be transformed into some metaphoric or symbolic statement, movement, image, or object which stands for that which is being represented. Art is not an isolated sector of human experience. It is intimately connected with and embedded in other aspects of superstructural components of sociocultural systems." Measured against Alland's and Harris's statements about art, the artistic endeavors of the adjacent-living, different Highlands' language groups are seen to express some basic themes and patterning for the groups. A brief review of both the fundamental graphic and plastic (three-dimensional) artwork furnishes contextual insights about the cultural systems in which the stone toolmakers lived.

Across all language boundaries simple designs are incised with small chert flakes and marsupial or rodent mandible-tooth gravers onto at least hardwood arrow tips. Some carvers state that their chevron designs symbolically stand for rows of sweet potatoes in the gardens. Others state that such patterns are vulva symbols to remind the people of the women they love. Whatever the messages, the designs are always simple and with only minor variations across the Highlands area. In the Yali and East, bamboo earplugs, bamboo containers, and smoking devices are often incised with these artful patterns, but such carving is less often seen on similar, locally made objects in the Grand Valley and West.

Heider reported the presence of red pictograph figures in the Dugum Dani Neighborhood (1970:184–89). In my fieldwork subsequent to that of Heider's, I have found several more locales of red pictographs on cliff faces, overhangs, and large boulder erratics, but find that overall, relatively few pictograph paintings are used within the culture. *All* such sites are sacred *(wusa)* and protected from outsiders. They are religious in nature and activated as parts of a specific ritual in which they serve to communicate between humans in the world of the seen with ghost-spirit entities in the world of the unseen. Other pictographs, that are not red in color, are sparsely present in sacred caves. They include both simple realistic and abstract symbols. None of the Highlands pictographs are done with the complexity and artistic grandeur of many prehistoric rock art paintings in other places around the world.

Two types of graphic artwork that flourish in the Highlands are body "mudding" with white, gray, yellow, and red clays and body finger painting with those same colors. Mudding is usually done for periods of mourning, to prepare for song-dance activities, and by some men for war. In body painting, basically only seminal individual symbols of dots, lines, crosses, curves, and circles are used without much derivation. In addition, stamped patterns from fern leaves and broken ends of certain plants from which the leaves have been plucked are used by some groups of artists. Esoterically, the crosses and circles convey symbolic meaning within some local groups, but that meaning can change, even within the same language group, from one geographic area to the next. An example is a simple cross, which in one area denotes that the people are "followers" of a certain big man, but not far away, similar crosses used in rock pictographs are considered to be a moiety symbol. Although the list is lengthy, symbolic communication of this nature seems to be geographically restrictive, and systematic codification, like that defined by James Faris among the Nubia of Africa (Bernier 1991), seems to be lacking.

Most anthropologists consider the skilled potter, loom weaver, wood carver, and sandal maker artists, and their wares works of art. In the same context, some of the symmetrical, evenly looped, and colorfully patterned women's head-back nets and the strapless ceremonial nets are works of art in the Irian Jaya Highlands. It would seem that for these people, who make no pottery or baskets, that netting furnishes the women an alternative medium with which to create and display artistic skills. In a male counterpart of art creativity and expression, the men plait fiber arm bands and the tightly handwoven cowrie-shell-decorated display and exchange bands. Among the men, many of the carefully thought-out items of adornment, such as their array of mixed media feather and fur head pieces, colorful head plumes of parrot and birds-of-paradise feathers, matted spider web and shell decorated necklaces, and chest bibs, contribute to each man's creation of his adorned body as an individual three-dimensional art piece.

Sculptured art consists of the tabular symbolic display-exchange stones that are selected, shaped, and usually ground at quarries before being traded into the use areas where they may be further ground and most of them decorated with fanciful bits of fur and/or different kinds of other materials that convey symbolic meaning (chapters 3 and 4). From the widely used sculptured and then decorated profane symbolic stones, certain ones are selected to be instilled with supernatural power and treated as ancestor stones in sacred places (chapter 4). In one sense these items may be thought of as three-dimensional pieces of religious art. The fundamental aesthetic qualities of both the profane and the sacred symbolic stones derive from their simple form and natural colors— stones of certain structures and colors being more desirable to individuals in one area, and stones of slightly different structures and colors being sought by individuals in other areas.

In the Yali and East (eastern part of the research area), some of these kinds of stones are painted with geometric designs when used for sacred purposes; a lesser number used by the Una people are even incised with simple circular patterns. In this same Yali and East region, tabular rectangular boards are incised with geometric patterns, painted, and used in much the same fashion as the sacred stones. This form of graphic art communicates religious symbolic meaning within the user populations and in one sense the objects are icons (chapter 4).

MUSIC. The Highlanders—both adults and children—sing for many occasions. The people, especially the men, sing when in communal work parties, while in groups moving along trails through the forest, at many of the almost endless numbers of pig-killing ceremonies, to accompany dances, at funerals, at the boy-girl get-together games, and sometimes when gathered in groups for just the fun of singing. Dirges are sung at funerals by both sexes and are also commonly sung by men at all-night healing procedures as well as at other sacred rituals within the men's houses. Brief dirges, punctuated with laughter and animated conversation, express the mixed feelings of women relatives as parts of the dress-the-bride ceremony. Chanting is an integral part of edai victory dances and in the vigorous "trance dance" that encourages a healing-shaman and sometimes his/her patient to go into trance.

The Highlanders do not whistle or hum, but the men produce an interesting, quite audible, raking noise by grinding their molars. A man produces this noise at unspecified times, as a person in a modern Western culture might hum to satisfy and please him/herself. I would suspect that abrasive wear would be detectable on molars habitually used this way.

The Highlanders have no instrumental accompaniment to singing or dancing. The only indigenous musical instrument is what is commonly called by modern outsiders the "bamboo mouth harp" (fig. 1.24). It is actually made from the *pithe* reed. The mouth harp is played by men or boys, never women, for solitary or group enjoyment but never to accompany a group of singers or dancers. The people have no percussion instruments, although the men do sometimes express agreement or pleasure by clicking their fingernails against their penis sheaths.

The reed mouth harps, 10–15 cm in overall length, are shaped with a small, sharp, unretouched chert flake or, in a lesser number of circumstances, with a rodent or marsupial mandible-tooth graver (see Hampton 1997:297–99 for details).

DANCE. Two commonly used dance patterns prevail within the Highlands cultural systems: (1) the common worldwide pattern of a line of female dancers opposing a line of male dancers and (2) groups of mixed males and females, or groups of either sex, running back and forth or around in circles, shouting and singing. In the line dancing, the dance steps are simple, with only up and down movements of the feet. A characteristic sing-chant accompanies the dance. The arms, hands, fingers, and other body parts make no distinctive movements and apparently do not have parts to play in the dancing.

In addition to the two predominate types of dance patterns just described, both of which purposefully fulfill needs within community life (Hampton 1997:299–302), there is yet a third style of dance that is rhythmic and energetic and is used to alter states of consciousness of both healing shamans and sometimes their patients. This dance, done by energetically jumping up and down while either standing or from a squatting position accompanied by a chantlike rhythm, is a part of certain nighttime healing rituals that involve trance and other states of emotion that transcend everyday experience.

Lomax and Arensburg (1977) would see a correlation between the Highlands' relatively low level of subsistence and the peoples' song, instrumental music, and dance. These authors and their colleagues have made one of the most ambitious attempts to document the direct ways in which music and dance are a part of human adaptations (Lomax 1968; Lomax and Arensburg 1977). Although Kaeppler (1978) criticizes the studies on technical grounds relative to sampling and coding procedures, Lomax and Arensburg leave us with a provocative theory that can be translated to possible evolutionary relationship between the relative low-level stage of subsistence of the Highlanders with their associated stone tools and digging sticks, to a more definable stage in the evolution of the performing arts.

Tools from Other-than-Rock Materials

The raw materials used in Highlands technology include rock, wood, bamboo, rattan, bone, grass, feathers, shell, *Pandanus* palm leaves, banana leaves and banana trunks, reeds, gourds, orchid fiber, palm fiber, beeswax, and seeds. The Highlanders never developed pottery nor basketry, although they did hand weave nets and other artifacts of culture without the assistance of wooden looms. The variety of tools made from other-than-rock materials is impressive. Those of wood and bamboo are culturally the most important. Their visualization and development was an important—maybe even essential—part of the evolutionary step that the Highlanders made some millennia ago from a hunter-gatherer cultural stage to a plant and animal husbandry stage. By extending the shaft of stone adze/axe blades from the length of their own arms and hands to a more powerful and mechanically efficient chopping tool by adding wooden shafts, fixed at advantageous angles to the cutting edges of the stone blades, the people were able to deforest large areas where they could concentrate the growth of food plants. With fire-hardened digging spades and sticks that vary in length from about 1 to 2.5 m, the horticulturists were able to manipulate the soil within the newly deforested areas and to create a complex of gardens with irrigation and drainage ditches. With the introduction of pigs to the island of New Guinea some 6,000 to 2,000 ya, the horticulturists, who were probably already growing taro and yams, included pig husbandry in their strategy of subsistence. The women, who never carry bows and arrows like most men routinely did, both as weapons against sudden raids or to be ready for spontaneous hunting opportunities, have the digging sticks as their near-constant companions. They are used by women not only in the daily routine of planting, weeding, aerating the soil, and harvesting, but also as formidable weapons of defense against surprise attacks. With the newly improved wooden-handled stone chopping and adzing tool, the people were able to cut and adze very large quantities of lumber with which to build their efficiently designed houses and to fence living communities and gardens to control their domestic pigs. The surgical sharpness of their bamboo knives was advantageous, if not essential, to the castration, disarticulation, and butchering of pigs as their animal husbandry practices became a featured aspect of this newfound way of life.

WOOD. In addition to the stone adze and axe blade handles and the all-important digging sticks, probably the next most used and important wooden tool is the large wooden tongs (1.2 to 1.8 m long) that both men and women use to carry heated rocks from the "open furnaces" to the outdoor steam bundles, where pig meat, sweet potatoes, and other vegetables are cooked at rituals and ceremonials (fig. 1.25). Smaller wooden tongs (from a split branch) of the same

Fig. 1.24. The reed mouth harp is the common indigenous musical instrument.

Fig. 1.25. Wooden tongs for moving heated rocks while cooking outdoors

BAMBOO. The sharpest cutting blades known in the prehistoric (or in modern times) are obsidian knives made by an Upper Paleolithic blade technique. These knives are superior in almost every way to modern surgical scalpels (Haviland 1993:79, 80). The next sharpest prehistoric knives are flaked blades made from a variety of cherts (flint, agate, silicified wood, and chalcedony) and certain orthoquartzites. Although none of the latter compare to obsidian blades for sharpness, such knives along with those of obsidian have served prehistoric humankind quite well over a long span of time and in many parts of the world.

The Irian Jaya Highlanders, however, have no supply of obsidian, orthoquartzite, nor even an adequate supply of large enough chert nodules from which to make stone flake knives of the sharpness desired for specific cutting chores. In lieu thereof, the Highlanders use the sharp, durable, and energy-efficient bamboo knife as a replacement for certain kinds of stone knives so commonly used in other parts of the world (Hampton 1997:242–49). The bamboo knife is the only kind of knife used by the Highlanders for surgical procedures on both human beings and pigs and for disarticulating, skinning, and butchering the large cassowary bird and pigs. In the research area, thousands of pigs are killed and eaten each year at the ongoing pig ceremonies. The pigs are killed in a procedure using a very sharp bamboo-tipped arrow, skinned with bamboo knives, and disarticulated with a stone adze and bamboo knives (sometimes with just bamboo knives), and the meat is then cut with only the use of bamboo knives. Quite a statement is made for our consideration when we contemplate a prehistoric animal kill or processing site at which no stone processing tools are found (see Pope 1994:163).

FIRE-STARTING TOOLS: ORGANIC AND STONE. One of the more intriguing missing archaeological links in the evolution of cognition and technology is tangible information relative to the times, places, and methods by which humankind first purposefully started fire. From ethnographic studies and the relatively

general appearance are routinely used by women in communal cookhouses to move charcoal, hot rocks, sweet potatoes, and other food items about in the fireplaces.

Wooden twig tweezers are used by men for plucking unwanted hair from their bodies. Twigs of similar small size are often used by men to set mouse and rat snares while traveling in the forest. Perhaps this practice originated with their ancestors when they lived in a hunting-and-gathering stage.

recent archaeological record, several kinds of fire-starting kits and techniques are known.

In the Irian Jaya Highlands research area, there are two techniques with two distinctly different kinds of fire-starting kits (figs. 1.26, 1.27, and 1.28). All language-speaking groups across the research area use the rattan-thong-stick fire-starting kit shown in the lower photograph of fig. 1.26. A roll of unsplit rattan, along with a split wooden stick that is held open near one end with a small rock, a short piece of another stick, or even a piece of bone, make up the two permanent elements of this kind of fire-starting tool. The necessary tinder (leaves, grasses, or strips of bark fiber) is not usually maintained as a part of the kit, but is collected whenever a fire is to be started. The thong is briskly pulled back and forth against the foot-held resistance of the split stick, until heat created by the friction ignites the tinder (fig. 1.27). The bundle of tinder that had been secured in the open fork of the stick is then carefully picked up and the flames encouraged by gently blowing on the tinder.

The second kind of fire-starting tool I named the "Wano bamboo matchbox" after the Wano people whom I observed using it while working in the Yeineri rock quarry area (figs. 1.26 and 1.28) (Hampton 1992c:95, 96). It is not even known throughout most of the different language-speaking groups within the Highlands research area. In addition to its use by the Wano in the Yeineri quarry area, I found that it is used by the Duvle-speaking lowland neighbors of the Wano to the north (fig. 1.3). A key coastal Melanesian informant reports that he observed this same kind of fire-starting kit in use by Melanesians who live in the interior of the "Birds Head" area in the extreme western part of the island of New Guinea (fig. P.1).

The "bamboo matchbox" consists of a single internodal section of bamboo stem that varies from about 28–36 cm in length for each fire-starting kit (fig. 1.26). The bottom of the tube is normally closed off by a natural bamboo septum, but, if broken in use, the hole is plugged with a wax (identification not known) the Wano call *ijuk*. At the bottom of the tube, dried, shredded leaf tinder is packed on top of a

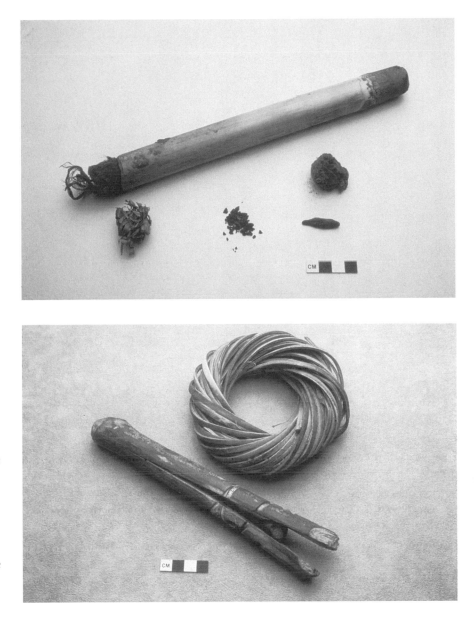

wad (or layers) of dried fiber hairs that are carefully harvested from new palm leaves of a specific palm they call *nibung*, which I have not identified. The hairs or "fuzz" tinder are called *gabuk* and *trivits* by the Wano users. Sprinkled in with this special, highly flammable material are tiny bits of charcoal made from the roots of breadfruit or *Pandanus* trees. A layer of tiny bits of the charcoal is usually accumulated before a small (about 3–4 cm long), river-smoothed, usually linear striking stone called a *yugum* is included. The type of rock material is apparently unimportant. The entire contents are capped with a wad of shredded leaf tinder.

Fig. 1.26. A bamboo "matchbox" and rattan-thong-stick fire starters

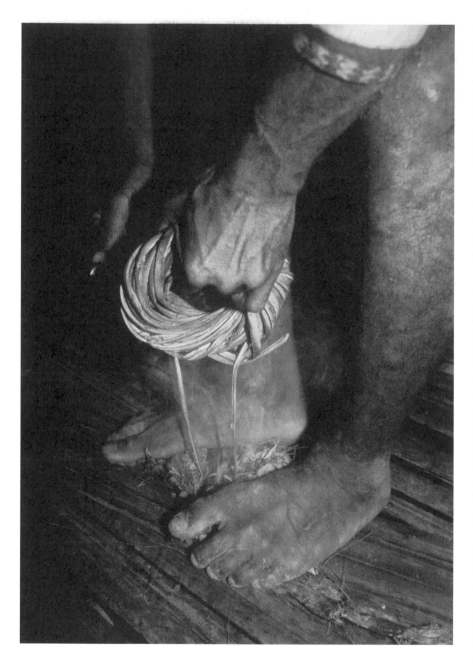

Fig. 1.27. Thong-stick friction ignites tinder.

bamboo that is both a container and a striking surface must be brittle from dryness to function successfully as the striking surface. It is presumed that the silicon dioxide (SiO_2) phytoliths within the bamboo play a role in creating a hard, brittle surface against which a stone striker can produce either a spark or heat-induced friction to ignite the special tinder.

BONE. The Highlanders make and use a large assortment of bone implements: boar tusk scraping tools, knives, awls, needles, and sometimes spoons (Hampton 1997:256–60).

BOAR TUSK SCRAPING TOOL. This tool is used to smooth down spears, bows, adze hafts, axe handles, digging sticks, and sometimes the hardwood tips of arrows. Both edges of the inner, concave surface of a boar tusk are sharpened with small chert flakes, the outer surface of another boar tusk, or a grinding stone to create two quite sharp cutting surfaces. With the two cutting edges, the tool can be used as a scraper in both the to-and-fro motions, but more often, a user will only scrape in one direction. When the edges become dull, they are easily resharpened with a chert flake or another boar tusk, which are kept in the same bark cloth or net bag with the scraper.

KNIVES. Bone knives are made primarily from the tibia of a pig and the cassowary bird, but sometimes from a dog bone. The cutting edges are honed down on grindstones and over time with resharpening and age become polished and a burnished brown color. The pig bone knives are mainly used to scrape and divide tubers (fig. 1.29). In the Grand Valley and West, both men and women seem to prefer the pig bone knife for this task rather than their stone knives, which they also have in their tool kits. Perhaps these bone knives are more available and less expensive from the many pig killings within their own compound communities and are also sharper than the ground stone knives that are traded in from a long distance. However, in the Yali and East, the people prefer their Langda-Sela ground stone knives, versus the bone knives for this same task (chapter 2). This situation may fit this theory because over-

In figure 1.26, some of the palm fuzz tinder protrudes from the upper end of the container. Below the container, on the right, is a small pile of the palm fuzz tinder, below that the yugum striking stone, to the left, a pile of the charcoal bits, and still farther to the left, the shredded leaf tinder "cap" for the bamboo matchbox.

To start a fire, the striking stone is held in one hand with bits of palm fuzz, charcoal, and leaf tinder that ignite from friction on about the third or fourth strike of the stone striker against the bamboo tube. The internodal section of

Fig. 1.28. Tingen Geri displays
a "Wano bamboo matchbox."

Fig. 1.29. Cutting and cleaning taro tubers with a pig bone knife

all the Yali own fewer pigs per house cluster than the Dani per compound.

People in both the Grand Valley and West and the Yali and East prefer the longer and stronger, daggerlike cassowary bone knives for dividing the pulpy red fruit of *Pandanus conoideus.* In addition to its use as a tool, the cassowary knives are used as weapons and also as decorated sacred objects.

AWLS AND NEEDLES. Awls and needles are made from the bones of marsupials, rodents, bats, and pigs. Whole marsupial, rodent, and bat wing bones are ground to shape and honed to sharp points on both portable and bedrock sandstone grinding surfaces; whereas the femurs and rib bones of pigs are first splintered, then select pieces are honed and polished by grinding. With aging and repeated sharpening and polishing, all but the bat wing awls and needles become a burnished brown in color. A needle for sewing is created by drilling a small hole in the unsharpened end of an awl with the point of an unretouched chert flake. The more durable archaeological remainders that attest to the presence of bone awls and needles within the cultural systems are not the implements themselves, but the traces they leave on grindstones when they are shaped and sharpened (chapter 2).

In addition to awls and needles, another small but important bone tool is the marsupial and rodent jawbone tooth-graver. These mandible halves-with-tooth are used to incise hardwood arrow tips, arrow shafts, bamboo earplugs, and both bamboo and gourd water containers. For incision work on most of these kinds of objects, chert flakes are also sometimes used.

Beeswax

Beeswax is used as a multipurpose glue, sometimes to assist in holding fixed arrow tips into reed shafts and to help "set" stone adze blades onto the wooden sockets of their hafts.

Profane and Sacred Uses of Fiber String

The most widely used natural product in the Highlands is rolled fiber string (fig. 1.30). String secures the essential items of attire on *all* adults. In addition to contributing to the com-

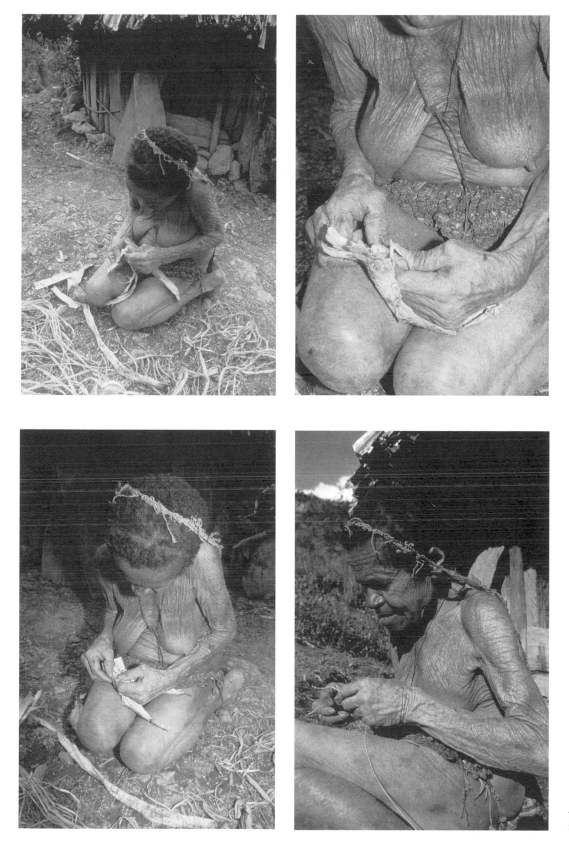

Fig. 1.30. Old Yali woman making string

positions of the variety of female skirts that are used among the diverse language-speaking groups in the Highlands, the women's important head-back carrying nets are all made of string. Several sizes of smaller net bags are used by males in which to carry small tools, sacred objects, cigarette-making materials, and miscellaneous items. The sociopolitically and economically important cowrie shell decorated display and exchange bands (*jerak*), as well as the strapless ceremonial nets, both of which are of basic importance to many ceremonial functions, are all made of string. String is sometimes used to bind adze blades to their handles. A list of other miscellaneous profane uses of string within the adjacent Highlands cultural systems is encyclopedic in nature.

The inner bark of certain kinds of trees and the shrub *Urticaceae* are the raw materials for much of the string. As with many other forest materials, the better quality of bark comes from trees that are located away from the more densely populated Grand Valley and must be traded into the valley from the Yali to the east, or from less densely settled areas to the west. In some cases, regardless of the language group area, small gathering parties of three to six go off for several days on collecting trips. The gatherers collect tree bark, using stone adzes to cut pieces of bark about 1 m in length or longer from the selected species of trees. Bundles of the bark are brought home for processing. The outer bark is scraped away from the inner core with bamboo knife scrapers, creating pieces of bark cloth that are dried in the sun or within the women's communal cookhouses. After drying, the pieces of bark cloth are beaten on a rock with wooden mallets (short pieces of tree limbs) to loosen the fibers, which are then accumulated into bundles for use without being rolled, or more often, for later use by rolling the fibers into lengths of fiber string. Both women and men roll fibers on their thighs to twist them into lengths of string. A lesser amount of string is made from fibers pulled off of sticks taken from certain bushes.

In figure 1.4, a married Dani woman on Sekan Ridge outside of the Grand Valley basks in the early morning sun as she uses the typical Dani-style hand-foot loom technique to weave a head-back net. The weaver's left hand has been mutilated at funeral sacrifices. Perhaps it is the loss of fingers that prompted the Dani and Western Dani to develop their hand-foot technique of weaving. In the woman's right hand, she holds two pieces of a broken bush stem from which she will pull fibers and splice into her rolled working string as she weaves. The Highlanders have no fixed wooden looms.

The Yali women seldom use the hand-foot loom technique of the Grand Valley and West, which is possibly due to the fact that they do not amputate their fingers. Instead, they stand or sit while weaving, holding and working the nets with both hands. Ancestors of the present-day Yali developed an innovative technique, unique to the Yali, which makes Yali head-back carrying nets a valuable trade item to adjacent-living, different-language-speaking groups. The Yali use thin plant-strip spacers that allow them to create loops of various but *uniform* sizes in each of their nets (fig. 1.31). The small-looped nets are desired by users outside Yali territory.

Women across the Highlands carry their babies, piglets, and heavy loads of food plants in their combination dress and utilitarian head-back nets. From a behavioral perspective, women carrying loads who are on the move on a daily basis are symbolic of one aspect of division of labor between the sexes. The use of string nets to transport and store (by hanging in cookhouses) these kinds of foodstuffs compares to the uses of basketry and pottery for similar purposes in areas where grains are the staple food products. Direct evidence for the uses of large quantities of head-back nets would likely be absent, however, in the archaeological record because of the decaying effects of the wet climate.

Relative to the division of labor, men, in addition to being responsible for the tasks of bridge, fence, rock wall, and house construction; preparing new gardens; and ditch maintenance, also do some of the more detailed weaving and braiding. They plait the fiber armlets, weave the cowrie shell display and exchange bands, and, within the Dani and Western Dani language speaking groups, make *all* of the braided string-orchid-fiber cording that is used for the women's wedding skirts.

An essential item of attire for most Dani and some Western Dani, both men and women, is a ritually empowered sacred fiber string necklace called, in mid–Grand Valley dialect, a dibat. A dibat may consist of a single (or several natural string fibers) or several fibers that have been rolled into a piece of string. On some wearers, the dibat is just the natural colors of the string, while on others they have been colored with soot-blackened pig grease. All dibat are generally thought to protect the wearer from harm and sickness. They are installed in ritual as a supernaturally powered countermeasure against the entrance of malevolent ghosts and spirits through the particularly vulnerable sternum area.

Dibat are empowered by a shaman at any of several sacred rituals where at least one pig has been sacrificed to encourage beneficent ghosts/ spirits to enter the necklace. Sometimes the dibat are installed at near-private ceremonies where an individual has raised a specific pig for the sacrifice and made arrangements with a shaman for the installation ritual. In addition, dibat installations are routinely carried out in conjunction with boys' initiation ceremonies, weddings, *ganekhe hakasin* ceremonies (refer to chapter 4), *wim ganekhe hakasin* ceremonies, or as a part of some shaman-directed healing procedures. Regardless of the ceremony at which the dibat is empowered and installed on a single person or on a group of individuals, this act is called in mid–Grand Valley Dani dialect a *dibat isin* (dibat, string; isin, to put on).

The dibat are worn as cumulative neck attire by some individuals. Other necklaces and some protective amulets are removed and exchanged frequently as items of dress, but if a dibat is removed, its power is gone. When a dibat becomes tattered, it may be ritually replaced. In certain cases, a person, particularly a shaman, may wear a single or a few empowered cowrie shells on a dibat. In such instances, if the dibat (string) itself becomes worn out, its power may be transferred to another dibat by reattaching the cowrie shell to a newly made dibat without the normal pig sacrifice.

Fig. 1.31. A Yali woman uses spacers to weave a quality net.

The accumulation of numerous dibat on the Sompaima mummy (fig. 1.13) were installed, one at a time, at various spirit installation and empowerment rituals of the kind that is described in the subsection entitled "The *Ganekhe Hakasin* Ceremony" in chapter 4. The various dibat installed on the mummy are both to protect and re-empower the ancestral spirit that is thought to be within. Perhaps one of the dibat might even have been put in place when a personified ancestral spirit was initially installed into the mummy. At that time, it is presumed (I do not know from informants) that the specific spirit of installation was that from the original "life-soul" matter of the person who died and was mummified.

Sacred Objects

The Highlanders recognize numerous kinds of sacred objects that focus their beliefs, many of which are utilized to manipulate supernatural power on the people's behalf (chapter 4).

Environment and Cultural Landscape

THE NATURAL ENVIRONMENT. The Grand Valley is a northwest-southeast-oriented, oblate-shaped flood plain (fig. 1.21). (The Grand Valley of the Baliem is sometimes referred to by others as the Baliem Valley. Hereinafter, I will continue to refer to it as the Grand Valley.) Marshy in many spots, the valley floor is a mosaic of sweet potato fields and irrigation ditches interrupted by a few low-lying hills of limestone and sandstone. The surrounding mountains rise from the valley floor, elevation 1,600 m above sea level, to heights of 2,500 to 3,000 m, while farther mountains rise to heights of 4,000 m and more. Snow can often be seen to the southwest atop the Trikora Crest (Wilhelmina Top) 4,750 m (fig. 1.32). A remnant receding Pleistocene glacier and snow is present on the Jaya Crest at the southwestern end of the study area. Swift tributaries of the Baliem River spill out of the surrounding mountains, abruptly slowing down as they reach the valley floor, and wind through the maze of sweet potato fields and networks of ditches to the centrally located Baliem River, which meanders the length of the valley with a deep, swift-flowing current.

Along the southeastern fringe of the valley from Pugima southward, past Seinma to the head of the Baliem Gorge where limestone rock erratics abound, an artful pattern of rock walls attests to the horticultural practice of the indigenous inhabitants (fig. 1.21). Here a karstic topography is also present on a limestone substratum with numerous sinkholes. Tuber gardens are sometimes planted right down to the bottoms of sinkholes.

Elsewhere around the margins of the valley a few scattered sinkholes in limestone terrain are indicative of underground streams that commonly emerge and disappear and sometimes issue forth from caves at the valley floor. Scattered pools with no visible inlets or outlets give further testimony to an underground system of water movement. Upriver, west of the Grand Valley, even the Baliem River itself disappears only to emerge out of the subterranean from what must be an extremely large, cavernous system.

Promontories and topographic ridges around the edges of the valley often accommodate caves at or near the junctures of steep slope faces with the valley floor.

At the southeast end of the valley, the Baliem River enters the steep walled Baliem Gorge, where it rushes in white-water torrents through narrow canyons as it descends out of the Central Highlands through territories of the Silimo, Hupla, and Momuna language-speaking groups onto the flat jungle swampland of southern New Guinea (figs. 1.3, 1.21).

The study area west of the Baliem River system, starting at Mulia on its east end, is bisected north-south by a relatively flat east-west travel route that approximately follows topographic contours at elevations of about 2,050 m from Mulia to Beoga where the route loses elevation west of the study area into the Enarotali-Paniai Lake area (fig. 1.32). At Mulia the people live on lower hillside slopes and valley floors at elevations that vary from 1,160 to 1,980 m. Rugged, high mountain peaks rise north and south of this route to elevations up to 4,040 m to the north and 5,030 m on the south at the Jaya Crest (Carstenz Pyramid), which is the highest point on the Island of New Guinea. The route lets down in elevation from the west end of the study area, north of the Jaya Crest to Enarotali at Paniai Lake. Here at the population center for the Kapauku people, the elevation of the swampy, flat Kamu Valley floor is 1,500 m, almost the same as the 1,600 m for the Grand Valley floor to the east. The surrounding mountain peaks in the Paniai area rise to well over 3,000 m.

CLIMATE. The study area, centered on about 4°S latitude, is characterized by the ab-

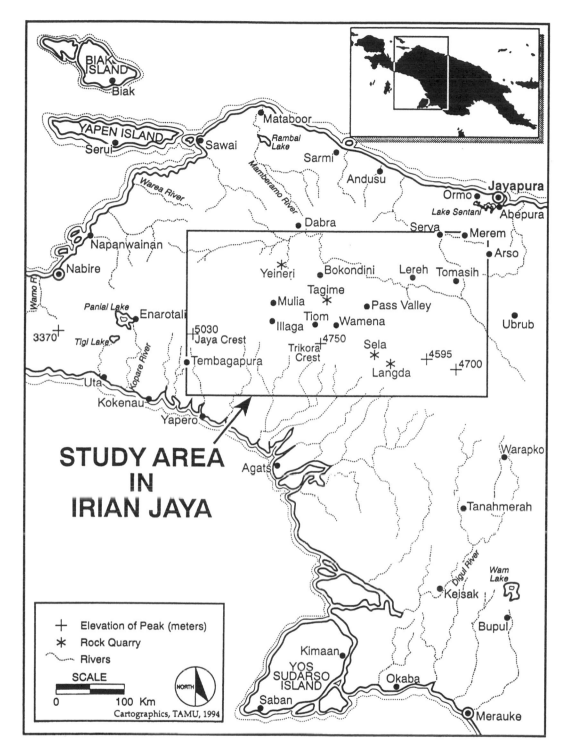

Fig. 1.32. Geographic reference points in Irian Jaya, Indonesia

sence of perceived seasonal weather variations by the local inhabitants (although November to April are actually the wettest months), nearly equal hours of darkness and daylight per day on an annual basis, moderate temperatures within the habitation zone (1,000–2,950 m), and abundant rainfall.

The inhabitants of the Grand Valley enjoy a year-round moderate climate. The absolute temperature range at Wamena is from 29.5°C to 6°C, with a mean daily range from 14°C at 6:00 A.M. to 24°C at noon. The mean relative humidity at Wamena is 98 percent at 6:00 A.M., 60 percent at noon, and 80 percent at 6:00 P.M.

Up the hillslopes from the valley floor the temperature ranges drop with increasing elevation. Frosts are not unusual at elevations above 3,000 m. On the higher mountain peaks snowfall occurs from time to time. Rainfall per year, as measured at Wamena, is 2,100 mm. There are approximately 245 rainy days (6.0 mm or more) per year.

At sunrise, fog often fills the topographic lows in and around the Grand Valley as well as in the narrower valleys away from the Baliem. As the sun rises this fog burns off, but higher on mountain slopes and around mountain peaks, skirts of clouds usually persist and build up during the afternoon and evening.

The fact that the Highlands of New Guinea is one of the wettest areas on the earth, while Australia is one of the hottest and driest, demonstrates poignantly the importance of climate as a controlling "context" when making archaeological interpretations. Referring to the first two sections of this chapter we see that the Australian and New Guinean populations arrived on the mega-island continent of Sahul as hunter-gatherers from a supposed common gene pool on the eastern extended edges of Southeast Asia (Sunda) by 40,000 ya. In Australia the technological evolution from that time included the early appearance of ground-edge tools but stopped short of a Neolithic revolution, whereas the people in the Highlands of New Guinea evolved from the same hunter-gatherer lifestyle to become sedentary horticulturists who practiced animal husbandry with all the attendant material baggage, subsistence strategy and tactics, economic customs, and political organization of a population that had evolved through at least the earliest phases of a place- and time-specific phase of the Neolithic revolution. With the caveat of knowing that both geologic and topographic differences in the two areas also affected the evolutionary strategy and tactics of basically the same people, the underlining (or overcontrolling) role of major climate differences must be recognized as a very important context in which we gather data and make archaeological interpretations.

FLORA. Flora of the tropical rain forest, which borders the lower edges of the Central Highlands, merges upward with the mountain flora of the foothills and lower mountain slopes. The giant swamp taro (*Cyrtosperma* sp.) and sago (*Metroxylon* sp.) of the lower environment is a food source for lowland dwellers. Coming up the slopes out of the lowlands, ridge crests are covered with dense growths of trees of the rain forest that merge upward into the midmountain forest.

From botanical work done on their discovery visit to the Grand Valley in 1938, Archbold, Rand, and Brass concluded that the midmountain forest was the most important floral zone on the higher portions of the Baliem (Grand) Valley floor and was dominated by oak (*Quercus* sp.) with some of the large coniferous araucaria (*Araucaria* sp.) (1942:282). Savannah grasses, more typical of lowland treeless areas, had taken over abandoned garden areas and burned-off slopes (Brass 1941:338).

From about the 2,000 m level on the mountain slopes surrounding the Grand Valley, the beech forest zone with its moss-draped trees extends up to the subalpine forest zone, which flourishes between 3,000 and 4,000 m (Archbold et al. 1942:282–83). Subalpine merges upward into alpine above 4,000 m on the taller peaks, and a receding Pleistocene glacial cap remnant is present atop the Jaya Crest (5,030 m) in the southwest corner of the study area (fig. 1.32).

Within the spread of the vegetation zones occupied, or at least harvested, by the indigenous people of the Highlands, virgin forests contain a great variety of tall evergreens, scattered softwood trees, different species of *Pandanus* palms, other palms, bamboo, rattan, shrubbery, vines, bromeliads, and many varieties of flowers, weeds, and grasses. Throughout the Highlands study area, many fallow slopes, extending to ridge crests and mountain peaks, are in various stages of regrowth and covered with shrubbery and grasses.

FAUNA. New Guinea, like Australia and Tasmania, was separated by oceanic stretches of water from Asia at the time when placental mammals evolved and dispersed throughout the Asian continent. It was not until the eastward extension of the Sunda shelf from Asia and the combining of Australia, New Guinea, and Tasmania into one continent at periods of maximum lowering of sea level during the Pleistocene that humans and animals like bats, flying foxes, and rodents are thought to have found their ways to New Guinea as representatives of placental mammals.

Throughout the study area the native mammals and reptiles present at the times of the first modern contacts consisted of several species of marsupials, including the tree kangaroo and bandicoots, both wild and feral pigs, the rare New Guinea "singing dog" and other species of dog, both small and large rats, as well as smaller rodents, bats and flying foxes, a few lizards, frogs, and some nonpoisonous snakes, including at least one variety of python.

Birds abound, including the large ground-running cassowary, numerous species of birds of paradise, parrots, cockatoos, the large New Guinea pigeons, hawks and a few other soaring birds of prey like sea eagles, two kinds of heron (one blue-gray, another white), cormorants, plus a variety of ducks and assorted song birds. In the subalpine and alpine zones some grouse are present.

The larger marsupials, such as the tree kangaroo and bandicoot; wild and feral pigs; and certain highly desirable birds, such as the ground-running cassowary and most birds of paradise, were hunted out of the Grand Valley and possibly other densely populated areas by the times of first contact with modern outsiders.

As one would expect, insects are numerous. Flies can be thick, especially around occupied areas where there is an abundance of pig scat. Bees and wasps are present as well as fleas, which are transported by pigs and infest both local dwellings and individuals' hair. Beeswax is culturally important, used as a glue for multiple purposes. Moths and butterflies of various sizes are present, which account for the numerous cocoons that are culturally used both as decorative objects and wrapping material. Many kinds of spiders are present. Some, like the *Cryptophora moluccensis* (identified courtesy Edwin Licht, University of Colorado Henderson Museum, Boulder, 1991) are quite large. Their webs are culturally important and are used to make necklaces, which, after empowerment through ritual, are thought to be supernaturally powerful and used to protect the body from ghosts.

Lakes and rivers, prior to the arrival of modern outsiders, were without fish but many were and still are teeming with crawfish. I suspect that the very large crawfish of the Baliem River might even be misidentified and actually be a fresh water lobster.

GEOLOGY. The central mountain chain that extends the length of the Island of New Guinea is a 150 km-wide band of jumbled peaks and valleys that rise abruptly from near-sea-level elevations to peak crests of elevations that often exceed 4,000 m and locally exceed 5,000 m in the study area (fig. P.1). Rock strata that are often severely folded, faulted, and crumpled are of diverse ages and lithologies.

This composite of diverse stratigraphy and complex tectonics comprise the geologic terrain to which the indigenous people adapted. From the rock outcrops, the people located and identified those kinds of rocks that were best suited for their tools and symbolic stones. Within the terrain of mostly steep hillsides and narrow valleys, they adapted to their horticultural lifestyle as they evolved from a hunting-and-gathering culture to a predominately sedentary and horticultural subsistence, practicing both animal and plant husbandry.

The central mountain chain was formed during the late Cenozoic by the convergence of the Australian Plate from the south with the Pacific Plate from the north. The southern part of the extensive east-west trending central Highlands of the study area consists largely of sedimentary rocks that range in age from middle Jurassic to middle Miocene and which were deposited on a north-facing continental shelf now raised high and deformed. At the top and youngest part of the sequence in the Highlands is the New Guinea Limestone group of Tertiary age and possibly uppermost Cretaceous (Visser and Hermes 1962:79). These limestones have been heaved upward to form the great mountain wall that surrounds the Grand Valley and some of the peaks and other topographic features of the extensive chains of mountains and valleys that extend the length of the Irian Jaya Highlands from the border of Papua New Guinea on the east to past Paniai Lake (Enarotali) on the west (fig. P.1). The sequence may be as thick in the study area as 1,600 m from its measurement at the type locality to the west (Visser and Hermes 1962:79). The limestone typically weathers gray and erodes to form pinnacle and karst topography. It is within the New Guinea Limestone that most of the sacred caves and rock shelters of indigenous inhabitants are located. Chert nodules from within the New Guinea Limestone and of importance to the inhabitants for tool chips are sparse and small, generally no more than 2–4 cm in longest dimension.

The New Guinea Limestone grades conformably downward into the underlying Kembelangan formation, which ranges from Paleocene to Cretaceous in age. The Kembelangan consists of four members, with lithologies of claystones, shales, argillites, silt stones, and some interbeds of quartzitic sand stones (Visser and Hermes 1962:70). A limestone is at the base of the oldest member. Metamorphism of the Kembelangan seems to increase generally from west to east in Irian Jaya. In lower units of the Kembelangan, claystones in the west change to shales, meta-argillites, and even some slates, phyllites, and finally mica schists and talc schists eastward. Belemnites, ammonites, and foraminifera are present. Ammonite content at some localities is extensive. Ammonites collected from river detritus of tumbled boulders and pebbles are often preserved as sacred objects by the indigenous inhabitants. River-rounded clay stone and argillite pebbles, with and without fossils, are also favored as sacred symbolic stones (detail in chapter 4). In one locale (Tagime quarries, fig. 1.32), meta-argillite boulders, recognized for their qualities of hardness and durability, are selected as source stones for tools as well as to be shaped into tabular symbolic stones.

Volcanic rocks have not been previously reported by geologists to exist within the study area, but andesite-basaltic rocks have been petrographically identified as part of this project by Guillemette, Medlin, Munoz, and Swope from rock samples in the Langda-Sela area, southeast of the Grand Valley (fig. 1.32). It is from select fine-grained, homogenous rock of this sequence that the Una and Kimyal people make their adzes and stone knives at the Langda-Sela quarries. Based on regional extrapolation from known volcanic rock sequences to the east in Papua New Guinea, these volcanics could be anywhere from Jurassic to Quaternary in age.

Whereas the south half of the east-west trending central mountain chain that makes up the Highlands of central New Guinea consists primarily of Cretaceous to Miocene-age Kembelangan and New Guinea Limestone formations within the central and southern parts of the study area, the mountain chain within northern parts of the research area consists of a Tertiary melange in which deeper water equivalents of shelf strata were jumbled with ophiolite slices and metamorphic rocks, including glauchophane-epidote schists, blueschist, greenschist, phyllites, and amphibolites. High pressure metamorphic rocks of slate and marble are also present. Along linear strike of the ophiolite-melange belt, some rocks at certain locales contain hornblende, garnet, epidote, and kyanite. The entire ophiolite-melange belt of the study area is known only from sketchy reconnaissance by Duncan B. Dow and extrapolations across the area from work reported at the Indonesian Petroleum Association Thirteenth Annual Convention (1984), Warren Hamilton (1979), Visser and Hermes (1962); and by my own excursions into or across the ophiolite-melange belt as I followed hypothetical trade routes and searched for rock quarries. In the Yeineri area (fig. 1.32), the indigenous people found just the right combination of rocks cropping out within this melange-ophiolite belt to establish a stone quarrying operation of some consequence, which is discussed in chapter 5.

TECTONICS. The earth movements that commenced in the latest Miocene or earliest Pliocene according to Dow and Hartono (1984:145) are still continuing today. Although most seismicity earthquake epicenters fall outside the area of study, to the north, northeast, east, and west two epicenters are located within the study area (Dow and Hartono 1984:149). Minor earth tremors occur every month or so, some strong enough to visibly shake houses. Major earthquakes are rare but often tremors are strong enough to cause mud slides carrying dense vegetal material down steep slopes. It does not take much shaking to initiate slides of water-soaked soil and shallow-rooted forest material on slopes near the angle of repose. In 1989, soon after I left the Kurima area, an earthquake initiated landslides that buried villages at great loss of life to the local inhabitants.

Probably unknown to the earliest inhabitants of the Highlands was the fact that volcanic activity and ongoing mountain building provided more nutritive soils to the scattered intermontane valleys than was available in Australia—just one of the multiple contexts that partially accounted for an early evolution from a nomadic hunter-gather lifestyle to that of sedentary horticulturists in the Irian Jaya Highlands.

BRINE POOLS (SALT). Salt (NaCl) is precious to the Irian Jaya Highlanders; its consumption a luxury. A special treat is to eat bits of salt with raw ginger and cooked sweet potato. Salt is a valuable trade item, with its value increasing the greater the distance from the salt sources. Within the study area I know of only two major supply points. Three other small brine pools only satisfy the hunger for salt of the closest inhabitants and a few passing travelers.

In the Grand Valley near Jiwika, the Ileukaima brine pool is a major source of salt for not only most of the Dani in the Grand Valley but also as a trade item (fig. 1.21). Much farther west, near Ilaga in the western part of the study area, another major brine pool furnishes salt via trade linkages all the way eastward to the Dani in the Swart Valley region (west of the Grand Valley) and as far to the west as the Enarotali area at Paniai Lake (figs. P.1, 1.32).

At the head of the Baliem Gorge, southeast of Tangma, small brine pools bubbling out of a slumped hillside area just above the Baliem River are visited by local inhabitants. I have heard of two other minor salt sources, one near the Yeti River between Hetagima and Kurima (fig. 1.21) and one in Yali territory near Angguruk, neither of which was I able to locate.

At Ileukaima, the brine pool, about 10 m in diameter and less than a meter deep, is next to a fresh water stream. In 1983 I sampled the water in the brine pool and found its salt content to be almost pure sodium chloride (NaCl), which is used worldwide as table salt. As far as a source for the salt water, I can only hypothesize that this and the other salt water springs are sourced by percolating underground water flows that dissolve salt (NaCl) from bedded salt within the New Guinea Limestone formation before emerging at the surface.

The brine at Ileukaima is extracted by using strips of dried banana that have been prepared at habitation sites before transport to the brine pool to be immersed in the salt water. These thin strips of banana trunk, their porous cellular structure now filled with brine water, are bundled up and carried back to the hamlets. Hard ashy salt cakes are produced by allowing the water to evaporate out of the banana trunk strips, leaving a salt residue in each organic strip. Then the strips are burned, leaving a salty ash residue that is molded into a salt cake with droplets of water and wrapped in a banana leaf. The salt ball is then ready to be transported for trade or stored for use. At the brine pool near Ilaga, the local people generally prefer to use banana leaves to soak up the salt brine. The leaves are then stacked and burned to produce the salt cakes. Control of the brine pools was an important factor of Highlands life. This subject is discussed in chapters 4 and 8.

THE CULTURAL LANDSCAPE. Understanding the cultural landscape within the study area is desirable before attempting to build ethnographically derived models of behavior regarding sacred stone tools and symbolic stones within the Highlands' cultures. The difficulty is identifying and understanding the hierophanies within a complex environment of seen and unseen entities. Eliade was probably the first to introduce the term "hierophany," which he believed was a fitting term because it is implicit in its etymological content, that is, that *something sacred shows itself to us.*

It is impossible to overemphasize the paradox represented by every hierophany, even the most elementary. By manifesting the sacred, any object becomes *something else,* yet it continues to remain *itself,* for it continues to participate in its surrounding cosmic milieu. A *sacred* stone remains a *stone;* apparently (or, more precisely, from the profane point of view), nothing distinguishes it from all other stones. But for those to whom a stone reveals itself as sacred, its immediate reality is transmuted into a supernatural reality. In other words, for those who have a religious experience all nature is capable of revealing itself as cosmic sacrality. The cosmos in its entirety can become a hierophany. (Eliade 1987a:11–12; emphasis in original)

In recent years scholars of non-Western belief systems have been trying to advance beyond antiquated terms such as "animism" and "animatism" when speaking of the conceptual relations between indigenous peoples and their cultural landscapes. Archaeologist Larry Lowendorf (personal communication 1994) believes that Irving Hallowell, the Algonquian anthropologist, made a well-known conceptual leap when he used the term *"other-than-human-person"* to characterize how Canadian Ojibway behaviorally interacted with entities in their nonbuilt environment for their material and psychological benefit. Earnest S. Burch, Jr., an anthropologist-ecologist, described the extensive domain as perceived by the traditional Arctic Alaskan Eskimos as the "nonempirical environment," with numerous and diverse phenomena (1971:148, 151). The entities the Eskimos regard as being "alive" range all the way from phenomena that are humanlike creatures, to animal-like, to completely invisible. In the study area of the Highlands of Irian Jaya, such entities are ghosts, spirits, and demons of the spirit world. By occupying both living and nonliving material objects, they may take on quite an array of appearances.

ANIMALS AND PLANTS. Animals (with the exception of pigs that are thought to have souls like humans) are said to be living bodies but without souls of their own. They may, however, *host* spirits. For example, demons of the spirit world, may reside inside a certain species of animal. Thus, for example, a representative of a certain kind of forest spirit may live in the body of a species of hawk; a water demon spirit may live within a particular kind of snake; or a spirit of the midmountain forest may dwell within the bodies of tree rats. There are hundreds, maybe even thousands, of these nonancestral spirits. They are accounted for in separate stories of the origin myth or just because they are known to exist.

Plants, like animals, are living and without souls, but they do *host* spirits.

Larson learned from the Dani and Damal in the Ilaga area that certain of the female demons of the forest "possess women by entering them through the vagina, thereby causing insanity or enabling them to kill by witchcraft. Women so possessed bewitch by leaving their own bodies in spirit (in the person of their own ghosts *ogoma*), either gradually consuming the spirit of a living victim (his *iniki*) or dramatically doing away with him through such calamity as drowning, crushing him with a falling tree, or through otherwise unexplainable misfortune" (1987:56).

Many female evil spirits are known to live in the lower forest, especially in stands of bamboo, having the ability to move out of their dwelling places to cause illness and death.

The numerous male evil spirits, called *kembu* by the Yali, Kimyal, and Una and *aap endak* by the Damal and many of the Dani, prefer groves of evergreens of the higher forest to scattered stands of bamboo below. The male spirits are believed to cause all sorts of ailments, aches, and pains, as well as death by illnesses such as influenza. Perhaps, aap endak (or kembu) are most feared by travelers because they are known to attack those who travel through their domain. Larson stated that "a lone traveler or hunter, for example, who dies of exposure on the high plateau is often said to have been killed by *aap endak*. Inexperienced travelers can become so fearful of the high forest demons they may even desert a lagging, sick member of their party to die in the cold for fear the demon killing him may also get them" (1987:57–58).

SUN, MOON, STARS, AND PLANETS. The most powerful of the "seen" sky entities are the sun and moon. Of the two, Mother Sun, called *Mo* by the mid–Grand Valley Dani is the most powerful. Her supernatural power is awesome, while that of her husband moon is of significance but of less importance. Among Heider's informants there was disagreement over the relationship between the sun and moon, as to whether they are husband and wife or brother and sister. Although the annual movement of the sun is not mapped in calendrical detail as it is in some other horticultural as well as later-evolved cultural systems farther from the equator (where the sun's position is important relative to growing seasons and associated rituals), its annual movement from summer to winter solstices is still recognized by its changing geographic positions on the horizon at sunrise and sunset. Its position at June solstice activates the evil female spirits of the lower forests to move uphill to cause illness and death. Similarly, its December solstice position on the mountain skyline activates the numerous male evil spirits of the upper forests to move down out of the high mountains to spread illness and death in the more densely populated regions below. This relationship between the "seen-sun" and the unseen evil spirits of the forest has consequences of importance to the lives of the Highlanders.

During the winter months, Mother Sun is thought to spend her nights, when she is out of the sky, in her winter home somewhere in the Jalemo to the east of the Grand Valley and south of Pass Valley (fig. 1.1). During the summer months, the sun spends the nighttime in her summer home in the Wadangku (alt. Wadlagu) compounds near the Grand Valley end of Pass Valley (fig. 1.1). Some informants say that after sunset each night she rapidly returns across the upper, invisible side of the sky to her house near the Grand Valley.

The moon, by most accounts the husband of the sun, guards the earth by night, which his wife, the sun, has warmed by day. The moon secretly reports back to his wife, the sun, the misdeeds of humans that he has observed during the night. The inference is that through control of the demonic spirit world, the sun can make retributions for wrongdoing.

Yali men and other informants scattered in the Highlands did not seem to attach much significance to the stars in the sky, but some felt that quartz crystals were fallen stars and often kept them among their sacred objects.

CAVES, ROCK SHELTERS, AND CREVICES. All caves, major holes in the ground, and many crevices are sacred—wusa. They are hierophanies, and entrance is prohibited to the uninitiated. These are the places of emergence of all life, both the seen and the unseen. It is within certain caves and rock shelters that the secrets of supernatural powers are discussed by men's groups, human skeletons are maintained, and certain sacred paraphernalia are kept for ritual purposes.

The leaders (big men) of hamlets or groups of hamlets often have their own sacred caves where they conduct ritual and go for private spiritual guidance.

UNUSUAL ROCK FORMATIONS AND STONES. Most unusual rock formations are perceived as places where spirits reside, or for other reasons are considered to be wusa and are, therefore, hierophanies and accorded due respect. Two such areas with which I am familiar contain sacred pictographs on cliff faces. At these locales, spirits in the rock are activated with special ritual every four or five years during the Waija boys' initiation ceremony.

Small rocks and river-worn pebbles of unusual shapes and colors are often picked up to be saved as stones with potential to receive supernatural power. Some will later be selected to be treated through ritual and imbued with supernatural power to be maintained and used for special purposes.

CHAPTER 2

Stone Tools and Profane Uses

Within the study area six kinds of ground stone tools are used (adzes, axes, knives, chisels [alternative names drill and gouge], stationary grinding slabs, and handheld grindstones) in addition to unground chert flakes, hammer stones, and anvils. Within one language group even an unusual stone-striker bamboo fire-starting kit is present (chapter 1). Not every kind of ground stone tool is used by each language-speaking group. The adzes, axes, knives, and chisels vary by shape, size, kind of rock, and color relative to quarry source. Of the six kinds of ground stone tools, the adzes and axes are the only percussive cutting implements. Both the adzes and axes are used with a chopping motion and are swung with percussive force to strike a blow with a cutting edge. All of the profane tools are described and grouped structurally into types in archaeologically useful terms to facilitate comparative studies in both the ethnographic present and with prehistoric assemblages. In the study area some of these tools and stone blades have important sacred uses in addition to their more commonly known profane uses. The sacred uses are discussed in chapter 4.

The quarrying complexes that are the sources for most of the stone used for both profane and sacred tools, as well as for the symbolic stones, are discussed in chapters 5, 6, and 7.

Two Major Distribution and Stone Tool Use Areas

During my first visit to the Grand Valley in May of 1982, I was able to start looking at tools and other artifacts of culture. I was immediately curious about the adze and axe tools, the different sizes, shapes, colors, and lithologies of the blades, all of which were ground stone.

During my next three visits to various parts of the Grand Valley and Western Dani territory to the west, the adze and axe blades that I saw, measured, and described, could be clustered into three groups by lithology and color differentiation. One group was black, which looked macroscopically like an argillite but because of

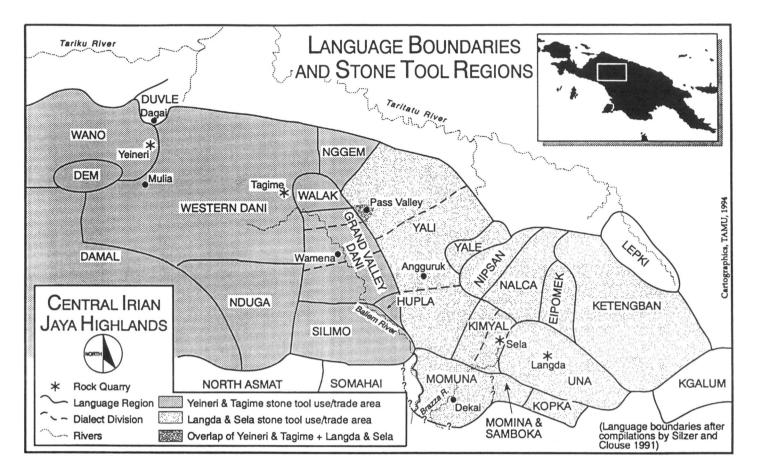

Fig. 2.1. Grand Valley and West and Yali and East stone tool regions and language speaking groups.

its hardness I presumed it to be a metasediment. A second group had a distinctly different color, ranging in individual specimens from predominantly green to blue. Some were dark; others were light-colored. Some were mottled, variegated, or solid in color. I presumed, again from macroscopic analysis, that these were probably similar to a greenschist, with mineral variations causing the color changes. A third miscellaneous group had individual blades that ranged in color from black to light green to tan; none of which looked like either of the other two groups, which were distinctively colored. The adze/axe blades that I was seeing were ranging in length for the black from 6 to 24 cm, from 4.5 to 39 cm for the blue-green, and from 6 to 20 cm for the miscellaneous category. In a dorsal plan view, shapes ranged from ellipsoidal to triangular for all three categories.

There was yet a fourth category of which I had seen only two adzes, but no separate adze blades. The blades were light gray-green, aphanitic, long and narrow, and looked like they might be andesite—distinctly different from the other three categories. The owner was a Yali man who, as a war refugee, had fled from his Yali homeland to Dani territory and was taken in by the mid–Grand Valley Dani. He continued to use his Yali adzes. He and Dani informants agreed that his type of adze was the only kind used by the Yali, so I felt that the unique stones were Yali and came from somewhere within Yali territory to the east of the Grand Valley.

As I continued to move among the people and about the study area, I confirmed that the black, dark green and blue variegated, and miscellaneous colored axe and adze blades, most with the same distinctive ellipsoidal to triangular shapes, but also some tubular shaped axe blades, were only used within the Grand Valley and westward. I also reaffirmed that the distinctive blades I had originally called Yali were used only to the east of the Grand Valley by the Yali, and yet farther to the east by other language speaking groups (fig. 2.1). This same kind of distribution that I was seeing in the ethnographic present could well be a distribution from prehistory.

Nomenclature

Adze and Adze Blade

The adze is the single most important tool of all the different language-speaking groups in the study area of Irian Jaya (fig. 2.2). For a definition of the implement and nomenclature I rely heavily on Blackwood (1964:13–14), deviating from her nomenclature or adding to it only in deference to clarity and an archaeologically oriented classification. As already pointed out in chapter 1, an adze is a cutting tool, the blade of which is hafted with its cutting edge transverse to the long axis of the shaft. This distinguishes the adze from an axe, which has a blade hafted so that the cutting edge is parallel to and in the same plane as the long axis of the shaft.

The haft is that part of the tool that forms the connecting link between the blade and the hand of the person using it (figs. 2.3 and 2.4). As shown in figure 2.3, the haft is cut from a tree where the branch forms the shaft and a piece of tree trunk, the foot. The bark is removed from the haft and the haft smoothed. The shaft is that part of the haft that is grasped by the hand or, more often, both hands, when chopping with the tool. The foot is that part of the haft that is transverse to the haft. The socket is that part of the foot that is flattened to form a surface against which the proximal end of the adze blade is lashed. The heel is the part of the foot away from the socket that joins the long axis of the shaft. Working with the Kukukuku in eastern Papua New Guinea (near Kosipe on fig. 1.2), Blackwood (1964:13) shows that the heel is a continuation of the long axis of the shaft and barely projects away from it. In the study area in Irian Jaya, I found that the heel usually projects a measurable length away from the long axis of the shaft, and that it generally varies from one-third of to the entire length of the socket. In a few cases I observed shafts

where the heels were nearly as long as the socket ends of the feet of the hafts. The haft angle is the angle between the shaft and the socket end of the foot and is determined by the angle at which the selected branch grows from the tree trunk. My measurements of socket angles throughout the entire study area varied from 50° to 85°, with one unusually curved haft where the socket angle was 95°, and several, also unusually curved hafts, where the socket angles were 33°, 38°, and 41°. The proximal end of the

Fig. 2.2. Dani man on Sekan Ridge with his large adze

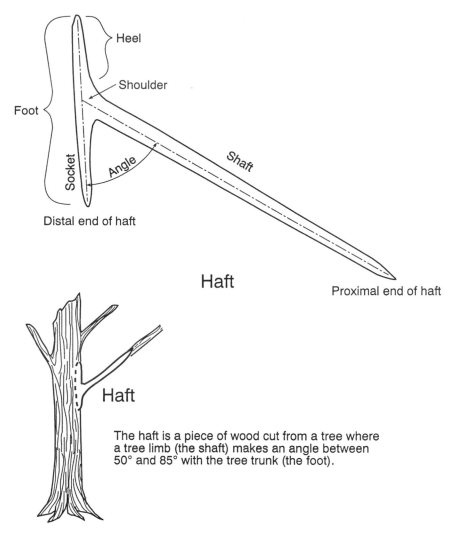

Heel

Shoulder

Foot

Socket

Angle

Shaft

Distal end of haft

Haft

Proximal end of haft

Haft

The haft is a piece of wood cut from a tree where a tree limb (the shaft) makes an angle between 50° and 85° with the tree trunk (the foot).

Fig. 2.3. The haft is part tree trunk and part limb.

haft is that nearest to the body when the tool is held in position for use. The distal end of the haft is at the socket end of the foot. In figure 2.4, a Dani man carries a piece of tree trunk and a newly cut haft from the forest to his home for further work. He will allow the haft to dry before flattening the upper surface of at least the socket end of the foot with an adze, and before attaching a ground stone adze blade.

The adze is the complete tool with the adze blade bound to the socket of the foot of the haft (fig. 2.5). Lashing the blade to the socket is called "hafting the blade." The lashing material is strips of rattan and/or string cording that secures the blade onto the flattened surface of the socket. The stone blade is secured to the distal part of the haft. The proximal end of the blade is the end bound to the socket. The distal end of the blade is the cutting edge. The dorsal

side of the blade is the side away from the shaft (called the "back of blade" by Blackwood [1964:13] and Hiroa [1930:333, 357]). The ventral side of the blade is the side facing the shaft (called the "front of blade" by Blackwood [1964:13] and Hiroa [1930:333, 357]).

When adze and axe blades are first shaped and the cutting edge of each blade formed and sharpened and then later, throughout the lifetime of the blade, resharpened, different characteristic structures are created at the cutting end of each blade. To facilitate communication and analyses of this important part of each tool, a set of terms is herein defined (refer to fig. 2.6). In longitudinal side view, the dorsal side of the blade is up, the ventral side down, and the cutting edge to the reader's left. The angle between a horizontal line and a line of a plane most nearly approximating the steepest part of the dorsal side of the blade, as it approaches the cutting edge, is defined as the dorsal bevel angle. The angle similarly described on the ventral side of the blade is the ventral bevel angle. The angle formed by the intersection of the dorsal and ventral sides of the blade at the cutting edge is termed the bit angle. In blades that are symmetrical in longitudinal side view cross sections, the dorsal bevel angle equals the ventral bevel angle. The sum of the dorsal and ventral bevel angles equals the bit angle, which measures the bluntness at the cutting edge of the tool.

AXE AND AXE BLADE. As Axel Steensberg says, in *Man the Manipulator,* "The difference between an adze and an axe depends on the way they are hafted, not whether they belong to the European Neolithic or New Guinea prehistory" (1986:11). In an earlier book, *New Guinea Gardens,* which is the result of three visits to what is now Papua New Guinea in 1968, 1971, 1975, Steensberg differentiated the Papua New Guinea axe from the adze when he showed that the cutting edge of the axe blade is hafted parallel to the longitudinal axis of the haft in the "fashion of the Neolithic Sigerslev axe in a perforated handle" (1980:14) (fig. 2.7C). The same definition holds true for the two types of axes that are used in the study area of Irian

Jaya, which are differentiated by the shapes of the distal ends of their handles. In both types, an axe blade is inserted into a hole near the distal end of the haft and held in place either by just a tight fit or with the help of pitch from the araucaria tree. In the most commonly used Highlands axe, or Type A, the distal end of the haft, where the blade is inserted, is bulbous in shape, tapering down to a more manageable handhold near the proximal end of the haft. This type of axe is shown at the top of figure 2.7. The second, or Type B axe, is distinguished by a rectangular shaped distal end, which, as mentioned in chapter 1, is sometimes used as a wedge when logs are being split. An example of the rectangular-ended Type B axe is shown in the middle drawing of figure 2.7. A type-sketch of the European Neolithic Sigerslev axe is shown at the bottom of the same figure. The nomenclature of the axe blade is the same as that of the adze blade, as presented in the previous section. When I cannot be definitive in typing loose blades as either adze or axe blades, I have chosen to call the blades adze/axe blades.

Knife

Knives are used by each of the language-speaking groups in the Irian Jaya study area. They are all ground stone and of differing shapes. None are hafted, so the knife blade is the total tool, and therefore referred to as the knife, rather than the knife blade.

Chisel

The nomenclature of chisels will be treated in a later section when these tools are discussed in more detail.

Methods of Determining Rock Lithologies

Within the study area the majority of ground stone tools originated from four widely scattered quarry areas: Yeineri, Tagime, Langda, and Sela, with another rumored quarry area in the vicinity of Korupun west of Sela (fig. 2.8). A sixth source, which I call "sources of opportunity," to be discussed in chapter 7, accounted for only a small number of tools. Langda, Sela, and Korupun (if the latter produced at all)

Fig. 2.4. A Dani carries a newly cut haft to his home.

produced lithics of the same lithologies, blade structure, and color, so they cannot be typed separately. I have not located a Korupun quarry on the ground and believe that people in that area may have only been a trading link between

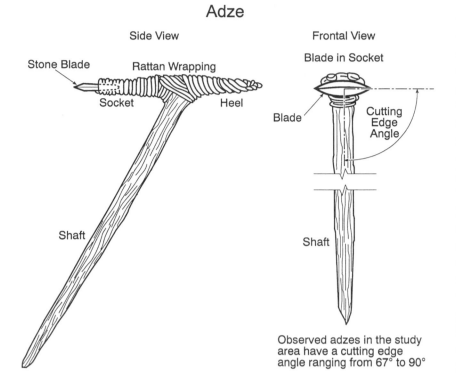

Adze

Side View

Stone Blade

Rattan Wrapping

Socket

Heel

Shaft

Frontal View

Blade in Socket

Blade

Cutting Edge Angle

Shaft

Observed adzes in the study area have a cutting edge angle ranging from 67° to 90°

Fig. 2.5. The adze is a complete tool with blade bound to haft.

the quarries in the Langda and Sela areas and some of the users of blades from those quarries. The sum-total of production from individually owned and operated quarries in the Langda area was major; whereas at Sela, relatively few blades were produced. The Yeineri, Tagime, and Langda-Sela produced lithics are distinctly different from each other by lithologies and color. The Tagime and Yeineri outputs are distinctly different lithologically, but alike structurally and, in both respects, different from Langda-Sela-Korupun(?) lithics.

I compared macroscopic identifications of

the black, blue-green, and miscellaneous clusters of lithics with outcrop geology to help confirm origins for those groups of lithics. After the quarry sites were located by on-the-ground surveys, through literature research, conversations and letter correspondence with different missionaries, and questioning of indigenous informants and my teams of helpers at numerous locations, I became reasonably satisfied that I had located all of the stone tool origins, with the exception of a possible Langda-Sela-type producer in Yali territory near Korupun. While at the quarry sites I collected representative samples for laboratory rock identification and other petrological analyses. From my collection of lithics I selected representative samples from the four clusters (black, blue-green, light gray-green and tan "Yali," and miscellaneous) by hand specimen examination. A few "type" examples were also selected from symbolic stones.

I wanted to be able to confirm my conclusions of the relationships of both tools and symbolic stones found among user populations throughout the study area to the specific source rock areas, determine the relative hardness of the different "type" lithologies; have the necessary mineralogic, grain size, and textural data available for possible future rock tool durability studies; and provide a base of data for comparative analyses of these different "assemblages" to tools and symbolic stones not only throughout New Guinea and Australia, but also to lithics assemblages found worldwide in the archaeological record. Professor James L.

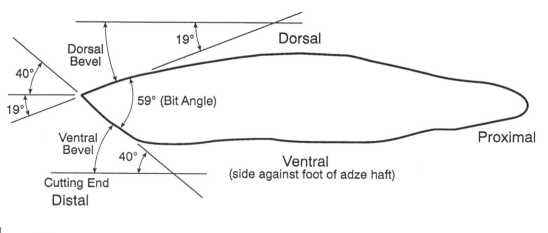

Fig. 2.6. Nomenclature for angles to the cutting edge of axe and adze blades

Dorsal Bevel

40°

19°

19°

Dorsal

59° (Bit Angle)

Ventral Bevel

40°

Cutting End
Distal

Ventral
(side against foot of adze haft)

Proximal

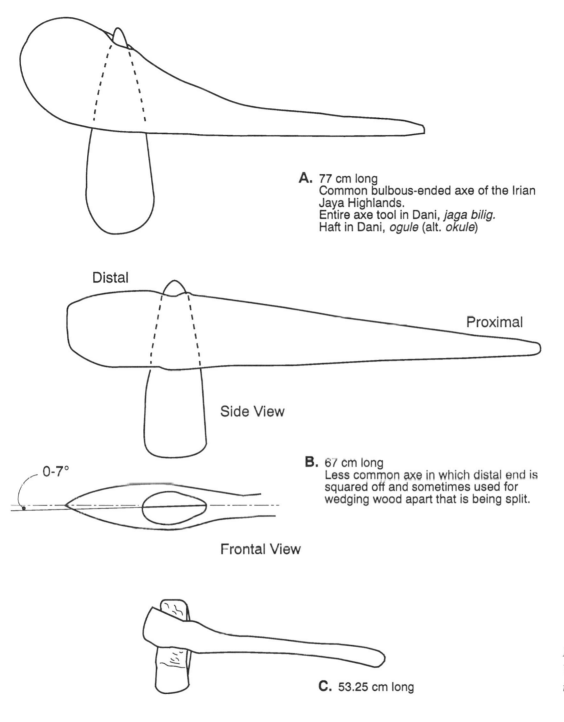

A. 77 cm long
Common bulbous-ended axe of the Irian Jaya Highlands.
Entire axe tool in Dani, *jaga bilig.*
Haft in Dani, *ogule* (alt. *okule*)

Distal

Proximal

Side View

0-7°

B. 67 cm long
Less common axe in which distal end is squared off and sometimes used for wedging wood apart that is being split.

Frontal View

C. 53.25 cm long

Fig. 2.7. Two Grand Valley and West axe types (A and B) and the Neolithic Sigerslev axe (C)

Munoz, doctoral candidate R. Jeffrey Swope, and graduate student Elizabeth A. Medlin, department of geological sciences at the University of Colorado, Boulder, agreed to undertake the rather major project of performing various analyses to describe in detail the total collection, with the exception of Langda-Sela-style knives, which were analyzed by Renald N.

Guillemette at the Texas A&M University department of geology electron microprobe laboratory.

After considerable macroscopic review of the samples collected in the field, a total of sixty lithics were chosen for laboratory work in Colorado. Initially, the team at the University of Colorado thought that a combination of pow-

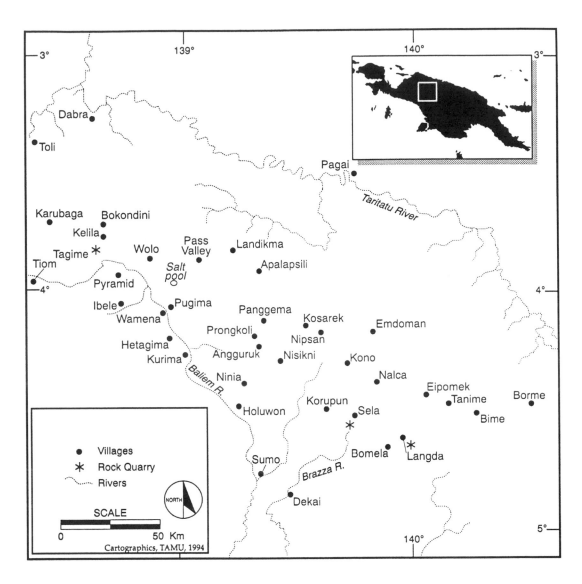

Fig. 2.8. Geographic reference points

der X-ray and hand specimen examination would provide adequate descriptions. Since most of the hand specimens are not easily identifiable because of the extremely fine-grained texture of the rock (a necessary quality for rocks used to fashion durable tools), it was determined that thin-section examination would be required in addition to the X-ray work. Powder X-ray data will identify the major phase, but it does not give grain size or textural information. The University of Colorado scientists and I jointly selected twenty-five of the sixty lithics for thin-section examination. This was done only after six months of laboratory work had shown the necessity of this step to be able to reach our objectives. I considered all of the lithics important artifacts that should be preserved in their entirety if at all possible. Only those specimens that are characteristic of each of the quarry sites were cut for a detailed analysis. Twenty-five samples were selected for thin section. The Colorado team photographed, on grid paper with one-half-inch squares, each artifact before it was cut. In summary, the artifacts were examined in hand specimen, in thin section, and by powder X-ray diffraction, with rock type name, mineral content, texture, grain size, and relative hardness noted. At one point in the work, Medlin and the United States Bureau of Standards, located in Boulder, Colorado, unsuccessfully explored the feasibility of determining relative rock hardness of select samples using the bureau's equipment. In the final analysis grain size and textural information obtained from thin sections proved to be essential in estimating the relative hardness of the individual lithics.

For Guillemette's work, representative knife blades were selected from the Yali use area as well as from the Langda quarry and use area, including one knife blade from Langda still in the manufacturing process. New chips from a Langda adze blade quarry site were included in the work. Elemental analyses were made with medium-power scanning electron microscopy and image analyses. By the use of the EDX system (Energy Dispersive X-ray Spectrometer) and the scanning electron microscope, an elemental analysis of each sample was made. Peaks in the energy dispersive X-ray spectrum were compared to known peaks in a petrology atlas (Welton 1984). The EDX results were compared with crystal structure in the SEM (scanning electron microscope) micrographs. A texture analysis was made and elemental analyses checked with thin-section work on the SEM.

Grand Valley and West

The large western stone tool manufacturing, distribution, and use region includes at least ten language-speaking groups within the study area: Grand Valley Dani, Silimo, Hupla, Walak, Nggem, Nduga, Western Dani, Wano, Dem, and Damal (fig. 2.1). The Tagime and Yeineri quarry systems furnished the majority of stone tools for users within the area; sources of opportunity only an estimated 3 percent. Yeineri- and even Tagime-sourced blades have been reported outside the study area westward to Enarotali (fig. P.1). However, to the east, Yeineri- and Tagime-sourced blades do not trade for profane uses past the Grand Valley Dani-Yali language speaking boundary; with the exception of the Pass Valley area (and a few other minor points of mixing along the language boundary). Other kinds of material goods trade across this boundary for use on both sides.

Axes and Axe Blades

Axes are used only in the Yeineri-Tagime quarries-sourced western use region; not at all to the east in the Langda-Sela-Korupun(?)

quarries-sourced use region (fig. 2.1). The Dani and others in the western region use both the Tagime and Yeineri manufactured axes for splitting large felled trees, sometimes for splitting smaller wood, but almost never for chopping down trees, for which they simply prefer the adze. In figure 2.9, a Dani is seen splitting a section of a felled tree trunk in characteristic fashion with a perpendicular type of percussion stroke. When splitting wood with an axe, men often work as two-men teams. One man straddles the log, and with perpendicular overhead vertical strokes, splits the log with the axe, working backward toward his feet, while his helper stands to his front and wedges the wood

Fig. 2.9. A Dani uses an axe for its normal purpose.

open with a stick pole. In the photograph where the man works alone, the axe handle is typical of the Type B rectangular-ended axe haft for the area (previously presented in fig. 2.7), into which a Tagime tubular-style axe blade has been inserted. The axe is a longer handled, normally heavier tool than the adze, and one would think its primary purpose originally might have been for felling large trees. However, Steensberg, working in eastern Papua New Guinea, observed:

In this area large trees with huge buttress roots were attacked from scaffolds similar to those constructed by the Hiowe, and in both cases adze-hafted tools seemed to have been preferred to tools hafted as axes. The reason for this may have lain in the overhead stroke of the adze in that it cut the tree higher off the ground, and also their predominately vertical movement would cause less vibration of the scaffold. Adzes were certainly the most common tools for felling in most parts of the New Guinea rainforest, and it would be interesting to investigate this further because the composition of primary and secondary woods in the Neolithic of Europe suggests that there was experience here of a similar kind. (1980:38)

Within the study area, Heider, working with the Dugum Dani along the north-central edge of the Grand Valley, stated that axes were primarily for splitting wood and did not elucidate other uses (Heider 1970:278). O'Brien, working with the Dani in the Konda Valley near Bokondini (fig. 1.1), said that in addition to the adze, "The Dani also use a stone axe, made from the same type of stone as the adze and also oval in cross-section, but usually larger and with an edge cut at the same angle on both sides. The axe is less common in the Konda Valley than the adze and is used only for splitting wood and never for cutting or chopping" (1969:37).

I would hazard a guess that at contact time there was a minimum of ten adzes per one axe and one to three axes per living compound. I found no restrictions against women using axes, but I never observed a woman using one. Twice I saw a woman using an adze to smooth or sharpen her digging stick, and informants said that women sometimes used adzes to chop wood.

The mid–Grand Valley Dani term for an axe is *jaga bilig* (alt. *jakabiliga,* both pronounced jaka bilik). A large axe blade (more than approximately 25 cm long) is immediately recognized as a jaga bilig and not differentiated from a finished axe, which also is identified by the same name. A large axe blade, with or without the haft, is the most valuable tool stone that the Dani possess and may be considered an item of wealth. Much effort has gone into the manufacturing process, especially the grinding of a large blade. The black axe blade from the Tagime quarries is identified as a *jaga bilig gu.* (*Gu* is a black colored stone pronounced ku.) A large blade (obvious by its size that it is an axe and not an adze) made at the Yeineri quarries is a *ebe jaga bilig.* The Dani generally favor the Yeineri-made axe blades over the Tagime blades.

Axe blades are of three distinguishable morphologies, each of which are produced at the two quarry areas: asymmetrical ellipsoidal, flat, and tubular. These morphologies combined with the quarry-specific lithologies account for a total of six axe blade styles: Tagime style, Tagime flat style, Tagime tubular style; and Yeineri style, Yeineri flat style, and Yeineri tubular style.

TAGIME AXE BLADES. Upstream, away from the Grand Valley, the Wurm River forks at the village of Tagi. A short distance up the right fork, the river bed and banks are laden with river-rounded, black argillite pebbles and cobbles of the Kembelangan formation, which contain numerous ammonite fossils. This material is unmetamorphosed or at least little-metamorphosed relative to the meta-argillite from which the best Tagime adze and axe blades are made. Adze/axe blades, chisels, and knives can be made quickly from the argillite, which is soft and does not hold a good cutting edge for long. In Dani terminology it is *aik dlek* (has no tooth). Tools of expediency are easily fashioned from this material but they wear and break quickly. Up the left fork of the river from Tagi, however, just a short distance from the river junction, river worn pebbles, cobbles, and boulders of black metamorphosed argillite are present, mixed with pebbles and boulders of the softer argillite. It is the meta-argillite that constitutes the favored harder material for tool manufacture, and it is in this area that the Tagime quarries are located.

The Tagime axe blades are black and made of meta-argillite cobbles and boulders that have been selected from the Tagime (river). The major minerals found by the University of Colorado team (Medlin, Munoz, and Swope) in the metamorphosed argillite are quartz and siderite, with chlorite being a minor constituent, and muscovite an accessory. The texture is very fine-grained. Based on thin-section observation of grain size and texture, the Colorado team attempted to make rough estimates regarding the rock's relative hardness to the Yeineri blades and the Langda-Sela blades. The team rated the Tagime metamorphosed argillite on a scale of "very hard (VH), hard (H), medium (M), and soft (S)."

In plan view, the Tagime-style blade shape is asymmetrical ellipsoid, with the distal, bit (cutting edge) end being broader than the proximal end. The proximal end is ground to a near point. In cross section the blade tends to be symmetrical-oblong in frontal (bit end) view and near-symmetrically ellipsoidal in longitudinal side view. The bevel angles are similar, and it is difficult to determine a dorsal and ventral side to each blade. The cutting edge tends to be straight or with a slight S-curve in frontal, cross-section view and crescent formed in dorsal plan view. The dimensions of one average Tagime-style axe blade are 23 cm in length, 7.8 cm maximum in width, and 4.0 cm maximum in thickness.

The Tagime flat-style axe blade is elongate-rectangular, with both sides of the blade being nearly parallel for most of the length of the blade. In figure 2.10, a western Grand Valley Dani user is seen modifying and sharpening a typical Tagime flat-style axe blade after receiving it from the quarry and prior to inserting it

into an axe handle. The sandstone grinding outcrop seen in figure 2.10 is one of many similar artifacts of culture that dot the landscape at convenient locations that are being relegated to the archaeological record as the Dani evolve away from a stone-using cultural system. For details concerning the morphology of the Tagime flat-style axe blade, which is the same as that of the Yeineri flat-style axe and adze blades,

Fig. 2.10. A Dani sharpens a typical Tagime flat-style axe blade.

refer to the section later in this chapter, "Yeineri-Style and Yeineri Flat-Style Adze Blades."

The Tagime tubular-style axe blade is as its name suggests, long relative to width and oval in cross section. In plan view, the cutting edge (or bit end) of the blade is crescent-shaped. In cross section, the bevel angles are nearly equal (fig. 2.6). In plan view, the proximal end of the blade is ground to a near point. The lengths of the blades that I saw hafted vary from 24 to 33 cm, with maximum widths per stone from 4.5 to 5.7 cm and thicknesses from 2.3 to 3.2 cm.

YEINERI AXE BLADES. The Yeineri axe blades vary in color from green to blue, with varying shades of each. Some are of near-uniform color; others variegated, and some mottled. All of the rocks at the quarry site are metamorphic from the ophiolite and melange belt previously described in chapter 1. Those pieces of rock selected by the quarrymen for tools and symbolic stones range from blueschist, to epidote

amphibolite, to epidote chlorite schist. The major minerals in the blueschist blades are glaucophene (blue color), plagioclase, and sphene. These minerals are noted in varying amounts. The minor minerals are chlorite, quartz, lawsonite, sphene, and epidote. Accessory minerals that were noted are calcite, epidote, quartz, sphene, pyrite, and opaques. The textures of the blueschist blades range from individual blades exhibiting very poorly developed schistosity to blades with wavy and good schistosity. All samples are fine grained. Other blades and quarry samples range from rocks that are termed epidote amphibolites, to amphibole schists, to epidote chlorite schists. In these rocks major minerals are epidote, amphibole, plagioclase, and chlorite; minor minerals are albite, chlorite, plagioclase, sphene, and calcite. These rocks range from very fine grained to fine grained with matted textures to crenelated layers to schistose. On the relative hardness scale (VH, H, M, S) the Colorado team subjectively rated the blueschist blades as hard (H) because the blueschist's dominant foliation seen in both hand specimen and thin section will lead to fractures along those cleavaged planes (glaucophane hardness 5–6 on Mohs' scale). The fine-grained, matted-framework texture of the epidote amphibolite was noted as the hardest, with individual samples being given ratings of "VH." Interestingly, while I was at the Yeineri quarry complex, a young quarryman took me to an abandoned quarry site within the complex that his deceased father had told him produced the hardest, best adze/axe blade stones of any of the rock outcrops (or boulders) quarried in the entire complex. Macroscopically I could not determine that the rock from this location was any harder than other specific locations that were either being quarried or that I had been told had been quarried in the past. On laboratory analysis, the rock thought to be hardest by the quarryman turned out to be epidote amphibolite, judged by the Colorado geological team to be the hardest, most durable kind of rock produced from the Yeineri quarries. The quarrymen's emic and our modern scientific etic analyses were the same.

Fig. 2.11. Large Yeineri-style blade in a bulbous-ended axe handle

The structure of the three Yeineri styles of axe blades are like those described in the previous section for the Tagime axe blades. I found a length range for axe blades of 20 cm to 39 cm. The maximum width of the longest blade, which is a Yeineri style, is 10.5 cm and maximum thickness 4.6 cm. Fitted into a Type A, bulbous-ended axe handle, a heavy tool is created (fig. 2.11). Twenty-two cm of the blade is exposed; 17 cm within the handle. Blades approaching this size are always hafted into the Type A, bulbous-ended handles, rather than the Type B, rectangular-ended handles. The handle is 77.6 cm long and 42.3 cm in circumference at its widest point.

Adze Blades

The adze blade is the most common tool blade produced at any of the quarries—in far greater numbers than axe blades. Whereas axe blades are all relatively large (about 20–40 cm long), without a great range in size, adze blades range in size from very small (length about 4 cm) to quite long (about 30 cm). The adze is the all-purpose chopping and adzing tool of the Irian Jaya Highlands used for such a variety of tasks as the heavy work of chopping down the largest trees in the forest and splitting wood to fine finish work on bows and spears and, within a segment of the population in the Tagime-Yeineri use and trade region, for amputating fingers in ritual procedures.

The two type morphologies of the Tagime- and Yeineri-produced blades are markedly different from the unique (in the Irian Jaya Highlands) Langda-Sela-style adze blade. The colors and lithologies are distinctly different for adze blades from each of the three quarries. The "tubular-" shaped axe blade produced at the Tagime and Yeineri quarries is not hafted as an adze blade, regardless of its length.

TAGIME-STYLE AND TAGIME FLAT-STYLE ADZE BLADES. Tagime produced adze blades are black metamorphosed argillite, with quartz and siderite being the major mineral constituents, chlorite being a minor constituent, and muscovite an accessory. The texture is very fine-grained. The Tagime very fine-grained

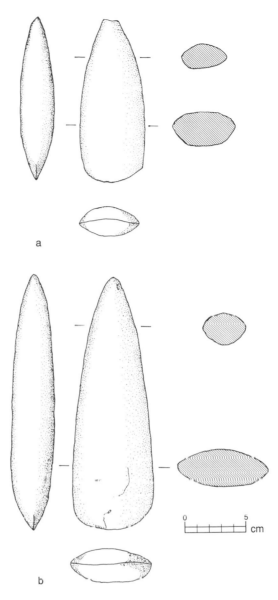

Fig. 2.12. Two typical Tagime-style adze blades

texture meta-argillite was judged by the Colorado team of geologists (Medlin, Munoz, and Swope) to be one of the two hardest rock types in the set of sixty samples selected for analyses.

The Tagime-style adze blade varies in plan view shape from asymmetric ellipsoidal for the longer blades, to semirectangular for some of the intermediate length blades, to triangular for the shorter blades. Figure 2.12 shows two characteristic asymmetric ellipsoidal blades. The distal, bit (cutting edge) end of the blade is always wider than the proximal, hafting end of the blade. In longitudinal side view, the cross section tends to be asymmetrically ellipsoidal, but with the ventral side often being flat to semiflat to facilitate hafting onto the socket of the haft. The dorsal (or upper) side of the blade in longitudinal side view cross section is arcuate convex upward. In frontal cross-section view the cutting edge of the blade tends to be a straight line or slightly convex upward and, in dorsal plan view, crescent-shaped, convex away from the distal (cutting end) of the blade. The dimensions of the longest Tagime-style adze blade viewed in the field was 23.2 cm in length, 7.8 cm maximum width, and 4.0 cm maximum thickness. The shortest Tagime-style adze blade collected is 6.0 cm in length, 4.0 cm maximum width, and 1.1 cm maximum thickness. For measurements of fourteen examples of Tagime-style adze blades, see table 2.1.

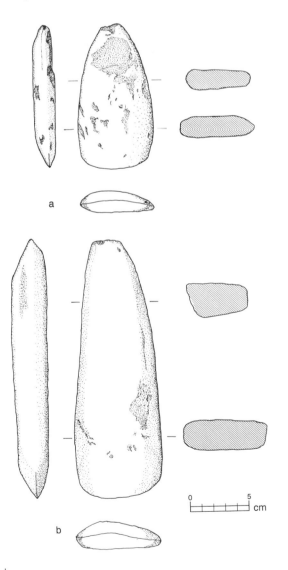

Fig. 2.13. Two Tagime flat-style adze blades

The Tagime flat-style adze blade varies from asymmetrical ellipsoidal to elongate-rectangular in plan view. The distinguishing characteristic of this style is that the dorsal and ventral sides of a blade are nearly parallel for most of the blade length (fig. 2.13).

Bit damage and fracture patterns are difficult to assess in both the Tagime-style and Tagime flat-style adze blades because cutting edge damage is rapidly repaired by grinding. Badly broken blades are made useable for other purposes or discarded. The broken Tagime-style adze blade shown in figure 2.14 with a use-wear chipped cutting edge had actually been discarded. I dug it up at the edge of a spring between two habitation sites. Whether the cutting edge damage preceded the transverse break across the tool, or whether the blade broke first and then was used as a hand tool and thought not worth the effort to keep in good repair is an interesting question. This is the most use-damaged Tagime blade that I have observed in the Grand Valley and West region.

YEINERI-STYLE AND YEINERI FLAT-STYLE ADZE BLADES. From Yeineri source rock, two styles of adze blades are made—Yeineri style and Yeineri flat style. The Yeineri-style adze blades vary in color from green to blue, with varying shades of each. Some are uniform in color, others variegated, and some mottled. The rock types of these adze blades vary from blueschist, to epidote amphibolite, to epidote chlorite schist. The fine-grained chlorite makes the rocks green. (For the major, minor, and accessory mineral constituents, textures, and textural considerations of the three different rock types that have been recognized in the Yeineri produced adze blades, refer to the previous section on Yeineri axe blades. For structure refer to the above descriptive material on the Tagime-style adze blade as it describes the same structure as that for the Yeineri-Style blade.) Table 2.2 shows blade measurements (maximum lengths, widths, thicknesses, and cutting edge angles) for a collection of Yeineri-Style adze blades. The maximum length from a collection of thirty-three blades is 13.9 cm, maximum width for that same blade 5.9 cm, and maximum thick-

Table 2.1. Measurements of Tagime-Style Adze Blades

Adze Blade	Length	Maximum Width	Maximum Thickness	Length to Width Ratio	Bit Angle	Dorsal Bevel Angle	Ventral Bevel Angle
1	7.5	4.0	2.4	1.9	—	—	—
2	9	4.2	2.0	2.1	—	—	—
3	13.5	5.3	2.9	2.5	—	—	—
4	7	3.9	1.5	1.8	—	—	—
5	23.2	7.8	4.0	3.0	—	—	—
6	8.7	4.5	1.5	1.9	—	—	—
7	14.8	5.1	3.0	2.9	—	—	—
8	—	4.4	1.5	—	—	—	—
9	24	6.6	3.1	3.6	—	—	—
10	6.1	3.9	1.3	1.6	—	—	—
11	11.1	5.2	1.8	2.1	—	—	—
12	6.6	3.9	2.0	1.7	—	—	—
13	7.3	4.3	1.3	1.7	55	14	41
14	12.4	6.3	1.9	2.0	35	29	6
Mean	*11.6*	*5.0*	*2.2*	*2.4*	*45*	*21.5*	*23.5*

Note: Maximum width of each blade approximates length of cutting edge; measurements in cm and degrees.

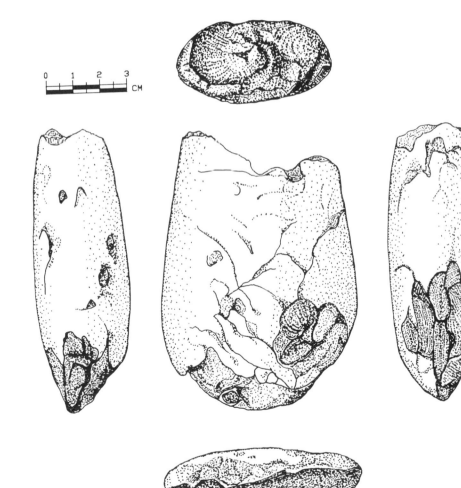

0   1   2   3   CM

Fig. 2.14. Bit damage and transverse snap of Tagime-style adze blade

ness for that blade 5.7 cm. The shortest blade in the collection is 4.5 cm, with a maximum width of 3.2 cm, and a maximum thickness of 1.0 cm. The length-to-width ratios are: for longest blade, 2.36; for shortest blade 1.47; and for all blades 1.8.

Regardless of the variance of plan view shapes, as indicated by the different length-to-width ratios, the longitudinal dorsal crestlines in cross section are usually gently arcuate. On the majority of Yeineri-style adze blades, however, a flat area is ground over some part of the central longitudinal line on the ventral side of the blade to facilitate a secure fit when binding the ventral side of the blade against the upper surface of the haft socket. Sometimes this flat area is not obvious, but upon closer examination it can almost always be defined.

On fourteen blades that were available for laboratory angle measurements, the mean ventral bevel angle is twice as large as the mean dorsal bevel angle (refer to fig. 2.6 for bevel angle definitions). On the majority of Yeineri-style blades, the ventral bevelled surface is

Table 2.2. Measurements of Yeineri Style Adze Blades

Adze Blade	Length	Maximum Width	Maximum Thickness	Length to Width Ratio	Bit Angle	Dorsal Bevel Angle	Ventral Bevel Angle
1	11.5	6.1	2.4	1.9	—	—	—
2	7.2	4.3	1.9	1.7	—	—	—
3	—	4.3	1.1	—	—	—	—
4	13.2	5.6	2.5	2.4	—	—	35
5	5.0	3.0	1.4	1.7	60	20	40
6	6.5	4.1	1.4	1.6	—	—	—
7	13.9	5.9	5.7	2.4	—	—	—
8	6.5	4.8	1.6	1.4	—	—	—
9	5.9	3.9	1.5	1.5	—	—	—
10	5.0	3.5	1.3	1.4	—	—	—
11	4.5	3.3	1.1	1.4	—	—	—
12	12.1	6.6	2.1	1.8	52	22	30
13	4.9	3.5	1.1	1.4	48	13	35
14	4.7	3.2	1.0	1.5	58	25	33
15	9.5	5.3	2.3	1.8	68	20	48
16	7.0	5.0	1.8	1.4	62	17	45
17	6.5	4.0	1.7	1.6	59	14	45
18	5.4	4.0	1.6	1.4	52	8	44
19	5.3	3.9	1.7	1.4	48	13	45
20	5.5	3.5	1.4	1.6	54	19	35
21	7.1	4.8	2.0	1.5	55	13	42
22	7.0	4.0	1.8	1.8	53	21	32
23	8.6	6.4	1.6	1.3	58	26	32
24	9.1	5.1	2.1	1.8	—	—	—
25	5.1	3.6	1.3	1.4	—	—	—
26	6.5	4.4	1.4	1.5	—	—	—
27	5.3	3.7	1.2	1.4	—	—	—
28	7.5	4.2	1.6	1.8	—	—	—
29	5.7	4.0	1.5	1.4	65	30	35
30	7.4	5.1	1.6	1.5	—	—	—
31	10.3	4.5	1.8	2.3	—	—	—
32	9.3	5.0	1.8	1.9	—	—	—
33	7.5	4.8	1.6	1.6	—	—	—
Mean	7.4	4.7	1.8	1.6	57	19	38

Note: Maximum width of each blade approximates length of cutting edge; measurements in cm and degrees.

ground flat, or faceted, as opposed to a more arcuate plane surface that creates the dorsal bevel angle (figs. 2.15, 2.16, and 2.17).

In the absence of finding this Yeineri-style adze/axe blade type separated from an adze haft or axe handle, the relative shapes of the opposing sides of a blade and the disparity of the sizes of the bevel angles (especially the presence of a high angle, flat faceted bevel on one side, near the cutting edge of a tool) would identify a blade as an adze blade rather than an axe blade and fix its orientation if it were to be hafted.

When adze/axe blades, or assuredly adze blades as determined by their small size, are first shaped in the Yeineri quarry, the bevel

Fig. 2.15. Yeineri-style adze blade with faceted ventral angle

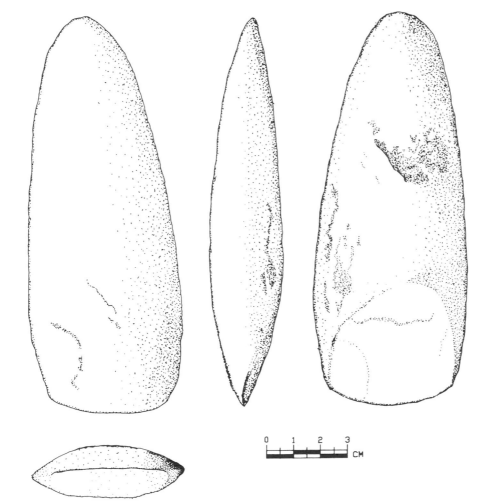

Fig. 2.16. Five drawn views of the blade shown in figure 2.15

Fig. 2.17. Dorsal views of seven Yeineri-style adze blades

angles are more nearly symmetrical than most of those found on blades in use areas. This means that with added value by further grinding en route from the quarry to final users or when resharpening by the users themselves, a more blunt bit angle is created and a greater disparity in the sizes of dorsal versus ventral bevel angles is created. Bluntness (bit angle, fig. 2.6) of the cutting end of the tool relates to both cutting efficiency through sharpness and to durability of the cutting edge. The more blunt, or greater the bit angle, the more durable the cutting end of the tool, but also the less sharp. The sharpest blades are thinner at bit end, and therefore more fragile. Perhaps the best balance between degree of sharpness and durability is achieved by the *user* for his specific tool use, rather than by the quarryman at the quarry site. At any rate the blades are sharpened quite often, and their shapes, therefore, are changed with use through time.

Especially for the kinds of rock used for these Highlands tools, even a small fragment knocked out of a cutting edge weakens the edge and makes it vulnerable to further chipping around the flaw. When slightly chipped, a user might proceed immediately to grind the edge of the blade at a convenient, permanently located stationary grinding slab or within his habitation site on either a portable grinding slab or with a handheld grinding stone. Adze blades are sometimes ground while in their hafts; although they are more often quickly removed from the hafts, resharpened, and replaced. In figure 2.18, two men are seen resharpening Yeineri-style adze blades at a much-used stationary grinding slab in a streamlet that meanders between their compounds and nearby slash-and-burn gardens.

When badly damaged, a tool blade might be set aside and knapped at a convenient time before laboriously regrinding such a blade over a period of several days before rehafting it. Since knapping is a skill not known by all men, a person not wishing to invest so much time grinding a blade that in the interest of work efficiency really should be knapped first, might have to wait even as long as a week or more for a knapper. Whereas all men are not skilled knappers, all men know how to shape, sharpen, and polish by grinding. Most unsymmetrical and unusually shaped adze blades are caused by breakage and then damage repair, rather than by original shaping at a quarry source.

Fig. 2.18. Two Dani men resharpen adze blades.

The line drawings of three Yeineri-style adze blades and the distal end of one Yeineri-style axe blade in figure 2.19 show the results of the three most common kinds of use wear fractures of Yeineri-style blades. Drawing (a) shows the remnant half of an adze blade that was

fractured longitudinally by a percussive blow in what was described as normal use. The fracture that broke the blade into two pieces follows a rock cleavage plane that parallels the longitudinal dimension of the blade. When I first observed this broken blade, it was hafted and

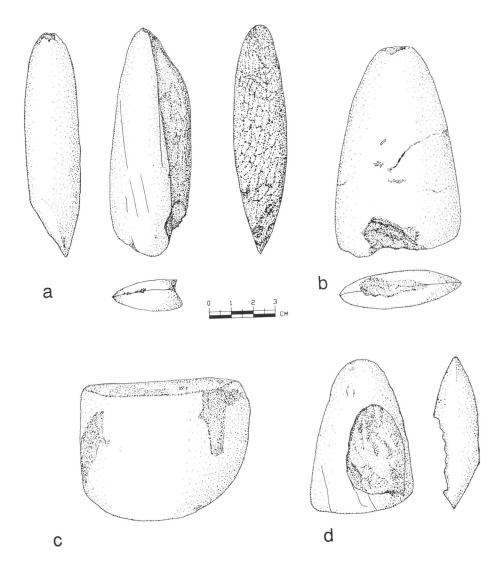

a

b

c

d

Fig. 2.19. Use damage on Yeineri-style adze blades

being used as an adze for select tasks. Drawing (b) illustrates a blade with percussive cutting edge use damage, in which no attempt has yet been made to regrind the blade. Drawing (c) is the distal end of a Yeineri-style axe blade that reportedly broke outside of the axe handle while the axe was being used in the normal fashion to split wood. The break appears to be a bending/compressive-type fracture that was initiated relatively far from the contact area (Olausson 1982:48–52). The owner of the axe blade smoothed the sharp fractured edges around the perimeter of the break, and his wife used this reclaimed tool as a sweet potato scraper.

The Yeineri flat-style adze blade is elongate-rectangular in plan view (fig. 2.20). The cutting edge in this view is approximately a straight

line, sometimes slightly convex away from the cutting edge end of the blade. The other or proximal end of the blade is usually rounded rectangular in shape in the same plan view and narrower than the cutting end of the tool. In longitudinal cross-sectional view, the dorsal and ventral sides of the blade are nearly parallel for most of the length of the blade, narrowing only toward the cutting edge of the blade where the surfaces are ground down with increasing bevel angles approaching the cutting edge to create the cutting edge. In frontal cross-sectional view the cutting edge is a straight or nearly straight line, sometimes slightly convex upward (toward dorsal side), and less often with a very elongated, modified S-shape. This fundamental tool blade shape of a flat, elongate tabular blade style is basically caused by quar-

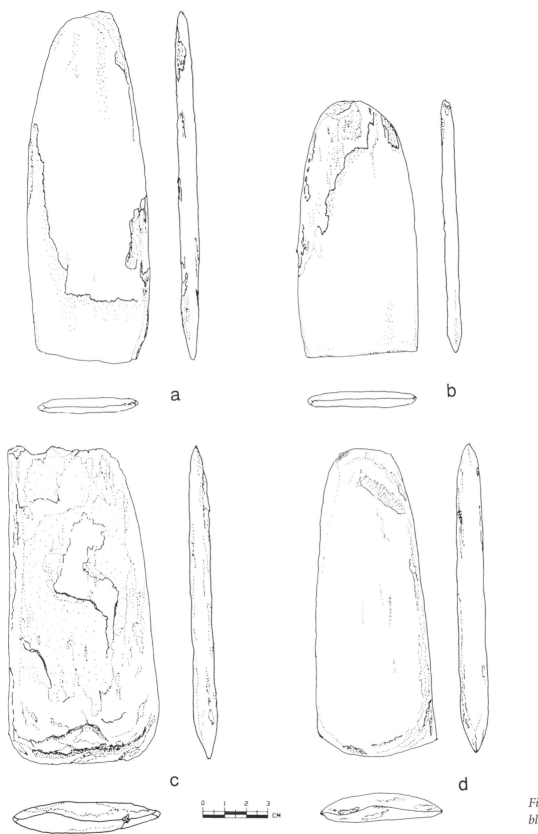

a

b

c

d

Fig. 2.20. *Yeineri flat-style adze blades*

Fig. 2.21. *Yeineri flat-style and Yeineri-style adze blades*

overall ophiolite sequence as other Yeineri metamorphosed rock strata. Such black blades might also be made from rock obtained from sources of opportunity elsewhere along the ophiolite-melange rock belt, but not from Tagime. The light green colored blades are an epidote, chlorite schist that is very fine-grained with a slaty cleavage. When the pibit pibit is flaked and then ground to an ellipsoidal shape in longitudinal cross section, it falls within the category of Yeineri-style adze/axe blade, but when completed along flat cleavage planes as a flat, tabular adze/axe blade, it is a Yeineri flat style (fig. 2.21). The upper photograph in figure 2.21 shows four Yeineri flat-style adze blades and a Yeineri flat-style blade blank. The blade blank has been knapped and is ready for grinding. The light colored specks are pyrite crystals. In the lower photograph, two of the flat-style-finished adze blades are compared to two "typical" Yeineri-style adze blades. The flat-style blade that is second from the left in the upper photograph is enlarged in the lower photograph to show the color and shape of a typical pibit pibit flat-style adze blade (Hampton 1997: fig. 207). The Colorado geologic team (Medlin, Munoz, and Swope) rated the epidote, chlorite schist (pibit pibit) as of medium hardness relative to the other adze and axe blade materials that were analyzed. In figure 2.22, two Yeineri flat-style axe blades on the left are compared to a typical Yeineri flat-style adze blade to show that the only distinguishing characteristic is the longer length of the two axe blades, which are 30 cm and 26.5 cm long, respectively, versus 18.5 cm for the adze blade.

Adzes

To facilitate reading the text in continuity and then making visual comparisons of the different styles of adzes and hafting techniques, all newly presented figures of adzes are presented as a group at the end of the section.

Both Tagime and Yeineri adze blades in the west as well as the Langda-Sela blades in the east are hafted by their respective toolmakers and users in much the same fashion. In both cases the blades are lashed directly to the feet of the wooden hafts, regardless of blade size, with

rying slabs of blade blank material along the parallel bedding/cleavage planes of the compact, fine-grained metamorphic source rock. Rock such as this can be relatively easily quarried and split into slabs and thin plates. This is the same kind of metamorphic rock series that is often selected for the flat, rectangular shaped *je* symbolic display-exchange stones (chapter 2). Most of the Yeineri flat-style blades are of the same varied green and blue colors as the Yeineri-style blades, but with the additions of a lighter slate green (called *pibit pibit*) and a black colored blade that from color alone would appear to be a Tagime blade. The black colored Yeineri flat-style blades, however, are distinct from the Tagime black meta-argillite by lithology. They are a slate that was formed by metamorphism of a black shale in the same

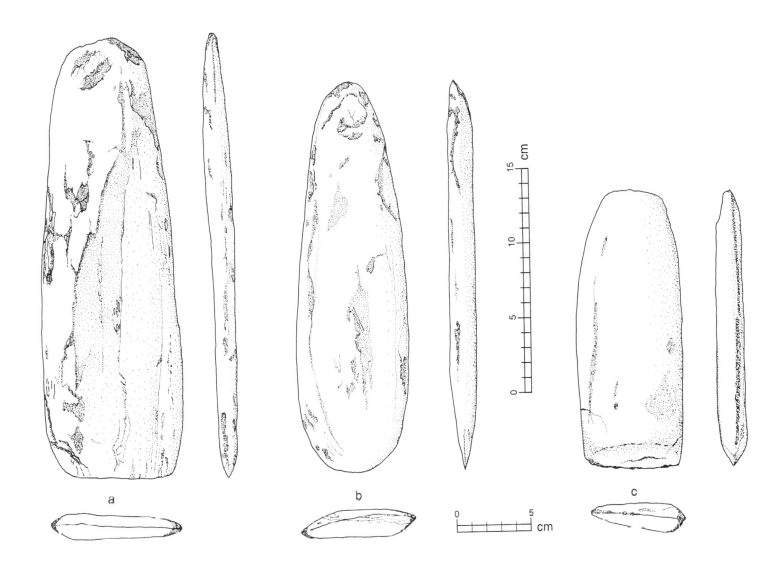

b

c

15 cm

10

5

0

0   5
cm

thin strips of rattan; in the case of the Tagime-Yeineri blade users, sometimes with string cording or a combination of string cording and rattan. This is different from hafting techniques used by some highlander groups to the east in Papua New Guinea, where both adze and axe blades are bound into detached (from the hafts) wooden split sockets that are then bound onto the T-shaped heads of the hafts (Sillitoe 1988:43–44).

In the study area a secure joinder between the blade and the haft is accomplished by a method wherein a blade is laid onto the distal end of the flat or slightly concave surface of the socket of the foot of the haft in a nested condition in carefully held thin strips of wood, bark, and/or bark cloth as the blade is securely

wrapped onto the socket. Sometimes, however, the blade is wrapped directly onto the socket without these other materials. The Tagime-Yeineri users also sometimes use the pitch from the araucaria tree as a resilient glue to help secure the blade into its nest of fiber material at the distal end of the socket.

I noted that cutting edge angles formed for Tagime-Yeineri-style hafted blades vary from 70° to 90°, with a mean angle of 82°; and for Langda-Sela-style hafted blades from 67° to 85°, with a mean angle of 79°. The users of the separate socket technique of mounting blades to hafts in Papua New Guinea create their desired blade angle by rotating the entire socket-held blade to the desired position before lashing it to the haft.

Fig. 2.22. Two Yeineri flat-style axe blades and one flat-style adze blade

Fig. 2.23. Three different handle styles on Grand Valley and West adzes

The haft is made from a piece cut from the trunk of a tree to include a branch that is growing at a proper angle and of a proper circumference to make a suitable shaft (fig. 2.3). The part of the tree trunk above the branch forms the socket of the foot. The branch forms the shaft. The stoutness of the shaft, indicated by its circumference, varies considerably from adze to adze, as does the socket-to-shaft angle. For hafted Yeineri-style and Yeineri flat-style blades, the socket-to-shaft angle was found to vary from 51°, to 78°, with a mean of 67°. For Tagime hafted blades the socket-to-shaft angle was observed to vary from 56° to 76°, with a mean of 66°. For adzes hafted with Yeineri-style, Yeineri flat-style, Tagime-style and Tagime flat-style blades, the handle stoutness was found to be about the same. For these adzes the shaft circumference was observed to vary from 5.1 to 11.5 cm, with a mean of 6.35 cm. Some shafts are straight. Others are curved, in which

the convex curvatures may be toward either the proximal or distal ends of the foot. Sometimes rather large blades are hafted in relatively small hafts; while at other times the size of a blade seems disproportionately small to the large size of a haft. The trade or barter value of an adze tool relates to the size of the blade but not to the size or quality of a haft.

As the hafted adze blade tools evolved, numerous principles of physics and mechanical engineering must have been manifest in tool changes, until the makers and users developed the kinds of adze tools that we see today. When chopping down standing trees with forceful overhand strokes, certainly cutting edge length and shape, angle and force of impact, mass of tool head, and limberness of tool handle (shaft) must fit into a calculus for chopping efficiency. At the moment of blade impact with the object being cut, the wooden shaft will bend and then on follow-through, as the blade is removed from the tree trunk surface, rebound. This spring effect might help flick cut chips away from the cutting surface. The straight or crescent shape and dimensions of the cutting edge of the blade must also play a significant role.

The three shapes of shafts that are used in the Grand Valley and West adzes are shown in figure 2.23. Note that rather than use rattan strips for binding, the users of the two tools on the left have bound their blades to the foot of each tool with braided fiber string cording of the same kind that is used to tether pigs. The Yeineri-style adze blades are shown both hafted and unhafted so that a viewer can get an idea of the relatively small proportion of the blades that are bound to the socket. The upper and lower blades are displayed with their dorsal sides toward the viewer and the middle blade with the ventral side toward the viewer.

Relative to the way that these adzes are constructed and the mechanics of their uses, it is pointed out that for adze blades that are of average length or longer, less than one-third to less than one-half of the length of the blade is bound to the socket (figs. 2.24, 2.25, and 2.26). Mechanically a tool so hafted must be used with a straight forward or straight downward motion so that tangential shear will not break the blade sideways out of the socket. Also, haft wear, if present, would only occur on the proximal one-third to one-half of the blade, which could be helpful information when attempting to reconstruct the kind of hafting from only an archaeological remnant blade.

In an experiment, Siba worked hard to haft a Tagime-style adze blade in fourteen minutes. Prior to hafting, he resharpened the cutting edge of the old blade and flattened the ventral surface to ensure a flat plane that would bind tightly against the upper flat surface of the socket. He examined the work on the blade from time to time while grinding and allowed the haft and rattan wrapping material to become tough and limber by soaking them in the river beside him. Because of the ideal shape of the blade for hafting (symmetrical, arcuate dorsal surface and flat ventral surface), Siba did not feel that he needed to use the normal "nest-

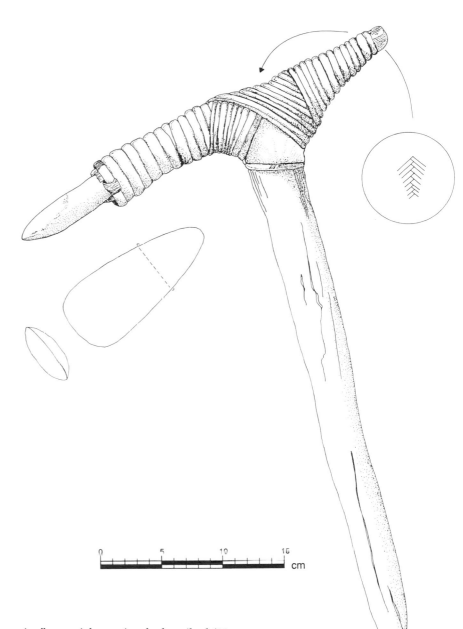

ing" materials previously described (Hampton 1997:360–63).

Siba then demonstrated how he could create two bow staves by splitting a downed sapling into two equal parts by deft strokes with his adze. The cutting edge of the adze never missed an imaginary line down the longitudinal center of the sapling as Siba quickly moved beside it and completed the job in less than a minute (fig. 2.27).

The next step in making a bow is adzing the stave to proper size before scraping it smooth with a boar tusk scraper and/or chert flake. As stated earlier, tool size does not always appear to an outsider to be commensurate with the task that it is used for, and it is difficult to guess

Fig. 2.24. Grand Valley and West adze with Yeineri-style blade

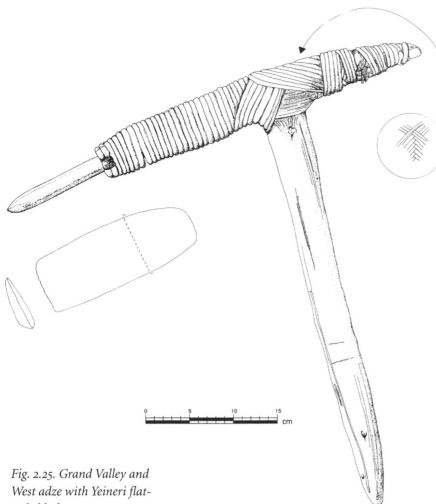

Fig. 2.25. Grand Valley and West adze with Yeineri flat-style blade

what size adze will be selected by a particular person for a specific task.

Knives

Knives used by the Grand Valley and West language speakers are made from the same kinds of rock as the Yeineri axe and adze blades, from meta-argillite sourced rock in the Tagime quarry area, and a small percentage as tools of expediency from the quickly worked softer black argillite of the Kembelangan formation. The users told me they prefer Yeineri dark blue-green and slatelike blades to the Tagime-made knives. The knives are generally rather small, thin, and irregularly shaped. They may be narrow elongate oblong or rounded rectangular. The average dimensions of the knives that I saw were 8.6 cm long, 4.4 cm wide, and 0.35 cm thick. The largest Dani knife that I saw is 33 cm in length, 8.5 cm maximum width, and 0.35 cm

thick. This knife blade is a light gray-green color and appears to be made from micaceous slate. The smallest blade that I saw that was owned by a Dani is a dark blue-green blueschist (or amphibolite) blade that is 9.2 cm long, 2.2 cm wide, and 0.2 cm thick. A similar-sized blade (10.8 cm long by 3.7 cm wide by 0.1 cm thick) is a silvery micaceous black slate. Its thinness is probably an attribute of the rock's original fissility.

The smallest dark blue-green knife described above is shown at the top of the photograph in figure 2.28, the middle knife is a Yeineri-sourced black slate-like material, and the lower knife is the largest knife (33 cm long), which was previously described. At the time that I discovered it, the owner had begun to cut it into two pieces with a chert flake tool to make two knives. He said that he used this knife primarily to split the *Pandanus* red fruit and had given up the task of making two knives from the one because cutting the knife in two was taking too long.

The knives are never hafted and are ground and polished smooth. Sometimes just one end is ground to a sharpened edge. Other times an end and an entire side are sharpened. The edges are not honed down to a cutting edge as sharp as the axe and adze blades. They are handled without much danger of cutting a user's hand. The variable structure of the stone knives in the Grand Valley and West region is different from the characteristic more oblate shapes (in plan view) of stone knives made and used in the Yali and East region.

Stone knives in the Grand Valley and West are a bit of an enigma. They are definitely present within the culture, but they are rarely seen being carried or used. To the east, an observer would describe the Yali, Una, Kimyal, and their neighbors as stone knife users, but not the Dani or Western Dani. Whereas the Yali and others in the east use their stone knives to process taro for planting and eating, the Dani and Western Dani prefer bone knives to stone for the same purpose. People of both the western and eastern cultural groups prefer bone knives made from the leg bones of cassowary birds to stone knives for cutting up the red

Pandanus fruit. Both cultural groups use adzes and bamboo knives for dismembering pigs for cooking but always bamboo for butchering—never stone knives. Women of the Grand Valley and West use a variety of "sandpaper" grasses, bone knives, and very small flat-style adze blades as vegetable scrapers to clean yams, sweet potatoes, and taro in preference to the conventional stone knives. So where does this leave the stone knife as a tool of importance among the Dani and Western Dani? Perhaps the stone knife in the Grand Valley and West is relatively unimportant in the cultural system—yet available for profane uses by those people who favor it over other options.

Chisels

A small, tubular-shaped (circular to oval in cross section) ground stone blade, sharpened at one end, is used as a chisel (alt. names drill and gouge) to cut holes in axe handles *(okule)* where the axe blade is inserted (fig. 2.29). This is the chisel's only profane use. Sacred uses of chisels will be discussed in chapter 4. Since the Yali and East group do not use axes, they have no use for a chisel of this type nor do they possess any (expect perhaps a few that are se-creted away as sacred objects). The Dani call this chisel a *pulu.* For use in chiselling axe handle holes, the pulu is sometimes mounted into a small straight handle that may simply be a rattan-bound notched short stick, as shown in a sketch by Heider (1970:277). The pulu blades are produced at both the Tagime and Yeineri quarries, and also in lesser quantities, as inferior tools of expedience from the softer argillites of the Kembelangan formation.

Chert ("Flint") Flakes

In both the western and eastern use regions, small chert nodules from the New Guinea Limestone are broken into small flakes using the bipolar reduction technique. The sharp, unretouched edges of individual flakes called *moli* (in mid Grand Valley Dani dialect) are used for numerous tasks. In this Highlands area where bamboo is an extremely important re-source (chapter 1), the chert flakes take on a special significance relative to the bamboo

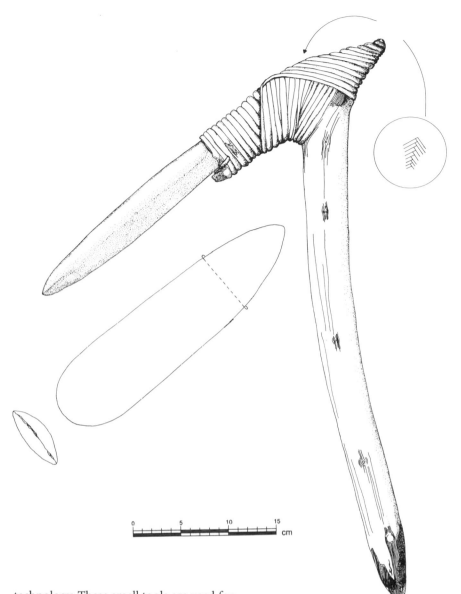

technology. These small tools are used for cutting and shaping, smoothing, incising, and boring most of the bamboo artifacts; including bamboo knives, culturally important ritual pig killing arrow tips, small surgical tips that are used for bloodletting, surgical probes, tuber and other kinds of scrapers, awls and needles, internode water and object carrying tubes, and earplug ornaments. The chert flakes are used for splitting and paring bamboo strips and rattan for bow strings as well as in the final phases of bow manufacture for paring and smoothing bow staves. The blades are used for shaping and smoothing both hardwood and the lesser used bone arrow tips, as well as incis-ing the wooden tips with artful designs. The chert flakes are used, along with adzes, for shaping and smoothing bone knives. Bone and

Fig. 2.26. Grand Valley and West adze with Tagime-style blade

Fig. 2.27. Siba splits a limb for bow staves.

Fig. 2.28. Grand Valley and West Yeineri-sourced knives

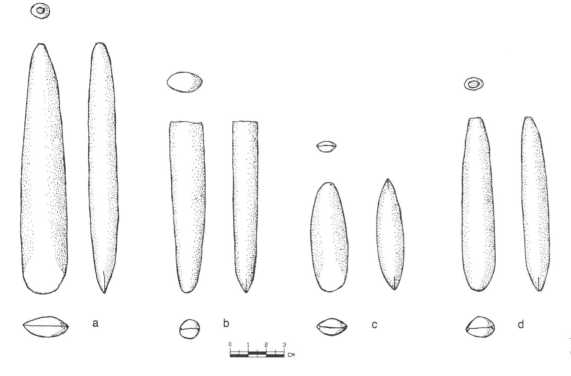

a   b   c   d

Fig. 2.29. Four line-drawn Grand Valley and West chisels

wooden awls are cut, shaped, and smoothed with chert flakes. Chert flake points are used for drilling holes in bone awls to make needles, to bore tusk scrappers so they can be conveniently tied with a piece of string, and for drilling holes in pieces of shell (fig. 2.30). The flakes are also used for sharpening the inner concave cutting edges of boar tusk scrapers. The only indigenous musical instrument, the reed mouth harp, is carefully cut and fashioned with a chert flake (fig. 2.31). The reed selected for a mouth harp is first sliced to furnish an adequate piece and then the three tongs of the instrument are cut and carefully shaved to produce just the

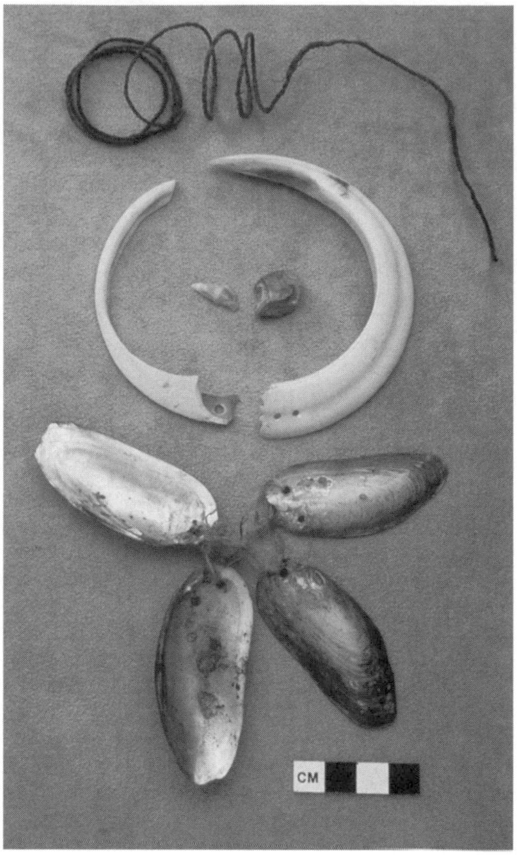

Fig. 2.30. Chert flake tools are used as borers.

right tone before a hole is bored on the other side of the end internode to accommodate a carrying string.

When the cutting edge of a chert flake becomes dull the user simply throws it away and either obtains a fresh flake from his tool kit or removes a chert nodule or already-reduced core from his tool kit and, using the bipolar reduction technique, breaks off new pieces. The tool users demonstrate little control over the size and shape of the flakes they produce. The process is really a random one. However, it does not take long (seconds to a few minutes) to obtain a flake suitable for a particular purpose. Often to start the process, an unworked nodule is wrapped in a banana leaf to protect the pieces from being lost when the core is struck randomly with a hammerstone. A whole new series of flake tools is produced this way.

Because no large chert nodules are available, small flakes must suffice. Pieces in which the long dimensions are in the range of only 2.0 to 3.5 cm are the norm. Larger flakes up to 5 cm

long are rare but sometimes available. The chert nodules that are the source for flakes are often obtained locally by users but are sometimes traded for. The cultural significance of this tiny tool is out of proportion to the very small size of the cutting flakes. Put into archaeological context, this may be a point to be remembered. How many millions of tiny razor-sharp chert flakes are scattered unnoticed throughout the archaeological record? Might this small type of simple flake tool be an important adjunct to the bamboo technology that Geoffrey Pope proposed was important as early as 1,500,000–200,000 ya in an easterly direction from the Movius Line and corresponding to the natural range of bamboo in Asia?

In terms of a Highlander's tool kit, one or several chert flake tools might be found with the following items: perhaps a chert nodule or two, perhaps none; one to three pig tusk scrapers on which the inner edges have been honed to razor sharpness; one or several bone awls and needles; one to three short bamboo knives; one or more marsupial or rodent lower mandible tooth gravers; a lump of beeswax; a stone chisel; and perhaps a small sacred stone or other small object (may simply be a rounded river pebble or a small adze blade) wrapped in a cocoon cloth to empower the entire kit. If bits of root or leaves are also present with these kinds of tools in the archaeological record, their presence should not be disregarded, as they may hold significance to an archaeological interpretation that will be discussed in chapter 4.

These kinds of tools are usually wrapped in an inner piece of cocoon cloth, with or without an additional wrapping of bark cloth, before they are all enclosed as a tool kit with a piece of dried outer bark of a banana tree and then tied with a fiber, banana trunk strip, or a piece of rolled fiber string. Such a tool kit is often carried from place to place in a small net shoulder bag. Two examples of these kinds of tool kits, all of which include chert flake tools, are shown in figures 2.32 and 2.33. The photograph in figure 2.32 shows a chert flake supply kit that a craftsman would carry along (or keep available as a supply source in his house) and from which he could select a tool for a specific job or for the replacement of a tool that has been dulled and was being discarded. The mandible graver shown next to the two flake tools outside the kit has been secured to a piece of aromatic wood and, after empowerment, is maintained with the tools to exude supernatural power and maintain the profane chert tools in good condition (further discussion in chapter 4). The tool kit shown in figure 2.33 reveals five kinds of tools that are wrapped in a very small parcel: boar tusk scraper, unusually large chert flake tool, a stone chisel, a bat bone awl, and three rodent mandible gravers. The two small clumps of *jiwi* root are included with the profane tools as an empowering element (chapter 4).

Hammerstones

River-rounded hammerstones are abundantly available along the courses of the many streams and rivers that pick up loads of rock as they wind their way from the slopes of the highest peaks across the study area and finally spill out of the Highlands onto the skirting swamplands below. Hammerstones of different shapes and hardness are, of course, used in the tool knapping process and will be discussed with quarrying and tool manufacturing in chapters 5, 6, and 7. In addition, river rounded hammerstones and anvils are used for various other tool-specific tasks, the most important being to break pig bones to obtain the desirable marrow for eating and for cracking *Pandanus* nuts. Hammerstones are often just picked up as tools of convenience when the need arises, but at least one rounded hammerstone and stone anvil pair are always maintained in each men's house near the hearth for cracking pig bones and *Pandanus* nuts. I have also witnessed the anvil and/or hammerstone used as a base (or in one sense, as a minialtar) in the men's house on which to burn tree resin *(hotali)* used in sacred rituals. In addition, one or often more, hammerstone and anvil pairs are kept in each women's common cookhouse.

Fig. 2.31. Shaping a reed mouth harp with a chert flake

Fig. 2.32. A chert flake supply kit with a sacred object

Fig. 2.33. Chert flake tool kit

Stone-Striker Bamboo Fire-Starting Kit
This intriguing fire-starting tool has been discussed with other bamboo tools in chapter 1.

Yali and East

East of the Grand Valley, the Yali and East stone tool use and trade region is inhabited by the following language-speaking groups: Yali, Yale, Nipsan, Nalca, Kimyal, Una, Eipomek and Ketengban (fig. 2.2). The Kopka, Momina, and Samboka, and the Momuna, also shown in figure 2.21 as being part of this group, technically reside along the steep Highlands-lowlands geographic interface and in a sense are neither Highlanders nor lowlanders. Trade relations, including the trading of stone tools, are definitely maintained between the more formally defined Highlanders and these adjacent living groups.

East of the Grand Valley in the Yali and East use and trade region, only stone adzes, knives, chert flakes, and hammerstones are used. For percussive cutting work, the Yali and East people are completely dependent on their adzes. They have no axes. Since they have no axes they have no use for the chisel axe-hole cutting tools. Their knives are abundant and are more routinely used than knives in the western area. Both Yali and East adze blades and knives are distinguishable from counterpart tools used in the Grand Valley and West by structure and lithology.

Langda-Sela-Style Adze Blades

In the study area of Irian Jaya, as well as throughout the entire New Guinea Highlands, the Langda-Sela-style adze blades are uniquely shaped—they are long and narrow relative to their widths (color plate 5 and fig. 2.34). From collections of blades measured, the mean length-to-width ratios for Langda-Sela-style adze blades is 3.3 versus 2.4 for Tagime-style adze blades and 1.6 for Yeineri-style adze blades. Perhaps part of the reason is because, for the users, the adze tool (hafted blade) suffices for both the percussive and planing tasks for which both axes and adzes are used by people to both the west in the Grand Valley and West region.

The majority of the Langda-Sela adze blades observed throughout the use area are light gray-green in color. A smaller number are a very light brown. Both rocks are aphanitic and uniformly colored. Other than by color, the two cannot be differentiated macroscopically in the field. Diman Balyo, the head quarryman at Langda, along with two other quarrymen from neighboring quarry sites in the Langda area, agreed unanimously that the gray-green rock makes better adze blades than the buff-tan (light brown) rock. The quarrymen all said that the buff-tan rock comes from along the same Ey River, but that it is more difficult to find. Other quarrymen from other quarry villages in the greater Langda area later affirmed both

points. In the laboratory, the University of Colorado team (Medlin, Munoz, and Swope) could distinguish, at least subjectively by their visual relative hardness analysis, that the unmetamorphosed light gray-green igneous basalt/andesite blades might be harder and more durable than the same or similar colored

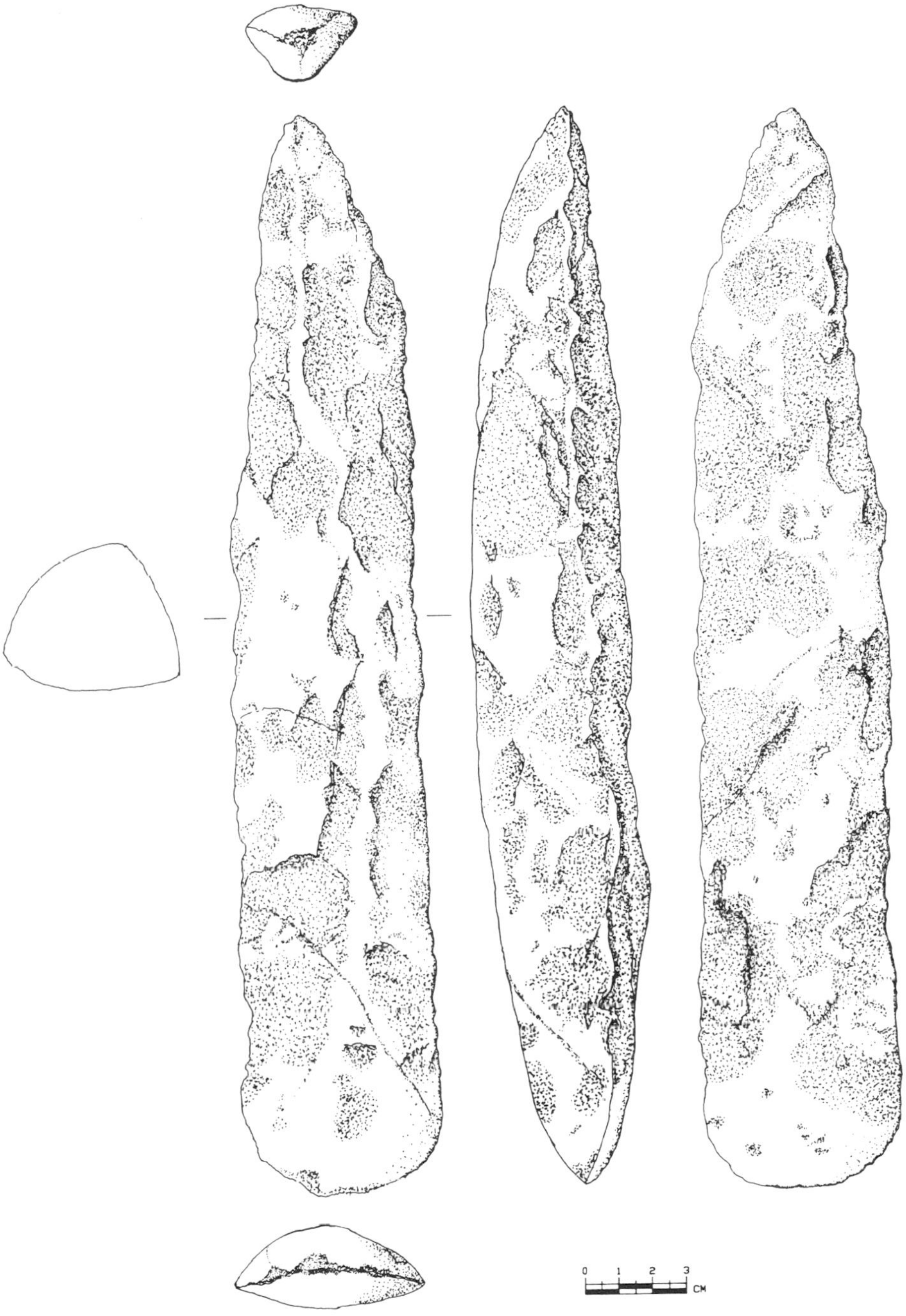

Fig. 2.34. Drawing of views of Langda-Sela blade shown in color plate 5

highly altered igneous metamorphosed basalt/andesites (which they termed metabasalt/andesites) and the highly altered metamorphosed tan rock. Macroscopically relative hardness/durability is not a differentiation that can be made by a modern outsider in the field, although the indigenous toolmakers seem to be doing this themselves.

Those blades in the user areas that appear to be dark brown to sooty black have probably taken on that additional surface color while being used, both from possible minor mineral alteration and from being anointed with pig fat and hung in a smoky environment under the low ceilings of the men's houses. The subtle color variation of used but clean blades from a light gray-green to a very light tan of some of the selected quarry source material boulders occurs within the geographic limits of the Langda quarry complex but cannot be used to distinguish Langda from Sela blades, which also produces light gray-green and light tan blade quality source boulders. The various blades, depending specifically on where they came from in the quarry sites, are either metamorphic, with a rock name of metabasalt/andesite (a highly altered igneous rock), or unmetamorphosed igneous with an assigned rock name of basalt/andesite. Major mineral constituents in the light gray-green and some of the light tans are CPX; plagioclose (small euhedral), plagioclase, amphibole (ragged subhedral), and pyroxene (medium-sized, anhedral to euhedral). A minor constituent of chlorite is present in one macroscopically representative sample from the Sela quarry. Minor accessory minerals are opaques, chlorite, epidote, and quartz. One blade sample contains an anomalous blue chlorite as an accessory mineral. One brown blade representative of a group that is thought to be naturally colored is classified as metamorphic-igneous (highly altered) with a rock name of metabasalt/andesite. The major mineral constituents are actinolite and fine-grained albite, which differentiate the specimen from others in the collection. Textures of different blades and flakes from the quarry sites are described as fine-grained, seriate (igneous texture); interlocking fine-grained equigranular to fine-grained fibrous in and around veins; to subophitic, fine- to medium-grained (mesh of interwoven fabric appears to be very strong); to subophitic/elongate interlocked, fine- to medium-grained; to subophitic, fine- to medium-grained. With powder X-ray analyses, albite, chlorite amphibole, actinolite, albite, and possibly kaolinite were found.

The structure of the Langda-Sela-style blades clearly distinguish them from all others manufactured and/or used within the overall study area. Figures 2.35 and 2.36 show the dorsal and ventral views of a collection of Langda-Sela-style adze blades. In longitudinal dimension the blades are elongate rectangular to elongate triangular. They are narrow relative to their lengths. In both dorsal and ventral plan view, the side edges in a longitudinal direction are parallel to subparallel throughout the medial portions of the blade. Near the cutting edge end of the tool the sides may almost imperceptibly flair out away from the blade to accommodate the widest portion of the blade at approximately the chord of the subcrescent to crescent-shaped cutting edge. At some point between the midpoint of the blade, in a longitudinal direction and the proximal hafted end of the blade, the outside blade edges commence to converge to form a narrow slightly rounded or even pointed blade end. In longitudinal side view, the dorsal (upper) surface of the blade is arcuate in shape from the cutting edge to the opposing proximal end of the blade. From the approximate midpoint of the dorsal surface (highest point of the dorsal arc), the arc angle increases as it approaches the cutting edge of the blade to form, at its greatest angle of divergence from the horizontal, the dorsal bevel angle. In a similar fashion the dorsal arc angle increases in magnitude away from the crest of the arc toward the proximal end of the blade. In the same longitudinal side view cross section, one can see that the ventral side of the blade (side hafted against the foot of the haft) is flat to subflat and nearly parallel to the dorsal side. This forms a practical hafting platform on some portion of the medial part of the blade or toward the proximal, hafted end of the blade. At the distal, or cutting end of the tool, the ventral bevel angle is almost always larger than the dorsal bevel angle. Only in the shorter blades do the shapes of the blades in longitudinal dorsal plan view become sometimes oblong and sometimes even triangular (in the very shortest blades). This change in shape seems to be caused by the fact that apparently the tool-makers and users designed blades that would maintain blade cutting edges with a length of at least 4 cm, regardless of how short the blade was originally or had become through use, wear, breakage, and resharpening (see table 2.3 for important blade measurements and dimension relationships). This approximate minimum cutting edge length seems to hold true also for the Yeineri and Tagime styles of adze blades. Mechanics studies, beyond the scope of this book, are required. Within the scope of the subject of cutting efficiency, two features of cutting edge structure may be especially pertinent. From a frontal view of the cutting edge, it is seen that the cutting edge is a straight line or more often a convex-up (toward dorsal side) curve. Further, it appears that the cutting edge of the blade is angled (by flaking and grinding) so that when normally mounted on the socket of the shaft, for a right-handed user, from the user's perspective, the right side of the cutting edge of the blade strikes the object lower than the left side. It may also be pertinent to tool efficiency that in frontal view—ventral side down, dorsal side up—that the upward arcuate shape of the cutting edge of the Langda-Sela blade is more pronounced than in either the Tagime- or Yeineri-style adze blades. In the most pronounced curvatures, the cutting edges of the Langda-Sela adze blades even approach the shape of a semicircle.

The textures of the Langda-Sela blades are classed as fine-grained, seriate (igneous texture); subophitic, fine- to-medium grained, mesh interwoven fabric that appears very strong; subophilitic/elongate interlocked, and fine- to medium-grained for the light gray-green Langda-Sela blades and quarry stone; and interlocking fine-grained equigranular to fine-grained fibrous in and around veins for the tan blades. The metabasalt/andesite quarry chips from Sela and metabasalt/andesite blades

are ranked as "hard" on the research scale (VH, H, M, S); whereas the Langda unmetamorphosed basalt/andesite quarry chips and basalt/andesite Langda blades are judged to be "very hard," due to the rocks' fine-grained interlocking texture. Macroscopically the Langda-produced and Sela-produced blades cannot be differentiated.

The Langda-Sela-type blades are distinguishable from both the Tagime- and Yeineri-produced blades not only by their color, lithologies, and structure but by the mottled patterns of polished and unground areas on the blades. On a Tagime and Yeineri blade most

Fig. 2.35. Dorsal view of fourteen Langda-Sela-style adze blades

Fig. 2.36. Ventral view of fourteen Langda-Sela-style adze blades

Table 2.3. Measurements of Langda-Sela-Style Adze Blades

Adze Blade	Maximum Length	Maximum Width	Maximum Thickness	Length to Width Ratio	Bit Angle	Dorsal Bevel Angle	Ventral Bevel Angle
1	26.9	4.8	3.4	5.6	49	13	36
2	18.6	3.4	2.3	5.5	42	12	30
3	16.2	3.0	2.5	5.4	40	19	21
4	27.0	5.3	3.4	5.1	59	15	44
5	11.1	3.0	1.8	3.7	45	16	29
6	21.7	4.5	2.5	4.8	57	18	39
7	13.7	4.7	3.0	2.9	66	22	44
8	16.2	4.0	2.7	4.1	65	20	45
9	21.8	4.4	2.8	4.9	62	22	40
10	15.8	5.8	3.3	2.7	43	22	21
11	19.5	4.8	3.0	4.1	63	25	38
12	17.0	4.4	3.0	3.9	48	17	31
13	9.2	4.1	2.3	2.2	65	17	48
14	10.5	4.0	2.8	2.6	70	25	45
15	10.4	4.6	2.5	2.3	70	25	45
16	9.9	4.1	2.6	2.4	65	26	39
17	16.2	4.5	2.8	3.6	55	15	40
18	11.9	4.4	2.8	2.7	61	21	40
19	9.2	4.4	2.3	2.1	72	12	60
20	9.2	3.8	2.5	2.4	68	16	52
21	14.7	5.1	3.3	2.9	68	31	37
22	9.9	4.2	2.7	2.4	62	24	38
23	7.7	4+	2.2	1.9	25	05	20
24	7.8	3.5	3.5	2.2	64	23	41
25	7.2	4.0	1.9	1.8	66	16	50
26	8.1	4.5	1.8	1.8	61	15	46
27	10.0	3.8	2.7	2.6	63	15	48
28	10.3	3.1	2.2	3.3	47	10	37
29	26.7	5.7	3.4	4.7	49	14	35
30	20.1	5.0	4.0	4.0	76	30	46
31	10.6	4.1	2.7	2.6	75	20	55
Mean	*14.6*	*4.3*	*2.7*	*3.3*	*59*	*19*	*40*

Note: Maximum width of each blade approximates length of cutting edge; measurements in cm and degrees.

of the surface area is ground and polished, with only a few, if any, scattered deep flake scars left rough and unpolished. On the Langda-Sela blades, however, the overall motif is a patchy appearance with highly polished areas interspersed with declivities of untouched flake scars. The Una-speaking people in the greater Langda quarry area call an average Langda-Sela-style blade with scattered rough spots a *sabea* and a blade that is ground smooth all over a *humulu*. The details of structure of the complexly shaped Langda-Sela blades are more precisely determined by knapping before grinding commences than with either the Tagime or Yeineri blades. On the Langda-Sela-style blades this detailed knapping causes an adjoining continuum of small flake scars on all sides. Grinding and polishing of the flaked blades smoothes the rough highlights over most of the surface of each blade and grinds smooth both the dorsal and ventral sides of the blade near the distal (cutting) end to produce the desired shape of the cutting edge and a well-ground sharpness. The dorsal crest is rounded and smoothed by grinding, and the lateral edges are just "touched" and smoothed. Often the proximal back third of the blade that is covered by rattan strips when hafted is less well ground than the half of the blade toward the cutting end. Surfaces of highly polished areas are usually interspersed with declivities of untouched flake scars.

The Una people sometimes apply pulverized red hematite "paint" to some of the flake scars on hafted blades. This creates a bright red and light gray-green mottled appearance. When a blade that has been so painted is removed from its haft, both the red paint and the darker color of the dirtied, exposed part of the blade visibly distinguish the exposed part of the blade from that part that has been bound to the socket. When I first saw blades decorated this way in the Langda area I thought two things: This was done either as a recent innovative decoration to attract modern buyers, or it might have some ritual empowerment to protect the blade from breakage or enhance its use quality. The quarrymen informants at Langda said neither was the case. They had always done this—learned from their ancestors—as a mark of beauty and it has no sacred significance. When I was able to re-examine my collection of Langda-Sela blades acquired over a period of years from scattered locations throughout the use area, I noted that some of them exhibit a dull red look on scattered, unpolished flake scars. This coloring may well be dirtied remnants of hematite powder that was painted onto the blades after hafting. If that is true, I suspect that there is probably more to it than just a profane decoration for the indigenous users, as they would have had me believe.

Adzes

The Langda-Sela-style adze blades are hafted in much the same fashion as the manufacturers and users of the Yeineri and Tagime types have hafted their blades. Since the Yali and East indigenous inhabitants use no axes, their adzes perform all the same chopping and planing functions that both axes and adzes do for the people to the west. One might think, therefore, that for the chore of splitting large felled trees, which is done in the Grand Valley and West primarily with sturdy axes that the Yali and East residents might, in some fashion, duplicate the Dani axe, where the cutting edge of the blade is aligned nearly parallel or is parallel with the longitudinal axis of the shaft. Supporting this supposition is the fact that in eastern Papua New Guinea, to the east of the Yali and East region, some groups of people haft their blades in movable hafting sockets so the blades can be rotated to the configuration of an axe if that is desired (Sillitoe 1988:43–44). But within the Yali and East study region of Irian Jaya, this is not so. From my field observations with the Una, Kimyal, and Yali, it appears they haft their adze blades with almost the same adze blade cutting edge to longitudinal axis of the shaft angle (fig. 2.6 for definition) as is used in the Grand Valley and West. Neither mount their adze blades so that the cutting edge angle even approaches being parallel to the longitudinal axis of the shaft, which is a cutting edge angle of 0°, or the precise definition of an axe. The cutting edge angles of adzes in the Yali and East regions are seen to vary from 67° to 85°, with a mean angle of about 79°. For Grand Valley and West adzes, the cutting edge angles vary from 70° to 90°, with a mean angle of 82°.

The Yali of the central Yali dialect call both the adze blade and the adze a *yaha* (alt. spellings *yaga* and *yaka*). The foot underneath the rattan wrapping is called an *akal* and the shaft an *ambo*. The rattan wrapping is called *sabeap*. The largest yaha that I observed in the Yali area has a shaft 65 cm long, 11.8 cm in shaft circumference, and a foot that measures 44 cm long, with an overall foot plus exposed part of the adze blade of 53 cm. The shortest yaha has a shaft length of 43.8 cm, a shaft circumference of 5.6 cm, and a foot that is 33.4 cm long. The mean shaft length of ten representative adzes is 53.1 cm, mean shaft circumference 7.3 cm, and mean foot length 32.7 cm.

Like the Grand Valley and West, the Yali and East language-speaking groups use hafts of different sizes and that vary from straight to quite bowed. Appearances, geometrics, and size variations are similar between the two groups. Una-speaking people call an average size adze a *metikja* (alt. spelling *metikya*) and a very small adze a *manghwarja*. Straight shafts are called *sirikto* and curved handles *tingento*. Both straight and curved handled adzes are used for the same purpose.

In figure 2.37 on a photograph of a curved handled adze with the blade removed, it is noted by the distribution of the red-painted flake scars and discoloration of the exposed part of the adze blade (as previously discussed), slightly less than one-third of the blade is bound to the haft socket. In the line drawing of a straight-handled adze in figure 2.38, it is also seen that slightly less than one-third of the blade is hafted.

When hafting, the cutting edge angle is determined by the angle that the flattened hafting surface makes with an imaginary plane through the shaft and foot of the adze and then the way that the adze blade is bound to that surface. Sometimes a blade is bound to the haft socket without the use of organic material padding. More often banana trunk strips, strips of wood, pieces of leaves, and other vegetal materials furnish a choice of nesting materials that are used to haft a blade for added shock absorption and to assist in angling the blade when binding it to the socket to create the desired cutting edge angle.

When put into use to chop down a tree, the hands are held touching each other on the haft to be able to obtain full momentum on the downward stroke by creating a comfortable pivot point at the wrists. By forward flexing the wrists just before the blade strikes the tree, both the blade strike angle is controlled and mechanical advantage gained. At times, a woodchopper may work while holding the haft with only one hand; yet the pivot-point principle is still in effect.

Often two men work as a team to chop down a tree (fig. 2.39). The men calculate the placement of their chopping on opposite sides of the tree and the depth to which each will chop to encourage the tree to fall in the desired direction. When working alone on a medium- to large-sized tree, a woodcutter will change sides on the tree to create the same pattern of opposite side cuts, as if there were two men working together.

When chopping a tree down with an adze, the worker chops higher as his blade bites deeper. He wastes no energy chopping away the frayed material at the base of the cut, as is done by axe cutters when cutting down trees as they change the angles and strike points of their blows. Note the neat pile of chips created by the woodchopper at the base of the tree in figure 2.39. Perhaps the spring effect of the adze at the end of each stroke assists the woodcutter in flicking chips away from the cut. At the moment of blade impact, the haft shaft bends backward and then rebounds as the tool is pulled way from the cut.

Knives

Unhafted knives are used often by the Yali and others in the east region. They are primarily used for cutting taro plants for planting and for

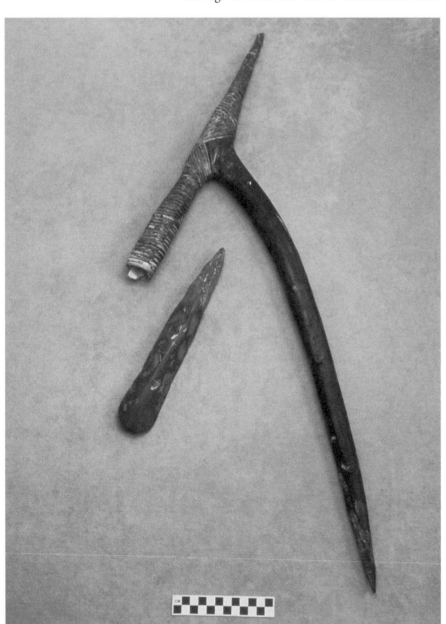

Fig. 2.37. Blade outside of its adze

scraping and cutting all tubers for steaming or roasting (fig. 2.40). Among the Yali, Una, Kimyal, and others in the eastern area, both men and women use and own stone knives. According to informants an adult person may own one or as many as five knives, but the average is about three. It was very common for a woman to have one or more knives with her in one of her head-back nets as she went to and from the fields and while doing her daily chores, just as a man routinely carried bows and arrows with him and quite often an adze over his shoulder as he moved about.

The knives vary from oblate to elongate oblong to narrow rectangular in shape. They range in color from light buff to light gray, sometimes light green, sometimes tan, and within a hamlet "assemblage" there are usually a few black knives. Some blades have narrow darker colored bands (from source rock color differences) exposed in interesting patterns on lighter colored blade surfaces. The knives are never hafted and are completely ground and polished smooth. Sometimes just one end is ground to a sharpened edge, and at other times an end and an entire side, and in other fewer cases almost the entire circumference of a knife, is edge-sharpened. Like the knives in the Grand Valley and West region, the sharpened edges are not as sharp as the sharpened edges of adze blades, and rarely does a user cut her/himself. The knives are originally shaped and sharpened and later resharpened on portable sandstone grinding slabs and at sandstone bedrock out-crops. Sometimes a handheld grinding stone is used for minor resharpening. In figure 2.41, a Yali woman shows me the two Langda-style knives that she was carrying in one of her head-back nets while on the way to visit a friend. When a knife breaks, if a piece of usable size remains, it continues to be used as is or it may be retouched by grinding the broken edge. Pieces that are considered too small to be usable are merely discarded. When knives break during manufacture or use, the people say the blade is "sick" and not that a malevolent ghost or spirit was involved in breaking the blade or that a knife blade-maker was at fault. The breakage is "just something that happens."

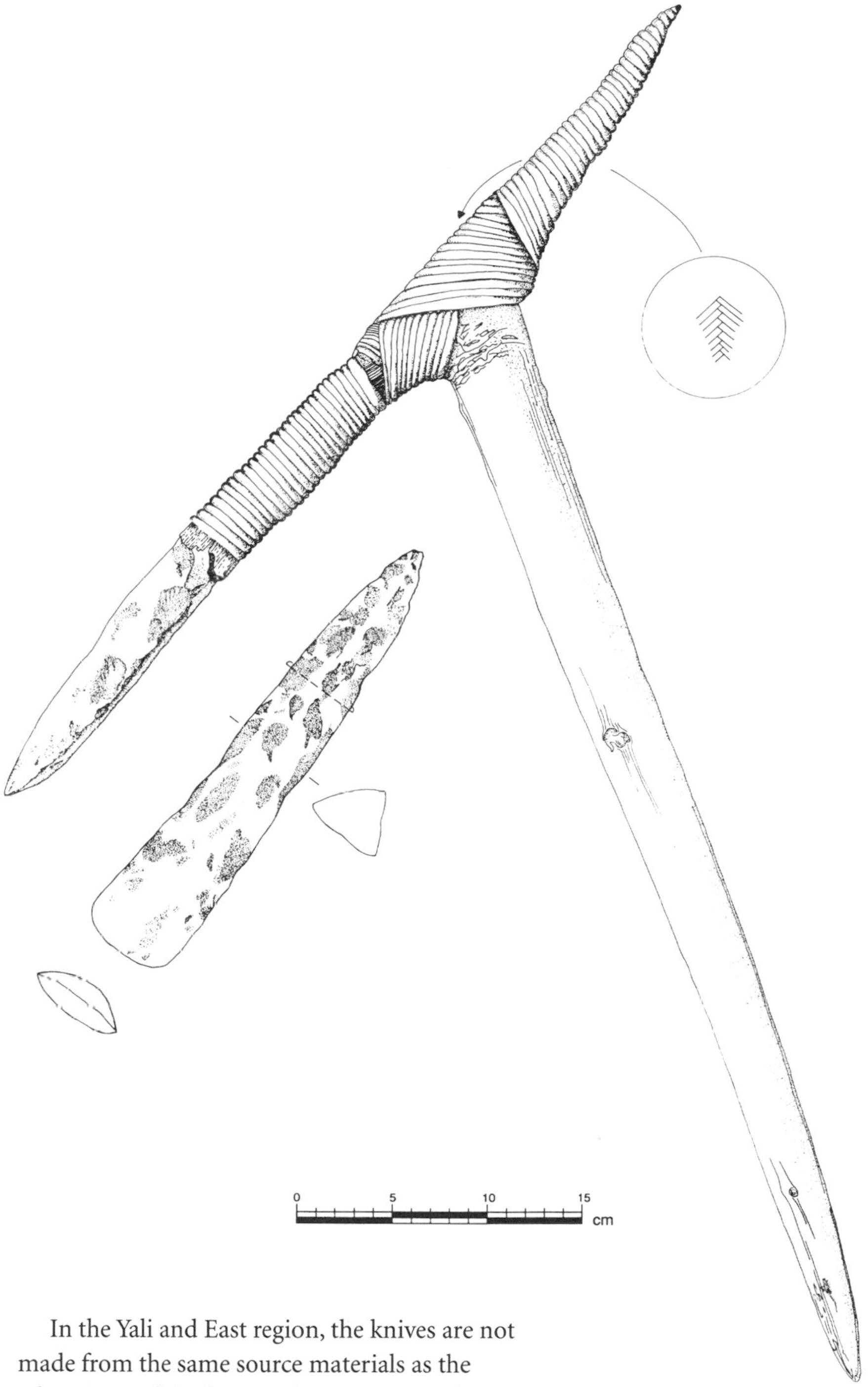

In the Yali and East region, the knives are not made from the same source materials as the adzes. Instead, in the Langda quarry area the knife material comes from rock outcrops up slope from adze blade quarry sites. The knives were found to consist of the major minerals muscovite, biotite, quartz, and albite feldspar. A titanium-bearing phase is also present as a minor unidentified accessory mineral. The micas, quartz, and albite are thought to be the result of metamorphic recrystallization (green-stone schist facies) and not deposited as detrital

Fig. 2.38. Line drawing of Yali adze and its blade

Fig. 2.39. Two Una men chopping down a tree

albite, missing the quartz and albite fractions, which are interpreted to furnish the hard, abrasive material for the cutting edges of the knives.

The quartz grains make up approximately 15 to 20 percent of the rock; individual grains are irregularly shaped, with long dimensions ranging from 5 to 10 microns. The quartz grain edges are deeply embayed and serrated. Visual analysis indicates that at least part of the serration is caused naturally and not from chipping by the thin-section grinding process. It is felt that the knives' durability and cutting effectiveness are caused by the bonding of the approximately equally spaced, abrasive sharp-edged quartz and albite in the micrograined, somewhat flexible muscovite and biotite groundmass. It is estimated that the microquartz and microalbite particles are spaced about 20 micrometers apart along the cutting surfaces and throughout the groundmass of the knives.

The genesis of the kind of metamorphic rock that was interpreted for the knives from laboratory analysis is quite compatible with the presence of the volcanic sequence in the Langda quarry area. The geologic relationship of the Langda area adze and knife blade quarries is discussed in chapter 4.

From hamlet to hamlet it was interesting to look at the knife blades as assemblages to be treated and contemplated as similar collections might be treated from archaeological excavations. One example of just such an "assemblage" was put together and photographed at the Yali hamlet of Pasikni, located not far uphill from Angguruk (fig. 2.42). (Pasikni is located toward Nisikni from Angguruk on the map but is not Nisikni.) The name of the owner of each of the knives was recorded so that interviews could be conducted. Of thirty-six knives, the longest was 20.3 cm (owner would not allow photographs) with a maximum width of 9.0 cm and maximum knife thickness of 0.76 cm. The shortest knife in the collection was 9.0 cm long and 3.3 cm wide at its widest point, with an average blade thickness of 0.3 cm. Not including the longest blade (20.3 cm), which was not photographed, but including the next longest blade, which was 19.2 cm, the mean length for the collection was 12.6 cm, mean width at

grains. The important quartz-albite grains are "wrapped" with the micas and shielded from observation under the SEM when viewed in unground, natural microchips taken from the knives. Only after grinding and polishing in the thin-section process do the quartz and albite grains become visible in cross section. Without a polished thin section, one might erroneously interpret the rock to be composed almost entirely of the silicate minerals muscovite and

Fig. 2.40. A woman and a man scrape and cut taro tubers.

the widest point on each blade 4.7 cm, and the mean blade thickness 0.53 cm. These knife blade dimensions are comparable to a collection from the Una people at Langda. At Langda the longest blade was 20.0 cm with a width at its widest dimension of 6.0 cm, and with an unusual maximum thickness of 2.2 cm in the center of this differently shaped blade, which is oblong in cross section rather than with the normal parallel sides. By comparison, the next longest blade at Langda, which is of normal proportions, was 11.0 cm long, 4.6 cm wide, 0.65 cm thick. The shortest blade in the collection was 10.8 cm long by 5.1 cm wide, by 0.6 cm thick. The thinnest

Fig. 2.41. A Yali woman's two knives

Fig. 2.42. Knife blade collection at the Yali hamlet of Pasikni

blade at Langda was 0.3 cm thick. Not including the unusual long blade at Langda, the mean length for the collection is 13.2 cm, mean "maximum" width 5.0 cm, and mean thickness 0.56 cm. To facilitate comparison, the dimensions for the two collections are set forth in table 2.4.

Chert ("Flint") Flakes

The Yali and East indigenous inhabitants have a similar supply of chert nodules as the Grand Valley and West inhabitants. They obtain and use unretouched small chert flakes in the same manner as do the people to the west. For de-

Table 2.4. Comparison of Stone Knife Blade Sizes at the Hamlets of Pasikni (Yali) and Langda (Una)

	Pasikni (cm)	Langda (cm)
Longest	20.3	20.0
Widest	9.0	6.0
Thickest	0.76	2.2
Shortest	9.0	10.8
Narrowest	3.3	4.0
Thinnest	0.3	0.3
Mean length	12.6	13.2
Mean width	4.7	5.0
Mean thickness	0.53	0.56

tailed information refer to the previous discussion of "Chert ("Flint") Flakes" under the Grand Valley and West in this chapter.

Hammerstones

The river-tumbled and -rounded hammerstones are available and used in the Yali and East region, just as they are to the west. Refer to the previous discussion for details.

Stationary Grinding Slabs and Mobile Hand Stones

The largest ground stone tools that are present in the Highlands are permanently located grinding slabs (select spots on bedrock outcrops and large erratics) and smaller portable but stationary grinding slabs. Another, although smaller, tool of abrasion is the mobile handheld grindstone. All play a key role as tools of abrasion in lithic reduction. Most are also used to shape, smooth, and sharpen bone knives, bone and wooden awls and needles, and certain hardwood arrow tips.

By way of definition, both the permanently located grinding slabs and the portable grinding slabs are "stationary" in that they are ground-supported when objects are ground against them, while the "mobile handheld grindstones" are just that, handheld while they are used to grind or abrade objects that are either held in the other hand, held with the feet, or supported on the ground or against another rock.

The primary sources for almost all of the grinding stones are outcroppings of sandstone beds within the Kembalangen formation. Sandstone is the lithology of choice for all grindstones and the *necessary* lithology for heavy grinding and shaping. The distribution of bedrock grinding sites and source locations for supplies of portable grindstones is thus controlled geologically by the presence of Kembalangen sandstone outcrops and the scattered presence of Kembalangen sandstone erratics. At certain locales, where men gather for purposes other than grinding, silty limestone erratics are sometimes used as grinding slabs of convenience for minor "touch-ups" on stone and other tools.

Within the controls of the geologic distribution of the desired sandstone grinding material, favorite bedrock and large erratic boulder grinding spots are developed near habitation sites, within rock quarry areas, at commonly used work or meeting spots (such as the salt pools), by habitually used war overlook positions, and at other locales of convenience.

When grinding, water is almost always used to lubricate the grindstones and to help create a grinding paste with eroded particles from the grinding rock. For this reason, grinding slabs are located along the banks of rivers and other bodies of water whenever possible. Often the grinding surfaces extend down into rivers on rock outcrops or are on large rock erratics out in small streams or places of water accumulation. At many such locales throughout the Highlands, the grinding area changes size as water levels rise and fall. When away from an adjacent water supply, water is carried to the grinding spots in both bamboo and gourd water containers and in spongy clumps of moss that are gathered for that purpose. Often a worker will have a helper who stands by to drip

Fig. 2.43. A stationary grindstone at the Ileukaima salt pool

Fig. 2.44. Two stationary grinding sites in the Grand Valley

water from a water-laden sponge of moss onto the grinding surface as a tool is worked.

The bedrock and large erratic boulder grinding areas are the most durable and permanently located artifacts of culture that will remain in the archaeological record to attest to the present ground stone technology. Already these artifacts are becoming archaeological objects because of the increasing disuse of stone tools. Inactive sites are identifiable by the presence of algae and lichen, which quickly cover the grinding surfaces. Some sites are already buried by organic debris and can only be located by inhabitants who know of their uses in the recent past. Within the constraints of the geological distribution of sandstone outcrops, the identification of ground stone tool users and, theoretically, their use area boundaries could be mapped in the archaeological record by the distribution and interpretation of similar grinding sites in prehistoric cultures.

One grinding site "of convenience" to the local inhabitants in one part of the research area is shown in previously presented figure 2.10. Three other permanently located grinding sites, at widely scattered locations, are shown in figures 2.43 and 2.44. These sites as well as numerous others in the Irian Jaya Highlands region are similar in appearance to classic grinding slabs of the Neolithic in Europe.

On the grinding slab in figure 2.43, which is located along the north-central edge of the Grand Valley beside the Ileukaima salt pool (see fig. 1.21), there is no evidence of sharpening marks other than from axe and adze blades. Although barely discernible, however, in the photographs of the two sites shown in figure 2.44, linear-use wear marks are present that were made by sharpening bone awls and needles, and in the upper photograph probably hardwood arrow tips as well. Such use wear patterns are clearly seen at yet two other sites shown by photographs in figure 2.45. Through repeated abrasion the linear V-shaped grooves were worn into the grindstones by bone awls and needles and by the sharpening of certain kinds of hardwood

Fig. 2.45. Hardwood arrow tips and bone awl grinding patterns

arrow tips. In figure 2.46, at yet another permanently located bedrock grinding site, a man interrupted his work of shaping and sharpening a Tagime flat-style axe blade to demonstrate that the axe blade would not fit in the deep V-shaped linear grooves. He said that the grooves were made by shaping and sharpening bone awls, needles, and arrow tips.

Two portable sandstone grinding slabs and a handheld grindstone are shown in the two photographs in figure 2.47, along with examples of the kinds of tools, which when re-

Fig. 2.46. Deep grinding
grooves caused by sharpening
bone awls

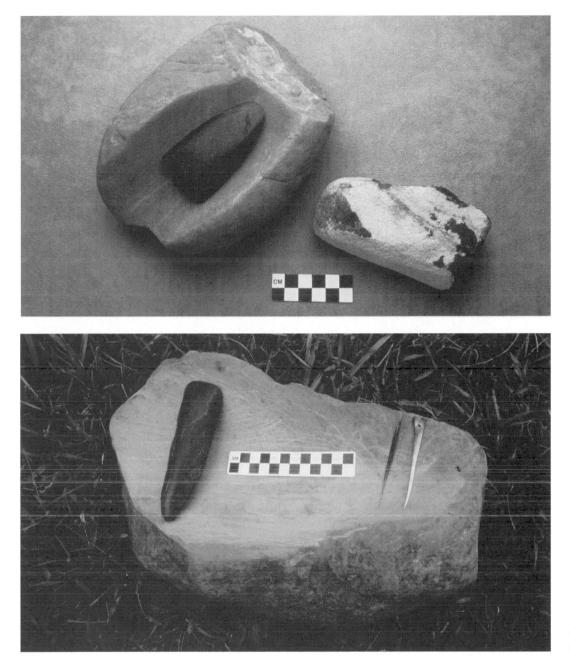

Fig. 2.47. Mobile grinding slabs and handheld grindstone

peatedly ground, shaped the grinding surfaces of the stationary slabs. It is pointed out that the simple concave grinding surfaces on the slabs are similar in shape to surfaces that are formed on grinding slabs worldwide by plant-food processing. In the upper photograph in figure 2.47, the grinding surface was shaped by grinding Yeineri-style adze blades, a type ex-

ample of which is shown on the grinding slab. In the lower photograph the concave grinding surface on a Yali slab was formed by grinding Langda-Sela-style adze blades. At the closed end of the Yali grinding slab, a bone needle is laid beside the narrow V-shape groove to show the kind of tool used to create the groove.

CHAPTER 3

Symbolic Stones and the Sociopolitical Framework in Which They Move

It is the hard, durable artifacts of culture, such as those of stone, that are most generously preserved in the archaeological record. Throughout prehistory, the recorded presence of symbolic stones, when they could be identified, not just stone tools, has intrigued us. We have thought much about the symbolic stones, understood a few occasionally, and written of them prolifically. It is similar objects from stone that because of their characteristics of durability and strength are generally created by the indigenous people of the Highlands of Irian Jaya for both profane symbolic uses of great sociological importance and as their most sacred and supernaturally powerful symbolic entities. But a most intriguing paradox exists herein: the most perishable of materials—bits of fur, feathers, and plant remains—are used to decorate and imbue both the durable profane and the sacred stones with symbolic meaning and thereby to visually transmit important added cultural information. In addition, the uses of a simple fiber string, stems, and blades of grass, a few leaves, a certain small root, and a bit of tree bark are essential to focus and maintain the continuum of supernatural power

from unknown places in the domain of the unseen into those durable stone objects that have been selected to be made sacred. The fragile organic materials are often destroyed in the archaeological record, so hence no thought can be given to them and their cultural context. At other times, bits of fur, feathers, a string, a few blades of grass, leaves, or a small stick are found with prehistoric remains, but usually they are not understood and little thought is given to them. To us, they are not as dramatic a discovery as the stone objects, most of which have been shaped by human hands. But here in the Irian Jaya Highlands we have the fragile artifacts as well as the durable stone ones. We are just now beginning to see through the veil of mystery to understand something of the symbolic relationships between these particularly fragile materials of the natural world and the durable objects we call symbolic stones. Because of the important relationship of the fragile and the durable—the bits of fur, feathers, the blades of grass, string, small sticks, leaves, and the symbolic stone—this chapter and the next will include a discussion of both profane and sacred organic material as well as of the stones themselves. What I will be describing is an ethnographically derived "kind of Rosetta stone" (phrase from Binford [1983:24] on stone tools) that will allow archaeologists to expand and evaluate our boundaries of interpretations of the dynamics that were associated with similar and, indeed *like,* combinations of objects that have been found worldwide.

Sociopolitical Organization

If at any instant in time we could see all of the symbolic stones, sacred and profane, and other sacred tool stones that are present in the Central Highlands of Irian Jaya, we would probably be amazed at both the quantity and variety. Yet their uses and physical presence at different places at any one time are quite structured and adhere to a predictable social format. The Highlanders' sociopolitical organization provides the hierarchy and framework within which the stones move. Certain events, set in motion at specific times and places by the edicts of the most influential leaders (the big men, or *gains* of different groups), provide the impetus and need for the uses of certain stones, both profane and sacred, at ceremonial functions. Other stones with well-known uses and some with specialized supernatural powers flow through a ceremonial continuum that is controlled by other leaders of lesser influence. Some shaman specialists have authority to use their stones in ways that are prompted not only by the requirements of ceremonial regimen but also by the unpredictable happenings of daily life. Other stones with special significance and power are utilized in daily routine by the common folk to promote health, happiness, and to help them carry out their individual responsibilities with some measure of success.

Within the social and political organization there are repositories for all of these stones, places where the profane stones are properly stored for the times when they are needed and wusa places where the empowerment of sacred stones is enacted through magical rites. Some of these stones are maintained for secret rituals within the places of storage as well as to be removed from storage from time to time by

shamans of authority for other uses. For the general population there are designated sacred stones that have been duly empowered but which can be maintained and used away from the places of special sanctity, where the supernaturally most powerful stones are maintained.

The interplay of social needs in dealing with the unknown, calling upon the assistance of supernatural power through stones and other objects to accomplish social ends, is indeed complicated. The starting place to gain an understanding of the cultural framework, within which the use of symbolic stones, profane and sacred, play their cultural role, is to briefly look at the sociopolitical organization. The social realms within the different adjacent-living language groups (fig. 1.3) are generally organized on the basis of kinship. Across the pan-mosaic of Highlands cultures, exogamous, nonterritorial patrimoiety groups form the framework for spousal choice and participation in some ceremonies. Kinship is traced through both patrilineages (known male lines of descent back to a common ancestor) and patrilineal lines of descent back to a common traditional mythical ancestor. In some parts of the Highlands, patrilineages are quite well known; not so well known in a few areas where there is a rather pragmatic indifference to genealogies. For my treatment of the subject, I will refer to both patrilineages and groups linked by patrilineal lines of descent as patrilineages. I further point out that what I refer to as patrilineages, Heider calls "sibs" (1970:65–67). Patrilineages are nonterritorial, which facilitates the formation of social-kinship trade linkages across both political and language boundaries. Segments of patrilineages are, on the other hand, territorial when they combine to form political units and, at the compound and hamlet levels (house cluster and wards in the Yali and East region), the men's socioreligious groups that control the sacred stones that are so fundamental to the vibrancy of the cultures.

Within the overall sociopolitical organization, the Highlanders are organized politically on the basis of territorial units that cooperate in wartime and are formed on the basis of patrilineage combinations. These units, called alliances and confederations in the Grand Valley and West region, partly interfere with the social groups formed at the compound and hamlet levels. It is the blending of the groups of the two levels, even with their disharmonies, that comprises the infrastructure within which the symbolic stones are traded, maintained, and used.

The territorial units in the Grand Valley and West region, from largest to smallest, within which the symbolic stones play their important roles are the alliance, confederation, hamlet, and compound; in the Yali and East area, according to Koch, they are the district, village (hamlet), and house cluster (1967:43–59). Koch, in his work at the Pasikni village near Angguruk, did not report the presence among the Yali of powerful political leaders at a "confederacy" or "alliance" regional level as are present in the Grand Valley and West. I deduce this to be because only in the Grand Valley and West were there population centers (greater Grand Valley and farther west outside of the study area in the environs of Enarotoli) with sufficient wealth to support the hierarchy of larger political organizations. (For further discussions beyond the scope of this research on the subject of social and political organizations the reader is referred to: Broekhuijse 1967, Hayward 1992, Heider 1970, Koch 1967, Larson 1987, O'Brien 1969, Peters 1975, Ploeg 1966, and Pospisil 1956.)

Alliance

In the Grand Valley and West region (fig. 2.1), as previously mentioned, the two important political territorial units are the alliance and the confederation. "The alliance is the maximal unit within which ceremonial, political, and social activity take place" (Heider 1970:77). Within the Grand Valley, people refer to members of alliances other than their own as foreigners or *dila-mege;* those people within their own alliance are called *aguni juma-mege,* or "people of this place, local people" (Heider 1970:77). Within the Grand Valley (fig. 1.21), at the time of Heider's initial work (1961–63) there were about a dozen of these alliances. Alliance boundaries are frontiers where two alliances meet. As Heider

pointed out interalliance frontiers may be war or peace frontiers, depending on the current relations between the two alliances.

Peters (1975:53) in his work in and around Wamena enumerated the five largest war alliances in the Grand Valley. He said that one of these, the Loko-Mabel alliance, was made up of at least eleven combinations and led by the most important man in this group of "confederacies," the gain (big man) Gutelu. (Peter's patrilineage combinations are similar to Heider's "confederacies.") Gutelu, as the big man of his own confederacy and the leader (most influential big man) of the Loko-Mabel alliance, had much influence within the entire Grand Valley and even beyond, as we shall see in chapter 4. Because of Gutelu's high position at or near the apex of the hierarchy of leadership influence within his own cultural system, I relied on Gutelu and his collection of sacred cultural artifacts as a symbolic model for personages of this political position. In chapter 4 Gutelu's personal sacred objects are examined in detail.

Two major activities involve an alliance in its entirety—war and initiating the *ebe akho* ceremony. Both are the responsibility of the most influential big man (leader) of the alliance. Both involve ritual and trigger the uses of symbolic stones. All-out warfare is a periodic alliancewide affair that results from the accumulation of numerous hurts and wrongs from previous conflicts or from the intrigue of a "political takeover"—the unseating of a big man or gain (alt. *kain*) who is the leader of a particular alliance. Ritual wars, although initiated and fought on the lower confederation level, are still the ultimate responsibility of the leader of the alliance.

It is only the most influential man in the alliance, as stated above, who has the authority to initiate the alliancewide ebe akho ceremony. The announcement and events leading up to the ebe akho in one alliance might influence other gain, powerful big men of other alliances, to commence their own ebe akho, during which wars are temporarily halted. This is a time among the Grand Valley and Western Dani when all outstanding war indemnities are settled, the final rituals for outstanding funerals are concluded, marriage ceremonies conducted, and the boys important *waija* moiety initiation ceremonies take place. Although held only once approximately every five years (five years during the time period of my personal experience, one in 1987 and the next in 1992), the ebe akho is the commencement of a grand round of ceremonies held down at confederation levels that encompass everyone in the alliance. As the ebe akho approaches, moratoriums are sometimes placed on the killing of pigs, so there will be enough when the ceremonies start. Wood is stockpiled at strategic hamlet locales for pig feast ceremonies that will be in the offing. The big men of the confederations and down to compound level are busy planning the activities for their many groups. The important profane je display-exchange stones are traded around and collected by those who will need a sufficient number to take care of their responsibilities when the ebe akho is finally commenced. Men's groups, whose responsibilities are to empower and maintain the sacred stones, dispatch their responsibilities to assure the spirits in the world of the unseen that all is in order and to solicit their help in secular affairs. The ebe akho is the periodic sociopolitical-religious culmination of pig feast rituals for which the people have been living.

The ebe akho is one aspect in which the sociopolitical systems of the Grand Valley and West and the Yali and East regions vary. Although pig feast rituals in the Yali and East follow some sort of a cycle, there is no periodic culmination in anything so all-encompassing as the ebe akho in the Grand Valley and West. For one thing, there are no massive weddings at periodic time intervals in the east as there are in the Grand Valley and Western Dani areas at the times of the ebe akho.

Confederation

The confederation is the most important sociopolitical unit within the Grand Valley and West region (fig. 2.1) (O'Brien 1969:185; Heider 1970:79). According to Heider, in the Grand Valley alone, there were some thirty confedera-

tions (1970:79). O'Brien mapped seven "confederacies" in the smaller Konda Valley where she worked near Bokondini (fig. 1.1) (1969:191). Bromley, who lived in the Grand Valley from 1954 to 1993, estimated that the population included in a single confederacy might range from fewer than 1,000 to perhaps as many as 5,000 (1960:252). Larson stated that, "the population of the subconfederacy forms the community in Dani. These are the people who assemble large work crews for land clearing and fence building, sponsor communal feasts, assemble warriors for battle, and . . . participate in group ritual to counteract illness in the past" (1987:131). As with the Damal and Western Dani of Larson's area of research in the Mulia-Ilaga area (fig. 1.31), it was at the interconfederacy level that war prevailed throughout the study area between confederacies of opposing alliances. The leaders (big men) of the alliances had an overall responsibility, but it was really the big men at the confederacy level who bore the burdens of commencing and stopping wars. One wonders how much consultation and influence went on between the gains of the alliances and their confederacy war leaders who were involved in war between confederacies across the boundaries of opposing alliances. At the confederacy level and within the confederacies, war strategies were discussed and warriors furnished. Rituals involving sacred stones were conducted to manipulate their domiciled spirits to strengthen warriors, keep them safe, and even to go forth and kill enemies.

As people moved from compound to compound and hamlet to hamlet, they tended to stay within the geographic boundaries of their confederacies. "A tendency of patrilocal residence in terms of confederation boundaries is shown by the fact," according to Heider, "that most adult males are native to the confederation" (1970:79). Just as the people in compounds and hamlets, scattered about the countryside within the boundaries of the confederations, make up the living population of each confederation, it seems that the male adults' allegiance is to the confederation rather than to the alliance.

Compound and Hamlet

The compound as described in chapter 1 is the smallest unit of social, political, and economic organization in the Grand Valley and West region. A group of such compounds in the western area, joined together by common fences or stone walls, forms a compound cluster. A large compound cluster or group of compounds forms a hamlet. This definition of a hamlet is admittedly subjective and not definitive.

As previously mentioned in chapter 1, the Yali live in open clusters of houses, without formally fenced or wall-enclosed interior compounds. Leadership at this level is really about the same in each area, Grand Valley and West and Yali and East, with the most influential man of each compound or cluster being the big man for that group.

In the Yali area, Koch (1967:45) defined a ward as a cluster of houses consisting of a large men's house (*jouéi sóumó*) with a scattering of smaller family houses (*homea*) built within its vicinity. Two or more wards compose what I am defining as a Yali (or Una or Kimyal) hamlet. It is pointed out that what I refer to as a hamlet in both the Grand Valley and West and the Yali and East regions might be thought of and referred to by some researchers as a "village."

Compounds, compound clusters, and hamlets in the west and house clusters (wards) and hamlets in the east are composed of several or, more often, extended polygynous families or parts of families. Sometimes a person, a cripple, or a person who is *gebu*, will live away from his/ her nuclear family in another compound or house cluster. It is not uncommon, for example, for a young male adult who is feeling family "stress" to move from one compound (Grand Valley and West) or house cluster (Yali and East) to another to stay with an uncle.

Compounds in the Grand Valley and West range in population from a minimum of one nuclear family (two to seven people) up to a maximum population of about forty-four. In the Yali and East, the population range within house clusters is about the same. Populations in hamlets in both areas appear to range from about 50 to 250.

It is within the individual compounds of the western area and the house clusters (wards) that comprise the geographically separated habitation groups in the eastern area that most activities involving the uses of symbolic stones take place. In compound (western area) and house cluster (eastern area) courtyards and their adjoining structures, weddings, funerals, and curing ceremonies take place. For the larger funeral ceremonies as many as 200 to 400 people fill a courtyard. Select men's houses in some compounds of the Grand Valley and West and the jouéi sóumó ("big men's house" or *usa-évam,* "sacred house") in the Yali and East house clusters (wards) are the specified repositories for both profane and sacred symbolic stones. Within these houses empowerment and renewal rituals for the sacred stones are performed. Appropriate stones that are maintained in these houses are moved with proper protocol to be used in bridewealth, funeral, and some curing rituals, which are held within the compound and house cluster courtyards. The attendance and interaction of most of the people involved in these rituals come not just from the individual compounds or house clusters where the functions take place, but from a larger area or group of compounds and house clusters within which the people are in routine social interaction (usually within a single confederation).

Sometimes certain designated big men will have special sacred houses or villages apart from the normal communal dwelling compounds, where the sacred stones are empowered, maintained, used in ritual, and worshiped.

Within groups of compounds (in the west) or groups of clusters of houses (in the east) that are socially related by virtue of being in geographic proximity and within the same confederation ("district" within the Yali and East), various important men's groups are formed. These include, within the Grand Valley, but not much farther west and not at all to the east, the watchtower groups that built and maintained the watchtowers from which men of each group kept lookout across no-man's-land for attack from known enemies (chapter 1); the

Fig. 3.1. Three decorated Yeineri-sourced display-exchange stones (je)

men's groups that maintain the sacred stones for their members; and the *mogat ai* groups that construct and maintain, at least in the Grand Valley and West, the Highlanders' memorial "cemeteries" (chapter 1).

Profane Display-Exchange Stones

Although throughout the Highlands area, there are numerous stones of many shapes and sizes with instilled supernatural power that are sacred, there is one style of profane stone that stands out above all other symbolic stones for economic and profane social importance. These stones are the stone wealth display-exchange stones called je by their Dani users (fig. 3.1). They are profane or *weligat*. The Western Dani in the Konda Valley call this same profane display-exchange stone *jao*. In the Yali and East

region, it is known as *sie* or *siengga*. Other stones of this same style have been selected by their owners to be instilled with supernatural power through ritual and are sacred (wusa, alt. *wesa*). The latter stones are secretly maintained by the men and stored in their *ganekhe* cabinets never to be seen by the uninitiated.

Regardless of the ultimate designations (je, profane; or wusa, sacred) by the users, the manufacturers of these stones call them all je, profane, because as such they can be openly handled, traded, and seen by the uninitiated. It is up to each user within his own belief system to select those that he wants to use for sacred (wusa) purposes.

Along with pigs, *jerak* (long, narrow woven bands adorned with single or more rows of cowrie shells), large stone axe blades, both utilitarian carrying and strapless ceremonial woven nets, and loose cowrie shells *(jeraken)*, the je are among the most important wealth items (figs. 3.2 and 3.3). Within most, if not all, of the language-speaking groups within the study area, they are necessities for marriage and funeral presentations and important as usual parts of war indemnity payments. In fact, in the Grand Valley, informants say that a war cannot be stopped without the payment of large numbers of je. The exchange of ownership by public display and presentation of the je (and other wealth items) not only fuels the economy by the repayment of debts and the establishment of new obligations, but it appeases the ghosts and the ancestral and other spirits in the unseen world that are observing and listening to the proceedings. The many formal displays of these stone items of wealth before distribution also establish social prestige—when both humans and ghosts/spirits are alerted to the donor's identification by loud pronouncements by ceremonial leaders. It is the presentation of pigs and the exchange of je stones (sie, alt. siengga in the Yali and East) at marriage and funeral rites and for indemnity payments that fashions the continual circulation of wealth items within most of the research area.

Structure, Dimensions, and Nomenclature
The normal style and most commonly used je

are ground and polished, flat to nearly flat, elongate-rectangular or elongate-oval in plan view shape, and thin with approximate uniform thickness throughout each stone. The ends and side edges are often ground rounded and one end sometimes sharpened similarly to the cutting edge of an axe or adze blade (fig. 3.4). From a collection of ten of these normal style je and field measurements of twenty-eight others, it was found that absolute lengths vary from 19.5 to 89.5 cm, maximum widths per stone from 6.0 to 14 cm, and maximum thickness from 0.9 to 2.0 cm (table 3.1). The longest je-type stone found in my research belonged to the powerful gain Gutelu in the Grand Valley. It is 121 cm long. This stone is discussed in chapter 4 as a sacred object. A flat-type je that is less than about 40 cm in length is generally referred to as *je holi* by the Grand Valley Dani. Although the shorter stones are of less value for exchange, it is from among them that certain stones are more often selected to be instilled with supernatural power and made sacred than from the longer stones, probably it is simply just impractical or even impossible to crowd the ganekhe cabinets with multiple long stones. While reading this manuscript, D. Gentry Steele made the observation that "possibly the longer je are too economically important to transfer to the sacred world?" All Highlanders in the Grand Valley and West admire and favor the longer flat-type je for the funeral display and exchange stones, as well as for war indemnity payments.

When slightly curved, rather than being flat in longitudinal dimension, the concave surface, according to Heider (1970:288) is the front and is called *elokhegen* (cheekbone or face) and the convex or back side is called *opolikhe*. Each side edge is called *elak*. The narrow end is called *uguloak*, head or skull, and the broader end is called *alokhe*, anus. Numerous informants maintain that this physiological terminology does not indicate that the stones are anthropomorphic, but that this vocabulary merely gives the users a common reference language with which they can communicate about the stones.

In addition to the common flat-type je display-exchange stone, there is another kind of je called the *je puluen* or just *puluen* (figs. 3.5

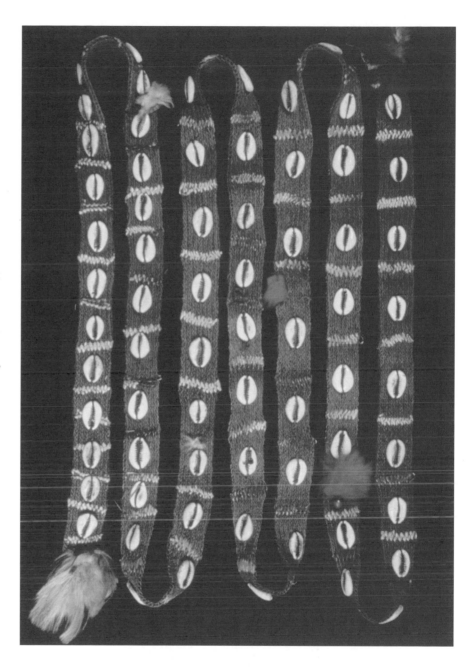

Fig. 3.2. A funeral display-exchange band (jerak)

and 3.6). It is less numerous than the flat-type display-exchange stones within the cultural exchange system and because of its short size is rarely seen displayed at funeral or indemnity payments. The puluen, instead, has a very special use in association with the sacred ancestral stones (which use is discussed in chapter 4). The puluen is on average much shorter and narrower than the flat-type je and is rounded in cross section. The nine puluen that I have been able to measure vary in length from 30 to 53 cm, maximum width per stone from 5.3 to 5.8

Fig. 3.3. An open strapless ceremonial net

the stone so I carried it to trusted informants to learn what they might know about it. All, including Wali of the mid–Grand Valley Dani, recognized the stone immediately as a *je omaken* (root je). One end had been ground to a rough sharp edge. This je omaken is variable dark green, with a bluish cast in spots and looks like rock from the same sequence as the typical good-quality Yeineri quarry axe and adze blades discussed in chapter 2. This observation was confirmed by a comparison of mineralogical work done on the je omaken courtesy of T. T. Teih (mineralogist, Texas A&M University) and the mineralogical work done on samples of Yeineri quarry stone and adze/axe blades and symbolic stones from within the Grand Valley and West region by the University of Colorado group. Wali himself said that although he had never seen one in his lifetime, he had heard of such. He ventured that perhaps two or more of the most influential big men among the Grand Valley Dani and Western Dani may have owned one. Wali thought that perhaps Gutelu had owned a je omaken. When I inventoried Gutelu's belongings at Jiwika in both 1991 and 1992, I did not see one, nor did Gutelu's sons make any mention of such an unusual stone; although they acted rather guarded when I questioned them. We can safely presume that such a stone is indeed a cultural rarity and that in former times the ownership of a je omaken would have only been by the most wealthy and powerful of big men.

Sources, Colors, and Lithologies

The normal flat-style display-exchange stones were manufactured primarily at the Yeineri quarry complex, a much smaller number at the Tagime quarries, and possibly some from sources of opportunity (fig. 1.3). None were made at the Langda or Sela quarries. Just as the adze, axe, knife, and chisel tools that came from the Yeineri quarry area vary in color from green, dark green, blue, variegated green and blue, so do most of the flat display-exchange stones. They come from the same ophiolite-melange belt at Yeineri as the profane tool blades. Lithologically, these exchange stones are composed of blueschist, epidote amphibolite;

cm, and thickness from 2.3 to 3.2 cm. The dimensions of seven of these nine puluen are presented in table 3.2.

The most unusual je that I have seen in all of the Irian Jaya Highlands is one that was brought to me for trade at a small compound in the northern Grand Valley. It is a long, tubular shaped stone (71 cm long by 13 cm mean circumference) (fig. 3.7). The owner of the stone could not give me any information about

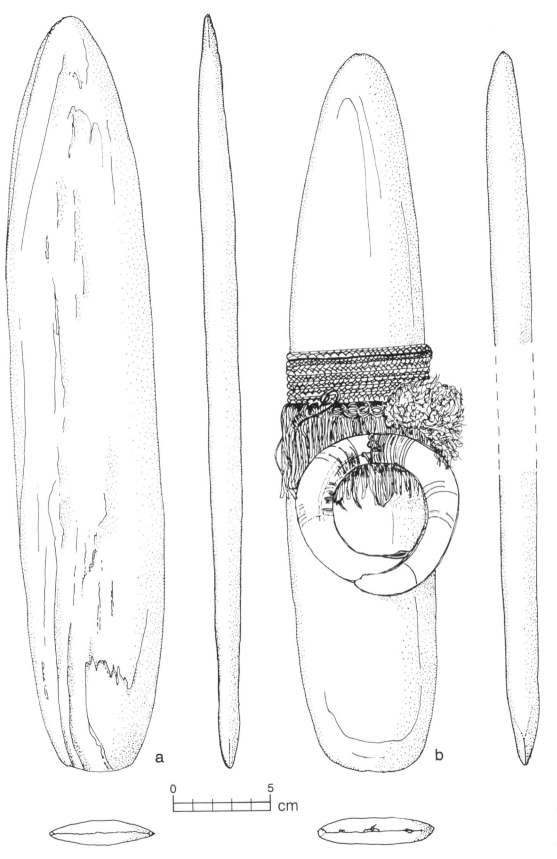

0   5   cm

a   b

Fig. 3.4. One undecorated and
one decorated display-
exchange stone

amphibole schist; epitote chlorite schist; and light green, gray, and black slate. Specks of gold-colored pyrite are sometimes present on the polished exchange stone surfaces. Some of the flat display-exchange stones that are used across the entire research area are composed of a micaceous schist, which also comes from the same source quarries. These stones are a silvery-gray color from the micaceous minerals in the schist. The puluen je or just puluen, as they are usually referred to, consist of a hard dark green to blue-green amphibolite rock that is also produced at Yeineri. All of the display-exchange stones produced at the Tagime quarries are a gray to black meta-argillite.

Some display-exchange stones (je) in the Grand Valley have traces of red paint (pulverized hematite or red clay) on them called *bimut* (alt. *pimut*). Informants in the Grand Valley generally profess ignorance of the origin or meaning of the red paint, which indicates that its use has sacred (wusa) connotations. Two

Table 3.1. Flat-Style Display-Exchange Stones (je) in the Irian Jaya Highlands

	Length (cm)	Maximum Width (cm)	Maximum Thickness (cm)
1	40.4	7.3	1.4
2	43.5	7.5	0.9
3	36.0	8.1	1.5
4	38.0	7.4	1.8
5	52.0	8.5	2.0
6	38.5	8.8	1.6
7	34.5	10.5	0.9
8	54.5	11.9	1.2
9	74.0	8.1	2.0
10	68.0	12.0	—
11	73.5	14.0	—
12	74.0	8.0	—
13	79.0	8.0	—
14	79.5	13.0	—
15	60.0	10.0	—
16	19.5	9.0	—
17	45.0	12.5	—
18	29.3	7.0	—
19	52.5	7.5	—
20	70.0	7.3	—
21	51.3	6.8	—
22	48.5	6.0	—
23	78.4	12.0	—
24	89.5	11.0	—
25	68.5	14.0	—
26	53.5	7.5	—
27	53.0	9.5	—
28	74.0	—	—
29	57.5	12.0	—
30	77.5	13.3	—
31	72.0	12.5	—
32	58.0	14.0	—
33	74.5	7.6	—
34	71.1	8.8	1.3
35	66.0	10.2	—
36	23.8	7.0	—
37	37.0	8.0	—
38	28.0	7.5	—
Mean	*56.4*	*9.6*	*1.5*

informants, one a north Grand Valley Dani and one a Western Dani, did say, however, that a red stripe is put on a display-exchange stone, which is then used by the director of each funeral to announce the forthcoming second stage of the funeral—usually four to six weeks after the first stage. Remnants of such a stripe could account for the barely visible traces of red seen on a small percentage of the display-exchange stones present in the Grand Valley and West. A Yali and, then a year later, an Una informant told me that in their areas, once a red stripe is put down the back of a stone it becomes sacred. The uses of red, white, and black paint on sacred symbolic stones in the Yali and East region will be discussed in the forthcoming section on sacred stones.

Within the Yali and East region the profane display-exchange stone (sie, alt. siengga) users either knew that the stones came from the Dani to the west or explained the sources for specific stones as places either mythically divine, or as spots of magical happenstance in "the forest," where a traveler or worker would "just find the finished stones." The Yali who lived near the Yali-Dani language boundary knew with certainty, however, that both the flat display-exchange stones and the je puluen came from the Dani and not from sources of opportunity or magical spots within their own areas. Koch, working with the Yali in the Angguruk area (fig. 1.3) says that, "Polished flat, oblongated stones, known as sie and traded from Hóvólama, have no utilitarian use but rather represent valuables chiefly transferred as marriage and death considerations" (1967:115–16). The border between the Yali people and the Dani to the west is known in central Yali dialect as *Hóvólama* and the people (Dani) to the west as *hóvóla-énap*. In contrast, I found that the Yali *tool* blades (adze blades and stone knives) came from the Langda-Sela quarry belt to the southeast.

Decorations

Some of the display-exchange stones are unadorned, but most are decorated with various objects tied around the stone's approximate midsection (figs. 3.8 and 3.9). The undecorated stones are usually (maybe always) the shorter

Fig. 3.5. Three representative puluen

stones that were unacceptable in a decorated format as parts of formal ceremonial displays. One or several handcrafted small objects and pieces of different kinds of material constitute the adornment. In mid–Grand Valley terminology the decorations on the display-exchange stones are called *etani*. Female skirt attire is a common motif, with some stones wrapped with bands varying from 3.5 to 6.0 cm in width of braided, brightly colored reddish-brown and/or yellow orchid fiber cording to replicate the mid–Grand Valley Dani brief wedding skirt *(jogal)*. Both the *sali* (alt. *gem dadli*) skirt made of flattened reeds and the fiber string skirts, so common on young girls scattered over broad areas and also worn by adult women in many areas are also much used. Miniature bark strand cloth skirts of two kinds, that are indicative of female attire in yet other areas, are often wrapped onto the display-exchange stones. Often both the miniature jogal, symbolic for adult married women in one area, and one or two other kinds of symbolic female skirts are wrapped onto the same stone. Some stones even have three kinds of miniature skirts wrapped onto them, in addition to a few brightly colored feathers and bits of fur. Fur pieces from the cuscus marsupial seem to be most preferred; although often bits of fur from either the tree kangaroo, tree rat, or ground living rodents are used. One or a few feathers, often from the parrot, are quite common. Even dried whole skins and heads of small red birds are used (fig. 3.10).

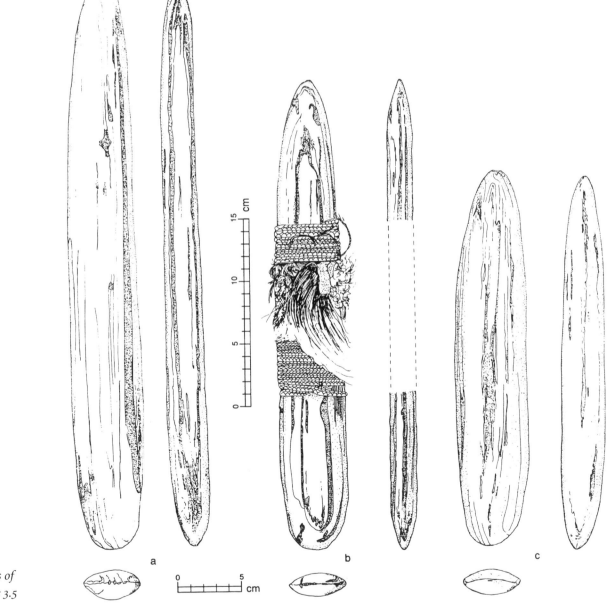

Fig. 3.6. View drawings of puluen shown in figure 3.5

Table 3.2. Display-Exchange Stones *(je puluen)* in the Irian Jaya Highlands

	Length (cm)	Maximum Width (cm)	Maximum Thickness (cm)
1	38.3	5.3	2.3
2	30.5	5.5	3.2
3	46.0	5.6	2.9
4	34.5	5.8	2.8
5	34.7	5.8	2.0
6	34.0	4.8	—
7	47.0	8.6	—
Mean	*37.9*	*5.9*	*2.6*

Rarely seen ornamentation on the profane display-exchange stone are boar tusks, pig tails, and the unusual appearing, tiny stick studded cocoon of the case moth called *pumpalep*. These decorations are, however, commonly present on the sacred stones (ganekhe in Dani, *owili* in Yali). Some Dani and Western Dani informants have asserted that pieces of *jerak* (woven band decorated with cowrie shells), pig tails, boar tusks, and cocoons cannot be used on the profane display-exchange stones (je), but that those items are reserved only for the sacred stones.

I have observed that one or more symbolic skirts are almost always included when feathers, bits of fur, and/or boar tusks, pig tails and cocoons are used as either profane display-exchange stone or sacred stone (ganekhe) decorations. It is always easy to look at a stone so attired, with obvious miniature symbolic replicas of female skirts, and often with splashes of color and "softness" added with bright bird feathers and bits of fur, and imagine a female anthropomorphic stone. Heider reported that "the terms for size, parts, and decorations of the exchange stones indicate an elaborate anthropomorphic symbolism. There are minor inconsistencies in the fact that it is especially the larger, or male, stones, which 'wear' the decorations, made of female skirt material. And, of course, a Dani female wears either a *jogal* skirt or a *dadli* skirt, while the exchange stones often have both" (1970:289).

This apparent inconsistency is no inconsistency at all. It is just that the ethnocentric *etic* interpretation is wrong, as far as the people are concerned. As it has been explained to me by informants scattered throughout different parts of the Highlands, there are no "female" and "male" display-exchange stones, just *stones*. All of the objects used to decorate the stones are individually symbolic in themselves, and taken

Fig. 3.7. A rare je omaken next to a flat style (je)

Fig. 3.8. Three unadorned exchange stones, the lower one a puluen

for example, the stones are often used as "bridal gifts." In such a case a thoughtful donor might decorate the stone with a *yogal* to indicate the transition of the bride from an unmarried virgin to a married adult woman. A *sali* (alt. *dadli*) skirt might or might not be added to represent memories of the new bride from times before she was married. At a funeral the female symbolic skirts might be added to *je* stones to visually show the ghosts and spirits that the women are also paying respect to those beings of the unseen world—not just the men. This message reportedly furnishes some degree of protection against malevolent ghosts and spirits for those women closely related to the giver of the stone. Fur and feathers are symbolic of the men involved. These are favorite items of adornment used by men. When a man adds feathers, especially parrot feathers, to the stone and bits of fur, he is really symbolizing mementoes of himself on the stone (or loved ones who are close to him), rather than dressing the stone as a man. Boar tusks and pig tails are considered male items and are sometimes used as mementoes of ceremonial occasions or to alert the ghosts that the pigs are being duly considered and cared for. The cocoons stand for the ghosts and spirits. For me, I use some things which are just reminders or mementoes of people I care for or of ceremonial occasions. I like to dress a stone for all of these reasons but I guess I think of the items mostly as mementoes.

Unedited excerpts from my field notes taken through the years from indigenous informants while I was observing display-exchange stones in traditional uses and questioning the meaning of decorative objects follows:

fur (this one from a ground rat) is for health of man . . . *sali*—a girl's skirt is symbolic for young girls, may they be healthy and strong . . . feathers for young boys to be healthy and become adults . . . wrapped *je* with orchid fiber cording to represent woman and because *je* is given as a bridal

in entirety as a decoration bundle, the items are representative of many of the facets of the Highlanders' life.

It was Pua, known to anthropologists from the film *Dead Birds* (Gardner 1963) and the book *Gardens of War* (Gardner and Heider 1969), who explained to me at length the decorations of the stones several years before he died in 1993. Pua said that there are no male and female stones as far as he knew. According to Pua:

gift . . . *sali,* little girls' skirts before they marry when they are virgins and for their health . . . *cus cus* fur bits—as a man decorates himself so he decorates a *je* . . . parrot feathers are for adornment—same as fur; these are for men's adornment—so also adorn *je.*

Winoco, one of the indigenous translators and helpers on many of my annual excursions to the Highlands, has heard me ask the same questions over and over again about the sex of the stones and the meaning of the decorative objects. He always shakes his head and says that his parents never told him anything about a *female* and *male* je stone.

Value

Within the Grand Valley, which is the geographic center and most densely populated area within the confines of the research area, I found correlative with the high population the greatest numbers of symbolic stones. I found general agreement that: (1) the longest display-exchange stone is the most valuable, (2) width is less important, (3) there are definite color and rock type preferences, (4) adornment does not enhance the value of individual stones for trading purposes, and (5) sometimes the most value can be derived by trading more than one display-exchange stone at a time or by combining a display-exchange stone with some other wealth item. The people of the Grand Valley use and like light green *(pibit pibit),* green-dark green, blue, and black stones. Most of the people who were interviewed in the Grand Valley preferred the Yeineri-sourced stones over the black Tagime. Some informants could enumerate between seven and nineteen different kinds of stones, taking into account length, shape, color, and lithologic aesthetics. Few could agree with others on many of their own named types of stones, with the exception that they all knew a pipit pipit (light green, slatelike rock from Yeineri), those that they classified as short stones (less than about 40 cm in length), and the distinctly shaped *puluen,* with its characteristic dark green-blue color and rock type. Wali and many in the mid–Grand Valley favor

the green pibit pibit. Wali pointed out that before trading for a stone he always checked its midpoint area carefully for hairline cracks, which might be points of weakness.

Although the profane display-exchange stones are traded for quite a variety of items throughout the entire network of different language-speaking groups within the research area (to be discussed in chapter 8), the common denominator for their value and all other

Fig. 3.9. Three decorated Yeineri display-exchange stones from the Grand Valley

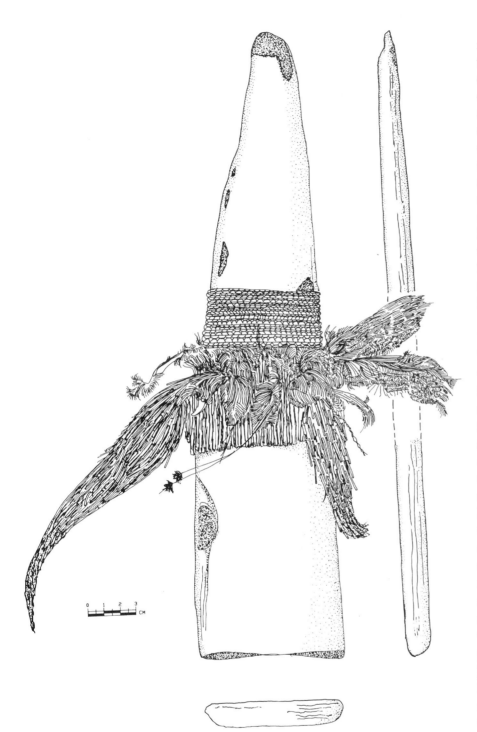

might be worth five pigs of assorted sizes or three big pigs. These values are, of course, general and subjective, with significant variables of each stone and each pig (age; sex; size; health; and when female, pregnant or not) that can effect any one exchange, but it does give an idea of the general value of a je in the Grand Valley and West region. The approximate same values seem to prevail throughout the Yali and East region. The last time I saw Wali in 1992, he was carrying a beautiful 3 m jerak in a net bag and his helper had a display-exchange stone. They were on their way to Pugima where Wali said he had negotiated a trade of his two wealth items for a pig and some Indonesian rupiah, which he badly wanted.

Uses

The profane display-exchange stone is the most visible symbolic stone. It has many uses: (1) funeral display and distribution, (2) war indemnity payments, (3) marriage wealth transfer, (4) as a stone of value for trading purposes, and (5) profane source from which to select *sacred* symbolic stones. Since the profane display-exchange stones lack the secret nature of the sacred stones they are stored in easy view, leaning up against the interior circular wall of the men's house. Except when being ritually displayed, exchanged, or personally examined, the display-exchange stones are almost always neatly wrapped in *gisakpel,* the dried outer bark of the banana tree (fig. 3.11). When going to ceremonials where the display-exchange stones will be used or just somewhere for trading purposes, women sometimes carry the stones, just another indication that they are handled like other profane objects. Some men maintain that the display-exchange stones cannot be traded outside of affinal groups and that they are reserved only for ritual use.

Fig. 3.10. An adorned green, pibit pibit Yeineri-sourced exchange stone

material goods throughout the entire Irian Jaya Highlands is pigs. In the Grand Valley and West area, a very large display-exchange stone, more than about 70 cm in length, might be worth a large pig. One medium-sized stone is equivalent in value to a medium-sized pig. Five assorted stones of varying individual quality

FUNERAL DISPLAY AND DISTRIBUTION. In the Grand Valley and West, a series of four funeral rituals that extend over a period of three to five years is initiated by the death of a person. The first stage of the funeral is held one to two days after death. The body is cremated at a ceremony where pigs are ritually killed and eaten. Grief is dramatically expressed by loud wailing and other ritual acts to both purge personal sorrow and to placate ghosts and spirits. In the Grand Valley and certain bordering areas, joints of fingers are amputated and small pieces of ears sliced off to purge grief and express sorrow, as well as to placate ghosts and spirits by showing this degree of sacrifice on their behalf. Joint and finger amputation is not practiced within the Yali and East area. Although all funerals within the Highlands area are similar, there is considerable variation in the ordering of events. Everywhere, however, ritual display and exchange of wealth items take place, and the use of the display-exchange stones is manifest.

The second stage of the funeral process is, like the first, held for individual deaths and takes place within a month or so after death. The *je wakanin,* or third stage, is held every year or two, involving one or more confederations, and is for all of the deaths within the larger area. The ebe akho pig feast, as previously mentioned, takes place every three to five years and, in addition to being the time for marriages and the boys' *waija* initiation ceremonies, is the final funeral rite within the alliance for all deaths since the last ebe akho.

At the first stage of a funeral, the display and passing out of the display-exchange stones, ceremonial nets, and cowrie shell bands may be delayed a day or two to allow donors time to accumulate necessary items. A death often prompts a flurry of rapid borrowing and trading of items of wealth such as the display-exchange stones, so that a donor will have what is needed. At the appropriate time in the funeral ritual, the big man in charge prompts the laying out of the funeral bundles with their display-exchange stones. There is a sudden rush of activity as men lay out their items in just the right way. Individual funeral bundles called *jetalek* in mid–Grand Valley Dani dialect consist of strapless ceremonial nets *(tegetagi su),* funeral display-exchange stones (je), and cowrie shell bands *(jerak).* First, fresh banana leaves and/or grass are laid out at the designated spot within the compound, then, on top of these are laid the tegetagi su, neatly folded, followed by the display-exchange stones (je), and then on top of them the long jerak (woven string bands decorated with cowrie shells). Later during the funeral ritual, these wealth items will be distributed to deserving people. It is customary for some of the display-exchange stones to be assigned to men who donated pigs for the funeral.

Fig. 3.11. Display-exchange stones stored in men's house behind mummy of Aikima.

At a small funeral, where a child of a common man or an unimportant adult has died, the funeral bundle may be small, with practically no objects, and perhaps, no display-exchange stone at all. Conversely, for a very influential big man or admired warrior killed in battle, a compound may be nearly filled with funeral bundles, all laid out in long rows.

Individual display-exchange stones are identified as to their importance by their length and position on the funeral bundle (fig. 3.12). In the Grand Valley and West, the longest, and therefore the most important, is laid out in the center. If there is one that is distinctly longer than the others it is called (mid–Grand Valley Dani dialect) *je oak* (je bone). Those slightly shorter and laid out to the sides of the je oak are called *je aie* (je leg). The small ones are laid out at the ends of the net piles and are called *ogosi*.

Informants in both the Angguruk-Pasikni and Pass Valley locales within the Yali and East region state that the Yali prefer a different configuration of their funeral display-exchange stones than that elucidated above for the Grand Valley and West. The northern Yali dialect speakers call the je display-exchange stones, *sie;* the jerak cowrie shell bands, *sulanggen;* and the tegetagi su ceremonial nets, *sum.* On each pile of ceremonial nets, the Yali feel that it is desirable to lay out seven display-exchange stones (sie) in a configuration that to them is symbolic of an entire human figure (fig. 3.12). On the center of the bundle and perpendicular to the long dimension of the underlying folded nets, a "second longest" stone called an *ilinggo* (for the heart) is positioned. The ilinggo is flanked on both sides by the "third longest" stones called *inggik* (for the shoulder and arms). To the outside of the inggik are placed the "longest" sie of each bundle, called *iok* (for the legs, including the feet), and finally on the outer edges of the display the shortest sie, called the *aho* (for the leg between the knee and the thigh). Next, numerous small display-exchange stones, about 22 cm in length, are set at each end of the bundle, next to the aho, before the sulanggen cowrie shell bands are laid across the top. It is argued by some Yali informants in the Pass Valley area that the ilinggo is the longest sie

stone in a presentation bundle, rather than the iok (fig. 3.12). I could get agreement among most Yali informants (using forearm, hand, and fingers as measuring devices) that the long ilinggo and iok stones vary from about 45 to 65 cm in length, with rarely one being longer than about 65 cm. A minority of Yali informants state that all of the sie in a presentation bundle except the aho are painted with red stripes and polished with special leaves before a presentation is made. I never had the opportunity to observe a Yali presentation.

To put the numbers and sizes of display-exchange stones presented at Grand Valley funerals into social perspective I will cite four examples; first a general statement about the funeral of Gutelu (alts. Kutelu, Kurulu), one of the most influential big men (leaders) who is historically known in the Irian Jaya Highlands; second, the funeral for Obaharok (alt. Obagatok), a big man of lesser influence but still one of the more influential leaders in the Grand Valley in recent times (Heider 1970:119; Sargent 1974); the funeral of Jagik, a lesser known leader, who died some time ago and was cited by Heider (1970:151); and, finally, the funeral of Pua, which is of interest and importance because of the longitudinal information of anthropological fame on Pua as the young boy swineherd in Gardner's film *Dead Birds* (1963) and the book *Gardens of War: Life and Death in the New Guinea Stone Age* (Gardner and Heider 1968).

When the powerful alliance big man Gutelu died in 1990, his family knew him as Iluagimo P. Gutelu Mabel. Gutelu had "converted to Christianity (Catholicism)." The "P" in his name stands for his Christian name of Petros, after the Apostle Peter. Daoke Mabel, Gutelu's oldest son, showed me photographs taken at the funeral in Gutelu's home compound in Jiwika. The main courtyard was filled with three rows of funeral bundles with five display-exchange stones (je) per bundle. Daoke said that there were a total of four hundred display-exchange stones displayed. Since, even in historic times, there were other big men in and around the Grand Valley of approximately Gutelu's political stature, I would presume that

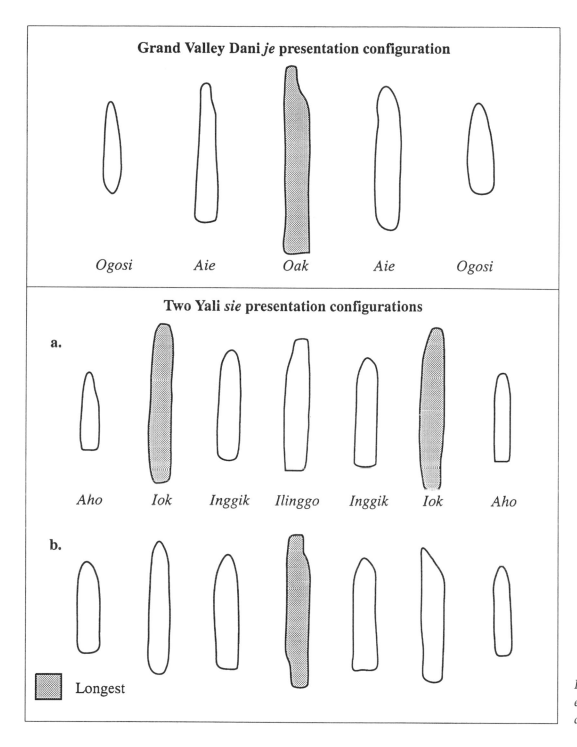

Grand Valley Dani *je* presentation configuration

Ogosi   *Aie*   *Oak*   *Aie*   *Ogosi*

Two Yali *sie* presentation configurations

a.

Aho   *Iok*   *Inggik*   *Ilinggo*   *Inggik*   *Iok*   *Aho*

b.

Longest

Fig. 3.12. Funeral display-exchange stone display configurations

at some big men's funerals more than four hundred display-exchange stones may have been involved. Daoke Mabel says that in the mid–Grand Valley area around Jiwika, only three display-exchange stones per bundle are required for marriage displays and payments, rather than the five that I have normally seen

and which were used, as described above, at Gutelu's funeral.

At the time of Obaharok's death, he and Wali were each other's father-in-law and son-in-law. Some years ago, they had previously each married a daughter of the other one in a move to formally cease hostilities between their two warring factions and to cement mutual support for social activities and political maneuvering. Obaharok died on December 2, 1992, and his funeral was held at his residence compound of Pabuma on December 3, the day after his death. The following information was derived from my interview with Obaharok's oldest son, Akabuga; Obaharok's youngest brother, Huliak; and Akabuga's uncle, Ananias (Akabuga's mother's brother) on March 28, 30, 31, 1993. At Obaharok's funeral there were ten funeral bundles (jetalek) presented, nine of them were comprised of ten ceremonial nets (tegetagi su), five display-exchange stones (je), and one cowrie shell decorated band (jerak). One jetalek consisted of twenty tegetagi su, five je, and one jerak. Upon Obaharok's death, Akabuga immediately became the big man, replacing his father as the man of influence, but by his own admission a man of lesser influence than Wali. Akabuga received one of the jetalek bundles at the funeral and distributed the rest of the wealth items from the other bundles. Reportedly, the longest stone of the jetalek bundle, which went to Akabuga, was laid out at the funeral as a je aie as shown in table 3.3 (not as the je oak, longest je in the bundle by common usage).

The reason for this was unexplained to me but well understood by Akabuga and his family. The laying out of a proper funeral bundle (jetalek) is complicated and takes the skill and experience of the indigenous inhabitants in each subcultural area within the study area to be able to effect an acceptable presentation. For each funeral bundle, which consists of tegetagi su, je, and jerak, there is a fundamental formula that is somewhat subjective but that still must be properly invoked in building the bundle before even contemplating the difficult-to-understand aesthetics of the stones, which also has some influence on the ways they are laid out. The formula defines the number of tegetagi su, je, and jerak that are used in any specific presentation. For example, the jetalek shown and the stones defined with measurements in table 3.3 consisted of ten tegetagi su on the bottom, then five je, and on top one jerak. But if the longest je is "very, very" long (longer than the one shown here), then there must be twenty tegetagi su underneath and two tegetagi su on top of the bundle. The length that a display-exchange stone (je) must be to mandate this requirement is only defined subjectively in terms understood by the "people." If the two end je are too short (again length not defined objectively), then, by social custom, they are not to be adorned. The symbolic value of such a jetalek, both to please the people in attendance and the ghosts and spirits that are hovering about, would be less than when all the stones are adorned. Akabuga and his uncle stated that all of these display-exchange stones were passed down from their ancestors, and that they are maintained the way received— "dressed if dressed and naked if naked."

Akabuga and his family, in trying to answer my questions, pointed out that they call the narrow end of each stone *ekat,* the longitudinal sides *alel,* and the wide end *ukut,* but that this nomenclature (in the central-eastern part of the Grand Valley) is not used to describe the stone as a person but just to define various parts of the display-exchange stone as an object for communication purposes. This family reiterated what I had been told by others, that

Table 3.3. Flat-Style Display-Exchange Stones *(je)* That Went to Obaharok's Oldest Son

Functional Name	Length (cm)	Width (cm)	Color	As would be named at Yeineri Quarry
je ogosi	73.5	14.0	light green	pibit pibit
je aie	74.0	8.0	very light	pibit pibit
je oak	79.0	8.0	green	pibit pibit
je aie	80.0	13.0	green	pibit pibit
je ogosi	60.0	10.0	dark green	?
Mean	*73.2*	*10.6*		

there are no male or female stones and that size, shape, and "dressed" or "not dressed" makes no difference.

In this example of a top quality funeral bundle (jetalek), four of the five je stones are of one kind known to the Yeineri quarrymen as pibit pibit and quarried as an item that they feel are favored by the users in the Grand Valley over stones of other colors. (Additional information about the pibit pibit will be brought out in chapter 5 under the discussion of rock quarries.) The fifth display-exchange stone on this particular jetalek is also from the Yeineri quarries, but of a different type.

Heider (1970:151) pointed out that at the funeral of old Jagik, a former big man, old enmities were removed when several display-exchange stones, carrying nets, strapless ceremonial nets, and shell bands were brought to Jagik's funeral by people who had done him injury in the past. Those wealth items were presented in the courtyard, along with other funeral bundles, and, as is the custom with all funeral bundles and display-exchange stones, the name of the donor was clearly and loudly shouted over the items for all people, ghosts, and spirits present to hear.

Pua died on February 5, 1993, reportedly of natural causes. Pua's funeral was held in Suroba with his older brother Siba officiating on February 7, 1993. Of the traditional wealth items, twenty-five pigs (which were for the ceremony), ninety tegetagi su nets, twelve je flat-style display-exchange stones, one je puluen display-exchange stone, four jerak, one cymbium shell mikak, one nassa shell walimo bib, and one cuscus headband were presented and distributed. Siba, Pua's older brother, received four flat-style display-exchange stones (je) and one puluen je-style display-exchange stone from the distribution. I was able to see and photograph all five display-exchange stones in their dried banana bark wrappers, then measure and examine four that Siba removed from their wrappers for this purpose. Siba explained that the fifth stone was received from one of Pua's uncles, Hibit Marian, with the restriction that neither Siba nor anyone else would touch the stone without permission from the uncle. I

suspect that there are traditional wusa obligations involved.

Siba showed me how the five stones were laid out for display on the funeral bundle (table 3.4). In the context of funeral display nomenclature, the two longer stones were centered and classified as je oak, the two stones on either side of the centered je oak as je aie. The shortest stone, set to one side of a je aie, was considered an ogosi in the context of the funeral bundle presentation, but a je puluen in the areawide symbolic stone classification based on stone structure. Siba was delighted that the ogosi was a je puluen. He told me that as soon as he saw it he started planning to empower it through ritual as a special stone to replace a sacred puluen that had disappeared from his ganekhe.

Heider (1970:158) relates that on the day before a funeral resumes (in the Dugum Dani neighborhood) with the second stage (four to six weeks after the first stage), the funeral leader paints a stripe on the sill of the men's house with red clay and then holding a display-exchange stone on which he has also painted a red stripe, stands in the courtyard and shouts "Walo wetno" (come bring pigs). The word is spread by courier and word of mouth. The second stage is a one to three day ritual in which pigs are killed and eaten, ritual acts are performed, and the grief over the loss of a loved one or friend continues to be expressed and purged. Heider feels that this second stage, like the first, has the explicit function of placating the ghost of the deceased. Although he points out that this is also the time that mourning clay is removed (1970:158), I observed instances where this was not true and those in mourning would tell me that they would continue to stay in mourning and wear clay until they personally felt that the ghosts had been properly placated and that they also were feeling prepared for personal renewal. Only in rare instances could I find that display-exchange stones were displayed at this stage of the funeral, other than the use of a single stone to announce the "call" for commencement of the ceremony.

The third stage of a funeral takes on a different complexion. The purposes of the first two

Table 3.4. Funeral Display-Exchange Stones *(je)* That Went to Pua's Older Brother, Siba

Functional Name	Length (cm)	Width (cm)	Color	Quarry
je aie	—	—	—	—
je oak	78.4	12.0	light green	Yeineri pibit pibit
je oak	89.5	11.0	black	Tagime gu
je aie	68.5	14.0	dark green	Yeineri
je ogosi	53.5	7.5	dark green	Yeineri puluen
Mean	*72.5*	*11.1*		

stages are to purge the grief of those "close" to a single deceased and to placate the ghost of the dead person and ghosts in general. The third stage recognizes all of the deceased within one or more confederations since the last large alliancewide funeral ceremony was held. The third stage is held about once every year or two. Its cyclic period commences with the alliancewide funeral ritual, which is held as one of the numerous ceremonies that are a part of the alliancewide ebe akho, held every three to five years. This third stage is the *je wakanin*—the carrying of the je display-exchange stones.

Preceding commencement of the je wakanin, announcements are sent far and wide, even to people outside the alliance who had responsibility for local funerals during the period of time involved. Then for several days there is much coming and going between compounds as display-exchange stones, ceremonial nets, and cowrie shell bands are carried from compound to compound and collected into funeral bundles, one for each funeral, by the men who were responsible for those funerals. The exchange of goods is extensive.

Although the ceremony starts in individual, scattered compounds with the gathering of the wealth items, the people ultimately converge in groups on a designated compound of an influential ceremonial leader within the confederation in which the ceremony is being held. Men, women, and children carry the ceremonial nets, the cowrie shell bands, and the je display-exchange stones to the designated compound. This is the *je wakanin*—the carrying of the je display-exchange stones.

As the groups move into the compound of the ceremonial leader, the women's nets containing wealth items are placed in the area that will later be used for display. The women leave the courtyard and gather in the women's houses and communal cookhouses to watch the proceedings.

In one such ceremony that Heider observed (1970:161), each bundle of ceremonial nets was neatly folded and then laid out in a line along the long axis of the courtyard. The display-exchange stones, three to seven to a bundle, were then properly formatted on each pile of nets. In one line there were about 25 piles of nets, with about 108 display-exchange stones. In the shorter line about 12 piles of nets with 59 display-exchange stones. Then, one by one, cowrie shell bands were carried carefully from the men's house to the lower compound and laid on the long lines of nets and stones. Heider reported a few moments of silence while the ceremonial leader walked the lines and inspected the stones. Then he returned down the line, touching each bundle with foot or hand, while loudly shouting out the name of the dead person it represented. He returned to an upper courtyard and shouted various kin terms, following each with an approving loud "thank you" *(wa)*. (It was by shouting of the names of the deceased and various kin terms that the ceremonial leader was both assigning the exchange goods to relatives of the deceased and alerting the ghosts and spirits as to what had transpired.) The atmosphere then changed. Men and women swooped down on bundles, packed them up, and returned home. The next day in their own courtyards they again laid out the bundles, with display-exchange stones well exposed, and went through the approximate same ritual of display and exchange before enjoying a meal of steamed vegetables. (For another perspective and example of a je wakanin ceremony in the Grand Valley, the reader is referred to Peters [1975:109–11].)

The fourth stage, and ending ritual of the three to five year funeral cycle, is but one ceremony of several that are held in the alliancewide ebe akho in the Grand Valley. Elsewhere in the Irian Jaya Highlands the funeral ritual cycle also covers a time span of about three to five years, but nowhere does the cycle end in a climax of ceremonies that is so important as it is to the Dani in the Grand Valley. As a part of the ebe akho, mass marriages are performed; the important waija moiety boys initiation ceremonies are held; enmities between enemies are sometimes settled (or at least tension relieved); the "ritual killing of many pigs" is enjoyed with food for the attendees; pork is sent to relatives and friends who are outside of the areas of participation; the castration of pigs is highlighted; mock battles are fought for different purposes; new bark string and bark strip necklaces are empowered to protect the wearers from the untimely entrance of ghosts; and, to end the funeral cycle, the je display-exchange stones are carried to a compound of importance within the alliance to display both to the people and to the ghosts and spirits of everyone who had died within the alliance since the last ebe akho. There is feasting in memory of people who were killed by the enemy, for people who had died of natural causes, and an "overarching ceremony" for the ghosts of all people who had died; truly an important manifestation of ancestral worship as an integral part of the complex Dani belief system.

WAR INDEMNITY PAYMENTS. After every war in which revenge killings have occurred, indemnification ceremonies are obligatory. In ritual wars, the "owners of the wars" and/or confederacy big men leaders are responsible to make indemnification. I found that generally throughout both the Grand Valley and West region and the Yali and East region that profane display-exchange stones are an important part of these payments to relatives of the dead and even to men who had been wounded but who had recovered. In the primary war indemnification ceremonies, certain rituals are wusa—these will be addressed in the next section in context with all of the various uses of sacred stones.

Larson, in his work in the Ilaga area, reported in *The Structure and Demography of the Cycle of Warfare Among the Ilaga Dani of Irian Jaya* that resolution of conflict, after a death balance had been achieved, was accomplished by a series of highly ritualized payments between allies in each alliance.

The first was called "distribution of dead birds," made less than a month after the truce in memory of those killed in battle. War leaders in each alliance simultaneously sponsored a separate feast for their respective allies at which they distributed both the feathered head-pieces and live pigs owned by warriors killed in battle on their side. Those who received were close kinsmen of the "owners" of the war or close allies who also called for battles during which victims fell. They did so with the understanding that they would make an "axe-pig" (yewam) indemnity payment to the agnates of the victim as soon as they could raise enough pigs to sponsor the payment. The second was made by the same war leaders in each alliance 8 or 9 months after the truce. It was a massive payment called "paying for the cost of the war" (wim anep yakwi). War leaders slaughtered and distributed more than 70 large, full-grown pigs to individual allied leaders as compensation for wounds their men had suVered during battle. The last and largest were the yewam indemnity payments, made during a 6–18 month period which began about 2 years after the dead birds distribution, at a time when gardens planted since the war had time to mature so pigs could be fattened for payment. . . . The ceremonial yewam payments were intercommunity festive events attended by hundreds, sometimes thousands, of persons decorated with bird plumage and painted with red ocher or blackened pig grease. While many danced or performed mock-battle maneuvers, scores of pigs and much other exchange wealth were presented to the agnates of the deceased who, in turn redistributed the payment to kinsmen to whom they were related as agnates, affines, or cognates. (1987:167–69)

At these final payments, pigs, display-exchange stones, and other wealth items were distributed. I quoted Larson at some length to describe in detail the framework for indemnification ceremonials so that the reader can visualize just what is being replicated by numerous esoteric groups scattered throughout the entire research area, during which thousands of pigs, display-exchange stones, and other wealth items must have been kept in circulation during the ritual warfare era just by war indemnity payments alone. Within different Una, Kimyal, and Yali groups I was told that wealth item payments at similar war indemnification ceremonials consisted primarily of pigs, utility nets, display-exchange stones (sie or siengga), cowrie shell bands, and sometimes utilitarian adzes and cakes of salt.

TRANSFERS OF WEALTH ITEMS AT TIME OF MARRIAGE. Bridewealth transfers (previously called "marriage payments" in dated material) are customary in almost all parts of the Irian Jaya Highlands, although the details of transfer ritual and the kinds and number of items are variable. Pigs, display-exchange stones (je to the Grand Valley Dani and part of the Western Dani, jao to other Western Dani, sie or siengga to the northern Yali, and sie or siengga to the Kimyal and Una), ceremonial nets, bands of cowrie shells, and loose cowrie shells are the wealth items most consistently used for bridewealth transfer throughout the Irian Jaya Highlands. Other items that are customary parts of the transfers in many areas, sometimes used in others, and little or never used in a few areas, include loose cowrie shells (jeraken), utility carrying nets, stone axes and/or large axe blades, adzes and/or adze blades, stone knives, nassa shell bibs, bailer shell necklaces, braided orchid fiber cording, bows and arrows, salt, vegetables, and sometimes services (labor).

In intragroup transfers, made both at marriage and at death, display-exchange stones have both symbolic and economic utility. Like pigs, nets, and cowrie shell bands (jerak), they are one of the most universally used wealth items as a part of bridewealth (and headprice) throughout the entire study area. O'Brien, working with the Konda Valley Dani near Bokondini (fig. 1.31), said that from a life-cycle perspective "marriage payments are the largest in a series of payments between affines" (1969:530). In a total of seventeen marriages taking place in the Konda Valley area between 1960–62 in which O'Brien felt she could document the total components of "payments," she found that out of a grand total of 318 items used, there were 61 pigs and 64 display-exchange stones (jao) for a mean of 3.6 pigs and 3.8 display-exchange stones that changed hands per marriage.

Farther to the west, working with the Dani, Western Dani, and Damal in the Mulia Area (fig. 1.31), Hayward found that the groom "drawing upon his own resources and along with the help of his kinsmen" (1992:237) makes the betrothal payment (kwe awu), which consists of four to five pigs, three to four display-exchange stones (je), and ten to eleven shell bands. These "payments" are made to the parents of the bride. At the next wam lengganak wakwi ceremony the bride can be skirted (fig. 1.10). While the girl is being skirted inside, the girl's father is making the "father's payment" (kwe owak) outside in the courtyard. This "payment" made by a girl's father to all those individuals who had earlier sponsored her mother's own skirting ceremony typically consists of gifts of seven to eight pigs, two to three display-exchange stones (je), and approximately eighteen to twenty shell bands. According to Hayward, "the primary purpose of this payment is to express appreciation to the members of the wife's family, via reciprocal gift giving, for their support and investment on behalf of both mother and daughter" (1992:239). A groom's "payment" *(kwe onggo),* made a few years after a girl's skirting ceremony, to her father and his kinsmen is to reciprocate specifically for the "payment" they made earlier at the girl's skirting ceremony. Such a transfer of goods may or may not include the presentation of display-exchange stones.

Larson (1987) found that similar marriage customs and "payments" prevailed in the Ilaga area, as did I throughout the entire Grand Valley and West region during the course of my research.

Throughout the Yali and East, marriages are generally formalized with similar rituals as in the Grand Valley and West. Bridewealth bundles are laid out. Display-exchange stones (sie, alt. siengga) are displayed and presented. Differences include the absence of the "dress-the-bride" ceremony, which is held only in those areas in the west where married women wear the orchid fiber corded skirts. Also, in the east, marriages are not put off until the periodic alliancewide ebe akho ceremony, which is not conducted as such in the east, although their important pig ceremonies do adhere to a ritual cycle. In the central Yali Angguruk area (fig. 1.31), Koch reported that, "A man will often augment the value of the initial *ongkama* (pig) transaction (part of marriage formalization) by adding valuable display-exchange stones *(sie),* cymbium shell segments, and new nets" (1967:61).

Big man Morahidek Kombo and several advising Yali elders said that at a wedding, the parents of the bride never ask for a "price," the wealth transfer is decided by the groom's side. In a wedding, where the groom is marrying a daughter of an influential big man, the wealth transfer might be approximately ten ceremonial nets *(sum);* seven normal size (about 47–64 cm) display-exchange stones (sie), plus numerous small sie (about 22 cm); approximately four cowrie shell bands (sulanggen); and about three nassa shell necklace "bibs" *(walimunggen).* At the Yali marriage ceremony, the groom's family displays the wealth bundle as described above outside the men's house of the groom's father. The bride-to-be and her family are in-vited to come view the display. The bride's parents bring *he yihiruk,* which is one live pig and a pig that has already been killed. The live pig is given to the groom's parents, who care for it and then later return it to the bride and groom as a symbol of giving them a "good start in life." The dead pig is cooked and eaten. Only the bride-to-be and the groom's family eat the pig. While eating, the family of the bride-to-be examines the wealth bundle. After the meal the bride-to-be's family picks up the display items and goes home. This wealth bundle transfer is called *he onggo.* After the he onggo, the bride and groom are considered married and the bride moves to the husband's ward (house cluster) and lives in the same hut with the groom's mother. Prior to the he onggo it may have taken the groom and his family as long as a year to collect the sie display-exchange stones and other items of wealth for the he onggo.

Near the eastern part of the Yali and East area, the Una inhabitants also use display-exchange stones as important items of marriage wealth transfers, but among the Una, the Langda-Sela-style adze tool has also become important as a marriage wealth transfer item. I am told by Una informants that at least thirty adzes must be presented to the bride and her family.

PROFANE DISPLAY-EXCHANGE STONES AS SOURCES FROM WHICH TO SELECT STONES FOR SACRED USES. At the quarry sites, the quarrymen only know that they are quarrying the flat display-exchange stone (je) and the elongate ellipsoidal shaped je puluen to be traded as profane stones to user populations. They profess to know little about the ultimate uses of the stones. Perhaps this practice stems from a much earlier prehistoric evolutionary stage when only rock for profane stone tools was quarried, not rock for symbolic stones. Today, once in use as a profane display-exchange stone, it is up to the user's prerogatives to select, from time to time, particularly desirable stones to be converted through ritual to the supernaturally powerful sacred stones.

CHAPTER 4

Sacred Symbolic Stones and Empowered Stone Tools

The broad range of sacred stones in all of their functional simplicity and complexities are the most powerful tools that the Highlanders use to deal with the ghosts and spirits that are omnipresent. Herein is an opportunity to understand all that we can about the *detail of function* of the sacred stones and other accompanying material objects within the cultural system in which they exist and the cultural behavior that is prompted by their presence. A reasonable amount of scholarly information is available regarding both the identification and behavior associated with icons and other sacred objects (including idols) that are present worldwide in historical religions, but there is a serious gap of information regarding the identification and uses of such kinds of artifacts made of stone, bone, ivory, clay, and wood that are present in the prehistoric record and that we often perceive to be religious in nature.

As was pointed out in the preceding section, some sacred stones are selected from the broad choice of available flat-style je (sie and siengga in the Yali and East) (fig. 4.1) and the elongate, ellipsoidal je puluen profane display-exchange stones, but many are selected from a plethora of other kinds of rocks. Some supernaturally powerful stones are river tumbled pebbles or small cobbles that may have impressed their original owners by their smoothness, degree of rounding, other unusual shapes, colors, or any combination of the foregoing. Some are ammonite fossils (cephalopod mollusks), molds and casts of their interestingly coiled shells, with lobes and saddles, which would appear as objects of interest and mystery to almost anyone (fig. 4.2). Natural quartz crystals—some transparent, others translucent—are objects that glisten and sparkle, surely entities already with mystic power that are to be treated as wusa, with care and caution. Sheer aesthetic appeal may cause someone to feel that a natural stone might already be wusa, or with proper treatment can easily be imbued with supernatural powers. Perhaps a felt divination prompts a stone owner to make a stone of this type sacred.

In addition to all of the above described

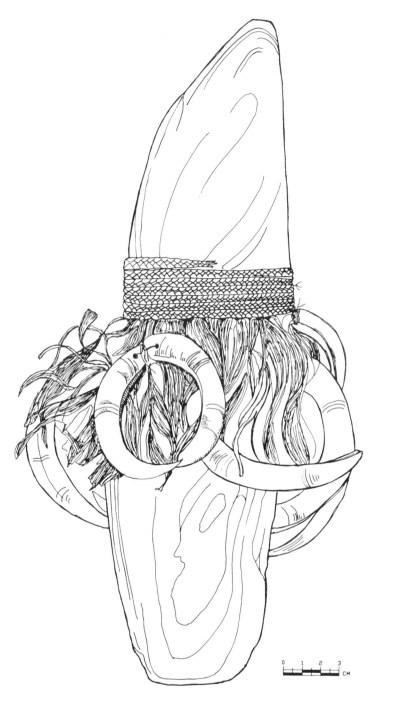

Fig. 4.1. A short flat je-type, typically decorated sacred ancestral stone

to be transformed into sacred objects. Axe and adze blades, knives, and chisels of common current usage are sometimes selected because it is thought by the owner that the object so selected had performed some task in such a way that it had already expressed an inherent supernatural power. Others make sacred a tool that was a special memento from a favorite relative, or a tool that has special aesthetics that impress the owner. Sometimes an event or act involving the stone tool causes the owner to feel that there had been a divination directing the owner to create a sacred object out of that tool. In addition, many, perhaps most, of the sacred stone tools and blades in the ganekhe cabinets are inherited objects, already within a collection of sacred ganekhe stones, about which the living recipient knows only that the special wusa object had come from an ancestor. Within the Una tradition (fig. 1.3), stone adze blades and knife heirlooms that are of slightly different lithologies than those used today were converted to sacred stones and maintained in that context, rather than used as profane tools like their ancestors before them had done. It can be seen that there was, and is, always an attractive choice of stones to be converted into sacred objects for use as ancestral spirit stones or as tools with supernatural powers.

Once stones are selected for sacred use, they are transformed from the profane to the sacred. With proper ritual, spirits are put into the stones and then through manipulation of the powerful spirits within the stones, many facets of life are kept in order. After the metamorphosis by ritual from the profane to the sacred, the stones are not identified, talked about, or used in their original profane context. They are now hierophanies. Only when *spirit* (supernatural power) abandons an object, usually through neglect by its owner, does the object again become profane and so treated.

Within the multitude of functionally different kinds of spirit stones used in the Highlands, one type is used to house venerated ancestor spirits. Ancestor worship, at the core of the complex Dani belief system, is manifest by the way these ancestor stones are empowered, maintained, and utilized. These most sacred

choices of stone objects, shaped both by geological process or by the hands of humans, certain commonly used stone tools and tool blades, like certain profane display-exchange stones (je, puluen, sie, or siengga) are selected stones (with the exception of the sun spirit stones, which are discussed later in the chapter) are kept within the ganekhe cabinets and are treated ritually with the highest regard.

Wars are fought and won and warriors kept safe with the assistance of spirit power directed through ritually empowered stones. Wounds and illnesses are healed with the assistance of healing powers from the power stones. Successful births of healthy, large litters of the all-important pigs are encouraged with specially designated sacred stones. Too much rain is discouraged and the disappearance of flooding rains are mandated through ritual with stones. Sweet potato and other crops are fertilized with supernaturally powered stones. The recognition and routine uses of sacred stones with supernatural power are just as fundamental to ways of life among the Irian Jaya Highlanders as the use of profane stone tools and the raising of sweet potatoes.

Considerable detail will be presented regarding ownership of the stones, architecture of the *place* of the stones, spatial relationships of these *places* to community, and then their spatial relationships to both sacred and profane objects within *place*. Finally, the cultural behavior will be reviewed that directly involves interaction of the stone owners with the stones, both in those places where the stones are maintained and elsewhere. From this order of presentation it is hoped that general principles will evolve to serve as baselines of thought when making interpretations of behavior and belief systems of extinct cultural systems from material goods.

Ownership of the Stones

Sacred objects, including most of the sacred stones, are individually owned by men, but maintained, manipulated, and worshiped within small socioreligious groups, which number from an unusual minimum of three to as many as twenty-two, with the typical group varying from six to eleven. These are the ganekhe (mid–Grand Valley Dani dialect) groups mentioned in chapter 1. Every adult man belongs to one of these groups. The ganekhe themselves are the individual, sacred,

Fig. 4.2. Sacred ammonite fossils

and secret (outside of each ganekhe group) objects and packets of objects that are maintained in the special ganekhe cabinets within certain men's houses. (Ganekhe literally translates to "sacred stones" but within a broader context, the indigenous users of the term expand its meaning to include all of those sacred objects kept within the ganekhe cabinet.) Henceforth, I will use the mid–Grand Valley term ganekhe to refer to such objects and packets throughout the entire Grand Valley and West region. A man's ganekhe is his entire ganekhe packet with one or several ganekhe objects inside.

Each adult man has within his ganekhe at

least one stone that is sacred (wusa) and super-naturally powerful. I have even observed that the "worthless ones" *(gebu)* and the physically deformed possess ganekhe and belong to a ganekhe group. Thus, the cultural system has provided a social mechanism for every initiated male to belong to a religious group, in spite of possible mental or physical frailties, and through the ownership of a ganekhe stone to participate in a very personal way in the worship of ancestor spirits, the Highlanders' "god-power." However, all females, and young boys until initiated, are precluded by taboos imposed locally by the different cultural groups across the entire research area from being involved with these sacred objects or with ritual within the confines of sacred space. At the time of initiation, this taboo is formally removed from young boys. Within the religious variance of Highlands' cultures, there are circumstances, however, when a ganekhe object is owned and manipulated on behalf of a female (to be later discussed).

Each ganekhe group is composed principally of members from a segment of a given patrilineage. Within the Grand Valley and West (fig. 2.1), I suspect that membership of each group is composed solely of members of a single patrilineage, but in the pragmatic ways of the Highlanders there are exceptions to this generally enforced rule. In the Yali and East region (fig. 2.1), the issue of membership in the religious groups that control the stones becomes a bit clouded because some of my own observations throughout a broad area are contrary to Koch's statement that "men's house" membership is from multiple lineages and his inference that this membership also composes the stone-controlling religious groups (1967: 117). Regarding the importance of lineage, ownership of the stones, and ritual, O'Brien, working a considerable distance west of the Grand Valley with the Western Dani stated that, "The ceremonial function of lineage derives from its corporate ownership of sacred objects, most commonly various small kinds of stones, or 'spirit bones,' used in ceremonies associated with war, death, sickness, and fertility" (1969: 90–91). My observation is, as previously stated,

different from O'Brien's in that even within O'Brien's area of research, I conclude that the ganekhe packets and objects are individually owned, even though they are communally stored and then treated as corporate entities when manipulated in group ritual. Each man, if he moves to another location, has the right to remove his ganekhe from a sacred cabinet and instill it at another location. Also, for personal devotionals and to assist in carrying out group-honored social and political functions, individuals do possess some control over the temporary removal of their own ganekhe objects from a ganekhe cabinet. This issue of individual versus corporate ownership of super-naturally powerful spirit stones is important to our comprehension of the religious concepts that are at play within the Highlanders' belief system. An understanding of the complex role of stones in this construct is a prerequisite to establishing boundaries (perhaps even a model) from which we can manipulate calculated guesses about belief systems and cultural behavior within the archaeological record and also to use the data for comparative analyses between the Highlanders' belief system and the religions of others.

Houses for the Stones: Both Profane and Sacred Space

We take the built environment for granted; yet we create worlds of meaning through the buildings we construct. Architecture is a powerful medium for representing, ordering and classifying the world. For over a decade archaeologists have been using concepts of the symbolic use of space, but until now there has been no single field of study of this field, or its interaction with architecture and anthropology. (Pearson and Richards 1994)

An average men's house, whether in a Dani compound or a Yali or Una house cluster, is at once, from a modern Western theological perspective, a seeming paradox. For the Irian Jaya Highlanders, the men's house with its sacred space and objects is the *axis mundi*, the center of the world where Highlands men put the world in perspective and develop definitions and understanding of the cosmos. It is the primary living quarters for men and initiated male children, with all of their normal household activities, and, as such, the storage area for all manner of profane items of dress, adornment, tools, and valuables, including the je display-exchange stones. At the same time, it is the sacred house of worship for male religious groups wherein their *most* sacred stone objects (ganekhe) are maintained and the place where the men retreat to obtain holistic measures of comfort and to experience *sacred* sharing. Much of the Highlanders' ceremonial activity focuses on the ganekhe within the sacred houses. The women are completely left out of this experience.

The architectural style and construction of the men's house in the Highlands is almost always the same within the bounds of each language group, whether a normal men's house, with its dual profane and sacred roles, or in certain cases, a sacred house built specifically to house sacred paraphernalia and to be the focal point of religious ritual.

The big man (leader) of each socioreligious group, who is responsible for the care and uses of the sacred objects, determines the locale for the repository of sacred objects—the ganekhe—that belong to the members of the group. Usually the men's house in which he resides is this repository, as well as the place where the men residing in that particular men's house also maintain their profane je display-exchange stones (sie or siengga in the Yali and East region).

A big man of particular influence beyond the confines of the compound (or Yali house cluster) may even control more than one ganekhe repository. This is especially true for those big men who are of sufficient stature at the confederation and alliance levels (see "Sociopolitical Organization," chapter 3) to gain control of war trophies, which may include bows, arrows, occasionally spears, sometimes items of a dead warrior's adornment regalia, even small clumps of hair, and, on rarer occasions yet, other body parts. Their men's

house (with a ganekhe cabinet in the rear) becomes also a storage vault for war trophies, which are treated as sacred relics stored to the sides of and from the ceiling in front of the ganekhe cabinet.

When men of influence construct special, well-hidden sacred houses or even an entire sacred compound for the sole function of a sacred ceremonial retreat, the geographic boundaries of land-holding segments of patrilineage (or at least areas of common political control) become important not just for political and economic reasons but for religious reasons as well. Land ownership is marked by natural features that easily identify boundaries. Hilltops, crests, ends and slopes of ridges, gullies and heads of gullies, springs, groves of trees and even single trees, all have names that might define boundaries and identify not only land-controlled areas for gardens and forest manipulated food plants, but also those areas in which sacred houses, caves, and rock shelters could be used to house sacred objects, including the stones.

A restriction or taboo prevails across the entire research area to prevent the uninitiated from walking on sacred ground or viewing sacred things. Missionary-writer Don Richardson reported the incident (possibly true) of a young Yali girl being hurled into the Heluk River to her death because she had unwittingly played on the sacred ground of a "*Kembu* temple" (conventional men's sacred house) (1977:22, 35–42).

Architecture, Contents, and Spatial Relationships

The men's habitation and sacred houses are small structures that contain human beings, collective unseen entities (ghosts and ancestor spirits), and numerous material objects, both profane and sacred. Interactions of the humans with each other, unseen ghosts, spirits, and material contents of the house translate to contemporary behavior within the cultural system. To gain the greatest advantage from a construct in the ethnographic present, one must keep in mind that to those humans living within these small quarters, the spirit and ghost entities are in many ways like another human species, competing for space and attention with *Homo sapiens sapiens.* To the Highlanders, the collective spirits have many of the same capabilities and behavioral patterns as the people. However, ghosts have, in addition, special abilities that allow them to be invisible to the normal human eye and to travel through barriers that would deter humans. The ancestral spirits can also perpetuate themselves with the help of their human lineage descendants in a symbiotic relationship through time without temporal boundaries. Many of the implications of the existence of the collective spirits on human behavior are manifest; while at the same time, the psychological effect on human beings of such unseen entities is little understood from a modern Western perspective. We do know, however, that fear of reprisal from the spirit world by breaking an absolute taboo or being attacked by spirits manipulated through sorcery against a victim can bring about the death of humans (McElroy and Townsend 1989:252–54). This fear of the ultimate consequence of action taken against them by ghosts and spirits is one of the strong motivating factors for adherence by the Highlanders to their strict regimen of *proper* ritualistic manipulation of the stones—certainly a factor to be understood when contemplating behavior within the Highlanders' men's houses.

Although it is only male spirits that are installed as personified ancestral spirits within the ganekhe stones and other objects, female ghosts and spirits are also known to be present in the world of the unseen, some of which were discussed in chapter 1. The personified male ancestor spirits that are domiciled within the ganekhe stones retain their specific identity and known place (in the stones) within the world of the seen only as long as descendent members of their *seen* patrilineages continue to revitalize the spirits' superhuman energy (life) through a continuum of renewal rituals. Whenever this "life-giving" continuum of rituals ceases, the personified ancestor spirits in the stones do not "die," they just "move out"—abandon the stones of domicile—to join the large number of other spirits that roam in perpetuity within the

milieu of the Highlands' landscape. To an individual in the *seen* world, the vacated stone has lost its special power (its spirit) and no longer has the supernatural ability to deal with circumstances or other entities in the world of the *unseen* on behalf of the owner of the stones. The stone is then, once again, a stone of only profane reality and can be treated as such.

The multitude of unidentified ghosts and male and female spirits that seem to abound everywhere throughout the landscape and to come and go from houses in the seen world are thought to be individually and collectively capable of both malevolent and benevolent deeds within the world of the seen. Consequently, a great deal of time and energy is expended to both contradict potentially malevolent acts on the parts of ghosts and spirits, as well as to foster beneficent help from the ghosts and spirits in endeavors promoted by individuals in the seen world. To an outsider, what is first observed is the tremendous amount of cultural energy that is constantly being utilized to keep malevolent ghosts and spirits out of houses, entire living compounds, potato fields, water supply points, stands of manipulated plants, and away from numerous cultural activities with the uses of seen ghost and spirit barriers; and to placate the ghosts and spirits by both thoughtful deeds and a never-ending continuum of sacrificial rituals.

The presence of ancestral spirits and the possibility of visits by unwanted ghosts certainly add to both physical and mental crowdedness in conditions that are already filled by humans and an array of both profane and sacred material objects. Cultural interpretations from only the material residue of interactions of household contents (humans, spirits, and material goods) are difficult, but to archaeologists, this is a difficulty that we must continue to surmount if we are to improve our qualitative interpretations of prehistoric cultural systems. As archaeologists, our increasing understanding of these things and also of the identifications and *interrelated roles* of profane and sacred stone tools and symbolic stones within both profane and sacred space will not only favorably impact our interpretations and thinking regarding the origins and evolution of architecture and religion, but more broadly, systemic interpretations of prehistoric cultural systems. With the objective of adding "missing links" of understanding between scholarly knowledge of historically known places of worship (with their icons and other sacred objects, including idols) and suspected prehistoric places of worship and sacred objects, a considerable amount of detail regarding the architecture, contents, and use of sacred space follows.

All of the different language-speaking groups within the research area build men's houses of architecturally planned and volumetrically compact space that within the boundaries of each language group are of similar dimensions and design. Raglan (1964) stated that houses were originally built as temples, not shelters or dwellings, and as recently as 1990, Highlands (1990:55) substantially agreed with this view. Rapoport's own views concerning the theory for religious origin modifies Raglan's and Highlands's position: "It is one thing to say that the dwelling has symbolic and cosmological aspects. . . and another to say that it has been erected for ritual purposes and is neither shelter nor dwelling, but a temple" (1969:40). Pearson and Richards stated that, "Part of the problem is undoubtedly the modern perception of clear distinctions between symbol and function, and religious and secular aspects of life" (1994:55). Certainly in the highly sacrilized lives of the Highlanders, with the omnipresence of collective spirits, the religious and secular merge until, to even an understanding outsider, the distinction becomes clouded and to the indigenous dweller himself, the distinction is lost.

In the Grand Valley and West, the men's house, as the focal center of male activity, is located across the central courtyard from the single entrance into each compound. From inside a men's house, any activity within the compound can be observed as well as people coming and going through the compound entrance. The men's houses are round hemispheres with plank board walls about 1 to 1.5 m high, grass thatched conical roofs, and a single entrance. Some have two openings through a small antechamber, while others have only a single entrance and no antechamber (fig. 4.3). These houses are the largest of the round structures in a compound or house cluster, being bigger than the women's (or family's) sleeping houses and different in shape from the rectangular women's communal cookhouses and the pig sties. Inside diameters of Dani and Western Dani men's houses fall within an absolute range of 2.5 to 5 m, with most between 4 and 5 m. In these same geographic areas, the inside diameters of the women's sleeping houses range from about 2.5 to 3 m. Normal Dani men's house occupancy varies from five to ten males, with an absolute range of one to seventeen. The openings through the antechamber into the men's houses are about 50 cm wide by about 80 cm high. Usually both openings are slightly raised from the ground and can be closed with one to three wooden slats. The small entrances make an archaeological statement about the stature of the users. Even so, the adult Dani males, given their mean heights (chapter 1) must squat low and proceed slowly to negotiate entry.

The antechamber serves several functions. It slows a visitor down as he maneuvers the small door openings to enter the main house room. Those inside have time to carefully look at a visitor, who, himself, is at a disadvantage as he enters into a dimly lit interior to which his eyes have not yet adjusted. For the residents the antechamber offers a convenient place to temporarily set tools during the day. It also serves as the first line of defense to keep unwanted ghosts from entering, especially during occasions of ritual. Hopefully, visiting ghosts will tarry in the antechamber rather than enter the house proper. Sometimes, it is used by people who have a message or some food to pass to someone in the house, but who do not have authority to enter. This small room also provides human visitors a place to pause or to have protection from the rain or direct sun. At times of courtyard pig sacrifices, this area may become especially crowded during typical sudden downpours.

Measurements of five men's houses at three

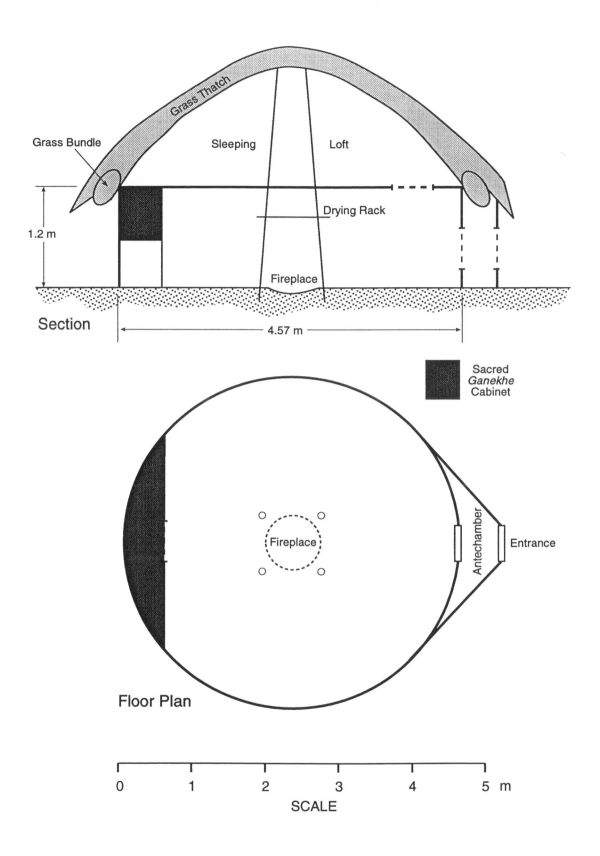

Grass Thatch

Grass Bundle

Sleeping   Loft

1.2 m

Drying Rack

Fireplace

Section

4.57 m

Sacred *Ganekhe* Cabinet

Fireplace

Antechamber

Entrance

Floor Plan

Fig. 4.3. Grand Valley and West men's house with antechamber

0   1   2   3   4   5 m

SCALE

widely scattered areas in the Grand Valley and west region, two in the Yali and one in the Una, were averaged to give the following dimensions for entrances: 50 cm wide by 80 cm high. Yali ground floors are raised off the ground by as much as about 60 cm. The inside diameters of Yali men's houses with the sacred stones (*jouei* and in secluded areas *sóumó*) vary from 4 to 5 m, the same sizes as the big men's houses in the Grand Valley and West.

The floors of the men's houses in the Grand Valley are usually at ground level, which is different from the slightly elevated floors of the women's houses and the greatly elevated floors of the men's houses among the Wano to the west. Planks stuck into the ground form the outer perimeters of all Highlands' houses. In the Grand Valley and West region, these plank walls stand about 1.5 m above ground level, higher in the Wano area. Wooden rafter poles lashed horizontally to the top of the wall planks form the support for reed flooring that is both the ceiling for the ground level room and the floor for a sleeping loft above. Ceiling height in the lower area varies from 1 to just slightly more than 1 m above floor level. As male adult heights vary from 1.5 to 1.8 m, vertical accommodation of a standing male is restrictive. Four center poles form the central support for the conical roof. Their bases are sunk into the ground to form a square no bigger than 1.2 m in both Dani and Yali men's houses, which outlines the space for a circular, earthen hearth.

In Dani houses, a shallow hole is scooped out of the ground and lined with a layer of clay, which becomes fire-hardened with use as a fireplace. In houses with raised floors, an earthen fireplace mound is built up to floor level from the ground. Above the hearth, the four center poles slant inward up through the sleeping loft to the apex to support the semispherical roof. A distinguishing feature of houses of the Yali and East is an adze-sharpened wooden spike that rises above the roof at the apex of each house. The spike is securely fastened under the thatch to supporting poles of the roof. This short "lightning rod" serves an important functional purpose, which will be discussed under a later heading with sacred

symbolic stones. (Such a wooden spike is not present on the roofs of Grand Valley and West houses.)

Inside each house, less than two-thirds of the distance up from the fireplace to the lower ceiling, a square plank board rack is lashed between the four center support poles as a convenient place on which to dry firewood or to dry and/or store various other objects. Bamboo knives, marsupial mandibles, tusks, a few arrows and other odds and ends are often found here. Rattan, bamboo, and vine lines are often stretched at various places between ceiling rafters to furnish support from which to hang or creatively stick personal dress items, accumulated wealth items (with the exception of display-exchange stones) from funeral and wedding exchanges, and, in certain specially designated men's houses, war trophies. Sometimes, wooden hooks are suspended from the ceiling and center poles from which also hang various and sundry objects. Articles placed on the rack over the fireplace or suspended near the ceiling soon take on a black tarry appearance. The same black carbon residue that coats the ceiling and artifacts, coats and contaminates the lungs of house inhabitants. Health complications caused by the ingestion of smoke is the number-one cause of natural death among Highland dwellers (personal communications with medical staff at the Wamena Hospital, Irian Jaya, Indonesia, 1989, 1991, 1992, and 1993).

Within the Grand Valley and among the Western Dani, it is the practice to keep both the ground level and sleeping loft floors covered with a comfortable mat of clean grass. In the Wano area and within the Yali and Una areas, the more conventional practice is to have either reed or wooden plank floors on the lower level, on which individuals can place their *Pandanus* leaf mats, and reed floors in the sleeping loft, upon which mats are also placed.

Access to the loft sleeping quarters is through a small opening in the ground-level ceiling that is set to one side of the entrance (from my experience, more often to the right as one enters a house). The sleeping loft is relatively free of objects, although a minimum of items may be hung from the center poles. The loft is warmed by the fire from below (in the Grand Valley and West region) and kept relatively free of night-marauding rodents by the dense smoke that accumulates beneath the unventilated tightly thatched roof. Sometimes in the sleeping loft, a false hearth with ashes is located under the grasses on the floor to accommodate ghosts who might pay a visit. In the Yali and East region, however, this is often an active fireplace for use by humans, located in the center of the room above the ground level hearth.

On the back wall of the lower floor, opposite the entrances into those men's houses where ganekhe are maintained, is a raised narrow wooden box, attached to and constructed as a part of the wall itself (fig. 4.3). A section of the circular wall of the house is the back side of the box. The front plank wall is festooned with a curtain of ferns that have been steamed along with pig meat from pigs ritually killed at sacred ceremonial feasts and, in some houses, also with the long, narrow leaves of the *jiwi* plant. In most houses a bundle or at least a number of plant stems ("sticks") are located at the edges of or across the single wooden door of the cabinet. This solid curtain of special materials that have been ritually treated at pig sacrifices not only shields the ganekhe stored within the cabinet from view but acts as a barrier to the penetration by malevolent ghosts or spirits. Access to the ganekhe cabinet is through a centrally located door that usually consists of one or two removable soot-blackened planks. Inside, the people's most sacred objects are maintained in great secrecy. Hanging below the elevated box are two, or in the cases of the most influential big men, three rows of pig mandibles, brown with age, suspended from rattan or bamboo thongs that are stretched wall to wall, horizontally between the front support legs of the cabinet. Leaning upward from the floor against the central front part of the box are often one to four display-exchange stones (je), usually individually wrapped in the conventional *gisakpel* banana trunk coverings. An unadorned je puluen stone rests upright against one of the front central support legs of

the box or is sometimes tied to the leg at floor level. This is just below the left side of the box opening located above. Sometimes one or two rattan thong-stick fire-starting tools are laid haphazardly here and there on the floor under the box, along with other objects such as digging sticks and bows and arrows. Bows and arrows may often be leaning against the outer edges of the box and against the adjoining circular house wall. Throughout the rest of the room are all manner of profane objects and a number of well wrapped sacred objects; some stuck between ceiling rafters and the loft reed floor, some hung from the ceiling, and some attached to the circular wall of the house.

A minimum number of profane objects are communally maintained in each men's house for the personal uses of its members. These may be considered house furnishings. Along the outer perimeter of the room and standing upright from the floor against the wall are one to four, usually aged, light brown gourd water containers and sometimes a gourd that contains pig fat for greasing the body. Directly in front of the fireplace (toward the entrance), a rectangular-shaped, shallow wooden bowl is conveniently placed in which to collect sweet potato and yam skins before feeding them to the pigs. (The Dani are strict about not eating tuber skins themselves.) On occasion, this functional wooden waste container is turned over and its surface used as a minialtar on which small sacred paraphernalia can be laid out for healing procedures and other sacred rituals. In the Yali and East region, it is the common practice to use bark from the casuarina tree to fashion this waste receptacle rather than to use a wooden bowl. Another object often present alongside the fireplace are one or two pieces of hollowed bamboo tubing, less than 1 m in length, through which a person blows to fan still-glowing embers into a flame or to encourage a new fire. Sometimes one to several stems of long narrow hollowed reed tubing lay by the fireplace to be used as cigarette holders. On the back side of and adjacent to the fireplace, often partially hidden from view by the loose grass floor coverings is a single smooth, river-rounded, usually linear-shaped hammerstone and an accompanying single river-rounded, circular but somewhat flattened anvil stone. This tool pair appears to have been carefully selected for the symmetry and the high degree of smoothness of each stone. Sometimes one or two hammerstone-anvil pairs are maintained along the side edges of the fireplace. The routine use of the stones is to crack roasted *Pandanus* nuts. Another use of the hammerstone-anvil tool pair is to crack pig bones for their marrow. Daoke Mabel and two of his brothers told me that the river-rounded, oblong anvil stone (12.7 cm thick by 15.2 cm wide by 20.32 cm long) on the floor in front of Gutelu's ganekhe cabinet was used for just that purpose. *Pandanus* nuts are usually cracked close to the hearth because the Dani are careful about keeping their house floors clean, and they throw the nut hulls into the fireplace. Just as the wooden waste receptacles are at times used to create minialtars for use with small sacred paraphernalia, the stone anvils are sometimes used in rituals as bases upon which to burn sacred tree resin *(hotali)*.

The array of personally owned material goods that make up the contents of a sacred-profane men's house would make definitive statements about their owners if found in preserved archaeological context: the occupants were in all probability of the Neolithic Stone Age because of the presence of only ground stone tools, no copper, bronze, nor iron; the inhabitants had yet to discover pottery or the use of baskets; and they collected bird plumage, fur, pig mandibles and an assortment of different-shaped linear gourds (used for penis sheaths), the function of which, without prior knowledge would be impossible to interpret. Whatever name one might assign to this culture, one would feel confident that the occupants were of the Stone Age, using ground stone versus flaked tools.

Although there are no physical partitions or visible markings to define an individual's space, each occupant of a men's house does have his own understood space on the wall, at the juncture of floor and wall, and sometimes on part of the ceiling, where he consolidates his belongings. Some flat and thin objects, like packets of

feathers, may be slipped under the grass floor covering, especially around the outer perimeter of a room. Axes, adzes, and display-exchange stones (in Yali and East, adzes and display-exchange stones) are usually leaned against the wall, but sometimes stuck between the curved horizontal reenforcing pole members and the vertical wall planks. Individual feathers and packets of feathers, feather and fur headdresses (sometimes protected in circular bark containers), packets of penis gourds as well as singles, tied strips of orchid fibers (for cording), nassa shell bibs *(walimo)* and bailer shell neck pieces *(mikak)*, white egret and black cassowary feather wands, envelopes of cigarette leaves, small gourds or leaf packets containing fat for greasing the body, small tool kits—all of these and other artifacts of culture are stuck or tied into wall plank lashings, wedged between horizontal reenforcing poles and the upright wall planks.

All kinds of packages of different sizes are tied to or hung on both wooden hooks suspended from the ceiling and on rattan, bamboo, and vine lines tautly tied between ceiling rafters. Some of the packages (both gisakpcl and leaf wrapped or unwrapped bamboo tubes) contain items for profane personal use, such as feathers, penis gourds, boar tusks, pulverized red hematite and ochre cakes for coloring purposes, and packets of flint chips. Men's net carrying bags are also often hung from ceiling hooks. These unwrapped items become soot-blackened over time. Other packages and bundles contain string nets, both those received at ceremonies of exchange and stored as items of wealth and those newly made to be used at a future time.

In those houses where the leadership is of such stature that war trophies are collected, some of these items are secreted from view as sacred (wusa) objects or just protected from the accumulation of smoke soot by being packaged and hung from the ceiling. Some packages might even contain items considered to be ganekhe, but storing these objects outside the cabinet is rare. The larger packages and bundles are usually hung at the sides or toward the back of a house. The area toward the back of the

Fig. 4.4. The smallest continuously occupied house in the Highlands and its occupant

between the fireplace and the entrance, with arrow-tip ends pointing toward the door. These are arrows that have been removed from wounded residents of the house. Empowered with the flow of energy from the ganekhe cabinet, they are capable of powerful countermagic. Also, usually stuck in the rafter lashing above the fireplace is a blackened arrow that is used at times of ritual gatherings as a wand, waved in the air to cleanse both humans entering the room and the room itself of malevolent ghosts. One or a few jiwi leaves on a short branch are tied midway on the arrow point and held over a fire in the hearth to activate the spirit power before the smoking arrow with leaves is used.

High on the front two center poles (toward the entranceway from the fireplace) other objects ascribed with supernatural power are often hung facing the entranceway as another line of defense between the house opening and the sacred ganekhe cabinet. In addition to various amulets, these are often the same soot-blackened neck gear (bark, spider web strips, and one or several pig tails fastened to a string) that are worn by the men to keep malevolent ghosts from entering their own throats. Whether or not this placement of amulets and neck gear within the houses on the front sides of the fireplace is indicative of a degree of anthropomorphism of the house I do not know. It is possible that the opening between the center posts and above the hearth is considered a vulnerable, throatlike passageway to the ganekhe cabinet with its edai egen (singing seeds of life) of the house. What is known is that it is desirable to keep unfriendly ghosts away from the ganekhe cabinet and that available precautions have been taken.

Architectural style of house construction in the Yali and East and the Grand Valley and West is quite similar, yet differences should be noted. In both areas, men's and women's houses are round with the men's houses having larger diameters than those of the women. Throughout the Grand Valley and West, roofs are thatched with grass; whereas east of the Grand Valley, the roofs are covered with either *Pandanas* leaves and their stems or bark strips

ceiling is reserved for packaged war trophies and/or other well hidden (by wrappings) sacred relics.

The area on the ceiling from the fireplace toward the door is kept free of large hanging bundles, as a matter of practicality to keep the entrance into the house unobstructed. Then, too, it provides ceiling space that can be used to set up a line of defense against marauding ghosts and spirits and as an avenue for the departure of friendly spirits on missions of attacking the spirits of the seen enemy (human beings). Foremost in this line of defense-offense are one to several soot-blackened arrows that are hung from the ceiling over the fireplace or from the casuarini tree. A wooden spike, as previously mentioned, sticks skyward from the roof apex of the Yali and East houses but is absent from houses in the Dani and West region. House diameters are nearly the same across the entire research area. The diameters reported by Koch (1967:118) at Angguruk-Pasikni in the geographical center of the research area for the Yali "big jóuéi ranging between 13 and 16 feet" (3.96 and 4.87 m) is representative of men's houses for the entire research area. In the Yali and East, it is common practice for the floor of the men's houses to be elevated about .5 m above ground level. Earthen, fire-hardened, clay-lined fireplaces are built up to floor level in these houses. Always in the Yali women's (or family) houses one or two enclosures, separated from human use areas, function as pig pens, but rarely is this found in a men's house. Whereas in Yali and East house clusters, the women's houses often stand relatively close to one another (as close as 2 m on occasion), the sacred men's houses are usually set apart by at least approximately 7.5 m. Thus, sacred space can be identified both by the relative size of dwellings and by spatial relationships within any house cluster. The smallest continuously human occupied dwelling that I ever encountered anywhere in the Highlands is 2.5 m inside diameter at ground floor level and 1.1 m from ground floor level to the room's ceiling, with an even more restricted sleeping loft (fig. 4.4). It is occupied by Uwehe Sama, an aged Yali woman (134 cm tall) and her two piglets, high on a hillslope above Pasikni.

Wali's Sacred Compound and Sacred House

Secreted on a flat area above a gentle rise toward the mountains, not far from the mountainside of Dutoba Ridge, is Wali's sacred compound. Known among the people as *Yalogon* (alt. *Yalohon*), it is sacred (*wusa*) and, therefore, little talked about. Yalogon translates to "you stay here," referring to the ancestor spirits who dwell in the ancestral stones (ganekhe) but have the inherent rights and ability to come and go. Yalogon is only about a forty-five-minute walk from Hupainma, the compound where Wali lives. In Hupainma, the men's house is known

as *pilamo* (alts. *pilai, bilai*) *Wali mege* (literally "house where Wali lives" or "house of Wali"). In Yalogon, the men's house is known as *pilamo* (or *bilai*) *Wali wusa*, "the sacred house of Wali." This is the place where Wali maintains the ganekhe for the men of the religious group he leads. Adjoining Yalogon compound (sharing a common fence) is another sacred compound that is shared by three other big men. They also maintain ganekhe and use the compound as their own ceremonial center for sacred affairs.

Wali once said that every big man with significant influence on the confederacy level has his own secret compound apart from the men's house where he normally lives. Due to the sacred (*wusa*) nature of the subject, I was never able to properly corroborate this with informants in other areas. Since I have visited (with permission of appropriate big men and their ganekhe group members) four other isolated secret compounds that are maintained for only sacred purposes, I suspect that there are numerous hidden sacred houses and even entire sacred compounds scattered about the Highlands landscape.

Most of the time these sacred places are quite literally "ghost towns," inhabited only by ghosts and unseen spirits of the unseen world and a single guard and his family; none of whom dwell in the sacred house but rather in another house within the compound. The job of caretaker and guard of a sacred compound and sacred house (pilamo wusa) with its sacred stones (ganekhe) is handed down from father to son. The responsibilities are considerable: the sacred house and its contents must not be profaned and the house must be protected from all but authorized visits. I have never entered a sacred men's house without being accompanied by its big man leader, nor elsewhere within the confines of a sacred compound without at least the presence of its designated guard.

While taking photographs and making notes, once at Yalogon and once at a sacred sun house compound with only the unobtrusive presence of the resident guard, I was impressed by the solitary stillness of the compounds. At times of inactivity these places become cultural artifacts, the stuff of which the archaeological record is composed: no life, only the opportunity to interpret life. While at those places I felt I was within the confines of sacred space. What could be learned from the architectural style, spatial relationships, and the kinds of material goods present that would be helpful in developing a model for cultural interpretations from material goods?

With the exception of the house where the guard lived and the sacred men's house, the other buildings of both compounds were void of material goods normally related to inhabited living sites. The designs of the compounds and

Fig. 4.5. Yalogon, a Dani sacred compound

their various structures are all within normal size, shape, and material variance of compounds being lived in with the exception of the sun house compound, where one house built on stilts is rectangular in shape with a board slat roof. Spatial relationships of buildings are the same. The view at Yalogon compound is across the length of the open courtyard to the front of the sacred men's house at the far end of the compound (fig. 4.5). The sides of the courtyard are lined with the same kinds of buildings that are present in a traditional "living" compound. In the central part of the courtyard, three piles of heating rocks are visible along with some wooden rock tongs and the nearby accumulated charcoal debris from numerous fires. Fanning out from the concentrated, centrally located pile of small pieces of charcoal, the ground can be seen to be darkened by surface scatter of tiny bits of charcoal and charcoal dust. The compound is not overgrown with vegetation as it would be if the compound were functionally abandoned. The grass near the compound entrance looks as if it had been cut or worn down by recent use, giving the compound an air of being temporarily vacated while its occupants were off in the fields or tending to other routine matters (a normal situation). It is only by examination of the interior of the buildings that one would realize that this compound is only being lived in by someone in one house. There are no pigs here, and the men's house, although containing many objects, does not appear to be lived in (absence of a normal quantity of items of dress and adornment, tools, and weapons).

Wali sometimes goes alone to Yalogon to meditate, experience vision quests, or to open the ganekhe cabinet and deal personally with the power in the stones. He may remain for several days, exposing himself to divination, worshiping ancestor spirits in privacy, seeking communion with the supernatural, and/or manipulating the supernatural for his own or group social ends. At other times, there are rituals involving the entire ganekhe group of which Wali is the leader. All members who maintain their own personal ganekhe in the cabinet are expected to be in attendance. They trek in from different directions, prepared to stay the duration of the ritual, be it part of a day or in continuum for several days. Women and children are sometimes enlisted to carry food, firewood, water, and grasses (for the steam pits) into the compound, but then they usually leave. For some ceremonies that take more than one day but at which nighttime attendance is not required, some of the participating men may leave to overnight in their own nearby compounds of domicile and return the next day. On other occasions, when larger numbers of people are involved in ceremonies where the activities for most of those in attendance are out in the courtyard, but in conjunction with which the head shaman and his group must manipulate supernatural power in the sacred ganekhe, people may come from a broader geographic area and overnight in the houses around the perimeter of the courtyard. A common cookhouse is available as part of the courtyard accommodations for occasions like this. As in other compounds, a ghost or spirit enclosure *(waro leget)* is present between the courtyard fence and the outer fence, set to one side of the back of the sacred men's house. Not far from the waro leget, a large pile of cooking rocks is also maintained.

From the exterior, big man Wali's pilamo wusa at the Yalogon compound looks just like any other Dani men's house. In the lower photograph of figure 4.5, Wali is standing in front of his pilamo wusa. He is adorned with a delicate white egret feather headdress and a broad white nassa shell chest bib of unusually good quality (by virtue of its large size) hangs from his neck to almost the base of his penis gourd. On each wrist, Wali wears a tightly plaited fiber band, which Wali himself has weaved onto his wrists. Soot-blackened, sacralized pig grease has been carefully rubbed onto Wali's face, shoulders, and chest as atonement to ancestor spirits for breaking faith with them—a private matter not to be discussed. For three months Wali appeared daily with the freshly applied sooty ointment, which he said was applied nightly by a guardian spirit. (I suspect Alula, a personal healer of Wali's with *wusahun* power, of being that "spirit.") To the left in the photograph is an

upright meat rack from which special pieces of butchered pig meat and pig entrails are hung during sacred pig feast ceremonials. In the courtyard in front of the pilamo wusa to one side of the meat rack is an outdoor altar where pigs are ritually killed as sacrifices and sweet potatoes and other edibles are accumulated during ceremonies. The stripe on the roof of the house is a growing vine and not a painted symbol.

The interior architecture and the sum total of objects within the pilamo wusa identify it as a sacred men's house. It is distinguished from any men's house (also with a ganekhe wall cabinet) that is located in an occupied "living" compound by the paucity of the presence of profane items of dress and adornment, tools, and weapons.

A series of photographs taken over a three-year period of the undisturbed (by me) interior of Wali's pilamo wusa, adds visual detail to the previous summary of the architecture, contents, and spatial relationships within a typical men's sacred house. This pictorial review, in addition to providing visual insights, sets the archaeological stage before the "dead" material objects are brought to life with cultural behavior that is observed in the following sections entitled "The Ganekhe *Hakasin* Ceremony" and "Typical Use of A Religio-Medical Kit: Wali Treats Alula."

Figure 4.6 (1989) is a view from inside the entrance looking across the centrally located fireplace to the back wall. Nearest the entryway, one sees the usual barkwood receptacle for potato skins in front of a partially visible bamboo "bellows" fire tube, a piece of firewood, the fireplace outlined by the four center poles, another piece of firewood, and then the back wall. Hanging down from the front side of the wood storage rack over the hearth is a barely discernable small packet of sacred objects—unidentified talismen—meant to block the paths of potentially malevolent ghosts that may have penetrated the house entrance. At the top of the picture, the lower part of the wooden slat door to the ganekhe cabinet is visible. Hanging below the cabinet door on a rattan thong stretched between the cabinet's two front

Fig. 4.6. View from doorway into Wali's sacred house (pilamo wusa)

wooden legs is a row of pig mandibles. Of importance to note but not seen is an upright, dark green puluen stone leaning against the left edge of the front of the right center leg (to the reader's left) of the ganekhe cabinet. The sharpened distal end of the stone rests on the house floor; its pointed end upward, toward the sacred stones (ganekhe) in the cabinet above. Almost always, wherever there is a ganekhe cabinet within Dani culture, a puluen is traditionally set against or tied to this same positioned cabinet leg, always in the same spatial relationship to the ganekhe objects in the cabinet above. The orientation and placement of this functionally important type of stone is more visible in later figures. Maintained on the floor just behind the fireplace but masked from view by a piece of firewood and grass floor covering is a single river-rounded, oblong hammerstone and a very smooth disk-shaped stone anvil.

The significant objects and their spatial relationships in the back two-thirds of the sacred house are depicted in the next six figures, commencing from central-left along the left wall and ceiling to the ganekhe cabinet itself, then across the ganekhe cabinet to the reader's right and back along the right wall toward the entrance. Figure 4.7 (May 30, 1991) shows spatial relationships of those objects present on the left side of the room. Hanging from the ceiling on the left is a newly wrapped bundle of ceremonial nets, received at a recent funeral exchange ceremony by one of the members of the socioreligious ganekhe group that uses this particular sacred house and who says that these nets can be recirculated at future exchanges and need not be permanently maintained. Just to the right of the net bundle, a Yeineri flat-style adze is stored against the center of the wall. The proximal end of the haft is stuck between a wall plank and its horizontal bracing beam. The Yeineri flat-style adze blade has been bound to the socket of the adze by a wrapping combination of both rattan strips and braided fiber string cording (not a common way of binding an adze blade to a haft, see chapter 2). This single adze is kept in the sacred house for easy access when butchering pigs at sacred rituals and for chopping firewood. Wali says there is no sacred connotation to the adze. One, sometimes two, are always kept for the same purpose at all sacred houses.

Next, seen in figure 4.7 hanging from the ceiling are two narrow, partially soot-blackened bundles of bamboo knives that are opened and used only at sacred ceremonies. These knives are sacred implements, differentiated from profane bamboo knives by a wrapping around a section of each knife to form a handle, which on occasion may include one or more attached feathers or pieces of other organic materials. At certain ceremonies one of these knives is used to make the initial incision when skinning a sacred pig after it has been singed and is ready for butchering. The knife is used to cut through the skin and fat layer on the under side of the pig from snout to anus as the first step in the butchering process. Then any number of profane knives may be used while butchering the pig for steaming. In other men's houses I have observed that one or more sacred bamboo knives are often stored nearer the ganekhe cabinet than the packet of sacred knives shown here. Next, from the ceiling hangs a squash gourd of *holy water,* used *only* for the steam bundle at sacred (wusa) ceremonies. Stuck in the soot-blackened rafters above the water gourd are two barely distinguishable gisakpel wrapped packets that contain profane bamboo knives, conveniently handy for any suitable cutting chores in or near the sacred house. The long narrow package hanging from the ceiling between the water gourd and the large round net is a packet of penis gourds, which one of Wali's brothers hung there. These penis gourds are for personal profane use.

The nearby round bundle presents a different situation. It is a very large carrying net (*nogen*) that contains an assortment of exchange bands (*jerak*) that were distributed to Wali at funeral exchanges. The longest jerak (perhaps 8 m, not measured) of the collection has taken on sacred connotation and will stay in the pilamo wusa as a relic and not be exchanged again. However, the other, less important jerak, may be removed from the sacred house and reused at the owner's discretion,

Fig. 4.7. Left, backside of sacred house (pilamo wusa) and ganekhe cabinet

although at this time they, too, are considered to be relics. Behind the round bundle of jerak are several smaller packets of unknown contents. A straight penis gourd can be seen laying on the grass-covered floor in the same area. One small, out-of-sight gourd container, next to the end of the ganekhe cabinet contains sanctified pig fat that is reserved for ritual function to anoint sacred objects. The very long, slender gisakpel wrapped bundle hanging from the ceiling near the left side of the ganekhe cabinet contains several long ceremonial nets of the kind that are laid out as the base for ceremonial display bundles (fig. 4.8). Between this rather elongated package and the round net of jerak to its left can be seen several objects standing against the end of the ganekhe cabinet, including a bundle of exposed reed arrows. The upper ends of the arrows are soot-blackened (on close inspection they even appear charred) and the bases are tightly wrapped with a protective covering of gisakpel. The blackened portion of the arrows indicates that they were once stored in the ceiling or possibly laid on the center rack over the fireplace. The black soot

residue on arrows can at times be used to distinguish functional profane arrows from those that are war trophies that have been relegated to the rafters of a men's house, their presence there for the comfort of ghosts, spirits, and human beings as artifacts of war.

In figure 4.8 (May 30, 1991), the left side of the fern-curtained ganekhe cabinet can be seen, with its closed, centrally located door, to the reader's right. In figures 4.7 and 4.8, a long packaged je stone can be seen leaning against the left center leg of the ganekhe cabinet, below the ganekhe cabinet door. A puluen stone, first photographed tied to the cabinet leg in 1989, is observed in figures 4.7 and 4.8 tied to the same cabinet leg, but partially shielded from view by the long packaged je. The puluen is reportedly tied to the leg of the ganekhe cabinet so that the spirit in the stone will not cause the stone to depart. (The people feel the spirit within such a stone not only can leave its stone body from time to time, but that the spirit stone as an entity has the ability to also depart and move about.)

The two photographs shown in figure 4.9

Fig. 4.8. The left side of the ganekhe cabinet with boar tusk mandibles

(May 30, 1991), with Wali in both, are to be viewed as a composite pair that together show the entire front side of the sacred ganekhe cabinet. The same oblong hammerstone can be seen casually laying on the grass in front of Wali's left knee in figure 4.9 that was first photographed in 1989. The front wall of the cabinet (facing the sacred space within the sacred house) is curtained with an abundance of hanging ferns that have been steamed and sacrilized with ritually killed pigs at sacred ceremonies. A scattering of long, slender jiwi leaves are sparsely intermingled with the ferns. In the center of the cabinet is the door, which in this case consists of a single adze-smoothed, fire-smoked, blackened wooden plank. In some cabinets, the door is a single board, as it is here; in others it consists of two boards. On both sides of the door is a curtain of bunched reed sticks, present on many ganekhe cabinets, but not used on all. In a similar fashion, although the hanging ferns are always present on ganekhe cabinets, the long jiwi leaves present as part of the curtain on Wali's cabinet are not. The front legs that support the cabinet well up off the floor are also the vertical supports for horizontally tied wooden poles, rattan, or bamboo thongs from which pig mandibles are hung beneath the cabinet. In this case, the smoke-aged, pig-grease-rubbed, sometimes soot-blackened mandibles fill two complete rows below most of the cabinet, with a single row of five below the cabinet door. In all men's houses and sacred houses (pilamo wusa), these mandibles serve as icons and are mementos, sacred relics, kept in perpetuity out of respect for the spirits of the pigs that have been ritually sacrificed on the outdoor ground altar in front of the pilamo wusa, and as tallies to show humans, ghosts, and ancestral spirits that sacred sacrificial ritual is performed with regularity. Young boys being initiated to uses of sacred space and religious objects within the men's houses learn from the pig mandibles as icons, embellished with anecdotal stories told by their elders. Those mandibles hung below the left side of the cabinet door are from pigs that were sacrificed at ceremonies that focused on: (1) driving malevolent ghosts and spirits from

habitation compounds, gardens, or other specific locales; (2) promoting health and fertility among women and the birth of healthy offspring; (3) ensuring the good health and bountiful reproduction of pigs; and (4) creating fertile gardens and abundant and healthy crops. The pig mandibles to the right of the cabinet door and below the cabinet were collected from rituals held for war purposes (success in battle, "good" warriors, and the safety of each warrior in the group while he is fighting). Any overflow of mandibles from below the ganekhe cabinet are hung on the house wall to the right and left sides of the cabinet. Wali maintains that man-

Fig. 4.9. The left and right sides of the ganekhe cabinet

influence of their leader to attract the donation of numerous large pigs for sacrifice. (It is pointed out that in the Yali and East region, pig mandible mementos are often hung outside underneath the roof overhang, rather than on the inside of the men's houses, as they always are in the Grand Valley and West.)

Of functional significance in Wali's sacred house are two small objects out of view behind Wali and stuck in a vertical position in the ganekhe cabinet curtain. One is a small feather that functionally is a wusa wand that is used to cleanse (deactivate) the hands and bodies of contaminating spirits at those times when a person is involved with certain sacred objects or procedures (to be discussed more fully in the next section on "function"). The other, slanting downward to the right and behind the feather, is a sacred bamboo knife that has one red feather (called *nararin*) and one white feather (called *taktak*) bound to that portion of the knife used as a handle. The red feather on the handle of the knife has symbolic meaning. It transmits to viewers that when the knife is used to make the first long cut of the skin and underlying fat layer on the underside of a pig (from snout to anus) that the meat from the pig is for *all* to eat who are participating in the ceremony.

To the left of Wali, hanging from the wall, are some drying cigarette wrapper leaves for the use of whoever put them there (fig. 4.9). Above the leaves, the jawbone end of a small pig mandible, stuck into the construction materials of the house wall, is visible. Below is what appears to be either a leaf-wrapped roll of thong fire-starting cord or rattan loop headband. Above it are two recently gisakpel-covered bundles of funeral display nets, and above them a small packet that contains something that is sacred and could not be discussed by its owner.

The many flat objects that are lashed tightly against the ceiling, only slightly more than 1 m above the floor, are coated with a black tarry residue from fireplace smoke. Wali says that the soot-browned bundle contains ceremonial exchange nets from a funeral distribution (fig. 4.10, 1987). This bundle is located alongside a blackened package that is said to contain war

Fig. 4.10. Ceiling, only slightly more than one meter above the floor

dibles from all pigs killed at sacred ceremonies in front of those men's houses with ganekhe are preserved. If they fill up one structure, then another men's house or sacred house must be constructed by the headman responsible for the rituals that produced the mandibles. The number and sizes of pig mandibles present around the margins of a ganekhe cabinet are an indication of the number of rituals performed by any given ganekhe group and an attestation to the trophy arrows. Both bundles are located on the left side of the house, near the ganekhe cabinet. The package of war trophy arrows are being maintained as a sacred war trophy relic. Both bundles are present in this same position at the time of the 1991 photography (fig. 4.7) and were also observed again in 1993.

Figure 4.11 (May 30, 1989) documents a moment of *great* anticipation on my part: the opening of the ganekhe cabinet and a look at the contents in an undisturbed context. Silometek, the guard of the ganekhe cabinet, is removing the door. Silometek has both the delegated authority from the ganekhe group leader and the ritually transmitted wusahun power to be able to maintain the ganekhe cabinet and to handle the stones. (Note the puluen stone tied to the front-center leg of the cabinet near Silometek's left knee.) Once the door had been removed, I was allowed to hold my camera inside the cabinet and take three photographs of its contents. There were ten conventionally wrapped ganekhe bundles on the grass covered floor of the cabinet, three standing unidentified objects, and two carelessly wrapped packages. Both before and after I held the camera inside the cabinet and released the shutter (three times), my hands and body were cleansed with a feather wusa wand (removed from its position on the front of the cabinet) that was waved over them, while both Wali and Silometek whispered esoteric formulae.

The moment to me was tense. The contents of the box is *most* sacred. In figure 4.11, three of the ten ganekhe packets that were within the cabinet look simple enough, but their unseen power is of mythical proportions, and they are not to be tampered with outside of wusa connotations. What, specifically, are the contents of the packets, and what would be our interpretations if they were found in the archaeological record?

Gutelu's Compound of Residence and Men's House at Jiwika

I have made naked the *power* of *The Stone* by removing it from the *ganekhe* cabinet and shedding it of its *gisakpel* wrappings. It now

Fig. 4.11. Opening the cabinet door reveals its contents.

stands upright against the center of the *ganekhe* cabinet, facing the people of the Valley [Grand Valley] so that *its power* may go forth unobstructed to make fertile all of the fields of the Valley that they may produce abundant crops of sweet potatoes, even those of my enemies, that all of the people will be of good health and without sickness, that the pigs will multiply and become abundant, with many healthy piglets, that there will no longer be wars and that the people will be safe. This I have done for the people. Maintain *The Stone* in its upright position against the *ganekhe* cabinet where I have used my authority to place it—so that *The Stone* can continue to exude its *power* to the benefit of all of the people. Defile not the salt pool [Ileukaima], but maintain it in its natural condition. Neither modernize it, nor let anyone construct buildings near it. I have set the boundary. [Gutelu Mabel's instructions to Daoke Mabel and his other sons, shortly before he died in February 1990. Gutelu (pro. Kurulu) was one of the most powerful big men living in the Grand Valley at the time modern outsiders began to move in and interrupt the Stone Age lives of the Grand Valley Dani.]

Gutelu's compound (fig. 4.12) at Jiwika is located at valley floor level, on the east-central

edge of the Grand Valley near the Mountain Wall to the east (fig. 1.21). The important Ileukaima (*ileu*, salt; *ai*, water; *ma*, place) brine pool, under Gutelu's control, is about a forty-five-minute walk/climb almost due east of Gutelu's compound up into the higher edge of the mountains. The route from Gutelu's compound is eastward across a short area of flat ground and then up the steep valley through the trees. Access to the salt pool was historically through the courtesy of Gutelu. Back a short distance into the mountains, still farther east away from the Grand Valley near the river toward Pass Valley, is the location of Wadangku, a sacred "sun house" compound controlled by Gutelu for religious purposes. Gutelu's compound is located at the junction or funneling point of three access routes to the Ileukaima salt pool from the Grand Valley floor and near two mountain routes from Yali territory. One of these is a main trade route between the Yali at Pass Valley and the Dani in the Grand Valley. By virtue of Gutelu's political power as the big man (gain) of a major Grand Valley alliance, his control and leadership of a sacred sun propitiation ceremonial center, and his control of the important Ileukaima salt pool, as well as regional trade routes between the Grand Valley and West and the Yali and East regions, it is logical that Gutelu had significant knowledge of goods that traded between the Yali and the Dani of the Grand Valley. Gutelu was the direct Dani recipient of artifacts traded from the Yali and then either retained for his own use, the use of some member of his patrilineage, or traded onward to other Dani. Did Gutelu, as a mighty gain of the Grand Valley Dani, use Yali stone tools and other objects for either profane or sacred purposes and, if so, for which, or both?

Let us look at the inside of Gutelu's men's house at Jiwika and at many of his belongings. Commencing in early June of 1991, one of Daoke Mabel's brothers acting in Daoke's absence, accepted the idea that it would be advisable to inventory his father's belongings. Work was commenced in June of 1991 and carried out intermittently over a three-year period from 1991 through May of 1993. In one sense, as work

Fig. 4.12. Gutelu's primary residence compound, located at Jiwika

progressed, I felt that we were conducting an archaeological excavation of an assemblage of artifacts that had been owned by a known high-level leader of the cultural system within which he lived.

Gutelu's compound at Jiwika (fig. 4.12) is architecturally the same as many Dani compounds, with the exception that the central courtyard is bigger than most, as is Gutelu's men's house at the far end of the courtyard. The presence and spatial relationship of six piles of burned rock are pointed out in the figure. In an archaeological construct in which only stones would be preserved, these might be the only remnant clues of the compound and cultural system within which these items were used. All of the individual cooking rocks are gray-colored limestone that were collected and then carried by about a thirty-minute walk from the base of the Cretaceous New Guinea Limestone formation, which crops out at the valley floor juncture with the rising mountain wall just west of Gutelu's compound. One pile of rocks (which could be interpreted as a small midden if found buried in the archaeological record) behind the tree in the left foreground is somewhat light-colored relative to the gray of the other piles of rocks, indicating newly sourced materials that have only been heated once or a few times. Two of the rock piles on the right are actually located against the courtyard-bounding wooden fence and two house walls. The surface of the front two-thirds of the courtyard is "grayed" with the dissemination of charcoal particles from the numerous fires that have been built through time to heat these rocks that are then moved from the fire to the steam bundles used for cooking. Today in the central portions of the Grand Valley where there are no rock walls or other structures, as the Dani move about from compound to compound and in the process abandon compounds, they move their tools and symbolic stones with them, leaving behind only a scattering of burned rocks (which are even themselves sometimes moved) as the only rock remnants of habitation.

The architectural design of Gutelu's men's house is the same as that of big man Wali's

sacred house at Yalogon (just reviewed) and of other men's houses scattered throughout the Highlands of the Grand Valley and West, only bigger. The ceiling is 124 cm high, about 15 cm higher than the average Dani men's house. Numerous banana (gisakpel) bark and other wrapped packages hang from the ceiling, the four center posts around the fireplace, and from the firewood rack above the earthen fireplace. Objects stored in Gutelu's men's house are similar to those in Wali's sacred house, only there are more of them and some of the packages are larger. The ganekhe cabinet across the back wall of the building looks the same as in Wali's and those of other men's houses, but with a thicker curtain of ferns and a few leaves (jiwi) and reed sticks that shield the contents of the cabinet from the view of people who are inside the room.

From wall to wall, below the sacrilized fern curtain of the ganekhe cabinet in Gutelu's men's house, with the exception of an open space in the center, there are three horizontal rows of crowded mandibles, most from large-sized pigs; whereas, at Wali's sacred house there are two rows of mandibles, several of smaller size than the smallest ones hung in Gutelu's house (color plate 7, May 10 1993. The top row of mandibles is difficult to see.) In Gutelu's men's house, like in Wali's sacred house, the rows of pig mandibles to the left of the cabinet door are maintained as sacred relics from ceremonials where help from the spirits was enlisted on behalf of social health and fertility (of women, female pigs, and "mother earth"); those on the right for the safety and success of warriors in battle. To the right of Gutelu's ganekhe cabinet, the back half of the right house wall is filled with crowded rows of pig mandibles (fig. 4.13); at Wali's sacred house there are only two mandibles displayed on the wall to the right of the ganekhe cabinet and none on the left. (The holes present in some of the pig mandibles in color plate 7 and figure 4.13 were human-made, through which to push out the tusks.) In the men's houses in compounds with big men of less social and political stature than either Wali or Gutelu, I have observed there are always fewer mandibles and

Fig. 4.13. Crowded rows of pig mandibles

hands, camera, and body were cleansed with a *totok* (alt. *tolok*) feather wusa ritual. I had seen this extraordinary stone in its mandated position just to the right of the ganekhe cabinet door in May and June of 1991; April, May, and June of 1992; and May of 1993. Apparently, it has never been moved, although objects around it have been. It was placed just to the right side of the ganekhe cabinet door opening, so that the ganekhe cabinet could be used without disturbing it, which was Gutelu's strong wish, made known to his family shortly before he died.

To the left of this unusual stone in color plate 7 (May 10, 1993), standing on the floor and leaning against the left side of the ganekhe cabinet opening, is a beautiful, highly polished, large puluen stone; symmetrically pointed on the proximal up-end and rounded and semi-sharpened on the distal end, variable dark green in color, with linear, eroded grooves. What might be remnants of a stripe of sacred red hematite paint (red *bimut*, alt. *pimut*) can be seen in one of these grooves in the upper-central part of the stone. This *very* sacred stone, because of its functional role as a communication link between the world of the "seen" and the world of the "unseen," is maintained in this *select* position in front of the cabinet as a special ganekhe stone, between the ganekhe stones in the cabinet above and the sacred and profane space of the men's house without. In a functional sense, the puluen, when in its position in front of the ganekhe cabinet, might be called a *"priest* stone." For example, when a ganekhe group leader, who is both in one sense a priest for the group whose function it is to "make sacrificial offerings and perform other religious rites as an intermediary between deity and worshipers" (Neufeldt and Guralnik 1988:1068), and a shaman, whose role is to influence both good and evil spirits (wherever they might be) on behalf of the group, prays before the ganekhe cabinet to the ancestor spirits, who are deified within the stones, his supplications are to the puluen, who transmits these prayers to the spirits within the ganekhe cabinet. Thus, there is a twofold communications link between the common man of the seen world and

often of a smaller size than those present in either Wali's sacred house at Yalogon or in Gutelu's men's house at Jiwika. Thus, a simple "archaeological" statement is made about the status of leadership, relative to at least one kind of sacred artifact of culture.

The first time that I was in Gutelu's men's house in Jiwika was in May of 1991, a little over a year after his death in February of 1990. I was astounded at the length of the unwrapped je stone leaning against the right side of the ganekhe cabinet opening. (This is *"The Stone"* referred to in Gutelu's instructions to his sons before his death in 1990.) Underneath the many rubbings of pig grease, I could see that *The Stone* is dark green (maybe pibit pibit). The Mabel sons told me that it was the longest such stone in the Grand Valley. Later, in June of 1991 when I photographed it, I learned the story of this particular stone from Gutelu Mabel's sons. *The Stone* is an elongate, rectangular, typical Yeineri dark green slatelike stone, 13.5 cm wide and about 121 cm long. A bit above midpoint, *The Stone* is wrapped with twenty turns of typical Dani yellow orchid fiber cording. As it is soot-blackened and has had many pig fat rubbings, I could not discern (with the aid of my flashlight) any other markings or decorations. I was not allowed to touch *The Stone*, so I could not measure its thickness or view its back side. Both before and after I photographed it, my

deified ancestral spirits of the unseen world: (1) from the people to the shaman-priest and (2) from the shaman-priest to the puluen stone and on to the spirit stones in the ganekhe cabinet. This role of a stone-spirit intermediary between the seen and unseen worlds is even more complex than it might seem from only this superficial understanding of that fact. The puluen is believed by the people to be, in a very responsible sense, the "eyes and ears" of the ganekhe-housed ancestor spirits. It is the puluen spirit who reports to the ancestor spirits in the stones the conduct of the profane aspects of "house" life. When ritual is being performed within the house and it is being used as sacred space, the puluen also observes and reports. At certain spiritual "renewal" ceremonies, the ganekhe packets are carefully removed from the ganekhe cabinet and the stones manipulated in ritual in front of the cabinet. At those times, the spirits in the stones themselves, sense what is going on within the sacred space of the house, but they do not know whether or not proper ritual protocol is being adhered to within the courtyard outside of the house. At these times, as well as at other times when the ganekhe packets are left inside the ganekhe cabinet, but ritual pig sacrifice and feasting is going on outside of the house, the puluen might be carried outside where it can observe the happenings and report back to the spirit stones within the cabinet.

The large, classical axe seen in color plate 7 and figure 4.14 was a favorite of Gutelu's that he stored on the floor of his house, within the bounds of the ganekhe cabinet. It was removed with the other items for me to photograph as a part of our inventorying project. This aged, brown bulbous axe handle with its large green and blue-black variegated-colored Yeineri-style amphibolite axe blade, with time, may become a modern symbol for the "Dani of the Stone Age." It is a type of rare tool of grand proportions that is rapidly disappearing from the Grand Valley. Daoke Mabel says that this one is now sacred. In the immediate Jiwika area, Daoke Mabel knows of only one other of similar size and beauty, and that is owned and maintained by an elderly man living in a

nearby compound. As previously discussed in chapter 2, the only use of this kind of axe was/is to longitudinally split tree trunks and large limbs; not to cut down trees or to chop wood.

During the early years of my research (1982–87), I often photographed between one and four je stones, almost always wrapped with traditional gisakpel wrapping, and often an unwrapped puluen stone leaning against the front, central part of ganekhe cabinets. In figure

Fig. 4.14. Gutelu's bulbous-type Dani axe

Fig. 4.15. The Stone, *Gutelu's most powerful spiritual object*

and also of the Gutelu *"Stone."* They could, however, be removed from this wusa context as ganekhe guardians and changed back into profane context and used as profane stones. If and when this is done, remnant spiritual power would make them especially good funeral display-exchange stones. The gisakpel wrapped stone, leaning against the leg of the ganekhe is sacred. "Gutelu's spirit is in this stone, and the stone is placed so that Gutelu will always be with us in the ganekhe house" (Daoke Mabel, May 11, 1992). The pibit pibit guardian stone between the wrapped stone and the Gutelu *"Stone"* was reportedly acting with spiritual duties on behalf of the puluen stone that was not present. Note that against the left front leg of Wali's ganekhe cabinet in his pilamo wusa at Yalogon (figs. 4.7, 4.8, and 4.9), there is a single, long, wrapped je-ganekhe stone. Wali would only say it is a sacred guardian of the cabinet. I point out that a puluen was also present behind the gisakpel-wrapped stone and tied to the leg of Wali's cabinet.

As in Wali's sacred house (and others examined in the course of the research), many bundles and wrapped objects hang from the ceiling of Gutelu's house, with the most sacred being those at the back of the house and hanging nearest to the ganekhe cabinet. A part of the ceiling, before the central cabinet door, is free of hanging objects, the intent being to keep that space open for the movement of people and the manipulation of objects in and out of the ganekhe cabinet during sacred rites. Around the wall perimeters of the ceiling toward the back of the house, the situation is different. This space is crowded with many personal and stored ceremonial relics (for detail, see Hampton 1997:517–25).

Photographs of the contents of three ganekhe packets (from the ganekhe cabinet) are shown as examples of Gutelu's ganekhe. (The contents of ganekhe packets from Wali's ganekhe cabinet are shown in a forthcoming section entitled "The Ganekhe *Hakasin* Ceremony.") Figure 4.16 shows, according to oral history as related by Daoke Mabel (1992), the adze blades, which are the original *jaga* (adze blades) of the Grand Valley that were handed

4.15 (May 11, 1992), to the right of the Gulelu *Stone,* is an unwrapped green-blue Yeineri-style je stone (7.6 cm by 74 cm). To *The Stone*'s left is a green pibit pibit je stone (9 cm by 71 cm), and to the left of that, nearest the center-left leg of the ganekhe cabinet, is a packaged stone that is 10 cm wide by 66 cm long. I was told that the two "je" adjacent to Gutelu's *Stone* had been sacralized and in the context in which they were being used, were guardians of the ganekhe down through the ancestral chain to Gutelu. All other adze blades, according to Daoke, followed. The upper photograph in figure 4.16 shows blade G-1 carefully nested on a few special leaves inside a reddish-brown cocoon cloth wrapper. The cocoon cloth packet was folded tightly and lay on a doubled-over piece of bark cloth inside a small man's carrying net. This packet, tied with string, constitutes a single "ganekhe." It is pointed out, however, that most ganekhe packets consist of an inner object or objects wrapped with or without a cocoon cloth, then two or more wrapping cloths of tree bark, all enclosed in a banana trunk (gisakpel) or *Pandanus* leaf outer wrapper and tightly tied with narrow bands of gisakpel, rattan, or string cording. The adze blade (G-1), wrapped with one single grass strand and piece of bark fiber string, lays within the cocoon cloth on several slender brownish colored leaves (jiwi and wolo by mid–Grand Valley terminology). I have not, as yet, been able to scientifically identify the jiwi and wolo leaves. The adze blade is a typical dark green Yeineri style. Included in the bundle is one black pig's tail. The ganekhe packet in the lower photograph of figure 4.16 contains two small adze blades, one a dark green-black Yeineri style (G-2), and the other a green-black Yeineri flat style (G-3). The Yeineri-style blade (ventral side up) is both wrapped with a knotted grass stem and also tied with a thin strip of bark fiber, onto which a nassa shell has been slipped. Two wolo (Grand Valley terminology) leaves are tied with about eight loops of a grass stem to the dorsal side of the Yeineri flat-style blade (dorsal side up). Both blades rest on several wolo and jiwi leaves, inside their multiple wrappings of two kinds of bark cloth, a layer of modern cloth (unique in my experience), and an outer cocoon cloth that was folded tightly within a banana trunk (gisakpel) outer wrapping.

Note that I was not allowed to touch any of the three stones in these two ganekhe bundles, nor any other *sacred* stones in the course of my research regarding these most sacred of objects. After these two bundles were closed and rewrapped, the hands and bodies of those involved were cleansed spiritually with a tradi-

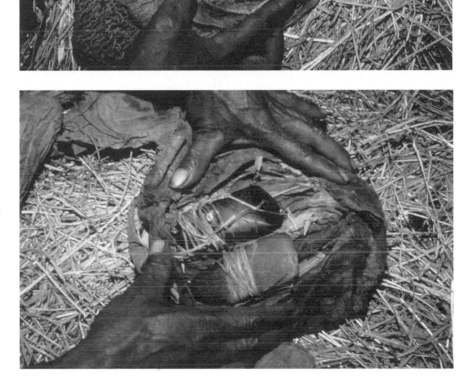

tional feather wusa wand totok procedure. Although I had not touched the objects, my camera and hands were also cleansed in a similar fashion, with a shaman waving the feather wand over my hands and camera as incantations were recited.

Ganekhe Packet No. 28 (author's identification code) is perhaps one of the informationally more significant (fig. 4.17). Underneath the traditional gisakpel wrapping is an outer dark brown-colored bark cloth, then a lighter-colored, stone-beaten, buff-colored, bark cloth, on top of which are three ganekhe stones. As in the previous two packets, the

Fig. 4.16. Two Gutelu ganekhe packets that contain Yeineri-style adze blades wrapped with strands of grass and fiber string

Fig. 4.17. A Gutelu-owned ganekhe packet contains three tool stones, each wrapped with numerous loops of grass.

stones lay on several leaves of the same kind of plant (wolo) as is tied to stone G-3. In addition to the stones and leaves, there are two buff-colored pig tails within the packets. Daoke Mabel informed me that the white moldy-looking coating on the stones is not "mold" as I thought when the packet was opened, but is white clay, rubbed onto the stones for ritual purposes. (From top to bottom, I coded the stones Nos. G-4, G-5, and G-6.) I did not touch the stones as I crouched over them for measurements (tape held away from the stones), visual analysis, and two quick photographs. Stones G-4 and G-6 are Langda-Sela-style stone knives, similar to those that I have seen in common use as profane cutting tools throughout the entire Yali and East region. Knife blade G-4, at the top of the photograph, is about 4 cm wide (widest point) and 18.5 cm long. It is gray(?) in color. Knife G-6, at the bottom of the photograph, is about 4.2 cm wide by 9.7 cm long and gray in color. The ganekhe stone between the two Langda-Sela-style knives is a green-black Yeineri flat-style adze/axe blade about 32.5 cm long by about 7 cm wide. Knife G-4 is wrapped with about thirteen loops of a special grass; axe/adze blade G-5 with about eighteen loops of grass, and knife G-6 with about nineteen loops of grass, and underneath the grass, several loops of a bark fiber string. The stone objects with their grass blade ties, two pig tails, and leaves are wrapped in three inner layers of a heavy bark cloth, one a dark brown, and the other layers a

buff color. When secured as a ganekhe packet, the bark cloths are folded over the contents of the packet and then secured in an outer layer of tightly folded dry outer covering of a banana trunk (gisakpel). This entire packet is tightly bound with narrow strips of gisakpel when stored. Some similar looking ganekhe bundles are secured with a strong bark fiber braided cording (kopi in the mid–Grand Valley dialect) of the same kind that is used to tether pigs. Another significant, but difficult to photograph quickly, of the Gutela ganekhe packets contained a traditional Langda-Sela linear adze blade as the ganekhe stone.

In color plate 8, a relatively large bundle is seen suspended against the right wall of the men's house, just to the right of the right end of the ganekhe cabinet. Whereas all other large bundles are hanging from the wall or the ceiling with their long dimensions vertically, this bundle hangs with its long dimension horizontally. Above the bundle, some soot-browned and blackened pig mandibles hang against the wall with a small scattering of fern leaves. It would appear that the motif of the closed ganekhe cabinet to the left of this bundle has been extended along the wall beyond the closure of the ganekhe box to include this large bundle. Actually, *it is being* treated as a ganekhe packet—the largest that I have had the opportunity to observe, although it is maintained outside the ganekhe cabinet. Do the contents include one or more long stones, a number of individual ganekhe packets, or what? On June 12, 1991, I was told what was in the bundle, but the bundle was not opened. In 1992, I again photographed the bundle in its same hanging position but was not allowed to see its contents. On May 10, 1993, a brief cleansing ritual was performed and the bundle opened. First, it was laid on the grassy floor of the house. After the tie strips of gisakpel bark were unwound and the outer covering removed, one could see a very large, conventional ganekhe bundle inside a beautifully crafted carrying net. It was immediately apparent by the tight, evenly spaced loops that the net was crafted by the Yali, not the Dani, Western Dani, Damal, or Wano (chapter 1). An unusually large ganekhe packet was removed from the nicely crafted carrying net. It was neatly tied with dark brown braided fiber cording (kopi). As the packet was laid open, its torn outer covering of dark brown bark cloth was placed on the grass-covered house floor. Next was a large newer-looking buff-colored piece of bark cloth, followed by the typical reddish-brown bark cloth that I was becoming accustomed to seeing used as an inner wrapping of ganekhe objects. The inner three layers of bark cloth wrappings form a cushioned "blanket" on which leaves (jiwi and wolo) and grass furnish the nesting material upon which lay seven pig-fat-anointed, soot-browned and -blackened human jawbones and three clavicle, two of which can be seen in the lower photograph of the figure. The front of each jawbone is wrapped with many individual loops of grass that may have been put on the jawbones at different times, as distinguished by color variances of the grass loops (color plate 8). White teeth can be seen emerging through the grass stem wrappings on at least two of the jawbones. The long, slender leaves that can be seen lying in the packet on the outer sides of the jawbones are from the jiwi plant. Leaves from this plant are often maintained with sacred ganekhe objects as well as used for other sacred purposes. As can be seen in color plate 8, the human jawbones lay nested inside of each other. In whispered voices (so hopefully the ghosts and spirits would not hear) the story of the jawbones was told.

Since the same story was related to me during the two preceding years, and again in the year of 1993 when I was first allowed to see and photograph the jawbones, it would seem that this is at least what the Gutelu Mabel descendent sons wanted me to know and believe. These seven jawbones, according to the story, are from seven male ancestors, each one from "the" big man of seven contiguous generations, genealogically flowing and contemporaneously touching in the ganekhe packet from the viewers left (oldest) to right (most recent). The jawbones from the seven big men, each the son of a previous big man, are relics of an unbroken chain of patrilineage descent. The jawbone on the reader's left comes from the first *human*

from which "all" succeeding humans descended. According to several similar origin myths told within the Grand Valley and West region, the first human was preceded by a mythical "god-power" (chapter 1). The first human spirit power, located within this first jawbone is so sacred, so spiritually powerful, that it is taboo to speak its name. (Hence, I was never told the name of this "first human spirit power.") This first jawbone represents (domiciled within) the people's *most powerful* ancestor god-spirit, whom I will henceforth call Unspoken-Name. Second from the left is the jawbone of one of the sons of Unspoken-Name who is known as Aula (alt. Aulusa). The third jawbone is from Aula's son named Walimo (alt. Bukale), the fourth jawbone from his son known today as Umo (alt. Wumo), the fifth jawbone from Umo's son Akalunonggo, and the sixth from Akalunonggo's son who is known as Filiak. From oral history, it is said that Filiak did not want to be cremated, but requested that upon his death the people mummify his body and henceforth keep it forever. As we can see, the people did not do this; instead, they preserved only the jawbone and cremated the remainder of his body. The seventh or end jawbone on the right is said to be from Filiak's son Yagathbuk (alt. Haliheli). According to this genealogy, Yagathbuk was the father of Wamena from whom the Highlands' town of Wamena (first a traditional compound, then a hamlet, and now a growing modern town) derived its name. Wamena was Gutelu Mabel's father and representative of the eighth generation in line of descent. Consequently, by the Mabel patrilineage origin myth, Gutelu is in the ninth generation from the first human in the Grand Valley, and Gutelu's son, Daoke Mabel, a member of the tenth generation. Three of the Mabel informants say that the three short bones alongside the jawbones in the ganekhe bundle are human collar bones (clavicles) that were from people eaten by the ancestors (two seen in color plate 8). These bones are called *agosiok*.

Under questioning about the bundle of human jawbones my informants replied that Unspoken-Name consumed all of himself by cremation except his jaw, so the people decided to make it sacred and saved it. This is the origin, as related by the Mabels, of the custom of cremation in the Highlands. The custom of saving human jawbones by the Gutelu Mabel patrilineage was apparently abandoned at the death of Wamena. But the practice of ancestor worship strongly endures as one aspect of the Highlanders' complex belief system (chapter 1).

Within the Mabel brother's story of their genealogy and the revelation of ancestor worship by the preservation and sacralization of ancestor jawbones, the Mabels briefly mentioned cannibalism but did not elaborate on the subject. From my own research during the period 1982–84 in areas away from Jiwika, I suspected that cannibalism was an integral part of ancestor worship (at least in scattered areas throughout the Grand Valley and its environs). Indigenous informants of different Grand Valley and West language groups made innuendoes relating cannibalism to ancestral religious ritual, and two different informants stated that "select parts" of deceased ancestors were "sometimes" consumed to perpetuate "life power" (chapter 1). From a theoretical viewpoint, it would seem that such an act of holy communion at the time of death of an ancestor would, from the actors' perspectives, either help a recipient receive supernatural spirit from an ancestor or at least establish an early rapport between the living and the ghost/spirit of the recently deceased. If this were the case, even in only isolated incidents, a seeming paradox exists regarding the practice of cannibalism in the Highlands because of other incidents where enemies' bodies are known to have been cannibalized as parts of victory celebrations or to disgrace the dead enemy's living cohorts (chapter 1). The literature contains numerous references to theoretical aspects of cannibalism and practical premises such as that cannibalism was practiced to offset protein starvation. Further presentation on the topic is outside the scope of this book.

A House Plan for Its Material Contents and Places of Worship

The spatial arrangement of artifacts of culture within both Highlander men's houses that are located in normal habitation sites, as well as those special sacred houses that are secreted away in isolated locales, adhere to a common house plan. To an uninitiated modern outsider visiting Highlands' men's houses, "the plan" might not at first glance be recognized, but it is there.

House content can be grouped into five categories for functional and spatial analyses: personal belongings, house furnishings, counter ghost/spirit objects, relics, and ganekhe cabinet and ganekhe objects. Personal profane belongings are maintained around the perimeter of the house floor, on the house wall, and attached to or hanging from the ceiling. The reader is referred to figure 4.18 to see the spatial relationships of the other four of these five categories of cultural artifacts, which are the categories that define the use of sacred space. In figure 4.18, the numbered artifact items indicate *representative* kinds of objects in each of the four categories and their location in space.

House furnishings on floor level:

(1) barkwood potato skin trash receptacle
(2) gourds for drinking water
(3) bamboo fire "bellows" tube
(4) reed cigarette holders
(5/6) hammerstones and anvils, and in addition to the numbered items, one or more thong and stick fire-starting tools

Counter ghost/spirit objects from ceiling or fireplace supports:

(7) packaged sacred objects with supernatural power
(8) supernaturally powerful spider web necklace
(9) stone amulets with supernatural qualities
(10) empowered string necklace (dibat) to protect the house
(11) sali stick to cleanse the area of malevolent ghost spirits
(12) power packet
(13) soot-blackened arrow

Relics hanging from ceiling or wall and on floor (some sacred):

(14) bundle of ceremonial nets from a
    funeral exchange
(15) bundle of war trophies
(16) wealth items from exchange rituals
(17) sacred bamboo knives (to be saved)
    and sometimes relic sanctified pig fat
(18) objects "from the ancestors"

(19) bundle of sacred relics (which in this
    special case contain Gutelu and
    Daoke Mabel's bundle of human
    ancestor jawbones and clavicles that
    are ganekhe
(20) jerak from funeral distribution
(21) sacred ancestor relics and/or trophies

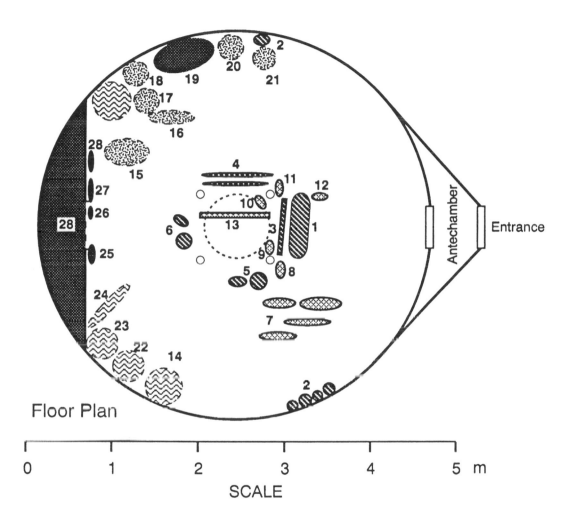

Floor Plan

SCALE
0   1   2   3   4   5 m

 House furnishings on floor level

Counter ghost/spirit objects from ceiling or fireplace supports

Religious relics hanging from ceiling or wall (some *wusa*)

Religious relics standing on floor (some *wusa*)

 Ganekhe Cabinet and *ganekhe* objects outside of cabinet

*Fig. 4.18. Placement of objects
defines use of sacred space.*

(22) bundle of war trophies

(23) bundle of nets with ritual attached pig tail mementos *(su walon)*

(24) bundle of arrows collected as trophies of war

Ganekhe cabinet and ganekhe objects outside of cabinet:

(25) puluen stone (guardian and "go-between"—see text)

(26) sacred je stone (guardian of the ganekhe)

(27) sacred je (in this case Gutelu's *Stone*)

(28) sacred je (guardian of the ganekhe, and/or ancestral spirit je)

(29) ganekhe cabinet, the box container for the sacred stones

In addition, mandibles from sacrificed pigs are maintained as religious mementos and icons beneath and sometimes to the sides of the ganekhe cabinet.

What we see by the plan at the back of the house is the ganekhe cabinet and its adjacent sacred objects. The ganekhe cabinet is the box for the supernaturally most powerful and revered items. Below and to each side of the cabinet is the space for religious relics. To the front of the house are those items with supernatural power that are advantageously located to protect the sacred space and its contents at the back of the house from potentially malicious intruders from the spirit world. In the following sections by examining function within sacred space, it will become clear that parts of the floors of the men's houses, usually used as routine profane space, are readily converted to altars during times of sacred ritual.

At the Highlands' people's places of worship (men's houses; scattered, isolated, and sacred houses; and sacred houses [pilamo wusa] with their adjoining courtyards) there are places for the most sacred and supernaturally powerful of objects (the ganekhe cabinets), places for religious relics, indoor and outdoor ground altars, places for the ganekhe religious groups with their shaman leaders, and places for the general people (both initiated and uninitiated (figs. 4.19

and 4.20). During religious ceremonies, the uninitiated (all females, very young boys before initiation) and outsiders are restricted to the compound courtyard, with its outdoor altar and nearby cooking pits. The shaman ceremonial leaders and members of the ganekhe group on whose grounds a particular ceremony is being held are authorized to freely come and go between the men's house and the courtyard, depending on their personal desires and ritual duties. Attendance at meditational rites may be restricted to only the leader of the ganekhe group of that particular sacred place and the resident guardian of the ganekhe. Most rituals are, however, conducted for all members of the ganekhe group, and others are for the ganekhe members and their guests. Some ceremonials, such as funerals, are open not only to invited guests of a particular ganekhe group who live nearby but also to both the initiated and uninitiated who might come from afar.

Spirit Power, the Power Circle, and Ancestral Spirits

From the viewpoint of a cultural systems analysis, the cumulative spirit power in the unseen world of the Irian Jaya Highlanders is formidable. Hundreds, maybe even thousands, of other-than-human-originated individual spirit types abound, all of which seem to be evil (chapter 1), the supernatural power of the sun is awesome, and the ancestral spirits never die but just increase in number. Both the positive and negative aspects of this power must be considered when people in the seen world are establishing, building, and maintaining social relations with the ghosts and spirits in the unseen world. Successful contradiction of malicious acts from the ghosts and spirits and some measure of control of the potentially positive power of ancestral spirits, as well as the perpetuation of the beneficial power of the sun can be understood as tantamount to success for those living in the world of the seen. How, to the esoteric groups dealing with this unseen supernatural power, is something so powerful, so potentially precious, beneficially perpetuated and controlled? It must have taken a great deal of evolved mental agonizing, group learning,

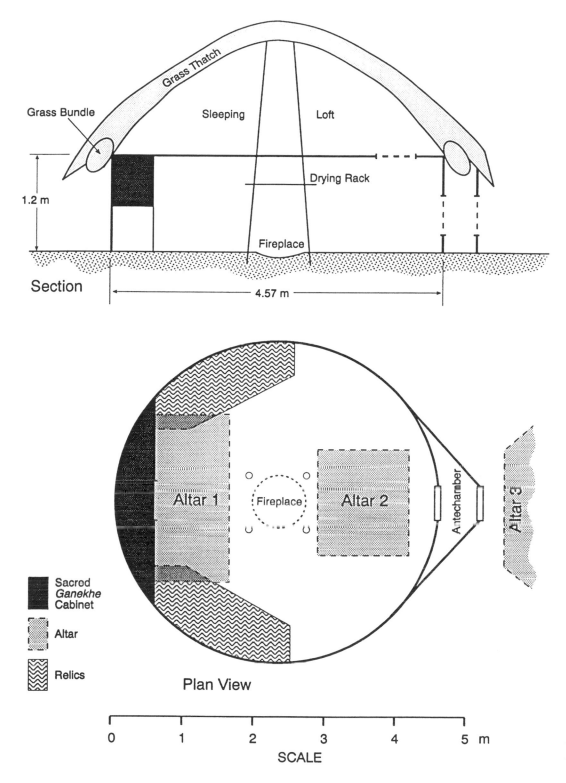

Section

Grass Thatch

Grass Bundle

Sleeping

Loft

Drying Rack

Fireplace

1.2 m

4.57 m

Altar 1

Fireplace

Altar 2

Antechamber

Altar 3

Sacred
Ganekhe
Cabinet

Altar

Relics

Plan View

0   1   2   3   4   5 m

SCALE

Fig. 4.19. Plan view of use of sacred space

and planning to first evolve a strategy for dealing with the world of the unseen and to then develop a tactical plan to activate the strategy. The strategy was to venerate, propitiate, and manipulate ancestral spirits, to propitiate the sun power, and to both placate and take contradictory measures against all malevolent ghosts and spirits. In tactically pursuing such a plan, do the people in general, or at least their shaman leaders, enter the world of the unseen to

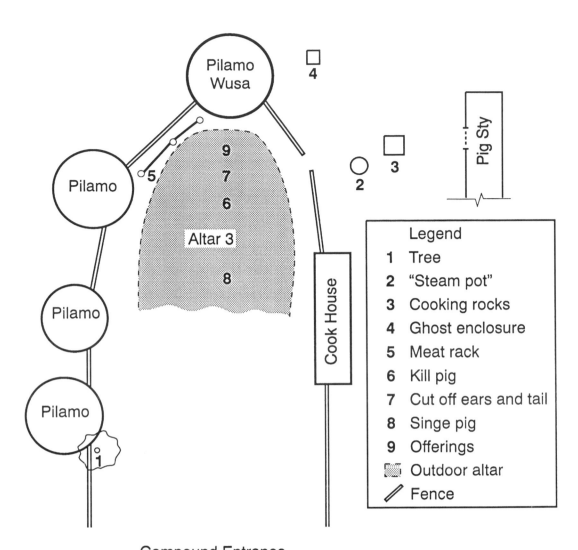

Fig. 4.20. Sacred compound at Yalogon

Legend

1 Tree
2 "Steam pot"
3 Cooking rocks
4 Ghost enclosure
5 Meat rack
6 Kill pig
7 Cut off ears and tail
8 Singe pig
9 Offerings
▨ Outdoor altar
╱ Fence

Compound Entrance

directly interface with ghosts and spirits to plead their cases? Are sacrifices and offerings made to placate the spirits and to attempt to gain favors from them through propitiation? Is it possible to identify general principles that are at play and have cross-cultural and temporal commonality, the hope being that by identifying such principles we can gain confidence in the uses of the material goods involved (and of similar ones preserved in the archaeological record) from which to interpret behavior?

Within the hierophany of the sacred space of the men's house, its contents, and adjoining outdoor sacrificial ground altar (figs. 4.19 and 4.20), the presence of supernatural ancestral spirit power manifests itself during ritual in grand proportions in a never-ending con-

tinuum or circle of power, or the *power circle*, as I call it. From time to time, additional power is added to the circle by the installation of another ancestral spirit into another ganekhe sacred stone or other suitable object. The individual and cumulative power that is already within the power circle is nurtured and rejuvenated by periodic ritual. At the same time that the power is being moved about in a seemingly complex symbiotic relationship between objects, pigs, and humans, it is being propitiated to commit heroic beneficial deeds on behalf of the religious ganekhe groups that attempt to control the power.

Individual ghosts (new power) are born into the world of the unseen at the time of death of each human. The soul matter (or edai egen, "singing seeds of life") departs the deceased to become a ghost. With maturity (subjectively understood only within the esoteric group), the ghost passes through a metamorphosis to become an ancestor spirit (chapter 1). At different times religious ganekhe group meetings are called by group leaders for the purpose of conducting one of several different sacrificial rituals. All members of the religious ganekhe group are expected to be present. During the rituals, supernatural power, which seemingly effervesces constantly from the individual ancestral stones (the ganekhe) and which also combines to form an aura of immense unified power within the ganekhe cabinet, is transferred from object to object, object to person, person to object, person to person, and object to object to sacred pig. The people in this power circle are the shamans (wusahun). To the people involved, the power is awesome. For an outside researcher it is difficult to know where to enter this never-ending flow of power to analyze and describe it from a nonparticipating secular view-point. It seems that this supernatural power, of and from the unseen world, just *is*. It does not seem to have a beginning or an end, but just *is*.

Supernatural power is added to the power source in the world of the unseen with the addition of each new ghost that has been created by the death of a human individual. The ghost is first thought to enter the ghost bundle *(wagun ai)* during a cremation (chapter 1). Some informants say that they feel each ghost first goes to the compound bone enclosure after each cremation to tarry a bit with its bone remnants before moving on to the sacred, secluded ancestral ghost house. Regardless, at whatever time that it is decided by a human individual to venerate a specific ghost-spirit and to formally recognize it as a personified *ancestral spirit,* that particular spirit entity is lured, from wherever it might be living, into a select stone, which at the time of installation becomes a personified ancestral spirit stone, a ganekhe. Ganekhe are passed down from generation to generation and it is not often that a spirit stone is replaced or a new ancestral spirit otherwise installed into a stone and added to a ganekhe collection.

A ganekhe is thought of and treated not just as a "house" where the spirit takes up residence (much like a human being in a traditional house), but as the *body* for the yet-living spirit *power* of a deceased human being. This is why ganekhe objects are sometimes thought and talked about as "spirit bones" within the indigenous population. Wali, Hanomuak, and Aluk say that when a new ganekhe is to be created, the sponsor lays out all of the stones from which he might choose: display-exchange je, profane tool stones, geologically shaped stones and oddities that he may have collected, and other candidates that might be acquired from within his family. The man then visually studies this collection and meditates (maybe for days) until a choice is made for him through a divination.

The Highlanders selectively choose ancestor spirits for veneration and installation into ganekhe from deceased leaders within their patrilineages of *ancestor beings,* omitting the spirits from men who were of small social or political consequence. They feel that if a man were a powerful gain that his departed spirit, if propitiated to advantage, would be a much stronger ally than, for example, the spirit from a man who was of less influence and power in his community.

As previously stated, the perpetuation of the life of an ancestral being (empowered single ganekhe stone) can be achieved by the inheritance and continued *maintenance* of stones already vitalized with spirit. The creation of a new spiritual being is through the selection of a body ("spirit bones," which is a profane stone, or rarely, another kind of material object) and the installation of a personified ancestral spirit into the body through an appropriate sacred ritual, often a ganekhe hakasin. The body, then, is the rock, which once installed with an ancestral spirit is the complete spiritual entity: the ganekhe. The room (or living space) for the spiritual entity is the ganekhe packet. The stone is nested and maintained in its packet with symbolic materials that its owner or caretaker (both the individual owner and the ganekhe group shaman leader) feels will ensure a measure of physical comfort and mental well-being to the spirit that dwells within. The Highlanders state that although there are female ghosts and spirits, it is only the male spirits that are installed into the stones to create ancestor beings.

It is felt by the ganekhe groups that the ancestor individuals (ganekhe stones) like to either stand or lay on their backs. Only during periods of temporary discomfort might an ancestor stone in a prone position roll over and turn or toss about (and thereby cause earthquakes, a belief of the local inhabitants). Thus, the ganekhe groups either stand the stones vertically or lay them on their backs. It is further felt that when the internal spirit power of any ancestor stone departs its body, to travel about and later return, it does so through the head. To be able to please and to not cause discomfort to the ancestors, the owners of the stones go to great lengths to orient the stones properly. If there is a slight curvature in a stone, it is felt among the eso-teric group that the concave side is the front of the individual, and should thus face upward when the individual is placed in a prone posi-tion. Sometimes, it is difficult even for the owner of a stone to remember which side he has identified as the front. In such a case he might lay a single feather on the front side of the ganekhe stone within the ganekhe packet. Occasionally, to assist those manually manipu-lating a ganekhe packet, a single feather or stem of a plant might be wrapped to the out-side of the packet to indicate the orientation of the stone within.

Once during a tremor in the middle of the night, I asked Wali why there was an earth-quake. He sleepily informed me that one of the ganekhe had probably rolled over. In the morn-ing when we could discuss the matter, Wali said that the after-shocks were caused because the ganekhe tossed and turned until it was again comfortable on its back.

Through periodic ritual, the ancestral spirit beings (personified spirits within sacred sym-bolic stone bodies) are fed, beautified, prayed to, sacrifices made to them, and their spirit power revitalized. Such repeated acts have been called "ancestor worship."

Spirits within Sacred Space

Four classes of guardian spirits live within each ganekhe cabinet and its adjoining space: (1) Pasoware, (2) Abut (alt. hale), (3) Asugum, and (4) Unspoken-Name. Pasoware is the universal guardian spirit that domiciles in each dibat, either worn around the necks of human indi-viduals (chapter 1) or tied around sacred ob-jects. Abut (alt. hale), considered to be the son of Pasoware, is, like Pasoware, thought of as a single spirit but with the capability of being present everywhere at once. Abut's sole func-tion is to protect Unspoken-Name, the most powerful guardian spirit of all. Asugum is thought of as the general clan power, whose job is to protect the many clans and individuals of the clans. Asugum might be thought of in a slightly different way as the ancestral spirit power that manifests itself as any of the numer-ous personified ancestral spirits, which are installed as individual entities into individual ganekhe stones. The fourth kind of guardian spirit is Unspoken-Name, which is so powerful that the people do not say its name. Unspoken-Name's function is to be the guardian of the human leader of the clan. Unspoken-Name, like Asugum, is an ancestral spirit that dwells within a ganekhe inside the cabinet. Three different informants, including Wali and Hanomuak, asserted that they themselves (as individual leaders of three different ganekhe groups) did not know which stone of their own ganekhe is Unspoken-Name. This was under-stood and respected by me as a ploy by these men so that I would not encourage any of them to identify the personification of Unspoken-Name within their own ganekhe cabinets.

The spirit within the puluen stone, which leans against the left central outer front leg of the ganekhe cabinet, is called Waganilan Wagnailan (alt. kinoke). This spirit entity is in all puluen stones and may be the second most powerful spirit that is among the array of an-cestral spirits that are centralized within the ganekhe cabinets. Waganilan Wagnailan is installed within each puluen in a sacrificial ritual, when the stone is anointed with sacred pig grease and the shaman leader directs the spirit into the stone. Waganilan (used hereafter as an abbreviation for Waganilan Wagnailan) within puluen is rejuvenated from time to time with sacred pig fat rubbings.

Although all four groups (or types) of spirits that domicile in and around all ganekhe cabinets are ancestral in nature, it is clear that each ganekhe group worships and installs individual ancestor spirits from their own patrilineage, including their own Unspoken-Name. Therefore, within a single patrilineage, separate ganekhe groups may be venerating and worshiping different specific ancestors, but all from the same patrilineage.

The Ganekhe Hakasin Ceremony

The ganekhe hakasin ceremony (ganekhe, sacred stones; hakasin, to make) is the most sacred and powerful ritual practiced by the Highlanders to deal with their fundamental life issues: health, food, procreation, and enemies. When called for by a ganekhe group leader to deal primarily with war concerns, the ceremony is formatted slightly differently and in mid–Grand Valley Dani dialect is called a *wim ganekhe hakasin* (*wim*, war). Supernatural power in the form of ancestral spiritual entities is present during either ritual. This power is simultaneously feared, worshiped, propitiated, perpetuated, and moved about. Meticulous attention to ritual doctrine is enforced by the ganekhe group leader, or else it is believed that the endeavor might not only fail, but the ancestral spirits become upset and take malicious action against the people.

Each ganekhe group conducts its own ganekhe hakasin at least once a year; although usually it is more often—whenever the ganekhe group leader feels the need. This is the time of the most holy communion for the members of the ganekhe group with their venerated ancestral spirits (god-power). Pig sacrifices and food offerings are made to the ancestor stones as they are venerated and propitiated in a most holy atmosphere in a sacred place, while the men enter into direct communion with the spirits in both the world of the seen and, by extensionalism, into the world of the unseen. It

is at the ganekhe hakasin ceremony when the power in the stones is rejuvenated and when supernatural power, both emanating from the stones and the shaman leader, is manipulated within the power circle. It is during some of these ceremonies that newly selected ancestor spirits are installed into their "spirit bones."

During the ganekhe hakasin ceremony, very audible and visual emotional peaks are reached by both the pigs being sacrificed and the human participants, as the humans strive to make contact with and beneficially influence the ancestral spirits. For years I have searched for the use of hallucinogens that the human participants in the Highlands might use to assist in these endeavors. To date, I have identified no chemical substance as a candidate for such function, other than ordinary tobacco, which is incessantly smoked but which I believe does not necessarily play a hallucinogenic role in the ganekhe hakasin, although at other times it is used to enhance a relaxed, dreamy state. I have observed people going into trance states with exercise-induced exhaustion, sometimes assisted by rhythmic chanting or the clapping of hands (chapter 1), but never any hallucinogenic experience promoted by the ingestion of natural (or other) chemicals. Wali and two others have alluded to the idea (but not directly stated) that he and certain others with wusahun can see spirits in the unseen world. How, I have always wondered.

There are about twenty members in Wali's ganekhe group at Yalogon, of which seventeen are listed below. All are members of the Wilil patrilineage: Wali Wilil, Silometek Wilil, Asudek Wilil, Elapinmo Wilil, Kolo Wilil, Sokalik Wilil, Ilae Wilil, Kuluka Wilil, Alela Wilil, Sikabelek Wilil, Tomali Wilil, Holitnabolok Wilil, Ababin Wilil, Tuanoba Wilil, Abitmo Wilil, Segiarek Wilil, and Wimoba Wilil. In addition, Wali considers those men, such as Hamomoak Wilil, a first cousin and leader of his own ganekhe group, and a few others who are close advisors, as having special rights to be involved in wusa consultation on matters of utmost importance.

By invitation, I arrived at Yalogon at about 8:00 A.M. on the first day of a ganekhe hakasin with only one indigenous inhabitant who had been approved by the ganekhe group as my assistant. Few people were in sight; only four men, whom I did not know. They obviously knew who I was, as they were members of Wali's ganekhe group. Two of them showed me to an abandoned pig sty in the compound garden, between the interior courtyard and the outer compound fence, indicating that this was my private space for the duration of the ceremony. Wali had not arrived as yet. I set my gear down, walked around the compound, and then entered the sacred men's house (pilamo wusa, fig. 4.20) carrying my camera, notebook, tape recorder, and a water bottle. Several old men, already in the house and seated to the right of the entrance welcomed me with the conventional greeting, "narok." I sat by the left side of the door where I could observe what was happening outside as well as in. There was a smoldering fire in the fireplace. The inside of the house looked as it always had at other times I had been there. Significantly, the same puluen I had seen before was leaning against a center leg below the lower left side of the ganekhe cabinet door. The four men inside the house carried on small talk. Aluka, a close friend of Wali's, picked up the bamboo tube "bellows" and gently blew through the tube against the barely glowing embers. I noted the presence of a packet of sacred sticks that was tied to the right front leg of the four roof support poles.

Outside, men began to gather, one or two at a time. A few women came, carrying nets of very large sweet potatoes and some greens and ferns. These were placed in a front corner of the interior courtyard near the sacred house. Other women carried bundles of grass, some of which they put in the interior courtyard near the sacred house, and some loads they carried through a courtyard gate to deposit nearby in the compound garden. After depositing their loads, most of the women left the compound, but a few entered the communal cookhouse (fig. 4.20).

I wanted to walk around outside to see what was going on throughout the compound, but I did not leave my spot inside the sacred house. If anything were to be done relative to the ganekhe cabinet and objects therein I wanted to

be there to observe. At one point I heard new male arrivals herding two pigs. It seemed that they may have taken the pigs back to the pig sty where I had stacked my belongings. Some pig grunts and a squeal alerted my attention to another man carrying another pig toward that same pig sty where I assumed the first pigs had been taken. These pigs were to be the sacrifices for the ceremony which was to ensue.

At about 9:00 A.M., Wali, walking alone, entered his sacred compound of Yalogon. He called out to members of his ganekhe group, who were either in the sacred house or seated in the courtyard nearby. His enthusiastic greeting of "wa, wa, wa" was answered with a chorus of "wa, wa, wa, wa" from the members of the ganekhe group. There were handshakes and hugs as Wali quickly moved about the courtyard greeting each man there in this traditional style, before entering the sacred house and going through the same procedure. Wali was obviously pleased. There was a smile on his face during the greetings, and the individuals of the ganekhe group responded with the same enthusiasm. They obviously enjoyed gathering to celebrate the ganekhe hakasin, the time of intimate communion with their much-worshiped ancestor spirits. Wali, at this moment in time, was acting in the capacities of a high priest and the shaman leader: he was the priest who would be the sacrificer and who would direct the sacrificial ritual. He was also the shaman who would enter the world of the unseen and plead the cases for his ganekhe group and others in the community.

When Wali entered the sacred house, in addition to me there were perhaps eight members of Wali's ganekhe group present. Wali acknowledged my presence with a smile and a modestly spoken narok. While exchanging information with his staff of ganekhe advisors and giving instructions, Wali sat on the floor and began to untie a very small gisakpel wrapped packet. This packet is called an ilelegeke (alt. jerabo). Inside were bits of sweet potato peelings, the ends of smoked-down cigarettes, and bits of unsmoked tobacco. I was told these are items that Wali's ancestor spirits had collected from enemy compounds and were then secretly placed in Wali's habitation men's house, after which Wali collected and carefully wrapped into the small ilelegeke packet. After Wali unwrapped the packet and showed the contents to his ganekhe group, he carefully rewrapped the items. Ritual recitations, directed to the ancestor spirits, were briefly recited by Wali and the men present in the pilamo wusa. All leaned forward toward the ilelegeke and pointed their fingers toward it. Then Wali hung the ilelegeke from the ceiling in front of the fireplace. It was placed alongside the soot-blackened ilelegeke that I had first photographed hanging at this same spot on May 30, 1991, but at that time did not know either its contents or significance. The newly hung ilelegeke was being put in place at the time of this ceremony to help direct the ancestral spirits to take action against enemies of the group. The materials reportedly collected from the enemies, act, as it were, in the same fashion as giving the scent to a hunting dog of the animal or person to be hunted. The hanging of an ilelegeke seems to be a part of the initiation of magical procedures that can be ongoing for a period of years—maybe even as long as an ilelegeke is left hanging in the line of flight of out-of-body spirits leaving the ganekhe to attack an enemy.

Other items at ceiling positions, which were also previously recorded, included: from left to right, a soot-darkened bundle of ferns from a 1991 sacrificial ritual hung in front of the front left center post; a vertically hanging narrow packet of sali sticks; from the wood rack by the right-front leg of the fireplace, a bundle of seven spiked cocoons (pumpalep); and in front of the previously mentioned blackened ilelegeke, a packet of wooden sticks that are sometimes used to toss to young people in the courtyard at the close of certain ceremonies. Two relatively newly hung cowrie shells (jeraken) are seen to the left, and a piece of medicinally used gami wood bark to the right.

Wali relaxed into a sitting position on the grassy floor while he adorned himself with a construction of brightly colored parrot tail feathers, that would become the upright focal point of a headband, and two yellow-white feathers that he carefully stuck into his red and white net cap. Very large sweet potatoes had already been laid on Altar 2, between the entrance and the fireplace, both as offerings to show the ancestral spirits what was to be cooked for them and to absorb supernatural power from those spirit stones within the cabinet before the sweet potatoes would be removed and cooked. Later the cooked sweet potatoes would be returned to the altar below the ganekhe cabinet where the spirits above would enjoy the essence from them, while the potatoes would commensurately be absorbing supernatural power from the spirit stones. The sanctified potatoes would ultimately be fed to wusa pigs that were being raised for yet another sacrificial ceremony. Wali was apparently pleased with the size and quantity of the potatoes. He continued conversation with those in the house and now and then would look through the entrance and shout instructions to members of the ganekhe group, who were building a pile of sweet potatoes on Altar 3 outside of the entrance to the pilamo wusa. These were also considered an offering to the spirits, but perhaps more importantly at this point in time in the early stages of the ritual, it was to show the spirits the effort that was being made on their behalf.

Wali suddenly turned quite serious. He was seated on the edge of a banana leaf near the fireplace while he contemplated a packet laid next to him. I did not know what was in that packet. A man crouched over and entered the house, shaking hands all around and quietly acknowledging "Wali" before he disappeared into the darkness of the back of the house. Wali replied "wa, wa." More men clambered in and seated themselves. I estimated that there were about twenty men crowded into the pilamo wusa—perhaps the entire ganekhe group. Wali talked rapidly, slipping easily back and forth into the wusa ane religious language, which had been handed down from the ancestors and which had been perpetuated among the shamans. Everyone else was silent. With head partially bowed, Wali simultaneously emitted a drawn out cry, then short, high-pitched crying yips as he pressed both of his eyeballs into their sockets with his thumbs. His hands were on each side of his head. He kept pressing his eyes with his thumbs. The look on his face was one of pain, mixed with ecstasy. I could not believe the degree with which Wali put pressure on his eyes. Tears began to run down his face. Wali, the shaman, the wusahun, had entered the "other world," the world of the unseen, and without the visible use of chemical hallucinogens but by the pressure-induced phosphene

Fig. 4.21. Three of the largest sweet potatoes lay next to the sacred packets.

experience (manuscript in progress). He was making this contact to act as intermediary for his entire group with spirits in the world of the unseen. As he maintained the pressure on his eyes, his head remained bowed in a state of deep concentration. Tears continued to run down his checks as he commenced the very sacred proceedings by expounding formulae. Others of the ganekhe group joined in and followed Wali's wailing. After a short time, Wali released the pressure on his eyes. The wailing continued and soon all were expressing themselves in a choruslike dirge, intermittently following Wali's sobbing incantations directed to the spirits—the cumulative god-power in the world of the unseen. Wali and his ganekhe group were now pleading before the ancestral spirits. They were saying that they were ashamed at the small size of the potatoes that were being offered, that they knew their sacrificial pigs were too little and too few. But in spite of all these inadequacies, would the spirits please forgive them and act positively on their behalf?

Abruptly, the wailing and incantations ceased. Wali raised his head and looked at the people in the house and told them how glad he was that they had come for this occasion. He addressed the group with enthusiastic repetitions of "*wa-wa-wa-wa-wa.*" Some of the men then moved outside the house to spread more grass in front of the sacred house, to ready the rocks for heating, the steam pit for cooking, and the outdoor altar for the pig sacrifices.

Inside the sacred house, Silometek, keeper of the stones, was directed to open the ganekhe cabinet and lay the ganekhe packets onto the banana leaves that had been set down in front of the cabinet on the area designated as Altar 1 (fig. 4.19). The stones, in their ten sacred packets, were removed from the cabinet and laid out in the same relative position in which they were routinely maintained inside the cabinet. After Silometek had correctly positioned the stones, he requested that Asudak, another member of the ganekhe group, bring him three of the biggest potatoes. Silometek set them on the altar next to the ganekhe packets (fig. 4.21). These potatoes would absorb supernatural power from the ganekhe objects before being cooked and then passed to certain ganekhe group members, who would later feed the pieces of sacralized potatoes to wusa pigs, which were being raised under their supervision. Other large sweet potatoes were brought into the pilamo wusa and laid out on Altar 2 to likewise absorb supernatural power from the ganekhe before being cooked with sacred pig meat in the outdoor steam bundle.

Activities associated with the ganekhe hakasin outside the sacred house took place within the interior courtyard in front of the entrance to the sacred house and nearby within the compound garden that is located between the courtyard fence and the outer compound fence (fig. 4.20). While Wali was still inside the sacred house, several members of the ganekhe group, following normal procedure, cleaned up the area around the permanently located ghost enclosure *(waro leget)* (fig. 4.20) while others cleaned out the previously used earthen fireplace and reconstructed an outdoor furnace to heat the cooking rocks.

In figure 4.22, a man in a yellow net string cap can be seen cleaning the old heating rocks and dried grass debris from the continuously used cooking pit. The largest rocks are those that had been previously used, after they had been heated in a nearby fire, to line the base of the 38 cm deep, conically shaped pit. Once the pit had been cleared of the previously used rocks and grass debris, the base for a new steam bundle was fashioned with a lining of three different kinds of grasses that had been carried and stocked at Yalogon earlier in the morning for just this purpose. Bundles of the fresh grass, used to line the cooking pit and to scatter as a ground cover for the outdoor altar, can be seen piled with freshly cut ferns and other greens in one corner of the compound near the cooking pit. Three different kinds of grasses were splayed out in a fan shape from the center of the pit as the new cooking pit was prepared. On the bottom was a kind of grass called *jalenka;* next, *silak;* and on top, *oojekka/kukaba.*

Nearby (#3 on fig. 4.20), a square-shaped open fire box was built in which to heat the rocks for cooking. This is the conventional

Fig. 4.22. The cooking pit is cleaned of rocks and debris.

outdoor open furnace in which rocks are heated for steam bundle cooking throughout the Highlands. First, a square of the desired dimensions was outlined on the ground with unsplit logs called *helege*. Second, a large number of cooking rocks *(hekit)* were spread within the square and covered with a ceiling of closely spaced split logs *(elem)*, which rested on the unsplit log perimeter of the fireplace. Next a second row of split logs *(ebe)* was laid parallel, one next to the other, and closely spaced in a transverse direction to the first layer of logs. These two layers of split logs furnish both a good supply of fuel for the fire that would heat the rocks and a sturdy floor on which to pile a second layer of heating rocks. The open furnace can be built higher with additional intermittent layers of split logs and rock or made of smaller outside dimensions, to fit the need. For funeral pyres, a special kind of wood, high in resin content, is used in similarly built open furnaces so that the fire will continue to burn, regardless of sudden downpours.

While part of the ganekhe group was completing the preparation of the cooking pit by piling logs in the outdoor open furnace for heating the cooking rocks, others of the ganekhe group greeted the few invited guests, who seated themselves on the ground in the central courtyard, leaning casually against the fence at the edge of ground Altar 3 (fig. 4.20). Most, perhaps all, were relatives of Wali's. For example, one was Siba Himan (Pua's brother), who is a nephew of Wali's by virtue of his mother being Wali's sister. Another big man, Hubi Walalua, a brother-in-law of Wali's, came from a compound on Sekan Ridge. These men had come out of respect for their deceased friends and to demonstrate their continued reverence to the ghosts and spirits.

Final dirges were wailed and incantations recited before Wali emerged from the sacred house. The ganekhe group, through this action and their own individual meditation, had prepared both themselves and the spirits for the live sacrifices that were about to take place. To the Highlanders, the moment of sacrifice is both an essential and fearful time. It is known that the ancestral ghosts and spirits must be placated by such acts, but the pigs are themselves mostly wusa, having been thoughtfully raised and given special care and attention. Many have become an extended part of the human family of any given compound. They have been nurtured, held, and cared for almost as nuclear members of a family. The pigs possess their own soul matter (edai egen). These souls, which are about to become pig ghosts by the sacrificial arrow, must be properly addressed in the sacrificial rites, so that the wrath of the ancestral spirits, as well as those of the pigs, will not become agitated or enraged.

At this particular ganekhe hakasin five pigs were sacrificed. Although the number of sacrificial pig offerings vary from ganekhe hakasin to ganekhe hakasin, at least one of the pigs must be a large sacred pig that has been raised specifically for this purpose and fed, from time to time, sweet potatoes that have been sacralized at yet other ceremonies. Usually all of the pigs for the ganekhe hakasin are sacred and raised according to proper protocol. At this particular ceremony, the pig donors were Wali himself, giver of the largest pig and one smaller pig; Wene Wilil, giver of a medium-sized pig; Abibmo Wilil, giver of a small pig; and, from outside the ganekhe group, Ulap Walilo. The small pig donated by Ulap was called the ilelegeke pig and was sacrificed specifically to ensure action by the ancestral spirits against the owner of the sorcery items (ilelegeke). The cooked meat from this sacred pig would only be eaten by a trio of members called the *aikmali*, consisting of Wali, Hanomoak, and Ulap.

During the early afternoon, while the steam bundle was being built, ganekhe group members were gathering numerous long, freshly cut blades of a special grass that were brought into the pilamo wusa, to be consecrated for use later that night and on into the early morning hours of the next day. Each grass stem was rubbed with sacred pig fat by Silometek and another of the authorized shamans, who at the same time chanted religious formulae. Supernatural power was being transferred into each stem of grass as it was anointed with the fat and chanted over. Seven to twelve stems were then stretched at one time above the banana leaf covering of Altar 2, in front of the fireplace, before each bundle was knotted and laid on the altar. Throughout the remainder of the day, these functionally important bundles would continue to absorb spirit power from the ganekhe packets that had already been laid out on Altar 1, below the ganekhe cabinet (alt. *opalek*), as would the three large sweet potatoes that had been set next to the ganekhe packets (fig. 4.21). That night and into the next day these grass stems would be used as the grass stem dibat that would be wrapped individually onto each of the sacred ganekhe objects, furnishing us analogues of behavior that we might consider when contemplating inferred behavior associated with similar grass stem-tied objects found worldwide in the archaeological record.

In this ganekhe hakarioki version of the ganekhe hakasin ceremony, it is considered quite important that an ilelegeke (or aikmali) pig be killed to please the spirits of the ancestors so that they will bless the people for what the people have done. If an ilelegeke bundle is presented, and an ilelegeke pig is not sacrificed, the ancestor spirits, according to Wali and Hanomoak, might go on a rampage and wreak havoc against the people—even against entire compounds of people. The aikmali staff is the group who is responsible for proper protocol of the ceremony. The meat of the ilelegeke pig is routinely dedicated to this group.

Earlier in the day before the pig sacrifices, the area of sacrifice, identified as Altar 3 on figure 4.20, was covered with freshly cut grass. Sweet potatoes had been set on this grass in front of the entrance into the pilamo wusa to both absorb power from the ganekhe within and to show the spirits and human attendees what was being done on behalf of the spirits. Beyond the grass-covered area of Altar 3, toward the central part of the courtyard, a fire would be lighted at the proper time on which to singe the sacrificed pigs before butchering them.

At the time of sacrifice, each pig, unless unusually large, is lifted above the ground of the altar and held feet down by the sacrificer's assistants. One or two men hold the rump of the pig, while the head is held by one or two others. The sacrificer, who is the leader of the ganekhe group conducting the rites (or the big man leader in charge of cross ganekhe group ceremonials), kills each pig in the same fashion. He leans forward toward the pig, or crouches lower in a similar position, braces himself, and shoots the pig in the heart just behind a foreleg with a very sharp bamboo-tipped arrow. As the sacrificer draws the bowstring, he almost touches the side of the pig with the arrow tip. Onlookers take on a solemn countenance. This is serious business. *A life is being sacrificed.* The ghosts and spirits are being placated. The procedure must be properly conducted. At the moment of impact of the arrow, the pig howls and cries loudly. It is set down on the ground where it runs or wanders around, mortally wounded, then falls over and dies. If the arrow misses the heart, the procedure is repeated. For me, the sacrifice is extremely unpleasant to watch, document, and listen to. At such sacrifices, I usually could sense varying degrees of this same emotion being felt by the ritual participants. I once asked Wali about the killing procedure which does not seem to necessarily bring death quickly. He replied that this killing method is a custom passed down from the ancestors; this is the way they want it.

When Wali shot the biggest pig, the pig did not die immediately. After it was dead, Wali recited religious chants and cried. The pig, although owned by Wali, was cared for by his daughter Aku, who was one of Obaharok's wives. The prolonged death of the pig was taken as a strong indication that both the soul/ghost of the pig and the spirit of Obaharok were objecting to Wali killing the pig. This was a very bad sign. Wali had to make supplications. He had to make amends for killing the pig. He earnestly promised Obaharok's spirit that at the next stage of Obaharok's funeral during the coming year, he would kill a pig for Obaharok's spirit that would be at least as big as the pig just sacrificed at this ritual.

The last pig killed was the small one brought by Ulap and designated as the ilelegeke pig. After it was killed, Wali again cried and esoteric incantations were recited, interspersed with Wali's sobbing. I have never heard Wali cry so

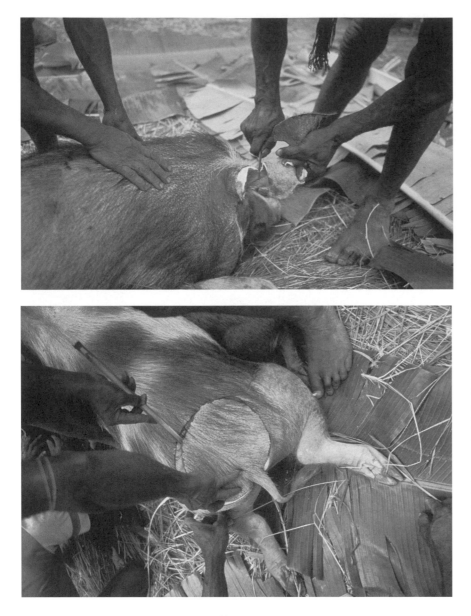

Fig. 4.23. The ears and tail are cut off with a bamboo knife.

respectfully treated—just as members of a living human family. After the pigs were so adorned, then, as is the custom at all sacrificial ceremonies, the pigs' tails and ears were cut off with bamboo knives (fig. 4.23). These sacred mementos of the occasion were laid onto a fresh banana leaf and removed to the sacred house, where they were displayed on Altar 2, in front of the fireplace.

Symbolically, the nogen placed on the back of a pig after sacrificial death is thought to protect the pig's soul-spirit from embarrassment before the soul departs the pig to become a ghost, just like a woman's carrying net, hanging down her back and over her buttocks protects her from mortification by humans. It is also thought that a net, pulled down over the gaping wound caused by removal of a part of the rump with the tail (on the larger pigs), will restrict bleeding. Blood spilled on the barren ground is a dangerous omen for onlookers. The moment the net is lifted off the pig, its soul-spirit departs the body to become a pig ghost. Butchering can then proceed without offending the pig.

Before the first pig was carried to an open fire, which was burning near the center of the courtyard, to singe off its hair, available members of the ganekhe group bent over the pig and pressed their hands on the pig in a group effort to beneficially influence human ghosts to act on their behalf because of the sacrifice. At about this time in the ceremony, the wood-rock furnace was lighted with burning tinder that had been ignited by a traditional thong-split stick fire-starting tool (#3 on fig. 4.20 and fig. 4.24). As the wood burned down, the rocks were heated until they were finally hot enough to be moved with large wooden tongs and a grass handle from the fire pit to the steam bundle (#2 on fig. 4.20 and fig. 4.25). Inside the pilamo wusa, the ears and pig tails were on display on an indoor altar in front of the fireplace, along with a pile of large sweet potatoes that were being empowered by the ganekhe, on the other side of the fireplace.

A circular area, within the confines of the larger grass-covered outdoor altar, had been designated as the butchering site for the pigs.

loudly or so vociferously. This is the way it is at a ganekhe hakasin in the Highlands. When dealing with the ghosts and spirits, feelings are not muted nor concealed. The ghosts and spirits are either rudely shouted at to get their attention or loudly wailed to in persuasive dirges.

After the pigs had been sacrificed, a woman's *nogen*, an essential item of female attire, was laid on the back of each pig. Symbolically, the dead pigs, each wearing a nogen, were on display to assure humans in the audience, the ghosts of the pigs, and the ghosts and spirits of ·departed humans that the pigs were being

This area can always be identified by a mantle of freshly cut ferns (sometimes, also with banana leaves) that have been transported from nearby for the occasion. (The butchering site is identified by #6 and 7 in figure 4.20.) In figure 4.26, one can see the pile of sweet potatoes (with a few yams and taro roots) on the grass matting of the altar before the door of the sacred house and adjacent to the butchering area, which is distinguished by a matting of fresh ferns overlaying fresh grass. The ferns themselves may have been growing in a wusa area that is preserved to furnish ferns for just such sacred rituals. These ferns play an integral role within the power circle because they catch the blood from the recently sacrificed pigs, often at a time before the soul-spirit has departed from the pigs, and it is these ritually used ferns that compose the organic curtain for the important ganekhe cabinet. None of the blood during butchering is allowed to be spilled onto barren ground—only on the fern or on banana leaves that are carefully placed to catch the blood. During the butchering process, the ferns are used to mop up blood from within the carcasses—this blood is supernaturally powerful. The bloodied ferns are then cooked in the steam bundle with the meat. Upon removal of the ferns from the steam bundle, some are spread onto the same circular part of the outdoor altar where the cooked pig meat will be laid for further distribution. Some are placed indoors over the grass of Altar 2, on which both pig meat and cooked sweet potatoes are set as offerings to the ancestral spirits of the ganekhe, before the tangible food is eaten by the ganekhe group staff. Some of these ferns may be eaten by participants later on when they are partaking of the sacred pig meat. Others of the sanctified ferns may be added to the curtain of ferns that cover the front side of the ganekhe cabinet. Power has been introduced into these ferns through ritual so that they, in turn, become a shielding curtain for the ganekhe. While hanging in place as the curtain on the ganekhe cabinet, the ferns continue to receive power from within the cabinet.

After burning the hair off the pigs, they are accumulated at the butchering site and ori-

ented so that their heads face the compound entrance and their tail-ends face the doorway of the sacred house. The largest pig is centered, its removed hide and attached fat layer kept whole after removing the meat, the mandible, and intestines. Informants at this ganekhe hakasin said that this common orientation of the pigs during butchering is so that the power of the pigs themselves is directed toward the entrance of the compound and acts as a contradiction to sorcery that might be practiced against someone at the ceremony. Also, the men themselves, while they are butchering, are in a good position to see anyone who might enter the compound. If an enemy would enter or

Fig. 4.24. Rocks are heated in an open furnace.

Fig. 4.25. The largest heating rocks are moved with a grass handle and wooden tongs.

the ganekhe cabinet, was carefully severed from the upper jaw. I have never seen an adze used for this purpose. An entire pig can be dismembered at its joints with only bamboo knives, although a stone adze is also usually used. It is only when a pig is halved along the backbone or broken apart transversely to the backbone that a stone adze is *always* used, along with a bamboo knife. For convenience, the tail of a small pig is severed from the body with a stone adze. For cutting up meat, ligaments, and tendons the Highlanders consider the bamboo knife superior to the stone knife (and even in most cases, where I have been an observer, to the recently introduced steel knife). Even when butchering larger pigs, a bamboo knife is the tool of choice (fig. 4.28).

The intestines and other innards were separated from the rest of the meat, placed on bamboo leaves, and carried to a water source and meticulously cleaned and voided of internal food and fecal material. Then, these choice pieces were carried back to the compound, some hung on the meat rack outdoors to dry overnight for use the next day (#5 on fig. 4.20), and some hung inside the sacred house for the same purpose. Choice pieces of meat were also hung from the outdoor meat rack as well as from the ceiling inside the sacred house. The intestines and meat hung inside the sacred house were saved primarily from the largest pig to be used as a food offering after being cooked the next day, with the spirits to partake of the essence of the meat and the ganekhe staff of the meat itself.

At this point in the procedure, spatial relationships of material goods within the sacred space of the worship area are reviewed. Outside of the sacred house, the pig meat was being readied for cooking on a circular mat of sacralized fern leaves (#7 on fig. 4.20). The pile of large sweet potatoes were still located at position #9 on the outdoor altar where, I was told, they continued to absorb power from the ganekhe spirit stones from within the sacred house. Inside the doorway of the pilamo wusa, the very large sweet potatoes were still displayed before the ganekhe, from which they absorbed sacred power. Wali appeared pleased,

someone whom they might suspect of coming to use sorcery against them, they can take appropriate countermeasures.

The men worked rapidly and efficiently with bamboo knives while butchering (figs. 4.27 and 4.28). While the pigs were being butchered, they were, as always, laying on the fern ground cover and not on just the underlying mat of fresh grasses. Here, as is the custom, first a pig was laid on its back and then one or two long cuts were made with a bamboo knife from snout to anus (fig. 4.27). The lower jaw (mandible), which ultimately became a sacred memento of the sacrifice to be hung below or to the sides of

presumably by both the state of the proceedings and the quality of the offerings. If one did not know Wali as a big man, he is identified as a person with supernatural power (wusahun) by the single cowrie shell worn on his dibat. A newly wrapped small power packet was commingled with the select, very large sweet potatoes on Altar 2 to also absorb power from the ganekhe. The ears and five pig tails from the sacrificial pigs were also present on Altar 2, laid out on a large banana leaf that was located between the potatoes and the fireplace. The tails from the smaller pigs would be wrapped in leaves to protect them from being burned, then dried by the fire and tied to a sacred net *(su walon)*, which is maintained in the pilamo wusa as a sacred relic. Sometimes a single tail or two are introduced to the ganekhe packets themselves or utilized in other ways as power objects. The tail from the largest pig, with the attached disk of pig fat, would be wrapped in a leaf bundle and steamed outdoors with the pig meat, the fat later cut away and preserved, to be used as a sacred ointment—the tail itself to be preserved as a sacred object like the other tails. On Altar 1, below the ganekhe cabinet, the ganekhe packets were still in their positions in an arrangement that was similar spatially to the way that these same ancestor stones were maintained inside the ganekhe cabinet. Alongside the ganekhe packets were the three largest sweet potatoes that had been set there earlier in the proceedings (fig. 4.21). Leaned up against the front left leg of the ganekhe cabinet was the unadorned puluen stone.

At this time in the ceremony, there were ten men in the sacred house. Of the ten, I noted that two, in addition to Wali, were shamans (wusahun), as indicated by the single cowrie shell that was strung on their dibat. All ten men were wearing dibat. Nine were dressed traditionally and one man in a T-shirt and shorts. One of the men also wore a piece of gami bark as an amulet around his neck. Most of the ten were smoking traditional tobacco in their carefully rolled leaf wrappers *(wisaken)*. All of these men ingested the smoke as they inhaled with an audible sucking sound, though I could not detect that the men were using tobacco to pre-

parc themselves for an hallucinogenic experience or that anything unusual was about to happen. Wali himself, as usual, was visiting enthusiastically with abrupt changes of tone of voice while the others of the group seemed to be listening to him and indicating, with brief utterances, concurrence with what their religious group leader was saying.

Then the mood changed abruptly. Inside the sacred house all became silent. Wali bowed his head, once again pressing his eyeballs with his index fingers and in a pleading voice began to make supplications to the ancestral spirits in the world of the unseen. He shed some tears. The group of worshipers, both sitting and squatting about the sacred space of the sacred house, lowered their heads. Most pressed their

Fig. 4.26. A pile of tubers is accumulated on the sacrificial and butchering site.

Fig. 4.27. Men work rapidly with bamboo knives to butcher small pigs.

own eyeballs with their index fingers and began to audibly respond to Wali's brief incantations. Wali and the men were jointly experiencing the dimensions of the unknown world, the world of the unseen by each of the group concurrently controlling his own phosphene experience. With emotionally toned supplications, amid flowing tears from Wali and brief, tearfully recanted dirges from the group, the ancestral spirits seen to be moving about in the indi-

vidually produced unseen world of phosphenes as well as those spirits felt by the group to be before them in the ganekhe, were addressed. Then, suddenly, the pressure was removed from the eyes. Wali stopped crying. The solemn mood of the group changed just as rapidly as it had begun. Wali looked up and called out with a different tone of voice, "*Wa, wa, wa, wa ne wa, ne wa, ne wa, ne wa, wa, wa, wa, wa, wa, wa, wa, wa.*" (In the context of this use, Bromley

[1981:176] feels that *"wa"* literally means "come" and that *"ne"* means either "you" or "place.") After offering emotionally presented apologetic supplications of inadequacies to the spirits, the shaman leader of the ritual group had changed his tone of voice and invited (almost demanded) that the great spirit "come to this place" to "see what we do for you" and to accept the sacrifice and offerings. Wali then gave verbal instructions to those of the ganekhe group within the sacred house before leaning toward the entranceway and shouting instructions to the men who were dealing with pig meat and the cooking pit outside.

Soon there was a flurry of activity around the cooking area (#2 and 3 on fig. 4.20) as a circular rim of fern leaves (and a few other special kinds of leaves) were spread within the cooking pit and around its margins, covering the long grasses that had been splayed out from the center in the shape of a circle on the ground. Next, a layer of fresh grass was laid over the leaves into the pit and around its edges. From the adjacent supply of hot rocks, the largest were first selected to be set into the bottom of the pit (fig. 4.25). Note in figure 4.25 that the first and possibly the largest rock to be transported from the heating furnace to the cooking pit was carried with a spontaneously made handle of grass stems, rather than the more conventionally used large split wooden tongs. The large rocks that were observed being tightly packed into the bottom of the shallow pit were insulated underneath and around their perimeter by the packed soil in which the pit was dug. In this position the large rocks furnished a massive heat source at the base of the oven from which the heat flowed upward through the steaming mass of repeated layers of sweet potatoes, grasses, pig meat, ferns, and smaller heating rocks. The grass and leaf interlayers that were added between food and hot rocks as the steam bundle was built vertically were sourced from nearby bundles, which had been soaked in water to keep the grass and leaves from burning and to add a source of moisture from which steam would be created. As the cooking unit grew, loops of rattan "rope" were tightly secured around the cooking bundle

to preserve its integrity. Each time a new loop of rattan was added and pulled tightly around the bundle, the splayed grass that formed the base was concurrently pulled up between the rattan and the bundle and laid over each loop and out away from the bundle, so that this outer side-covering of grass was slowly worked upward as the bundle grew.

People moved rapidly as a well-formed work party, building the bundle. No one person stood out as the leader in charge, but all felt free to give advice to each other. The process was a buzz of verbosity, but tempers rarely flared. Care was taken not to get burned with

Fig. 4.28. Bamboo knives are the tools of choice.

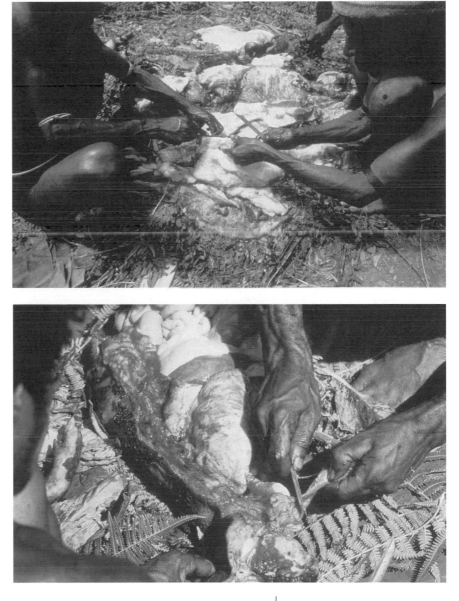

the hot rocks and not to burn one another. On this particular occasion of building a steam bundle, the participants were all male, but at many pig sacrifice celebrations, such as at funerals and weddings, women participate in the courtyard. In those circumstances, the men and women can join together as a common work party to build the cooking bundle, but always, it is the men who are solely responsible to kill and butcher the pigs. Both men or women can clean out the cook pit. When a new pit is to be dug, it is a man's job. The men build the outdoor open furnace and load it with fuel logs and the rocks that are to be heated. Men and women together carry heated stones with wooden tongs and add them to the cooking bundle, as sweet potatoes and other tubers, often greens, and chunks of pig meat are added—also by men and women alike. These are times of mutual cooperation by members of both sexes in a joint endeavor. Individuals of either sex may, from time to time, douse the contents with water from a gourd. The men are responsible to wrap and bind the growing steam bundle as it is being built. But in the special case of a ganekhe hakasin, all of the activities are considered to be wusa and there are no female participants.

At this particular ganekhe hakasin, as the steam bundle was nearing completion, the hide and fat layer of the entire carcass of the largest pig, called the *wam oat*, was flattened on the top of the cooking bundle. Next, grasses were added over the flattened pig carcass and overlain by heated rocks, then more grass was added. The contents were doused again with water. Then a layer of fresh banana leaves was laid across the top for insulation, after which still more grasses were added. The grasses that had been initially laid out in a circular fashion on the ground from the center of the then-empty cooking pit, were lifted above the last loop of rattan and folded over the top. Some more grass was scattered on top of the steam bundle and the final loops of rattan tightened around the outer circumference of the cooking "vessel" to secure it while its contents steamed. A couple of sections of the trunks of banana trees, a large wooden limb, and some dried gisakpel that was handy were haphazardly

thrown onto the top of the bundle, as a final lid to secure it. One participant looked on thoughtfully as he rested against his rock tongs.

While the meat and sweet potatoes *(hiperi)* cooked (for about one and a half hours), Agalela Wilil, came over to show me how he had cut off the tips of four of his fingers at a sacrificial funeral ritual in honor of his uncle Yagar Waliaken, killed by enemies in a battle at Minugibaka hill near Pugima. Agalela hobbled about with a club foot, with only a trace of toenail sticking up from the front of the club. It was not a propitious time for me to photograph this unusual (in the Highlands) deformity. Agalela said that his fingers were amputated out of a motivation of grief and to placate not only the ghost of his uncle but also the unified "big power." (I am unsure of his meaning of "big power.")

When the bundle was opened, amid loudly shouted instructions by Wali, the steamed ferns were placed on the front side of the outdoor altar to provide a circular ground cover on which to lay out the sacred food (#7 and 9 on fig. 4.20). Some fresh banana leaves, with a few edible greens and ferns were laid on Altar 2 inside the adjoining sacred house. Cooked food, consisting of pig meat and fat from the five pigs, sweet potatoes, and the few yams and taro tubers, was then set out in a conventional arrangement on the cooked ferns in front of the sacred house. Around the outer circumference of this ground altar-table, small accumulations of sweet potatoes were set out at spaced intervals. The largest sweet potatoes, which had earlier been blessed and sanctified, were held back at the cooking bundle. The intact pig skin with its attached layer of fat, the wam oat, was placed on the fern ground cover with its head end facing the compound entrance. Its tail end faced the entrance of the sacred house, just as it did during the butchering process. The rest of the cooked pig meat from the other four pigs was set out in piles in and among the accumulations of sweet potatoes and also in the center of the fern covered "table" area. The pig tails were placed directly in front of the entrance to the sacred house: the four from the smaller pigs were wrapped in a banana leaf and the single largest tail, with its still-attached chunk of fat, was set to one side, all with their tail tips toward the entrance of the sacred house. A single very large sweet potato was set next to the largest tail. This single "largest" potato would later be set inside the sacred house on the banana leaf and fern leaf covering of Altar 2 (fig. 4.20). At that time it would be blessed as an offering to the powerful Unspoken-Name ancestral spirit, who domiciles within one of the ganekhe stones. At a later time in the ritual, the potato would be divided by Wali into several pieces and sent back to more than one compound where the precious potato meat would be fed to living wusa pigs that are themselves destined to one day be sacrificed to the ancestors.

In just one day, this single large potato, while manipulated within the "power circle," had been displayed in an uncooked condition on both Altars 1 and 2 inside the sacred house where it had reportedly been appraised and supposedly accepted for a food offering to the ancestral spirits by Waganilan, the powerful spirit within the puluen stone. At the same time the potato was also absorbing spirit power from the ancestral spirits within the nearby ganekhe stones on Altar 1 (fig. 4.19). It was further sanctified by then being cooked with the ceremonial ferns and sacred pig meat before it was replaced on the indoor altar and its essence offered as food for the most powerful ancestor spirit of all who domiciled within one of the ganekhe stones. Again, simultaneously with this religious act, the tangible potato absorbed additional spirit power from the sacred stones before it was to be fed to sacred pigs that would one day be sacrificed for these same spirit ancestors, who were, on this very day, passing along some of their supernatural power to the pigs via this sweet potato.

But for now, the table had been set. Earth was its base. The freshly cut grasses on the ground in the area of the outdoor altar furnished a clean pad for the overlying "tablecloth" of fern stems and leaves. The table was arranged to include the sacred foodstuffs, the sanctified pig fat, and the pig tails, which would be preserved in the sacred space of the sacred house as religious relics from this particular occasion.

The adult male members of the ganekhe group and the guests assembled around the outer circumference of the fern covered ritual ground altar. A few men stood, but most were seated on the ground with folded legs or legs outstretched. Some even leaned against the adjoining courtyard fence as they waited for the special meal to begin. A few young boys played in the area of the cooking pit and open furnace outside of the courtyard (#2 and 3 on fig. 4.20). No females were to be seen; although some were quietly present within the communal cookhouse (fig. 4.20). This was to be a special meal as part of a very special ceremony. Overall the ceremony was a communion between a segment of the Wilil patrilineage with the clan ancestral spirits who were present inside ganekhe stones within the adjacent sacred house. It was this group and their few special guests who participated in the outdoor meal.

It was now about 3:45 P.M., and it had started to rain. Wali stepped out from the sacred house and walked directly to the wam oat where it lay on the fern-covered altar. As he started to cut the slab into strips of skin and fat with his bamboo knife, he shouted loudly at the rain spirits to stop the rain! It continued to drizzle but not to rain hard. The strips of cooked pig skin and attached fat are considered to be ritual delicacies. Momentarily they would be eaten with both relish and reverence as Wali passed them out to the attendees. (Such strips of skin and fat are also used as symbols for communication, such as at those times when designated couriers carry like-strips of skin-fat to big men throughout clan groups, and sometimes even to designated big men throughout a political confederacy to announce a call to forthcoming ritual events.) As Wali, the central figure on the altar, worked fast with his bamboo knife, the men in attendance began to partake of sweet potatoes that were before them and to sample small bits of pig meat. Now and again small boys would dash in from the adjoining area to be given a sweet potato or a bit of meat, and then dash back to "their" area to eat with their comrades.

Wali walked about in solemn pleasure handing out strips of pig skin and fat to each attendee. He continued to watch and assure himself that everyone was getting sweet potatoes, pig meat, and fat to eat. The light drizzle did not seem to dampen the enthusiasm of the occasion, but it did hinder my photography.

After everyone had been supplied with fat, some very large pieces of pig meat (by my estimate weighing about 7 kg) were carried by one of the staff of the ganekhe group into the sacred house. The remainder of the pig fat was then picked up by Wimoba, Wali's second oldest son. (Wimoba may follow in his father's footsteps as a big man.) Wimoba disappeared into the sacred house and deposited the pig skin and fat just inside the entranceway onto the floor covering of banana leaves and greens that had been spread over the floor of Altar 2 (fig. 4.19). At this time, Wali was still circling about outdoors among the ganekhe group and guests. A dwarf, who lived with Wali, was present, getting his fill of sweet potatoes and meat. The dwarf was healthy, happy appearing, quite muscular, but was deaf and dumb. He liked to arm wrestle with the bigger men who played roughly with him in a loving way. The dwarf and those about him communicated by "signing."

As eating and visiting continued outdoors around the area of Altar 3, a staff member of the ganekhe group carried a small whole-cooked pig from the fern-covered area into the sacred house to set it on the banana leaves of Altar 2. Silometek Wilil, the "keeper of the stones" for Wali and the group, spoke to all from the center of the fern-covered outdoor altar. He uttered a few sentences in an esoteric religious dialect and then assured those present that the ritual protocol of the ancestors was being followed. Everyone was assured that the sacrifices had been properly made and that "Your blood will not be spilled" by the act. Wali watched as a small bundle, consisting of the cooked shoulder of a pig, some fat and greens, were wrapped and tied into a banana leaf and left in the center of the eating area. This bundled food would be eaten later in the night during a continuation of the ritual proceedings, after all guests had departed Yalogon. From in front of the entranceway of the sacred house,

Silometek solemnly advised that later during the night the "holy communion" with the stones would be celebrated inside the sacred house. Four of the largest sweet potatoes were carried from the dismantled steam bundle and set in the center of the outdoor circle of fern leaves between the banana leaf bundle of meat, fat, and greens, and the door of the sacred house. Soon a fifth large potato was placed in line with the other four potatoes.

Two of the very large cooked sweet potatoes that had been carried earlier into the sacred house and blessed by a shaman in front of the ganekhe stones were brought out of the sacred house and added to the five very large potatoes that had just been accumulated into one pile. While this was going on the men continued eating. One man carefully cut his apportioned pig fat into very small pieces with a bamboo knife as he continued to eat with a loud sucking-chewing noise. The men were eating both yellow-meated and white-meated sweet potatoes. I do not know what happened to the few yams and taro tubers that had been cooked.

At this time, from the uneaten sweet potatoes (but not from the seven largest that had been recently accumulated in a single group), Wali distributed what were obviously choice potatoes to select guests and members of his ganekhe group. He loudly called out the names of certain individuals (thereby alerting both those human beings in attendance and the ghosts and spirits), identifying the especially devoted, "giving" members of the ganekhe group, before placing an especially large potato in the hand of each acknowledged recipient. This procedure is reminiscent of the way that jerak and je stones are distributed from display bundles at funerals (chapters 1 and 3).

At 4:00 P.M. the men were still eating, cleaning every morsel of meat and fat off the bones and pig skin. Wali called to Yamake, one of his wives who was in the cookhouse where she had been out of sight in seclusion all day with other women of the nuclear family. Yamake brought her carrying net and Wali lined the bottom of the net with cooked fern greens from the outdoor altar before he carefully loaded the seven largest sweet potatoes that had been accumulated at the front of the altar into the net. During the day those potatoes had been first blessed by Wali, presented as offerings to the ancestor spirits (ganekhe), and enriched with supernatural power that emanated from the stones. Now the potatoes would be carried to Wali's habitation compound and fed by Yamake to specific wusa pigs, which were being raised to be used as future sacrifices. Other men in the ganekhe group, who were going to return home for the night, loaded a few of the sanctified large sweet potatoes into their carrying nets as they said their good-byes and commenced to leave Yalogon, hoping to arrive home before darkness set in.

The inner corps, or "staff" of the ganekhe group stayed on at Yalogon to continue with the ongoing ritual and especially to be available later during the night for the intimate holy communion with the ancestor spirits domiciled in the stones and the rejuvenation of their power.

Ancestor Stone Packets
(Ganekhe) and Their Empowerment
At dusk, as the last of the ritual participants who were going home left Yalogon, the members of the ganekhe group who were staying for the nighttime activities split up, some to take care of corporate ritual matters and others to seek out privacy after a day of continuous activity. I suspected that two or three of the men returned to an adjoining sacred compound with its leader Hanomoak. Wali and three others of the ganekhe staff (plus me) retired to the sacred house where the others would quietly discuss matters of group concern and relax. The fire was stoked. After a short time, Silemotek Wilil, the Yalogon resident guard, took leave to go to his own house, which is one of those that opens onto the Yalogon courtyard (*pilamo*, fig. 4.20). Wali and the others remaining in the sacred house whispered to each other and napped from time to time. I, likewise, napped with them. We were spread out around the margins of the room. Cooked sweet potatoes, greens, and pig meat occupied the space on Altar 2. The ten ganekhe packets lay on banana leaves on Altar 1, just as they had been placed earlier in the day.

One or two men at a time would come and go in the outdoor darkness of nighttime and the almost completely dark room of the sacred house. The only light was from a flickering fire that outlined bodies as occasionally a man would enter, whisper for a few moments, and then depart. The brief conversations were always hushed, as the men wanted to avoid disturbing ancestor spirits that were also within the sacred space and that might also be resting or sleeping.

At about 10:00 P.M. the ganekhe staff gathered once again. Eight men, including Wali and Silometek, were there. Wali began to lead a subdued, intermittent dirge that was accompanied by utterances from the group. After a time, the men ate the sweet potatoes, greens, pig meat, and some pig fat in hushed, near silence.

At this point in time, the contents and spatial relationships within the sacred house were in order for the all night proceedings, during which the ancestral spirits in the stones (and a few other objects) would be empowered, rejuvenated, propitiated and at times pleaded with for assistance in human endeavors. *All* of the collective supernatural energy from within the ganekhe cabinet, *the power box,* had been removed as its individual entities in the form of the ancestral power packets had been laid out on Altar 1, in front of the ganekhe cabinet, in the same spatial relationship in which they were maintained inside the box. The collective supernatural energy of Asugum, the great clan guardian spirit, which is composed of the individual particulates of energy of all of its parts (the individual personified spirits that give spirit life to each of the ganekhe objects), was out of the box and was present as a unifying aura over and around the ganekhe packets. (Wali later whispered to me that Asugum was there, outside of the ganekhe cabinet, and that although he was a part of each of the individual spirit stones, he was also, always, everywhere.) Pasoware, the single guardian spirit that is in everlasting abundance and available everywhere, to be installed with ritual by wusahun into dibat throughout the Highlands, was there. He might be moving about in the air or occupying, at any given moment, any of the objects within the room or structural parts of the sacred house. But Pasoware was present and would come when properly summoned by Wali, the wusahun, or his authorized designee to be put into those dibat that would be individually wrapped around each of the ancestor stones. Abut (alt. Hale), the son of Pasoware, was there. This ancestral guardian spirit of Unspoken-Name (Wali's most powerful ancestor spirit), like Pasoware, had left the ganekhe cabinet and was out where he could function unencumbered by the box within the sacred space of the room, to protect Wali's primary guardian spirit from possible malevolent spiritual intruders. Wali, as well as Hanomoak, his most dependable advisor in such priestly matters, preferred not to tell me which stone was Unspoken-Name's body. But Unspoken-Name was most certainly there and now exposed, like all of the other ancestor spirits, to both benevolent manipulation by humans and to the potential dangers of malicious spirit intruders.

Overseeing all of this, as the powerful watchdog and communicator to the ancestral spirits in the world of the unseen, was the always-present Waganilan, which lives in all puluen that have been empowered with Waganilan and are maintained in an upright position against a front-center leg of ganekhe cabinets. In addition to his function as a watchdog for the ancestral spirit stones and a few other spirit objects that are sometimes maintained in the power box (ganekhe cabinet), Waganilan is a spirit that each of the ganekhe group leaders makes supplications to on behalf of himself and others in the community. Waganilan not only communicates matters appropriately to the proper ancestral spirits, but also has the power to act on his own to mete out both assistance and punishment to human members of the community.

In front of the puluen on Altar 1, the ten ganekhe packets were neatly laid out, in the same spatial relationships, one to the other, as the way that they were maintained when inside of the ganekhe cabinet. Inside of eight of the ten packets, a personified ancestral spirit stone was maintained and worshiped as an ancestral entity. In the other two packets, other kinds of

primary objects were so maintained and worshiped. The same kinds of other sacred materials that are present in Gutelu Mabel's ganekhe packets were included with the carefully wrapped spirit stones of Wali's ganekhe group, just as they are in other ganekhe packets throughout the research area. These are the kinds of things that the ancestors prescribed to both comfort the spirit entities of the stones and to augment the spiritual power that emanates from the stones. Wali and his ganekhe staff said that all of these particular spirit stones were passed down from the ancestors so that neither Wali nor his staff knew why particular stones were selected to be the bodies for certain ancestor spirits or why specific ancestors were selected for embodiment. In the Highlands' tradition, however, each ganekhe group leader and his staff must know the names of each of the ancestors that are embodied within each of the stones of the ganekhe for which they are responsible and be able to recognize each personified ancestral spirit stone.

Off to one side of Altar 1, lay a fresh supply of short strips of the white, cellular-looking material from the inner part of a banana trunk. According to informants, the juices from these inner pieces of banana trunk are the favored cleansing agent to wipe each spirit stone before it is anointed with sacred pig grease. These white organic cleaning "cloths" and their included juices are called *wakiapolo*. These strips had been already spiritually cleansed of the presence of possibly malevolent ghosts by a brief procedure administered by a wusahun.

By now a few packets that looked similar to the ganekhe ancestor power packets appeared adjacent to Altar 1 under the ganekhe cabinet. These other kinds of power packets had been placed there to be charged with the supernatural power that was emanating from the ganekhe. These packets were not going to be opened during this ritual, but were just placed there to absorb spirit power so that they could be used for their own social purposes (to be discussed in following sections).

Wali maintains that the empowering spirit for this sort of power transfer to other kinds of power packets is only the Unspoken-Name ancestral spirit, which Wali himself controls. Other informants have denied Wali's position, saying that beneficial power emanates from all of the ancestral spirit stones and that both nearby objects and people absorb some degree of supernatural power from all of them, especially at those times when power in the stones is being moved about—such as at the ganekhe hakasin. These informants further point out that the shamans of the ganekhe group are always present during empowering ceremonies, not only to ensure that proper ritual practices are followed and to help perform the ceremony, but to absorb from the stones a measure of spirit power to help them perform their social obligations.

Sanctified pig grease, both in the form of hardened cakes that are maintained in the sacred house and fresh fat from the largest pig that had just been sacrificed, was available for the stone-anointing procedure. (In some cases, individual pigs are identified while still being raised to be the sacrificial animals that will be killed in honor of specific ancestor spirits. The sacred pig grease from the fat of such animals is thus predestined to be used to beautify and anoint specific spirit stones at the time of sacrifice.) Some of the fat is saved to be used at a later time if another such designated pig for that particular ancestor spirit is not large enough for sacrifice during a future ganekhe hakasin. At the time of this ganekhe hakasin, the grease from the fat of the largest pig donated by Wali was used to anoint certain of the stones. The fat from one of the other pigs was also used. Grease from preserved, hardened pieces of fat were used for yet other ganekhe spirit stones.

A small pile of ferns (piteka) that was sanctified earlier in this ganekhe hakasin was available for the greasing of the stones, once the stones had been cleaned by rubbing them with white inner pieces from a banana trunk (wakiapolo). The stone-greasing ferns were first rubbed with the fat from the correct pig, concurrent with the anointing procedure.

During the night, Silometek Wilil would carefully open each packet, remove the ancestor spirit stone (two other kinds of objects in the cases of two of the ten packets), cleanse the stone and its previously tied-on bundle of dibat wrappings with wakiapolo, and then anoint the stone with grease from fat of the designated pig. To grease the stone, Silometek used a small clump of the ferns that one of his assistants, usually Asudek Wilil, had already daubed with the right pig fat. In a couple of rare instances, he put pig fat directly onto the stone and rubbed it about with the ferns (piteka). Objects, other than wolo or other kinds of leaves that accompanied the spirit stones in their individual packets, were also sometimes rubbed with the fat-saturated ferns.

This anointing procedure was said to beautify the spirit stones and thereby let the spirits within know that they were being properly cared for and were maintained in a handsome condition. In addition, the anointing process is felt to pass some spirit power back into the stones from the pigs and to rejuvenate the power of the ancestral spirits within. After the anointing process had been completed to the satisfaction of Silometek and staff and before laying each stone back into place in its packet, the symbolically most important function took place. One of the grass dibat stems was handed to Silometek by a nearby assistant. Along with his own accompanying recitations (inapefu) and a rapid blowing in short breaths on the stone (which were audibly enunciated with a sharply worded, "whoo, whoo, whoo, whoo"), Silometek looped a single strand of sacred dibat around each spirit stone and tied it off with a single knot over the front-up side (elokoma) of the stone. With this simple act of tying the knot, Silometek, assisted by Wali and others of the ganekhe staff, had once again secured the spirit power in the stone. At the same time, they had tied on a dibat that exercises its own ongoing power for protection of the spirit dwelling within.

At the first-time installation of an ancestral spirit into a stone or other object, it is the tying of the knot of the dibat that is the symbolic moment when the previously inanimate object is joined with the life of an ancestor spirit. This is when the object becomes a tangible "living" entity with supernatural power, instead of an artifact that is profane and dead, or, at best an object that inherently contains some sort of unidentified supernatural power that cannot be beneficially controlled. Just as the presence of a dibat on a human being signifies that there is life (edai egen) within the body, a dibat on a nonhuman material object signifies that there is a spirit life within the object. Without the dibat, the ganekhe has either not yet been empowered with an ancestral spirit or for whatever reason has been desacralized and can again be treated as a profane object—dead, without spirit and not to be worshiped or feared. By the repeated rejuvenation of personalized ancestral spiritual power within a ganekhe through numerous dibat isin procedures, a bundle of knotted grass stems (omatok) builds up on the spirit-stone entity. The knotted side of the grass bundle identifies the front side (elokoma) of any spirit stone or other object.

Throughout the night of the ganekhe hakasin, once the dibat isin procedure was completed on each stone, it was laid back down into its ganekhe packet, but the packet was left open, not to be closed, bound, and returned to the ganekhe cabinet until completion of the all-night ritual. An object in each of the ten packets from the ganekhe cabinet contains an identified spiritual entity, the particulars of which are set forth in table 4.1. Eight of the ten packets contain personified ancestral spirit stones, of which three were interpreted by the author as having formerly been Yeineri-sourced flat je-style profane symbolic display-exchange stones. One is a Yeineri-sourced puluen-style je before installation; three, Yeineri-style profane adze blades before installation, and one a Langda-Sela-style adze blade. Along with the Langda-Sela-style dibat-tied adze blade in the ganekhe packet is a rounded black stone without a dibat. Of the other two, of the total of ten ganekhe packets, one contains a short piece of a dibat-wrapped jerak cowrie shell band and a similar, but longer dibat-wrapped nassa shell string band. Eight named ancestor spirits were identified with their stone bodies ("spirit bones"). It is correct to think of the spirit-stone entity in two different ways: for example, at the top of the list in table 4.1, the spirit of an ancestor

named Pusawarek lives in the green stone, but also, "green stone" is thought of as being Pusawarek.

During the all-night rites when the attention moved from one stone ancestor to another, there was a near constant buzz of efficacious esoteric formulae, punctuated by the blowing sounds when a new dibat was being knotted onto a particular stone. Sometimes there were "uhs" and "ahs," accompanied by muttering as Wali and the others, at times individually and sometimes jointly, addressed Waganilan in the puluen and the ancestor spirits, either individually or as a group. Wali and the men asked for direct assistance on a number of subjects, such as raising many healthy pigs, requesting that the spirits stay close at hand to drive off malevolent spirits that may have been sent from an enemy, protecting the people from sickness or mishap, and the fostering of good crops. Sometime throughout the night Wali requested assistance on most of the major issues with which the Dani, as a group, must deal. While the stones were being manually manipulated, certain staff assistants would lean over Silometek or others working with the stones to cleanse hands (including mine) with the totok feather wand. This was an important part of ritual as these people, especially Silometek, moved from one sacred task to the next and as I photographed and made measurements without touching the stones. The background sound consisted of near-constant subdued talk and utterances of sacred formulae, as those people of the group who have wusahun powers communicated in this very intimate session with their spirit-powers.

Two days later in a much appreciated debriefing session, I was told in more detail of the meaning of some of the near-constant verbalizations during the empowerment of the stones. One important new aspect that came out in this conversation was that Wali, the wusahun, was not only making supplications, or requests to the spirits in the stones, but that with some of his wusa ane (little understood sacred language) he was passing a degree of his own supernatural power to the stones.

A brief review of a few of the photographs

Table 4.1. The Primary Contents of the Ten Ganekhe Packets from within Wali's Ganekhe Cabinet

Domiciled Ancestor Spirit	Width x Length (cm)	Color beneath Pig Grease	Former Function	Quarry Source
Pusawarek	8 x 37	green	je	Yeineri
Awadek	7 x 32	green	je	Yeineri
Kolo	6.5 x 44	green	je	Yeineri
Agit	5.3 x 9	green	adze	Yeineri
Nawit	4.9 x 10	green	adze	Yeineri
Wimarek	4.7 x 10	light green	adze	Langda-Sela
Unnamed	4.5 x 12	black	round stone	river
Awinilik	4.7 x 6	green	adze	Yeineri
Takali	6.2 x 47	dark green	puluen je	Yeineri
Unnamed	2 x 117	woven nassa	shell band	Culture
Unnamed	2 x 21	piece jerak	shell band	Culture

that were taken during the night of the empowerment rites of the ganekhe hakasin ceremony can broaden our visual perspective of the material goods, with similar kinds of artifacts as are found in the archaeological record. In figure 4.29, four of the total of ten ganekhe packets are seen lying on banana leaves at the front of the ganekhe cabinet. On top of two of the packets are the soot-blackened rattan headband hoops called *wasinade,* which were reportedly worn by Wali's grandfather. On the left side of the photograph, the right ends of two *hareken* power packets (to be discussed in a future section) are seen, advantageously placed to receive supernatural power from the ganekhe ancestral spirit stones. Note the black-looking puluen guardian stone leaning against the front central leg of the cabinet. At the top of the photograph one can see the lower ends of the bottom row of mandibles that are hung across the front of the cabinet. In the lower photograph of the figure, Silometek starts to unwrap the first ganekhe packet. Figure 4.30 reveals the contents of a typical ganekhe packet. Beneath the outer covering of *Pandanus* bark, the layers of reddish brown and buff-colored bark cloth (called *heisan,* reportedly traded from the Yali) are similar to the bark cloth layers revealed in the ganekhe that belonged to Gutelu Mabel. Inside the packet, the sacred stone is identified as the ancestor spirit stone called Pusawarek (table 4.1). It is a green-colored, 8 cm wide by 37 cm long, Yeineri-sourced je-type stone that is wrapped with an abundant clump of grass stem

dibat. Accompanying the stone in the packet are one pair of boar tusks, about fourteen black and blond-colored pig tails, several loose wolo leaves, and a single cowrie shell (jeraken). As esoteric formulae were recited by other nearby ganekhe group staff members, Silometek tidied up the dibat bundle (omatek) around the stone. He pulled back loose dibat grass strands toward the center, cleaned the stone by rubbing it with banana trunk juices *(wakiapolo)* and then anointed it with the appropriate sanctified pig grease. He rubbed this on with a small bundle of fern leaves (piteka). After Silometek completed the cleansing, anointment, and the tying of a grass stem dibat onto Pusawarek, Silometek's hands were ritually cleansed with the use of the feather (totok, alt. kut) that is maintained on the house wall for just such purposes. Throughout the entire night, the same feather wand was used over and over, in what is called a totok procedure, to cleanse Silometek's hands (and also mine and my camera) as Silometek moved from packet to packet to conduct his empowerment chores and as I photographed the contents of the packets. As the wand was waved over our hands, formulae were sometimes recited. The waving of the wand would remove supernatural power that had been absorbed from one spirit packet so that it would not be unwittingly passed on to cause a problem with a spirit in another stone.

The spirit stone in figure 4.31 is known as Awadek. As can be seen in table 4.1, Awadek is a

Fig. 4.29. The sacred stone packets lay on the altar before the ganekhe cabinet.

Fig. 4.30. The contents of the first sacred spirit packet to be opened are revealed.

green, Yeineri-sourced 7 by 32 cm je-type stone that is wrapped with a bundle of grass dibat. Underneath the grass bundle (omatok) that was formed by the accumulation of numerous dibat, a stick called a *jagat* is tied tightly to the stone with loops of what are either strips of bamboo or rattan. The jagat stick had previously been empowered and is used in this case to furnish Awadek with a measure of comfort and to demonstrate visually that Awadek is being properly cared for. Commonly, sticks such as this empowered jagat are used as devices to protect human individuals and others from illness and harm. In figure 4.31, after the stone was cleaned and then anointed with the

sacred pig grease, the hands of Silometek can be seen just after knotting the important dibat in place. Next, a grass stem dibat was tied onto a green, just-greased 6.5 by 44 cm sacred stone whose personified ancestor spirit is known as Kolo. The next packet that was opened revealed a dark green 6.2 by 47 cm Yeineri-sourced puluen-type je, wrapped with reddish brown cocoon cloth. The ancestral spirit within this stone is known as Takali.

Next, a 117-cm-long nassa shell decorated string band was cleansed, anointed, and secured with a grass stem dibat. Wali nodded his assent that this decorated string band contains a personified ancestral spirit, but he would not reveal the name of the spirit that dwells within. This so-called ganekhe entity, although certainly not a stone, and another "ganekhe" cowrie shell decorated band are similar to shell bands maintained by Gutelu in his ganekhe cabinet. The looping on of the dibat seemed to confirm Wali's affirmation that his shell-decorated string bands are personified ancestral entities, although he would not reveal their ancestral names. Wali's grandfather's black headband hoops *(wasinade)* were anointed with pig grease. A dibat loop was knotted onto a pair of sacred pig tails that were removed from a ganekhe packet for the purpose. This act indicated that a spirit dwelling within the bundle must be given attention and protected with a dibat. A boar tusk pair was first cleansed with a white piece of banana trunk cleaning material before being rubbed with a hardened, old piece of sanctified pig fat. The hardened piece of pig fat was maintained in a packet with a wolo leaf. The pig tusks were cleansed, anointed, and then put back into the packet with the ancestor spirit stone that they accompanied, but were not tied with a dibat.

After the ten ganekhe packets had been opened and the ancestor spirit stones, as well as a few other items of their contents, had been cleaned, anointed with sacred pig fat oil, and the grass dibat carefully tied around each ancestor stone (and a few of the other objects), each ancestor was appropriately addressed in the sacred language (wusa ane) and other (translatable) Dani formulae of "straight-talk."

Fig. 4.31. A grass stem dibat is tied onto an ancestral stone.

For the time being the packets were left open on Altar 1. Waganilan in the puluen stone watched over them. The ganekhe human staff moved away from around the front fringes of Altar 1, with all of its exposed supernatural power, to rest sitting on the floor and leaning against the wall of the sacred house or sitting around the outer edges of Altar 2, while they finished eating the last morsels of pig meat and fat. The only utensil with the food on the ground altar-table was a single bamboo knife. I asked Wali why no one ate the two large cooked potatoes that were located on the back edge of Altar 2, toward the fireplace. Wali did not want to talk. He did, however, whisper, "for the wusa." Later in the day, after sunrise and away from the sacred house, I was told that those potatoes were left there for a specific ancestor spirit (or spirits) to eat, while they in turn exuded their spirit energy into the meat of the potatoes. Wali would later take the potatoes and personally feed them to one or two sacred pigs that were being raised as future sacrifices to that or those specific ancestor spirits—just an example of the ongoing movement of supernatural power within the power circle.

Later that night, before sunrise, the stones were once again bound tightly; along with their accompanying leaves, sticks, boar tusks, and pig

tails, into their individual ganekhe packets and, following a prescribed methodology passed down orally from the ancestors, returned and secured into the ganekhe cabinet. Each ganekhe packet was returned to its correct spatial location and orientation in the cabinet. The ancestral entities must always be lying on their backs, front-side up when laid horizontally, or front side facing the front of the cabinet if stood vertically. In some cabinets, spirit stones representative of ancestors killed in war are maintained on one side of a cabinet, while those spirit stones representing ancestors who died of other causes are maintained on the other side of the cabinet. In certain other sacred houses entire ganekhe cabinets are devoted only to ancestor stones that contain the spirits of ancestors killed in war. In these cases, only ganekhe hakasin wim empowerment ceremonies are held in conjunction with such accumulations of ancestral power. Both the accumulated power within the ganekhe cabinet and the individual ancestor power stones are propitiated and manipulated to assist in dealing with war matters. Some (maybe all—I could not confirm) of the ancestor war spirit stones are laid in a cabinet with their head ends facing the entrance of the house. Reportedly this is to facilitate the propitiated ancestor spirits leaving through the heads of their bodies to kill enemy spirits. Once the invisible spirit of an enemy has been driven out of its living human body by another spirit, that human is vulnerable to being killed on the battlefield or in ambush. In addition, when orienting the stones within the cabinet and within the spatial relationships of the stones one to the other, the hierarchy of power of spirits within the individual stones was carefully remembered. Some spirit stones are thought by the members of each ganekhe group to be more powerful than the others. Such a presumption must be considered both in the placement of the stones within the cabinet and in the manner in which they are manipulated in empowerment and rejuvenation rites.

The Ancestor Guardian Stone (Puluen)

During times of the movement of the ganekhe packets, Waganilan, the puluen sentinel, remained in its usual upright position to protect the spirit stones at this time of vulnerability when they were outside of the ganekhe cabinet and to continue to report to them that proper protocol was being followed. If dissatisfied, this puluen sentinel might himself wreak havoc within the community. In addition to its importance as a sentinel and guardian for the ganekhe within the cabinet, the puluen also functions as a communication link between each ganekhe group leader and the ancestor spirit stones within the ganekhe cabinet. For example, when Wali wants to communicate with a spirit or spirits within the closed ganekhe power cabinet, he addresses his formulae or incantations to Waganilan within the puluen. Whether or not Waganilan can be addressed by other designated members of the ganekhe staff or possibly even all members of the staff I do not know. Wali says that Waganilan is "his" spirit. Others may not agree.

Waganilan is initially inducted into a puluen stone through a typical installation ceremony at which the properly raised sacred pig is sacrificed while a big man conducts the installation, following ancestor-formulated protocol and the significant blowing and utterances of formulae (inapefu). In effect, it is the wusahun who transfers the Waganilan spirit from the unseen world

into a selected puluen stone. It is also the wusahun who later maintains, feeds, beautifies, and propitiates the spirit that has been installed into the stone. Waganilan (alt. kinoke) is the pervasive spirit that is installed into all puluen stones, *not* different individual ancestral spirits who function for each individual ganekhe group.

Wali says that the puluen is maintained outside the ganekhe cabinet, not only to act as the guardian of the ganekhe within the cabinet and to be the communication link with humans in the world of the seen, but it is also to maintain good luck for their entire community. Although the puluen is maintained in a position outside the ganekhe power cabinet, it is considered a "ganekhe" stone and not a sacred stone of another category.

Wali maintains a special relationship with his puluen. Siba, the big man and ganekhe group leader within his own compound, told me that he, too, has this relationship with the puluen that leans against the center-left leg of his ganekhe cabinet. Wali stated that in his big man capacity with supernatural power (wusahun), he often goes alone to Yalogon to communicate with the puluen and ask for spiritual help for his people in matters dealing with health, both human and animal, and such social problems as fertility, food crops, and wealth. For example, before Wali might go to another compound to ask the big man leader of that compound to present a large pig at a planned forthcoming sacrificial ceremony, Wali might go alone to his sacred compound (Yalogon) to ask for assistance from the spirits through communication with the puluen. In such a case, Wali might remove the puluen from its guardian position in front of the ganekhe cabinet and carry it out into the area of the outdoor altar in front of the sacred house, anoint the stone with sacred pig grease, and commune with the spirit in the stone. Wali said that sometimes instead of just anointing the puluen with sacralized pig fat he might first rub the stone with sacred pulverized red hematite that is used as red paint (pimot, alt. bimot or bimut). (This is one of the few comments that I have had from a Dani, saying that red paint is rubbed onto either a je or a ganekhe.) Wali said that he might continue to anoint, manipulate, and talk with the stone for quite a long period of time. On one serious occasion, Wali said he went into communion with the puluen for a period of five days.

Supernaturally Powered Objects for Social Uses

The sheer number of stone and other kinds of supernaturally powered objects in circulation within the Highlander cultural systems at any one time is indeed profuse. In addition to the ganekhe packets with their ancestor stones, there are a vast array of other kinds of packets with their included power objects. Some such packets contain only a single stone with a leaf; others might contain as many as six to ten different kinds of objects, but almost always with at least one stone, the *power stone*. These power packets and objects might be thought of as sacred tool kits with sacred power tools, to be used to handle the kinds of personal, social, political, and natural problems that any cultural system has but for which there are no profane tools in the technological tool kits that can be helpful.

The supernatural spirit power within the individual items of this broad array of power packets is sometimes initially installed by wusahun-directed rituals and sometimes by absorption of the supernatural power that emanates from the ganekhe, by placing a designated packet inside of the ganekhe cabinet. Whatever the method of initial installation of supernatural power into items of these power packets, it is known that storing them near the ganekhe cabinet or exposing them to ganekhe packets during spirit-stone rejuvenation rites is advantageous to the maintenance of vital spiritual energy within the objects.

The broad array of these kinds of power packets, with their variety of included objects, are similar to other artifacts of culture that are used on a worldwide basis in other cultural systems. Many similar objects and packets of objects are also known from the archaeological record.

Within the Irian Jaya Highlands, although most of the more complex power packets and their contents are kept by men who have wusahun, a multitude of the more simple individual power objects, such as amulets and pig power balls, are owned and used by the numerous people who do not possess (or, are not) wusahun. Wusahun literally translates as "the sacred or supernatural power." Those men who rise to the level of "big man" learn about sacred (wusa, alt. *wesa*) objects, places, and activities from the time of childhood initiation and throughout their lives in the men's houses. Those who ascend to leadership and become shamans absorb wusahun along their journeys to achieve big man status. They then have the wusahun and are called wusahun. Some big men, as they continue their ascendancy in the hierarchy of political power, achieve or derive increasing levels of wusahun. Some of these big men become especially known for their wusahun (shaman) abilities.

Some men (and also a lesser number of women) who are adept at healing and who desire to become healers only, without social influence, can be trained and installed with appropriate wusahun by big men with such achieved abilities. Within the Highlands system of achieved and developed specialties there are different kinds of healers with different degrees of wusahun. Some have the wusahun to be able to deal only with simple illnesses. Others rise to a level with a recognized ability of more knowledge and a more powerful degree of wusahun. Some of these healers are known to control supernatural powers of such quality and strength that they can overcome the negative effects of even powerful black (malevolent) magic. An individual with a serious illness that he/she suspects has been caused by black magic of another or an individual who suspects that his/her soul matter ("the singing seeds of life") has been stolen by malevolent magic seeks out an appropriate "specialist" with sufficient wusahun to successfully restore the normal living spirit before a serious illness or death occurs.

In times of war, war leaders are assigned by a big man of at least Confederacy political level to act with authority and a precise set of duties. Wusahun is delegated from the big man who is in charge and has the responsibility for the war. In fact, wusahun, in varying degrees and operable over varying periods of time, is routinely instilled in different staff members who are always available for consultation while they carry out their assigned responsibilities—often with a special kind of power stone. At any one time and within almost any group of compounds or house clusters, the big man leader would be able to name several men who are known to have wusahun. He might have delegated it to them.

In addition to those in authority of leadership and the various kinds of healers, there is the vast array of common folk who must contend with their own personal problems on a daily basis: the women who carry their babies to and from the fields in carrying nets and are concerned about the children's health and safety, the horticulturists who want abundant crops, and the women who care for the pigs and want to promote the births of many healthy piglets. These kinds of concerns and other more routine daily situations are the actualities of life that the common folk must deal with and for which they, too, must have supernaturally charged tools to assist in their endeavors. The various power objects, amulets, and talismen that these kinds of people use are often thought to possess inherently generated supernatural power by virtue of the nature of the objects themselves. In other instances, power must be transferred into the artifacts by wusahun who possess the power to do those kinds of things. Any of these objects, whether inherently empowered or empowered through ritualistic installation by a wusahun, are felt to be beneficially strengthened by exposure to the ganekhe. Those objects kept by women can be rejuvenated by blessings from a wusahun and at times carried by a male relative to be stored near or, better yet, inside a ganekhe cabinet. The contained accumulated ancestor spirit power within the ganekhe cabinet seems to be *the* rejuvenating power for most of the power packets used in the Highlands.

Power packets range in size from as small as about 7 cm in length to as long as about 40 cm. Their outer covering is usually banana trunk bark (gisakpel), *Pandanus* bark, heisan bark, cocoon "cloth," a tightly folded small carrying net (nogen), or, in still rarer instances, a relatively small, purselike, woven fiber string bag.

The power packets, and their removable power objects, can be found scattered throughout the cultural system. Some are at points of temporary storage, some are at places of permanent installation, such as the ganekhe packets inside the ganekhe cabinets, and others are found being used by their owners at various activities to help keep life in order and to promote community success. A war leader might be using his power packet with its power stone out near the field of battle to prepare his warriors for success, a big man of a surgical team at a pig castration might have a power packet (or individual stone) lying nearby to protect the area from marauding ghosts, the groundskeeper for a ghost bundle memorial site *(wagun ai)* might carry a power packet to the site from a nearby compound while he is preparing it for a memorial service, a group of horticulturists with a wusahun in charge might carry one or several supernaturally charged adze blades to plant with potatoes in a new field to act as a "fertilizer" and ensure good potato growth, and a woman might be putting an empowered ballstone in the corner of a pig sty to ensure the health of a pregnant pig.

Religio-Medical Kits (Hareken) and Their Power Stones (Wamaket)

The religio-medical kit *(hareken)*, which always includes one or more power stones *(wamaket)* along with some other objects, is of utmost importance to those Highlands' healers who use supernatural powers in their healing procedures. The paraphernalia within a single religio-medical kit is quite variable. Healings, with the use of such a kit and its contents, are almost always conducted indoors in a healer's house, be it a men's house or a female healer's family compound house. In either case, a spirit enclosure (waro leget) is either attached to the back side of the healer's house or is set alongside, very near to the back of the house, both as a convenience to the spirits who assist in healing procedures and also to ensure reliable communication between the wusahun healer and the healer spirits who dwell in the waro leget.

Wusahun healers hang their religio-medical kits within a ganekhe cabinet from time to time, to renew power in their contents. Certain ganekhe group leaders are reported to even store their personal religio-medical kits in a ganekhe cabinet on an almost permanent basis. The primary artifact inside a religio-medical kit is a power stone of either natural or human origin. The main function of the power stone is to absorb and store supernatural power from the ganekhe at those times when the kit is hung (stood or lain) inside a ganekhe cabinet and then to be the power source for the other religio-medical implements within the kit, as well as a source for beneficially directed power from the healer to a patient. In addition to using the religio-medical implements from the kit (hareken) during healing procedures, both healer and patient are reassured by just the presence of the included power stone (wamaket).

The following classification lists the general kinds of materials and items that are included within Highlands' religio-medical kits (hareken):

1. Rocks
   (a) shaped by geological processes
   (b) shaped by human hands
2. Parts of trees and plants
   (a) pieces of wood
   (b) bark
   (c) leaves and stems
   (d) roots
   (e) seeds
   (f) resin
   (g) trees and plant fiber human-made string
3. Mammal and reptile parts
   (a) rodent and reptile skulls
   (b) rodent mandibles
   (c) rodent teeth
   (d) small bones and pieces of bone
   (e) pig feet
   (f) bat skulls and bones
   (g) pieces of fur
4. Bird parts
   (a) feathers
   (b) body parts with feathers attached
   (c) skulls
   (d) feet
5. Invertebrates
   (a) small snail shells and other fossils
   (b) pieces of shell
6. Natural paints (applied to objects).
   Example: from pulverized hematite

It is anticipated that similar religio-medical kits (or "medicine bags") put together by other people across both spatial and temporal boundaries differ in content at least because of environmental change.

The Highlands wusahun healers attempt cures by utilizing and demonstrating to others control of healing spirits along with the supernatural power from their power stones and the other objects from within their medical kits. The people of the Highlands, especially the healers themselves, feel that the broad classification of diseases being treated is caused by supernatural powers and, therefore, must be treated by the manipulation and application, if you will, of supernatural powers. To effectively identify religio-medical implements and comprehend related behavior within both contemporary nonliterate cultural systems and those that are prehistoric, it is necessary to understand cause (illness) and effect (treatment) through the eyes, ears, and minds of nonliterate medical practitioners ("Traditional Concepts of Life, Health, and Healing," chapter 1).

Nilik's Religio-Medical Kit (Hareken)
During the late 1950s and early 1960s, Nilik (pronounced Nee-leek and meaning "present at pig eating") Walilo was considered the most influential big man of the Walilo clan. He was considered one of the great modern gains (big men) of the Grand Valley, who at one time in the 1960s even attempted to usurp some of Gutelu's power. Nilik belonged to the waija moiety and lived to see the initiation of his grandchildren during the last valleywide ebe

Fig. 4.32. A religio-medical kit (hareken)

akho in 1993. Nilik, like most Grand Valley big men, had inherited the basics in his primary medical kit (hareken) from his father. Before Nilik died, he passed this wusahun healer's power kit on to a son. He and an older male relative of Nilik's generation showed and explained the power kit to me.

The package was opened to reveal and discuss its contents. Like most ganekhe packets and many religio-medical kits (healer's power kits), this packet is neatly wrapped with an outer layer of banana bark (gisakpel) and tied with a strong piece of braided cording. When the outer covering is laid back a single wusa wand feather and a hard narrow stem are seen stuck into the outside of a bundle of items neatly included within a wrapping of tree bark "cloth." I was told that the wusa feather and the hard narrow stem are placed there to both identify the top of the packet but more importantly for the wusahun healer to use to cleanse the air, people, and objects of any potentially contaminating spirits. The stick would be used to first cleanse the healing room, the persons within, and later anyone who enters. To function, one end of the special cleansing stem-stick is held in the fire, and when it is smoking it is waved around various parts of the room and

over and around the people within, as well as over any person entering the house at a later time. The feather (totok) is for use at appropriate times throughout the healing to cleanse the healer's hands and those of assistants as they move from one supernaturally charged healing task to the next (previously described, "The Ganekhe Hakasin Ceremony").

The two layers of outer brown bark cloth are known as *tage;* the innermost white bark cloth as *hisang* (alt. *heisan*). Both kinds of bark cloth are reportedly traded from the Yali. Centered in the packet, and resting on eight light brown wolo leaves (slightly aromatic and possibly medicinal), is a pair of power stones (wamaket). Figure 4.32 provides the overall view of the packet and its contents, and figure 4.33 shows the individual items that are present in the packet. The front of the power stone is shown in figure 4.32 and the back, down-side of the stone in figure 4.33. The elongate power stone is a typical dark green, Yeineri-sourced puluen-type je, 30 cm long by 5.1 cm at point of maximum width by 1.4 cm at point of maximum thickness. One end of the stone looks structurally like the cutting edge of an adze/axe blade in plan view, but it has not been sharpened to the degree of an adze or axe. The other end of the stone, which is considered its head-end, has been ground to a point. The pointed end rests on an H-shaped black argillite stone that has been well polished and configured by geologic processes. The front of the puluen-type stone is decorated with a bark strand miniature skirt, a boar tusk pair, and several loops of grass that are bound in the fashion of a grass stem dibat. Six large pig tails are fastened onto the under (back) side of the stone. Ten loops of grass are wound around the H-shaped river-tumbled stone. The long dimension of the H-shaped stone is 9.5 cm. A sacred bamboo knife, 15.6 cm long, with a fiber-wrapped handle is included in the packet. A trace of feathers protrude from under the handle wrapping on the cutting end of the knife. In addition to the boar tusk pair that is fastened to the puluen power stone, four individual boar tusks are included in the kit. None of these has an inner-sharpened edge, indicating that they were never used as profane scraper tools. Seven assorted pig tails, all smaller than those bound to the puluen power stone, are attached to a narrow strand stringer. Two black ammonite fossils make up the rest of the contents of the packet. Both fossils are river-tumbled and smoothed pebbles that have been broken open by the geologic tumbling

process to expose the fossils. The stone with the exposed fossil toward the viewer is 1.9 cm wide, while the other pebble fossil is 2.3 cm in its longest dimension.

The objects that are discussed in the following text are illustrated in figure 4.33. Both of the larger stones are considered to be power stones (wamaket). They are known to contain spirit power, which must be nourished and renewed and which transmits supernatural power to both inanimate objects and people about them. Although they do not contain one or more *personified* ancestral spirit, they do contain "spirit power," which must be protected. Hence, the grass blade and fiber string dibat are put about them just like a fiber string dibat around the necks of human beings and ganekhe stones, to protect the "life force" of the person, or, in the case of the ganekhe, the ancestral spirit within. In the case of this pair of stones, previously reliable informants pointed out that they did not know why the originating ancestor had selected them. They further stated that they had never thought of the power stones as an anthropomorphic spirit stone resting its head on a "pillow" (as a Western observer might surmise), or in any other way as even a possible conjugal pair of stones. They supposed the

Fig. 4.33. The contents of the kit shown in figure 4.32

ancestor selecting the stones had good reason for his choices, but that information was not known to them. These power stones and the other healing paraphernalia along with them would be used, just like other packets by other wusahuns, at the discretion of the owners. One routine use of the power stones is, however, to just be placed near the healer, usually in the packet, to exude beneficial supernatural power throughout a healing procedure. In some cases, during a healing, the wusahun might also set a power stone (within or outside of its packet) next to the patient or even give it to the patient to hold and thereby help with the healing process. Often special minipackets with a single power stone are made up by the healer for a particular healing procedure, at which the stone (in or outside of its packet) is presented to the patient as a "prescription" to help effect a cure.

The pig tails on the back side of the puluen-type power stone and those seen strung separately are the accumulation from separate healing procedures. It is customary for a pig to be sacrificed at a healing. The meat is ritually prepared and cooked for only the patient and the healer (wusahun) to eat. Often the attending wusahun will add the pig tail from the rite to his power packet, as had been done in this case. The larger pig tails on the puluen-type power stone were added from healing procedures at which the gain Nilik officiated, and the small tails are from smaller pigs sacrificed at healings officiated by Nilik's less-influential son who inherited the packet.

The boar tusk pair, seen on the front side of the power stone in figure 4.32, was thought by the informants to have been added to the power stone as wusa mementos of a healing ritual that had been officiated by the owner of the packet. They thought the fiber strand symbolic miniature skirt was added to the stone only as a discretionary added decoration.

The eight leaves (wolo) on which the power stones and other objects within the power packet lay are a bit of an enigma to the living population. The leaves smell slightly aromatic and are thought of as being in some way medicinal and spiritually powerful. This kind of leaf, as well as jiwi leaves, are included with the sacred stones in all kinds of power packets as well as with ancestral spirit stones in the ganekhe packets. According to informants, the leaves have been used this way since the times of "the ancestors." I have noticed that wherever spirit stones are packaged, across the broad research area, they are associated with these kinds of leaves. Some informants say that just as babies are laid on soft leaves in carrying nets, so are spirit stones cushioned with wusa leaves in their storage and carrying packets. The leaves, however, have meaning beyond this, for they are generally used along with stones and other power objects as part of altar paraphernalia during sacred rites. All adult males know that this practice was inherited from the ancestors. Some informants only say that, "we do it, because that is the way it has always been done." I have not yet confirmed scientific identification of the two leaf types and refer to them only by their Grand Valley Dani names, jiwi and wolo.

The sacred bamboo knife seen in the center of figure 4.33 can be identified as being wusa by its wrapped handle with included feathers. Its use is to make the initial cut on the pig (or in unusual cases, pigs) sacrificed at a healing.

It is difficult to distinguish ancestor packets (ganekhe) from healer power packets. I asked the informants who reviewed this packet with me, as well as other informants, including both Wali and Daoke Mabel, how they are distinguished. Their answers were vague, not because these informants avoided the question or chose not to answer it because of religious taboos, but because it is a difficult question to answer and there is honest disagreement among the group of informants. The descendants of Nilik, the big man owner of the packet who handed it down to this generation of adults, said only that the packet came to them as a healer's power packet, not as a ganekhe ancestor spirit packet. They were sure about this. Because one of the power stones is a puluen-type je, they all also agreed that the stone could just as well have been identified and transformed into a puluen ganekhe. With the dibat around the stone, perhaps differentiation becomes even more difficult.

Wali, on the other hand, says there is no problem at all as to differentiation. The packet is obviously a wusahun's power healing packet. The puluen-style je, although having dibat around it, which showed that the stone is wusa, not profane, could not be used as a ganekhe because a ganekhe cannot be decorated with a symbolic female skirt, only functionally je profane and other than ganekhe kinds of sacred spirit stones can be so decorated. This line of reasoning, however, is refuted both by the inclusion of a ganekhe stone with a hidden symbolic female skirt (sali) under a dibat bundle in Wali's ganekhe cabinet and by the verbal refutation by other reliable indigenous informants within the Grand Valley and West region. Regarding Nilik's healing power packet just reviewed, I feel that it would not be possible for an outsider to correctly classify it as to which kind of spirit-stone packet it is based only on its contents.

Religio-Medical Kit (Hareken) from Head of Baliem Gorge

In a small compound located on the east side of the Baliem River, southeast of Kurima, at about the point where the river spills out of the Grand Valley to start its rush through the Baliem Gorge (fig. 1.21), an elderly wusahun healer showed me his religio-medical kit (fig. 4.34). Like the religio-medical kit just reviewed from the mid–Grand Valley area (figs. 4.32 and 4.33), it contained two power stones (wamaket), but these were of a radically different nature than the two stones present in the mid–Grand Valley kit. These were spiritually empowered, Yeineri-sourced stone chisels. I have observed more Yeineri-sourced chisels than Tagime-sourced chisels used as supernaturally empowered objects throughout the Grand Valley and West. Denise O'Brien (1969), in her doctoral work on the Western Dani in the Konda Valley, a considerable distance northwest of the Grand Valley (Karubaga on fig. 2.8), adds that she was surprised by the numerous stone chisels present at a time when she saw practically no use of the chisels as profane tools: "I remained puzzled by their function, however, until my last few months in the field. The relative abundance of chisels became clear only when their ceremonial importance was divulged" (1969:90). O'Brien goes on to add that she found that the small unhafted stone chisels were used to represent slain men in war ceremonies.

The old wusahun of the Upper Baliem

Fig. 4.34. The contents of a religio-medical kit from the head of the Baliem Gorge

Gorge had other uses for the sacred chisel power stones, as did others whom I interviewed throughout my research. For the pair of chisels in the Baliem Gorge wusahun healer's kit there was a single important function in addition to empowering and protecting the other implements of the kit from outside ghostly interference. For the treatment of serious illnesses a sacred pig is always ritually killed to furnish meat for both the patient and the wusahun healer. While the pig meat, and often sweet potatoes and greens are steaming, the wusahun is usually inside his own house (or the house of the patient if he has gone on a house call) talking with the patient, diagnosing the cause of ailment, cleansing the area of possible ghostly or spirit contamination, and otherwise preparing for a treatment. The old, retired wusahun stated that when he did a healing he liked to first outline a circle with a narrow rattan strip (about 85 to 110 cm in diameter) beside the fireplace and next to the patient. Along the circumference of the circle he would put one of the empowered chisels (pulu) at a point nearest the doorway, with the cutting edge facing the house entrance. Then, opposite this chisel, along the circumference of the circle, he would place a second chisel, with the sharpened cutting edge facing outward from the circle. The purpose of the first power stone was to repel ghosts, unfriendly spirits, and other possible malevolent intruders at the entranceway. The power from the second was to protect the important pig meat that was prepared for the patient (which would be placed in the center of the circle) from ghostly contamination and "disease." The wusahun then would spread banana leaves on the ground in the center of the circle on which he would lay uncooked parsley (musan) and wurika leaves, which the patient and the wusahun would eat raw. Next, the cooked pork was added to the top of the greens. This wusahun liked to salt the pork to give his patient a culinary treat and to add strength to expel the cause of the illness. Some pieces of the cooked and salted meat would be set aside in one or two small banana leaf bundles for the patient to eat at a later time.

Before eating, the headbone of a water snake (heane), which is seen in the upper left corner of figure 4.34, would be laid beside the wusahun on the outer perimeter of the circle. The wusahun, squatting along the perimeter of the circle then would extend his arms as far as they would reach, symbolically embracing the circle on the ground and the food within. At this time, the wusahun said that he would audibly repeat formulae and blow short breaths directed at the food inside the circle to call upon healing spirits and the power within the stones to help him spiritually cleanse the food of "disease" and instill it with supernatural curing power. If conditions were "right," a meal would be eaten before the wusahun picked up the heane and rubbed it over the wound or "sick place," while at the same time blowing and uttering formulae. If a patient was suffering from a malaise or illness that could not be localized, the wusahun would start at the patient's head and work the heane down and out over the entire body, while at the same time blowing in short breaths onto the patient.

Another curing procedure that features the use of a single chisel power stone is for the wusahun to tie the power stone (chisel) onto a patient's lower arm with a string dibat while blowing the traditional short, sharp breaths against the stone and the patient's wrist. The sharpened end of the stone is tied facing the patient's hand, and it is believed to be effective in preventing the introduction of more illness while the patient is so vulnerable. At the same time the power in the stone reportedly reacts against the causal malevolent factors that are within the person to eject them and thereby get rid of the cause and cure the illness. (For such a procedure a sacred pig must be sacrificed and the chisel must be an item from the wusahun.)

Below the heane, in the upper left corner of figure 4.34, is a short pendant with five cowrie shells sewn onto a single narrow band. The healer sometimes uses this during a curing procedure to drive illness-causing elements from a patient's body. The healer says that the implement is supernaturally powerful and in favor with the spirits because each cowrie shell on the band represents a man killed by an ancestor. When the current owner's older brother owned the neckpiece, he would wear it from a string around his neck when he wanted to signal his staff and allies that he was preparing for war or an ambush against enemies. (I have heard similar stories about the symbolic uses of cowrie shells on narrow bands throughout most of the Highlands area.)

In the loop of the handle of the man's net string purse in figure 4.34 is a single piece of amber-colored tree resin. Tree resin (hotali) in mid–Grand Valley dialect is an item of fundamental importance in a medical kit. Different kinds of resin are used for different purposes. Most tree resin is clear or near-white when first collected, but it turns first yellow and then a dark but translucent brown as it ages. Pieces of resin (hotali) are thought to have a natural affinity as a power object for illness diagnoses, to have various uses in healing treatments, to be able to clear the air of malevolence by burning on the altar, and to use as objects of power in talismen and amulets. Every wusahun healer has a supply of the appropriate kinds of tree resin for a variety of eventualities. Only among the Wano people in and around the Yeineri quarry area did I find resin used on a routine basis as a light source, like a candle.

Below the brown cocoon wrapper is a fire-burned, soot-blackened marsupial skull, and to its lower right two single mandibles. All such skulls and mandibles must be preserved. This seems to be because of a general taboo present throughout the research area. In the Kurima-Upper Baliem Gorge area (fig. 1.21), the people feel that noncompliance will result in the death of some human within the community. The sharp front protruding tooth of the mandible is well known as a profane tool carver (or "tooth graver") and is present in almost every man's profane tool kit. The same kinds of mandibles are used as sacred power objects (hierophanies) throughout the culture. Note that the burned mandible on the left is looped with a bark string dibat. All three of these medical implements are available for discretionary use by the wusahun healer in any of his treatments, as is the small pig hoof with the reed insert. A fiber band dibat is also present on the reed stem insert to protect the spirit power within. A

discerning wusahun can show his concern for a patient by hanging a pig hoof power object above the entrance of a house in which a healing is being performed.

In the lower right-hand corner of figure 4.34, four silvery-white pelecypod shells are seen tied together on a tree bark fiber string. At the wusahun's discretion he can quickly fasten these objects onto a string around his neck or just hold them in his hand to use as a rattle to attract the attention of helper healing spirits. Sometimes when the wusahun wants to converse with these spirits and cannot get their attention (or wants to show a patient that he is conversing with the healing spirits on the patient's behalf), he rattles the shells. Since the healing spirits reportedly do not want these conversations with the wusahun overheard, the wusahun communicates with his mouth closed. Successful consultation with the spirits is manifest when a wusahun returns to a patient, purses his lips tightly, and blows short breaths in rapid succession onto the patient. It is then expected that the patient may recover as soon as the next day.

The religio-medical implements, shown in figure 4.34, as well as others added and subtracted from time to time, are tightly wrapped in the brown cocoon "cloth" wrapper (wulagap) and then carried by the wusahun in his net string purse. Such string purses are often used by older men but rarely by the younger men.

Typical Use of a Religio-Medical Kit (Hareken): Wali Treats Alula

Alula Wilil is a female healer (asiok) who can deal with only certain types of illnesses; supposedly not those requiring advanced skills of the more experienced healers. She lives in Abukulmo compound, not far from Hupainma, Wali's habitation compound, and works in the fields as a daily routine. Some years ago, while Wali was treating Alula for an illness, he received a divination that Alula should become a healer. Alula happily concurred. She received her wusahun from her older brother and her healing skills from Wali. On emergency calls to help a sick Wali, Alula need only walk down a short hillside slope trail to Hupainma. This is a comfort for Wali to know that an asiok is nearby.

One year, when I returned to field work and wanted to visit Alula, I sent a message up to Abukulmo from Hupainma. A message came back that Alula was sick and resting in her house *(honea)*, and she could not receive me. Three days later, I received word that Wali was going to perform a typical healing procedure on Alula at Abukulmo and that I could be present and photograph if I so desired. The healing treatment lasted most of one day. It started at 8:50 A.M. The indoor part of the ritualistic treatment took place in Alula's brother's house, which contains the powerful ganekhe cabinet and its contents on the back wall. Alula sat to the left of the fireplace, where various treatments were performed on her during the day. The area in front of the fireplace was converted to an altar, or preparation space, on which the implements from the medical kit were laid out and spiritually cleansed and their beneficial powers rejuvenated before they were used in the healing. A typical set of objects from a religio-medical kit (hareken) were used, including just one version of the very important wamaket, which is the essential power stone.

The medical team that performed the treatment consisted of Wali, as the wusahun healer, and six assistants, the primary one being Dogobma Wilil, an adult son of Alula's. As is the procedure at all healings of this type, a pig was ritually killed and steamed with sweet potatoes *(hiperi)* and greens in the courtyard adjoining the healing house. The sanctified meat was primarily for the patient but was also eaten by the wusahun healer and his assistants. Just before the healing, Wali slipped out of his holim and into a pair of running shorts and a blue sweatshirt and carefully donned a white net cap. (At this time during my relationship with Wali he would intermittently dress in his traditional attire or in simple modern clothing that had been introduced by recent Western outsiders—just a visible part of the acculturation that is occurring.)

Before actual treatment commenced, the altar space was prepared and cleansing and empowerment of the implements was initiated. A net carrying-bag holding the healing kit (hareken) was conveniently set near the fire-place. Most of the objects from the kit were removed and laid out on a short board between the net bag and the conventional fireside wooden trash container (fig. 4.35). From right to left, a packet of narrow jiwi leaves, a piece of gami bark, some freshly cut wolo leaves, a strip of gami wood overlying a piece of wolo leaf, and on the left edge of the board, a piece of hotali can be seen. Just off the board toward the fireplace is a nut *(nalelen)* set into a woven handle. A stone, disk-shaped anvil called a *helikit,* had been brought around from the backside of the fireplace and was the base on which a piece of tree resin (hotali) was ignited with a wooden stem (hite) lighted in the fireplace. During this part of the procedure, Wali uttered incantations to drive off malevolent ghosts and spirits. The stated reason for burning the hotali was so that, "evil ghosts and spirits would leave the area where the healing was to be conducted," a poignant early evolutionary manifestation of the burning of incense by many—perhaps most—religions worldwide today.

Dogobma laid down two large sweet potatoes on the space that was now serving as an altar. Wali, seated to the right, leaned over the sweet potatoes and with a laying-on of the hands quietly recited the religious blessing of the potatoes. The sweet potatoes, being on the altar, would continue to benefit from the power being transmitted from the ganekhe cabinet as well as by their proximity to ceremonial power transfers that were to take place on the altar. The sweet potatoes would then be steamed with the sacrificed pig and later be fed to a wusa pig that Alula was raising. (This wusa pig is the largest, 1.8 m long, that I have seen in the Highlands. It is being raised to be killed at a future unspecified but admittedly important healing ritual, where the cure of a patient will be considered of utmost importance.)

Soon Dogobma removed the power stone packet from the carrying net and unwrapped it. In this case, the power stone (wamaket) was tightly wrapped with light-colored isan bark in a packet that also included both old and freshly cut wolo leaves. This particular power stone (wamaket) is called, in its present context as a sacred stone, a *uken*. Before transformation from the profane to the sacred, it was known to the users as an adze blade *(habo)*. It is a small, green, Yeineri-style adze blade. In a similar fashion, the Dani users call the profane stone chisel (pulu), as described in the previous section, also a uken. They do not seem to differentiate a uken stone by its lithology, structure, or by its former profane use. The uken was maintained with wolo leaves. The fresh wolo on the small board altar with the bundle of jiwi leaves, the gami bark, and the piece of hotali were not only functional within this healing ritual but they were simultaneously being spiritually cleansed and empowered for future use.

It was only moments later that one of Wali's assistants made a piece of fiber string from yakik bark. Using this, he carefully made three loops with the string around the uken and tied it off as a dibat. Both the uken and its newly applied dibat were then generously anointed with sacralized pig fat. While this was happening, the assistant was blowing, in short quick breaths, onto the stone and intermittently muttering uninterpretable words. The freshly anointed stone was next handed to Wali, who profusely recited religious formula and also blew on the stone before it was set back down onto the wolo leaves in its open isan wrapper (fig. 4.36).

Next, a narrow woven neck band that had been decorated with a cowrie shell and a single row of nassa shells (walimok) was picked up from its place on the altar and rubbed lightly with sacred pig fat. Again, Wali blew and uttered religious formulae. Then, while holding the neck band, Wali audibly recited the names of all of the people in Alula's family who had died. The assistants joined in from time to time with agreeable noises. Wali and the group were advising the spirits that too many relatives had already died in the hope that the spirits would abandon any evil project against Alula and remove the cause of her illness. Wali set the neck band (walimok) down beside the uken and then burned a piece of hotali that had come from the medical kit. He next summoned the assistants closer as he urged them to put their hands on (or point toward) a piece of

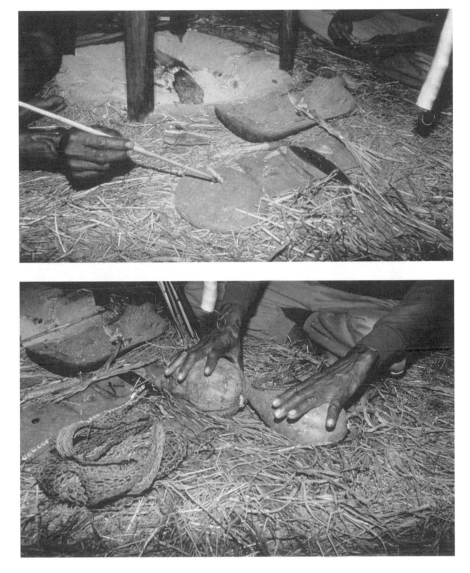

hotali that he held in his hands. Incantations and formula were again verbalized by Wali as he attempted to exorcise himself and his assistants of any malevolent spirits (negative power) that might be within them and to properly empower their hands for what they would do next. After Wali uttered a final loud, "out, out" as he clapped his hands, he, Dogobma, and Ikibadek rubbed consecrated grease on their hands before transferring it onto Alula's head, face, and body. The two power objects (the power stone, wamaket uken and the necklace, walimok) were still lying exposed on the altar during this procedure. This was the end of only one facet of the ritualistic healing treatment. Before going on to the next task, Wali cleansed

Fig. 4.35. The contents of one of Wali's religio-medical kits

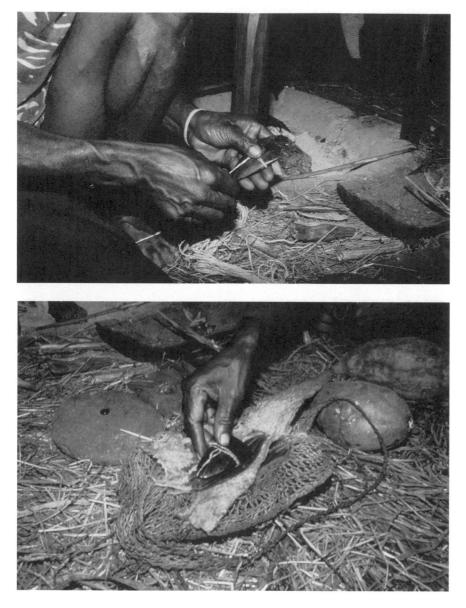

Fig. 4.36. *A fiber string dibat is tied around the power stone.*

his hands as well as those of the two who had assisted him in this part of the ritual by waving the feather wand (totok) and reciting more formula.

Then Wali and the men departed the house to make ready the rock heating fire and the cooking pit, and then to kill the pig. After the two hind legs of the pig were briefly looped with twine and tied, symbolically with a dibat isin, the pig was killed and its tail cut off with a bamboo knife. Alula emerged from the house and sat on the banana leaves, where the pig would be butchered. Ikibadek, another of Wali's assistants, carried the dead pig. Wali carried the

sweet potatoes as they circled around Alula to demonstrate for all the spirits to see what they were doing for Alula and to hopefully lure the good spirit back into Alula's body so she could enjoy the wusa food she was about to get. (Apparently the cause of illness had been diagnosed as the departure of Alula's spirit from her body.) Alula sat for a few minutes and then went back into the house. Ikibadek carried the dead pig over to the door and laid it down for a few seconds as a gesture to invite both Alula's spirit and that of the pig to enter the house where Alula was waiting.

Wali and two of his helpers entered the house to continue the healing inside while the others attended to chores in the courtyard. Wali settled down on the floor, setting the tone by uttering incantations. Next he picked up the cowrie shell necklace (walimok) from its place on the altar and proceeded over to Alula where he placed it about her neck. Then, he picked up the adze blade (uken), rewrapped it with wolo leaves into its isan covering, and, by placing it inside of a net bag that Alula had removed from her head and back, presented the adze blade (uken) to Alula. As Alula bowed her head while holding the net bag, with the included power stone against one shoulder, Wali did a blessing and laying-on of the hands (put one hand on each side of Alula's head) as he encouraged any bad spirits to depart and Alula's good spirit to re-enter. This was the end of the *eyageukalek*. The feather wand (totok) was waved again before Wali moved on to the next task.

While the eyageukalek was progressing inside, Dogobma and Sularek Wilil were laboring across the courtyard *(sili)* behind Alula's family house (honea). The two of them were fastidiously weeding the low ghost/spirit enclosure (waro leget) that was built against the backside of Alula's house. Old crumbling slats that formed the walls of this low enclosure were replaced with new. The small doorway of the waro leget was cleaned of moldy leaf debris. Dogobma stuck two sticks *(asusu)* from a *he* tree in the ground in the center of the waro leget. After the steam bundle was opened, a bunch of freshly cooked ferns was added to the top of the asusu, looking symbolically like a flag at the top of a flag pole. Friendly spirits were thus alerted that they had not been forgotten and that their spirit house had been cleaned. Other humans would also be alerted by this visible signpost to stay away from the waro leget. This is the enclosure from which Alula would call friendly spirits to enter her *house* at propitious moments to assist with her own healing procedures as a healer (asiok). It was hoped by this act of renovation and cleaning of the waro leget that friendly spirits would return and assist in helping Alula to a speedy recovery. As the two men left the now renovated waro leget and returned to the central area of the courtyard, it was with a feeling of satisfaction that they had played a role in helping to remove the cause of Alula's illness.

Meanwhile, Elegius Faluk was working at his chore of setting a long, slender limbless tree trunk, that had just been cut, into a freshly dug hole in the courtyard, to one side of Alula's house (honea). Before tamping dirt back into the hole to support the pole in an upright position, Elegius added a piece of newly blessed tree resin (hotali) to the hole. This was a gesture to ask the ancestor spirits to hold the pole upright and to move through it into Alula, who was about to climb onto it. This would be a way to help Alula in her fight to ward off evil spirits.

Inside of the house, Wali concurrently presented Alula with a bow and set of arrows for her use in a symbolic fight against the malevolent spirits that were causing her illness. It is thought that the bow and arrows might frighten away bad spirits and discourage them from attacking Alula in the future. Alula was led outside of the house to the tree-pole that she climbed onto, while clutching her newly acquired bow and arrows (fig. 4.37). (Note the black streak of paint [charcoal bits mixed with pig grease] across Alula's face that she wears with the authority of a healer [asiok] to attract beneficent healing spirits for desired communication.) As Alula stood for a few minutes, holding on to the tree trunk, Wali and his six assistants danced in a moving circle around Alula, sing-chanting, much as is done at some war victory dances (edai), but in this case the circular dance, with the patient in the middle, is

called an *akot wakanin* or a "bringing back of the spirit." Malevolent spirits were by this act hopefully scared off, and Alula's life-spirit encouraged to re-enter her body.

Cooked pig meat and sweet potatoes had already been laid out on banana leaves and greens on the floor altar before the fireplace by the time that Wali, with Alula and the entourage, had re-entered the house. Wali moved the

Fig. 4.37. As a part of the healing ritual, Alula stands on a tree pole.

ceremony along as he blessed a single white cockatoo feather, called a *yakik*. As Wali carefully inserted the feather into Alula's hair, just above her forehead, he muttered in the religious language (wusa ane) and urged Alula's good spirit to return to its place of normal residence in her forehead. Wali then carefully selected a fiber dibat that had been previously prepared and blessed. While blowing on the dibat and Alula, he affixed it about her neck in a *dibat iriyogi* procedure. Next, Wali selected a choice piece of sanctified pig meat and a large sweet potato from the combined food offering and held them before Alula while she took her first bites. An assisting wusahun pointed his hands toward Alula as she began to eat, and he recited formulae that urged the missing soul-spirit to return with the food into Alula's body. Alula, humbly postured, with the newly acquired power stone (uken) tucked within her head-back net and resting on her back, the recently acquired power nassa shell necklace, two old dibat, and the ritually powered new dibat iriyogi around her neck; the white cockatoo yakik feather stuck above her forehead, and a hand with the stubs of four amputated finger tips guiding the sacralized potato to her mouth, appeared ready to receive back the soul-spirit whose disappearance it was thought had caused her illness. No foods with chemical medicinal properties were used during the procedure.

As Alula began to eat, Wali and the other medical team also began to eat of the sweet potatoes (hiperi), greens, and pig meat that were on the altar. This ritual feast is called a *wamtatak nuwok*. That night the healers and others in Alula's compound, came together to traditionally sing and dance as a continuing thrust to cure Alula, their healer (asiok). In three days, Alula appeared to have regained her strength and she said that her edai egen was normal.

In the healing ritual to cure Alula, the rich interplay of the kinds of material goods that were used so often as symbolic tools in humankind's endeavors to deal with problems caused by unknown factors are apparent. We were able to observe material objects in the archaeological context of an assemblage, so to speak, and then in some detail the behavior that was prompted by function.

To gain a broader understanding of the range of stone objects with their interrelated other material goods as related to known function, refer to the appendix for examples of a representative set of the more simply constituted healing kits (hareken) and power stones (wamaket) that are commonly used throughout the Highlands; any of which are representative of similar objects that we often uncover in the archaeological record.

Power Stones and Packets for Other Than Medical Uses

In addition to the resolution of health problems with the assistance of supernaturally empowered religio-medical implements, there are a multitude of other kinds of specific problems and broader societal issues that must be faced with the assistance of power stones and empowered packets.

Throughout the entire research area, men and women alike may individually or as groups maintain a single or several different kinds of empowered but undecorated stones to promote individual or group well-being (including pigs). These kinds of power objects include river-rounded and polished pebbles, ammonite fossils, to a much lesser extent belemnite fossils, small pieces of white quartz, quartz crystals, other naturally shaped rock oddities, and small ground stone tool blades (both adze and knife). Sometimes pig tails received at a dress-the-bride ceremony or a shaman-directed healing procedure are maintained in a similar fashion. Of all of the kinds of rocks used in this context, the most common is the river-rounded pebble. These round stones are maintained mostly by women. They are held in such high regard by the women for promoting pig health and fertility and human family well-being that I doubt there are many adult married women throughout the research area who do not own one or more of them. Because these stones are sacred, a special effort is made to keep them hidden from children, who consider them attractive toys.

Among the Kimyal (fig. 1.3), all of the various kinds of these unadorned power stones are individually called *bumado,* as well as entire assortments of such stones that are maintained in small net bags (fig. 4.38). The stones are usually nested with vegetal fibers in the containing nets. The men hang bumado (entire bag of stones) near ancestor power stones (in the ganekhe cabinet) to continually empower the bumado. The group (of old men), who maintained the bumado shown in figure 4.38, stated that whenever they would open a new potato field, a man would climb a tree that was located in the center of the garden and cut a lower limb letting the white quartz rocks (bumado) fall with the limb to the ground. Then work could be commenced in the new field. Two or three of the old men, at least one with shaman power, would hide the white stones at the base of the tree, unbeknown to others who would work in the garden. The tree would be left standing, with its power objects at its base, until the garden was allowed to go fallow. Then the power of the stones would be rejuvenated and the procedure repeated at the opening of another new garden. The three old men thought that the white quartz stones were pieces of very old sacred pig fat that had turned to rock.

Among the Kimyal, all of these kinds of power stones (bumado) were empowered through sacred ritual by an appropriate Kimyal shaman *(sunruba).* Knowing that a sunruba had put spirit power in the stones, the people would use them with confidence. From time to time before most sacred rituals, but especially at times like a major harvest or the opening of a new garden, a big man (with supernatural power, sunruba) would direct that all people anoint their bumado with sacred pig fat.

The Kimyal, as well as other language-speaking groups in the Yali and East region, sometimes include small Langda-Sela-produced adze blades as bumado. When this is done, all flake scars must be ground down until the entire surface of the blade is smooth and polished. Such an adze blade used as a sacred power stone (bumado) by the Kimyal is called a *yogaba.* In addition to the completely polished Langda-Sela-style adze blades, the Kimyal also use small Yeineri- and Tagime-style adze blades

as bumado. Sometimes stone knives are used. Empowered adze blades (bumado to the Kimyal, *wamaket* to the Dani) are commonly used, not only by the Kimyal but throughout the entire Grand Valley and West and the Yali and East regions, as favored objects to be planted with both taro and potato cuttings in order to encourage their growth. The potential impact of this practice on interpretation of the archaeological record is significant. For the first five years of my field project, male horticultur-

Fig. 4.38. River-rounded power stones and a Kimyal bag of bumado

ists would sometimes tell me in answer to my standard question about the source of an adze blade: "I found it over there in a potato field." Visits to these sites revealed nothing helpful. At first my interpretation was that these people either did not want me to know where a particular adze blade had come from, or they did not remember—or they were purposely trying to mislead me. Then, I learned that indeed blades had been found in the gardens—as a remainder trail of fertilizing practices and not as lost or abandoned blades while clearing the forest or working the soil.

Power Stones with Woven String Handles

When empowered stones (and less often objects of other materials) are fastened with a meticulously woven jacket of string onto wooden or reed handles, the resulting sacred implement is called a *liru* (alt. *iluk*). Before being empowered through ritual and/or exposure to the ganekhe, most of the liru power stones are either profane adze blades or chisels.

The liru shown in the following sequence of figures are representative of this kind of power implement, which are not normally used as religio-medical tools, as are the healer's kits (hareken) and power stones (wamakets) previously discussed. Instead, they are more often used by wusahun, as well as the common people to deal with the myriad of problems of life. Wusahun often carry power packets with a liru included, as they go about any of a variety of special duties. A war leader in time of war might use a selection of several liru out on a battlefield site to drive off attacking enemy spirits and to keep his warriors safe. When a warrior is wounded in battle, the war leader wusahun may accompany the surgeon specialist who removes arrows, or he might be the surgeon himself. The fact that the wusahun carries an empowered liru or other power objects to assist at occasions like this is comforting to other involved individuals, even though the liru may not be visually apparent. When returning from battle, a wusahun often proceeds to hang one or more liru (or other power stones) that he has been carrying, inside a ganekhe cabinet to rejuvenate them; although the normal place

for storage of these implements is in the ceiling of the men's house.

In one use, liru influence social etiquette, even though these power tools may not necessarily be seen by those whom they are controlling. Often when hosting a pig feast, the big man in charge may be concerned that some people might attempt to eat more than their share of pig meat. Having this fear, the host—a big man responsible for the feast—may invite a particular wusahun who is known for his skills with handling protocol and social behavior to be a guest. A wusahun, so invited, usually does attend the function, but as a part of his wusahun duties, he secretly brings with him a liru, which he either hangs inside the men's house or carries with him as he circulates among the guests. One wusahun told me that on some occasions he would even hide a liru under the leaves of the ground altar where a pig is to be sacrificed. Seeing the presence of this particular wusahun, the people know that a power object is nearby, and that they must therefore be careful to exhibit proper manners and not eat more than their share of meat. To otherwise indulge would assuredly enrage the spirit within the liru who would cause the offender to become ill, or in cases of flagrant violations, to die.

In figure 4.39, nine liru are presented. For reference purposes I refer to the liru sequentially from left to right. Each liru has a string or string loop on one end with which the liru can be tied or hung from another object, such as a structural member within a house or as an amulet from a person's clothing. The woven parts of the implements are thought of as handles by most modern Western outsiders but not by the users of these power objects. To facilitate description of the liru, I will, however, refer to the woven parts as handles. The nine objects come from different male owners and were collected in the period of time from 1982 through 1991. The decoration present on each liru reflects a normal variation of the personal preferences that are expressed by each owner. Similarly, different personalized weaving styles are obvious by the variation in loop patterns that are seen on the individual objects. Most of

Fig. 4.39. Nine woven-handled amulets (liru), each with its power stone

these liru and others like them are normally maintained in combination with other objects, such as sticks, pieces of wood, or leaves, and carried about in neatly wrapped packets or small net purses, like the healing kits described in the previous section. Recognizing that the liru are sacred tools and that their included power stones are no longer identified by the traditional population in the context of the former profane function of each stone, I will however, for the purposes of this analysis, identify the power stones of each liru according to the classification previously used for their profane uses (chapter 2). In this set of nine liru, five of the power stones are small adze blades; three are Yeineri style and two Tagime style. Three of the stones are chisels; two are Yeineri style and one a Tagime style. One of the power stones is a black pebble, shaped only by natural process. It is probably either a mudstone or meta-argillite. Attention to detail in the woven jackets and decoration of power stones numbers two, five, seven, eight, and nine can be seen in the drawings in figures 4.40, 4.41, and 4.42.

In addition to adze blades, empowered chisels are also favored items to be used as empowered objects, not only without decoration or

embellishment but, like the adze blades shown in figures 4.39, 4.40, 4.41, with tubular-shaped woven "handles" (figs. 4.43 and 4.44).

The most unusual handle that I have observed on an empowered object while doing research in the Highlands was a dried section of leg skin from a cassowary bird (fig. 4.45). The length of the sacred object is 24.7 cm. The Tagime-style adze blade power stone that is tied into the piece of leg skin is 5.1 cm wide, with 3.9 cm protruding from the "handle."

Very small natural stones and other small attractive natural objects also often have woven "handles" of bark string, made with a loop or strand to facilitate their use as amulets, not only to be hung on articles of clothing and as adornment but also placed over entranceways or other places within the house. These sacred objects are used throughout the entire adult population without regard to the political or religious status of a using individual. These kinds of objects and materials are thought of as being natural spirit containers, although their power is usually also enhanced by ritual and/or exposure to the ganekhe. The specific objects most-used within both the Grand Valley and West and the Yali and East are quartz crystals; ammonite fossils exposed in broken, river-

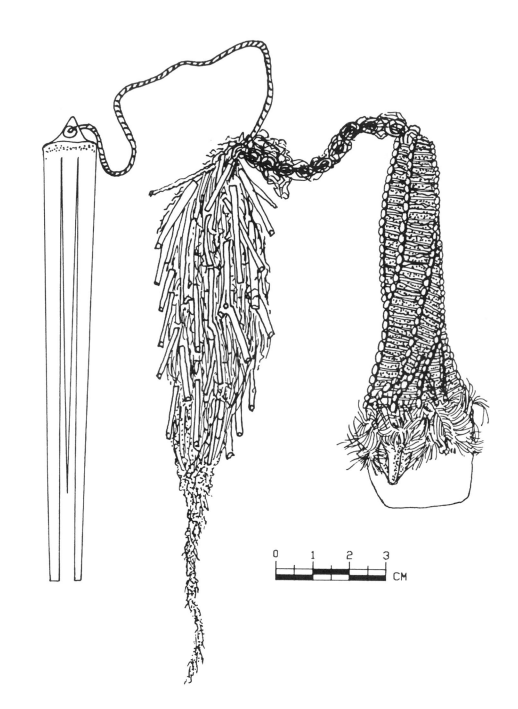

Fig. 4.40. The details of amulet number nine

tumbled pebbles; spherically shaped river stones; pieces of amber-colored, solidified tree resin (hotali); and small pieces of gami, sali, and jiwi wood. In figure 4.46, two of these commonly used amulets are shown along with the exposed, unwrapped types of materials from which they were made. On the left are quartz crystals, often called star stones, and on the right a piece of amber-colored, solidified, tree resin, which is highly regarded for use as a

power material. At times, the tree resin (hotali) is spoken about as a rock, a very special kind of rock that will burn.

In figure 4.47, Kocia Posia, at the head of the Baliem Gorge, is shown wearing an amulet attached to her carrying net. The power material in the amulet is a small stick of sali wood and is being worn by Kocia to protect the baby in her carrying net from harm. Another small amulet of jiwi root, carried in the bottom of the net, below the baby, is to protect the child from ants especially attracted by urine. Kocia said that for the general health and care of her children she also likes to use sali wood-powered amulets, routinely tied over the tie string of another young daughter's skirt and inside her house, above the entrance.

Sun Houses and Their Sacred Symbolic Stone
Within the Dani and Western Dani language speaking groups (fig. 1.3), the culturally most

powerful *individual* sacred symbolic stones are the least known. Peters, working in the early 1960s in the Grand Valley, learned that the Dani understood a beneficial relationship between sunlight and good potato crops, and that the Dani held the sun in great respect. Carefully pointing a finger at the sun, the Dani said, *"Mo ninajuk-en,"* which means "We shudder with awe for the sun" (Peters 1975:59, translation from German). The Dani would tell Peters no more. Heider, working northeast of Wamena in the Grand Valley at about the same time, recognized that the big men Maikmo and Gutelu both had close relationships with the sun and that Maikmo "has a special relationship with the sun *and* the moon" (1970:90–91). But Heider, like Peters, never put the people's relationship with the sun into a cultural systemic perspective. In Heider's review of the subject he points out the following:

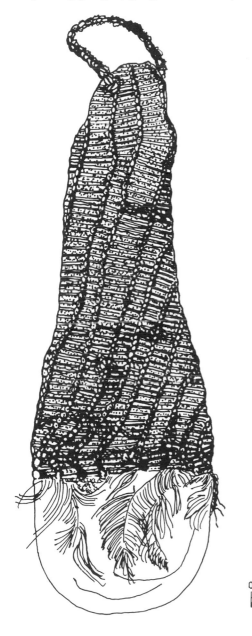

a

b

Fig. 4.41. Amulets (a) number five and (b) number two

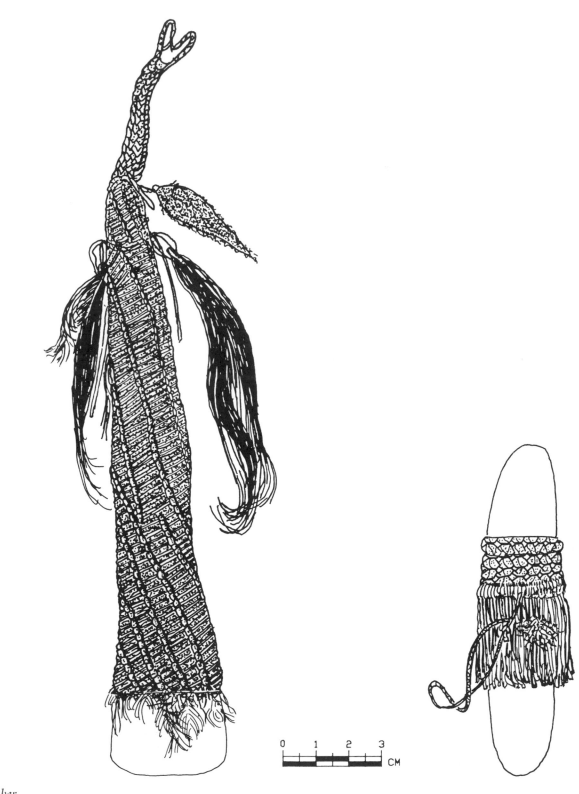

Fig. 4.42. Amulets (a) number
seven and (b) number eight

a

b

0 1 2 3 CM

Fig. 4.43. Empowered chisels are often used as sacred objects.

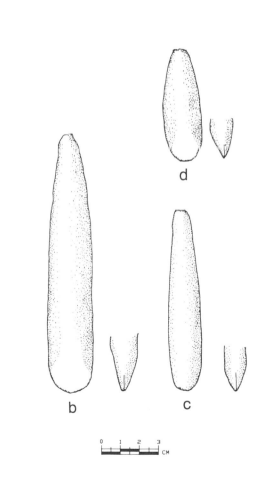

a

b

c

d

Fig. 4.44. A woven-handled chisel amulet and three empowered plain chisels

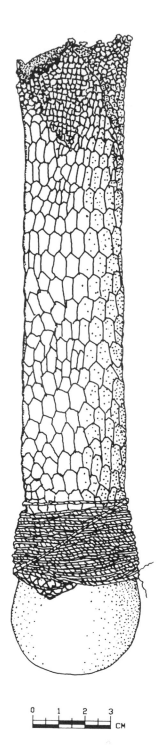

Fig. 4.45. An adze blade power stone with cassowary leg skin handle

0 1 2 3 CM

The sun is called *mo* and is a woman of terrible aspect: she has long hair, which is uncommon for Dani women; wears a married woman's skirt; she carries a spear, and wears men's decorations. . . . During the day the sun moves across the underneath of the sky. At sunset she sits down on a *dabul* (the

dried grass on the floor of a house) and retraces her steps above the sky to her home. In the winter months, when the sun is in the south, her home is in the Jalemo; during the summer months at Wadlagu, in the Pass Valley. . . . Most questions about the sun were met with professions of ignorance. . . . The Wadlagu compounds lie at the far eastern end of the Pass Valley, and it is here that the sun is said to spend the night. . . . Although I visited Wadlagu with Gutelu, I was not allowed to examine the house carefully and I took photographs with difficulty. This attitude . . . suggests the great *wusa*, or power, of the house. The house is about 2.5 meters high at the roof's ridge. It stands on stilts one meter above the ground. The wall and floor construction is of wood slabs. . . . The entrance is closely boarded. The roof is of two-meter semicircular bark strips, apparently from the trunk of pandanus trees. . . . The entrance faces west.

Gutelu explained that inside the house were nets, skirts, and other such feminine paraphernalia of the sun. . . . F. Verheijen, who visited the house after I did, reported (in a personal communication) that when he saw it, it was empty. It was not possible to learn more of the ritual or symbolism surrounding the sun. (1970:210)

The simple architecture of the house that Heider describes at Wadlagu (alt. Wadangku, as used by Gutelu Mabel patrilineage today) belies its true significance as a religious center where some groups of Dani and Western Dani come to conduct rituals to propitiate the sun. In a very real sense, these people belong to a regional "sun cult," who, in addition to the practice of ancestor worship, make periodic pilgrimages to the sun center to conduct rituals with pig sacrifices and vegetable offerings before a sun symbol. In 1989 and again in 1991, I photographed the rebuilt version of the "Heider sun house," which was burned to the ground in the war of 1977. The rebuilt house is a remarkable replication of its predecessor (fig. 4.48).

To many people in the Grand Valley and West, the sun is a woman called *mo.* Some

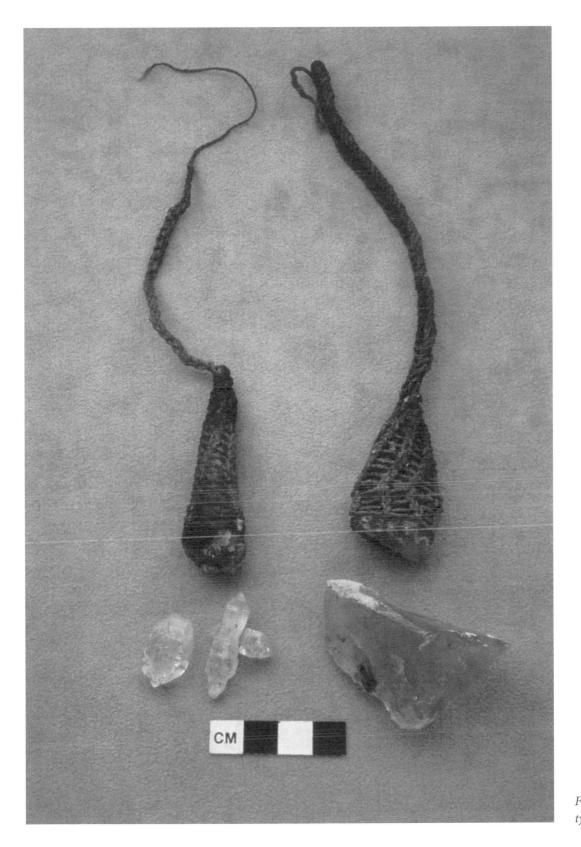

Fig. 4.46. *Two commonly used types of amulets*

Fig. 4.47. Kocia Pocia wears an amulet tied to her head net.

people refer to the sun as "our mother" (Nina-koja, alt. Naguja); while others call the sun Muliki. Throughout the area of the Grand Valley, the moon is called *sut*. The stars are called *husagal*. The people believe that all of these are important to the well-being of all forms of life within their cosmos, but it is the sun that reigns supreme as the most powerful life-giving entity of the three; the stars in this perspective being of little importance. Some people contend that although the sun is the single life-sustaining spirit-power entity, it is not female, but male. One thing that is agreed on by everyone is that the sun is very powerful and is held in awe.

The people believe that the sun, like all life forms, originated in the center of the earth. The understanding of the sun's current existence by the people in the Grand Valley is that the sun arises each day in her sun house in the lower Pass Valley area, travels across the sky, furnishing light and heat and "making the sweet potatoes grow," and returns to her house each night (fig. 1.21).

There is a story known by members of the Gutelu Mabel patrilineage that accounts for construction of the sun house at Wadangku (alt. Wadlagu) and sun propitiation. The

grandfathers passed this story down from father to son: Long ago (number of generations not specified), the sun disappeared; left the sky. (Had there been an eclipse?) When the sun returned and showed itself again, the people decided to build a house for the sun to encourage it to keep making its daily trips across the sky and thereby furnish its all important light, heat, and sun energy.

In the Lower Pass Valley, within an hour's walk of each other, there are three separate sacred compounds built just for sun worship, each with its own sun house. They are called Wadangku, Wagima, and Lukuluku. Wadangku has a sacred meaning that cannot be spoken. Wagima translates to "come," meaning "sun, you come." There was no translation available for Lukuluku. The sacred compound of Wadangku is often referred to as Wadangku Waga. Waga means "*the* sacred sun house." At Wadangku Waga, it is said that ceremonies are held to propitiate "the sun for the sun"; at Lukuluku, "sun for the war"; and at Wagima, "sun for the *waija*" (people of the *waija* moiety).

Control of these three sacred compounds within the regional center for sun rituals is by an interesting arrangement of leadership. For each sun house compound there must be a pair of leaders: one big man from the waija moiety and one from the wida moiety. At the Wadangku Waga the leadership consists of a big man from the Mabel patrilineage and one from the Logo (alt. Dloko). The leadership is the same for the Lukuluku, but for the Wagima sun house there is a big man from the Mabel patrilineage and one from the Dabi patrilineage. The Mabels are wida; the Logo (alt. Dloko) and Dabi are waija. During the era of the last great "big men," before the demise of the big man alliancewide leadership system due to the incursion of outsiders, Gutelu Mabel was the controlling wida representative of each of the individual sacred sun house compounds. Gutelu had parlayed political influence into religious leadership as well. All big men are known to have wusahun (supernatural spirit power), but Gutelu's was of the grandest proportions and most powerful.

Each of the sacred sun house compounds within the sun religious center has a resident guard, which is an inherited position. When I was doing my research at Wadangku Waga, the guard was Biolok Logo, who is the son of the man who was resident guard when Karl Heider visited Wadangku with Gutelu in the 1960s. Biolok told me that his only son would inherit the same job at the appropriate time. The other current guards (1980–91) are Englakhalok Mabel at Wagima and Dabuke Logo at Lukuluku.

Within the "sun cult" organizational system, each of the sun house compounds in the Lower Pass Valley religious center have subsidiary branches in and around Jiwika, a total of five branch sun houses in all. The Wadangku Waga (sun worship for the sun) has one branch sun house at Jiwika very near to Gutelu Mabel's habitation compound and another up the hill from Jiwika, near the compound of Obia, which is not far from the Ileukaima brine pool. The Lukuluku (sun propitiation for war) has one branch at Jiwika, and Wagima (sun propitiation for the waija) has one branch sun house on the hill behind Jiwika and another at Sunpaima, where an ancestral mummy is maintained. Outside this close-knit organizational complex, including the ritual center for the sun cult in the Lower Pass Valley and its branches in

Fig. 4.48. Close-up views of Wadangku Waga sacred sun house

and around Jiwika, there is evidence for sun cult presence throughout the Grand Valley, its surrounding mountainside fringe, and as far west as Mulia and Ilaga (fig. 4.49). Sun cult activities have been identified at Ilugum, Kelila, Bokondini, Karubaga, Mulia, Sinak, Mamit, Tagime, Tiom, Eragnyam, Winam, Obakma, Landikma, Ilu, Wolo, Yalengga, Pyramid, Poga, Ilugwa, Kurima, Tangma, Seinma, Ituga, Pugima, Wamena, and Hetigima. However, none have been reported from the Yali, but it is suspected by the author.

The cycle of sun rituals flows with the five-year ebe akho at which time representative big

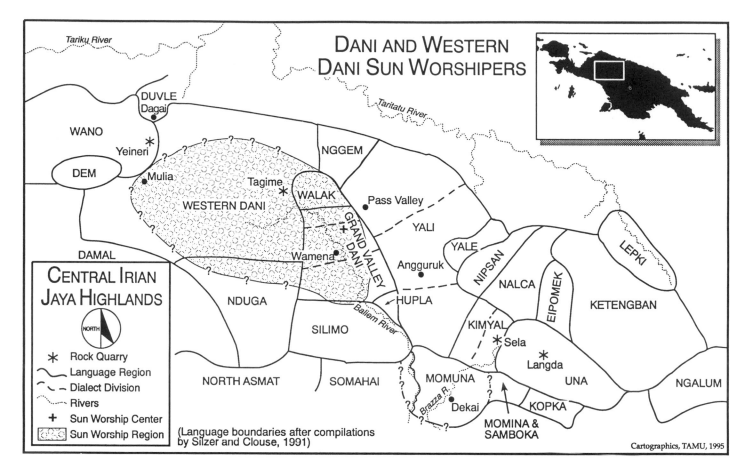

DANI AND WESTERN DANI SUN WORSHIPERS

CENTRAL IRIAN JAYA HIGHLANDS

NORTH

* Rock Quarry
Language Region
Dialect Division
Rivers
+ Sun Worship Center
Sun Worship Region

(Language boundaries after compilations by Silzer and Clouse, 1991)

Cartographics, TAMU, 1995

Fig. 4.49. Dani and Western Dani "sun cult" region

men from confederacies within the Dloko-Mabel alliance brought a big sacrificial pig and other food offerings to Gutelu at Jiwika where the group gathered before proceeding to Wadangku Waga for sun rituals. According to Mabel informants, at least one representative from each of the two moieties must be present at every sun ritual that is held at any of the sun houses in the Lower Pass Valley religious center. Regardless of current events, Gutelu reportedly officiated at a sun ceremony routinely once a year. Participants were obligated to bring sweet potatoes, bananas, and sugarcane to be used as offerings to the sun. Gutelu furnished a large pig for sacrifice. On a discretionary basis, other participants might also furnish one or more pigs. At any time, local groups of the sun cult from anywhere within the region might feel the need for a sun ceremony. On such occasions, they would send an envoy to Gutelu at Jiwika to make arrangements. Gutelu would usually allow safe passage to Wadangku Waga, even to enemies during times of active war—a pay-

ment of a pig and/or other items of food was understood. Any given big man throughout the region might feel the desire to initiate a sun ceremony at Wadangku for his group for any of the following reasons:

1. The sweet potato harvests had not been good.
2. It had been raining too much and that is spoiling the crops or will not allow a sunny planting time.
3. Flooded areas need to be dried. Only a series of continuous sunny days will dry the fields.
4. Illness abounds and several key people are sick or dying.
5. Children are sick or "look sickly."
6. Pigs are not plentiful or do not seem to be growing fast enough.
7. The soil in a newly opened garden does not seem "good" (I do not know on what basis such a judgment is made.)
8. Miscellaneous, personal reasons.

War matters, in a similar fashion, are taken to Lukuluku but must likewise have been taken there with Gutelu's approval and a payment of goods. When a group from out of the region would arrive at Jiwika for a sun ceremony, their offerings were divided, part to be used for a ritual to be held with Gutelu at Jiwika preparatory to the entire group (with Gutelu) proceeding from the Gutelu habitation compound to the sun cult center in the Lower Pass Valley. For the trip to the sun center, the participants traveled via a trail that enters the mountain wall directly behind Jiwika, rises up a steep hillside valley, and winds past the Ileukaima brine pool to the Lower Pass Valley sacred sun compounds. It was felt by Gutelu and others that the answer to the riddle of the presence of the brine pool that they passed is to be found at Wadangku Waga, "where the sun has made the salt and from whence the brine comes." So Gutelu, or more probably his ancestors, have tied the presence of the brine pool, within the people's belief system, to the "creator" sun. Just as Gutelu granted safe passage to the sun center for the devoted, so he would, for a fee, grant safe passage also to the brine pool. However, in times of war and with certain enemies, it is said that Gutelu steadfastly refused access to Ileukaima.

It is customary for big men within the region to continuously be raising one large wusa pig for sacrifice to the sun. If that particular pig dies for an unknown reason before it can be sacrificed, it is said that the pig must be cremated and not eaten. On those occasions it was expected by custom and by Gutelu that the big man concerned would pay a visit to Gutelu and explain the particulars. The two men together might decide that a sacrifice and offerings should be made to the sun, at which time sweet potatoes would be sanctified and fed to another pig that would be identified and raised as a wusa replacement for the pig that had unexpectedly died.

A few of the older people attest to a benevolent act on Gutelu's part. If a big man who came to Gutelu with a great need for a sun ceremony was of poor circumstance, Gutelu himself had been known to furnish all of the offertory items. (I presume that such an act on Gutelu's part was done with the understood precondition of a later pay-back because that is the way these kinds of matters are handled by big men in the Irian Jaya Highlands.)

One way that a big man within the region of membership of the sun cult notified other big men that he was planning a trip to the sun center to pay homage, in the interest of health matters, was to send by courier a single white cockatoo feather to those whom he felt might be interested in joining him in such an endeavor. A positive response was to send a large sacred pig back to the organizer, to be maintained by the organizer as a sacrifice to the sun, until the journey to the sun center was made.

Originally, the three sun houses at the lower Pass Valley sun center were rectangular (nearly square) closed wooden structures that were built on stilts (like Wadangku Waga, fig. 4.48). It seems logical that members of the sun cult would want to build their sun houses up on stilts, close to and with easy access to the sky where the sun travels during daylight hours. However, all three sun houses were destroyed by fire during the war of 1977. The two at Lukuluku and Wadangku were replicated on the spots of the original sacred houses. The house at Wagima (sun worship for the waija) was also rebuilt, but not in its original architectural style. It is circular with a thatch roof, like any other Dani men's house (except larger). Some waija representatives of the Wagima sun house leadership discreetly told me that their sun symbol disappeared at the time that their sun house was burned in the war of 1977, but they know that the sun still exists because it continues to light the sky and heat the earth each day. When the sun symbol returns, I was advised that an architecturally correct sun house will be rebuilt.

At Wagima, the circular sun house is located in a separate courtyard (with its own steam pits and a small cookhouse) that adjoins the primary courtyard of the Wagima sacred compound by a common fence. The sun house courtyard is reserved for rituals related to the sun. At Lukuluku and Wadangku Waga, the sun houses are an integral part of the inner compound fence, which encloses the main compound courtyards. Architecturally, the wooden sun houses are designed with one doorway for the use of human beings, which is securely closed with wooden planks. High on another wall, a small entranceway is usually left open for the use of the sun.

The mystery of the lack of evidence for a tangible symbolic presence of the sun spirit-god has been just that, a mystery. But, like the personified, worshiped ancestors with their symbolic stone bodies, the sun spirit was not to be denied its symbolic body. At Wadangku Waga it is a somewhat circular, flat natural stone covered with a mass of sparkling quartz crystals. Similar, sacred spirit stones were the symbolic stones that were also used to represent the sun body-spirit entity at the other two Pass Valley sacred sun houses. At Wadangku Waga, the spirit stone hangs in a simple nogen from the ceiling. These special sun stones are considered unique objects of the sun cult group's ganekhe. Whether or not clumps of multiple crystals or possibly individual crystals are maintained anywhere else throughout the region of the sun cult as sacred sun symbols within the ganekhe, I do not know. It is professed by members of the sun cult that the sun spirit departs its (symbolic) stone body in the sun house each morning, to travel the skies by day as the visible ball of bright light we know as the sun, and to return to its stone "spirit bones" body each night. Some few informants even maintain that the symbolic stone-spirit entity of the sun leaves Wadangku Waga each morning to travel in the sky. Those same informants always avoid the question, however, of whether they had ever looked in the sun house during the daytime to see if the "spirit bones" were still there.

The moon is called *sut* within most of the Grand Valley and among the Western Dani. According to Grand Valley informants, those ancestors who initiated moon propitiation referred to this revered spirit entity as *pae*. Although I know of no "center" for a possible "moon cult," currently there are houses especially for moon rituals secretly scattered about the cultural landscape. In mid–Grand Valley terminology these houses are known as *paéaila*

(or moon house). Some moon houses are structured like the rectangular sun houses, and some are round, grass-thatched houses, architecturally designed with interiors like the men's houses that have ganekhe cabinets. Such houses are known to exist at other places within the Grand Valley: near Aikima (where a mummy is maintained), at Pabuma where Obaharok lived, in the Dugum area, and at Abusa near the Baliem River. For rituals at which the moon is a featured spirit entity, and in all sacred houses (paéaila) where the moon is propitiated, a special symbolic object is reportedly maintained. It is reportedly a constructed artifact of three pieces that consists of a stick of wood that is kept in a short section of incised bamboo, which in turn is set within a water gourd. The gourd is hung in a net bag (nogen) from the ceiling, near the ganekhe cabinet or sometimes kept inside of the cabinet.

Painted Display-Display-Exchange-Type Stones and Sacred Boards in the Yali and East Region

Painted Display-Exchange-Type Stones and Sacred Boards in the Yali and East Region

East of the Grand Valley throughout the Yali and East region (fig. 2.1), most of the sacred flat display-exchange-type stones that I observed were painted with red, white, or black paint; some with combinations thereof. Some fewer stones were even incised. Two different Yali informants stated that during empowerment rituals a stone becomes sacred the moment a red stripe is added to a profane stone by a Yali shaman. When profane, it is called sie or siengga, but once painted, owili. East of the Grand Valley, the Yali also utilize incised and painted rectangular boards, which they call *sabalhe* in much the same fashion as the painted flat sacred ancestral stones.

The artistic addition of incising the stones, engraving boards, and painting these items in the Yali and East may be because the eastern part of that area is on a Highlands trade linkage or migration route, upward from both the north and south coasts of New Guinea (author's speculation, yet to be verified by grounded truth), between the more artistically inclined Sepik River inhabitants still farther to the east and the artistically inclined Asmat (north and east of Agats) to the south (fig. P.1).

The introduction of the rectangular boards (sabalhe) may have also been a solution to fill a supply deficit of the once possibly more desirable flat sacred stones, caused by distances and trade complexities with Grand Valley and West sources. As one moves eastward away from the Grand Valley Dani-Yali boundary, there is an increasing number of flat-style symbolic stones that originated from sources of opportunity, rather than from either the Yeineri or Tagime quarries.

In figure 4.50, a red painted, flat-style Yeineri-sourced gray schistose slate sacred stone (owili) is shown next to three red ochre painting chips (crayons) and a paquette of red hematite painting powder. Dimensional views of the stone are shown in the ink drawing of figure 4.51. The stone is 43 cm long by 12 cm wide by 1 cm thick. The left end of the stone in figure 4.50 is ground to a sharpened edge, but not honed as finely as if it were ground to be used as a cutting tool. The stone and the pieces of red ochre and the packet of hematite powder came from an unnamed hamlet near Pasikni, just south of Angguruk (fig. 2.8). The Grand Valley Dani traded their sacred red painting ochres and hematite from the Yali.

The ancestral spirit boards (sabalhe) are usually engraved with various geometric as well as other designs before being painted with red and/or white and/or black paint. The red and white pigments are mineral and the black from a natural berry. Representative dimensions for a single board is about 1.5 cm thick by 15 cm wide by 60 cm long. Some boards are larger. An example of painted boards (sabalhe) on the inside of a men's house that is located in central Yali territory is shown in figure 4.52. Grounded truth for the presence of the sabalhe is throughout an area that includes the hamlets of Korupun, Kosarek, Nipsan, Welarek, Gilika, Nalca, Kasin, Angguruk, and Apalapsali (fig. 2.8). Their presence in prehistoric times farther east than Langda is presumed, but I have not confirmed this assumption with on-the-ground research. Whether or not there is a relationship to the symbolic *churinga* of Papua New Guinea is not known.

At the eastern end of the research area, the

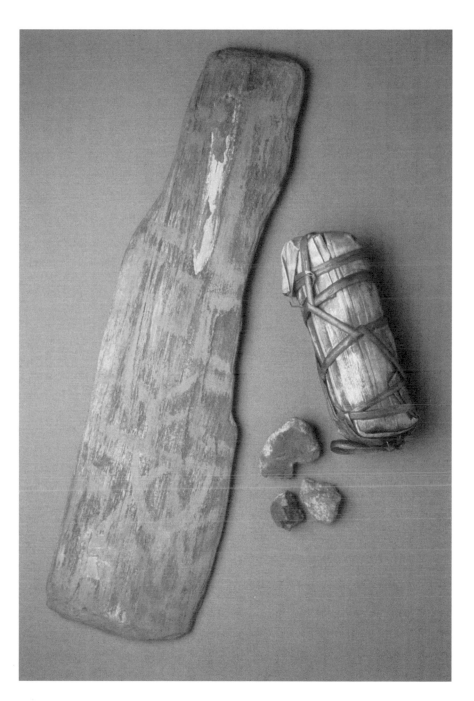

Una people call their empowered flat display-exchange-style symbolic stones *biri ya*. As with the Yali, most of these symbolic stones are painted. Some of the stones are instilled through ritual with ancestral spirit power, as they are farther to the west; while others are empowered and used in different contexts. For example, among the Una, in addition to "planting" adze blade style empowered stones with their sweet potatoes, the people plant empow-

Fig. 4.50. A red-painted, sacred exchange-type stone

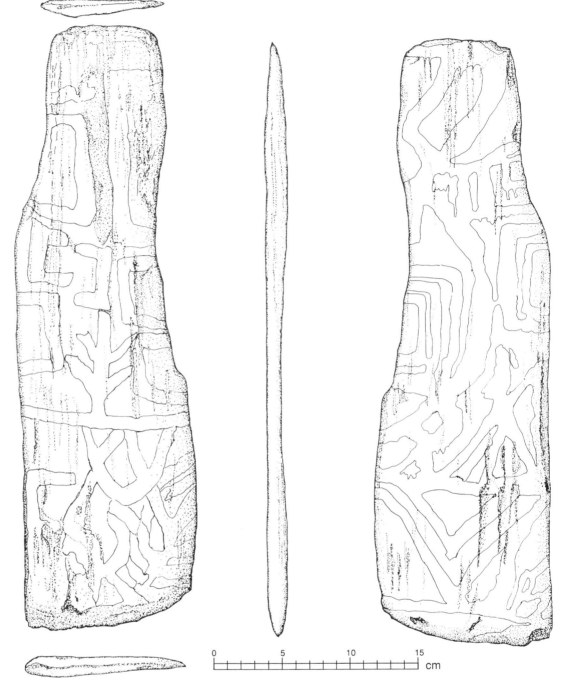

Fig. 4.51. Dimensional views of a painted owili stone (Yali and East region)

ered display-exchange stones (biri ya) with their crops to promote growth. Sticks are sometimes used to mark the locations of these stones so that they do not become lost. The Una biri ya in figure 4.53 is thought to have been obtained from a volcanic sequence source of opportunity within Una territory, not from a Yeineri or Tagime quarry. This 38.2 cm long sacred stone is 15.5 cm wide at its widest point.

On one side, it is incised with three concentric circles and painted with a white stripe that is perpendicular to the long dimension of the stone.

One example of an imported stone used by the Una is a black meta-argillite Tagime-style biri ya that is 10.3 cm wide (widest point) by 38.4 cm long. The meaning of a red and white painted design on one side of the stone is not known. The stone had been wrapped with nine loops of braided yellow orchid fiber cording called *sika,* which is distinctive of Una braiding. Among the Una, this type of cording is worn in necklace loops as men's adornment and never as married female skirting, as is done in the Grand Valley and West. Adjacent to the band of braided yellow cording on the stone is a miniature female skirt (*gem* flattened reeds), which among the Una is called a *le.*

Miscellaneous Sacred Stones in the Yali and East Region

Adze Blades (Biri Ya)

Like the Kimyal and Yali west of the Una but within the Yali and East region, the Una do not use Yeineri-style and Tagime-style adze blades as profane cutting tools, but they do use such tool blades as sacred empowered spirit stones. The Una with whom I talked did not know the source of the stones, only that they had inherited them. Like the sacred flat-style display-exchange stones, the Una call these former adze blades in the sacred stone context, *biri ya.* Typical of the adze blade biri ya are a green-black, Yeineri-style oblong-triangular blade that measures 6.9 cm wide by 12.7 cm long or a green-blue Yeineri-style blade that measures 3.8 by 10.2 cm. A group of six head quarrymen and big men from hamlets in the Langda area (including Diman Balyo, the head quarryman at Langda) advised that two uses of the Yeineri- and Tagime-style adze blade biri ya were to plant with their crops to encourage growth and to carry as amulets to help find good quarry stone. It was Weak, a Dani big man on Sekan Ridge on the edge of the Grand Valley who showed me a similarly sized and shaped green Yeineri-style adze blade which he said was a spirit power stone that he had inherited from his father and always had carried with him in former times during warfare to keep him safe.

Circular Ground Stone Disks

The Una, Kimyal and many of the Yali possess circular ground stone disks with centered perforations that the men use as sacred power stones. These disks look much like many of the shaft-hole stone implements that have been reported in the archaeological record worldwide. Similar artifacts have been called club-heads, battle axes, axe-hammers, mace heads, and pebble hammers. Such items have been mostly interpreted as profane stone tools or instruments of war; few as symbolic stones. The disks in the Yali and East region range from semi-square to round, about 10 to 16 cm in diameter and with center perforations that range from about 0.6 to 3 cm in diameter (figs. 4.54 and 4.55). The stones are cut and ground from pieces of gray, compacted volcanic tuff. Some are rubbed with pig fat and smoked, becoming light brown to gray-black in color; while others are left their natural gray. Some are incised with patterned grooves that are either left the natural color of the rock or painted with red, white, or black paint, or a combination thereof. Some of these stones are tube shaped, while others are honed down to a thin circular cutting edge on their outside perimeters. Those with large enough center holes (about 0.75 to 3.5 cm diameter) to fit over the exterior house center crestal poles (spikes) are called *bumkil* (alt. *tani bumkil*) by the Una people. These bumkil are slipped over crestal roof poles to ward off wind and rain, so that the roof will not leak, and to protect the house from being crushed in case the sky would fall. Others, especially those stones with very small center holes, are used as sacred power stones for other purposes.

Some of the disks that I have observed exhibit what appears to be both outer edge use wear and center hole shaft wear, much as one would expect if these stone disks had been used as profane stone striking or cutting implements with shaft holes (fig. 4.55C). I have not seen one of these types of disks used as any sort of a club head or chopping tool in Irian Jaya; although one Yali man told me that his father had used such an implement as a special kind of club head, and it is rumored that the Asmat used a club head similar to the one shown in figure 4.55A and nearest to the cm scale in figure 4.54 as a special tool to crush human skulls. Stone artifacts similar to the one shown in figure 4.55C are called club heads in a collection in the

Fig. 4.52. The use of sacred boards (sabalhe) on the wall of a Yali men's house

Australian Museum and in the Indonesian Government Museum in Jayapura, Irian Jaya.

Miscellaneous Una Power Stones
Having a nearby available source of layered volcanic tuff deposits, the Una selectively quarry small pieces of tuff that, like the circular disks with center perforations, they carve and grind into simple, small oblong and rounded stones which they use to ritually transfer spirit power and use as power objects. One example is a smoke blackened, rounded oblong artifact that is 7.6 cm wide by 18 cm long. A small "V" has been cut into one end, a red and white dot

Fig. 4.53. An incised and painted Una flat exchange-type sacred stone

Fig. 4.54. Four ground stone sacred power disks with centered perforations

placed on each side of two centrally located incised concentric circles, of which the inner has been painted white and the outer red. At the other end of the object, an incised grid pattern has been painted with red and white lines. This object and other similar objects are called *oboh*. The Una owner stated that he plants this stone with sweet potatoes and moves it from time to time to encourage crop growth. This same man owned a river-rounded stone (5 cm diameter) which he calls *amkil*. He says that an empowered stone like the amkil, planted between a taro plant and a sweet potato hill, encourages both to grow better. A round, flat stone that he maintains in the house beside the fireplace he called a *kwaningkil*. The man said that he would pray to the spirit in that stone for good sweet potato crops.

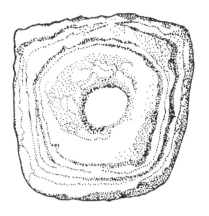

a

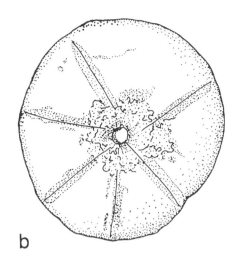

b

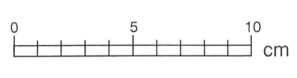

0   5   10

cm

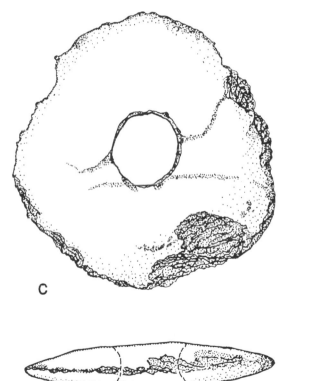

c

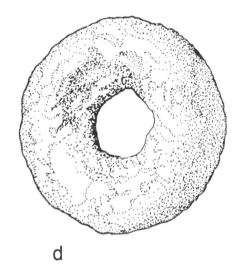

d

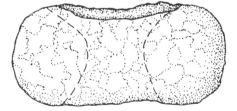

Fig. 4.55. Dimensional drawings of four ground stone disks with centered perforations

CHAPTER 5

Yeineri Quarries

The quarries are located in an unmapped part of the Highlands, not far from the ecological interface of the Highlands with the lowlands Dismal Swamp (fig. 5.1). Heinrich Harrar, a German explorer, is to my knowledge, the first Western outsider to have located the quarries area, which has been rarely visited by Westerners since, due to its remote location and rugged terrain. Harrar's expedition of 1962 was successful on its second attempt, after the first almost cost Harrar his life (1965:96–97). When Harrar finally arrived at the place that his porters had described as the "source for the stone axes," Harrar wrote in his diary (May 8, 1962), "The natives felled enormous trees and pushed them with great skill and experience over to the other side [of the Kiembe River], where there were rocks in all shades of blue and green" (1965:140). This was the axe blade source for which Harrar had been exploring. Harrar described the use of fire on scaffolding against a "big green rock face" to assist in the quarrying process (1965:141).

Whereas Harrar had followed a route northward from Mulia in his successful search for the "source for the stone axes," I chose to start my quest from Dagai (Duvle-speaking people) on the north, the lowland edge of Wano territory, and climb back uphill to locate the quarries (figs. 5.1 and 2.8). At Dagai, where the river tumultuously spills out of the steep mountains to flow quietly out into the bordering swamplands, it dumps a large load of gravel, cobbles, and boulders. From these river-tumbled rocks, a few are selected for the proper size and hardness to be rough flaked by the Duvle then traded farther downriver as adze and axe blade blanks. The elders at Dagai say that their ancestors supplemented this local supply of tool stones from time to time with the more highly prized, top quality adze and axe blade blanks from quarries upriver in the mountains. It was the upriver quarry or quarries that I was seeking.

Where the river pours out of the mountains, it is called the Dagai. In the Highlands to the south, where it cuts through a broad sequence of vertically tipped, complexly banded, hard metamorphic green-, blue-, and black-colored rock, it is called the Ye River or *Yei*. Some trans-

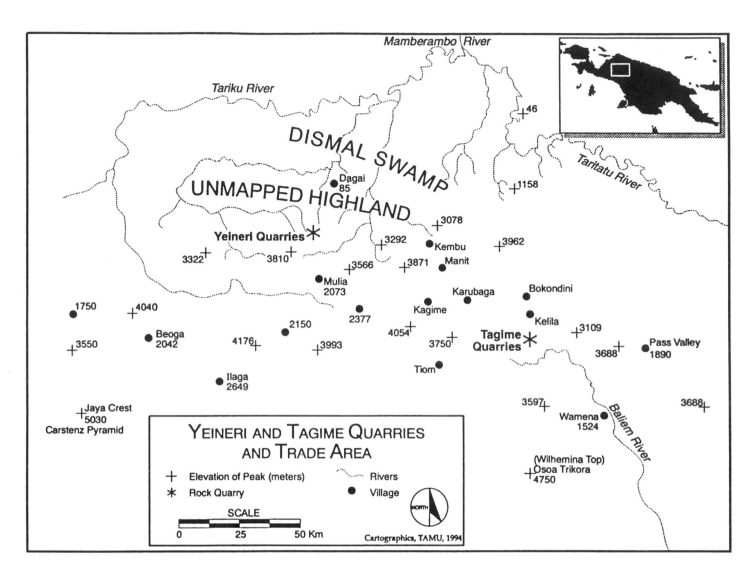

Fig. 5.1. Yeineri and Tagime quarries and trade area

late Yei to mean "source of the axe rock river." Some say Ye means "rock," others say it means "stone blade" or "exchange stone," or all three, and that "i" means river. There was never complete agreement. To the Wano Highlanders who control the quarry area, "neri" means literally "where the river begins," but the term Yeineri is generally understood by the Wano to refer to "the entire geographic area around the rock quarries" as well as to identify the Wano habitation site that is located within the rock quarry area from which the thriving stone-goods industry was operated.

Toward the end of the second day out of Dagai, my party and I (three Irian Jaya assistants and seven porters, five of whom were Wano and two, Duvle) climbed down a steep hillside to the river, known to the inhabitants at

that location as the Ye River (Yei). Somewhere around the rock shelter of the night before, the name of the river changed from Dagai to Yei, marking the north boundary of the Wano quarry belt. As we walked over and around boulders in the stream bed, a few Wano people appeared. It was apparent they had had advance notice that we were coming because they just smiled and pointed upstream. Soon the river divided around a large pedestal-shaped promontory. A trail could be seen winding its way up the steep hillside, finally disappearing into the trees. At the base of the hill a cluster of Wano men, carrying bows and arrows, told us they lived on the top of the hill and we should go there. This hamlet called Yeineri (after the river) turned out to be the center of this quarry operation.

My team and I had been following a swift-flowing, often white-water river up into Wano territory in search of a quarry or quarries. What I ultimately found was far more complex than just an operationally disconnected "quarry or quarries" but an integrated, although some-what informally operated, quarrying and manufacturing system that, even in recent times, supplied a variety of stone tools and profane symbolic stones to different language-speaking groups in the Highlands to the south and southwest and also downriver to the lowlands Duvle people to the north.

Yeineri consists of a scattering of both round, wooden-walled, thatched roof houses and rectangular, wood-sided houses with raised floors, one doorway, and thatched roofs. The mix of house types indicates a transitional adaptation of housing style to the environment, between the warmer low, round, thatched roof houses built on the ground that are used by the Dani and Western Dani at higher, cooler elevations and the Duvle, open-sided, thatched roof rectangular houses that are built on stilts in the hotter climate at still lower elevations to the north. The elevation at Dagai (Duvle inhabitants) is 85 m above sea level. I estimated the elevation at Yeineri to be about 1,200 m (plus or minus 150 m). For comparison, the elevation of the Grand Valley, which is inhabited by the Grand Valley Dani, is 1,600 m above sea level.

The focal point of the hilltop hamlet is a round, wooden-walled, thatched roof men's house, which is approximately 8 m in inside diameter, much larger than the 3 to 5 m Dani houses. When we first entered the hamlet, Teniak Wenda, our Wano trail guide disappeared into this house where he resides along with fifteen other Wano men. The floor of the house, built 0.9 m above ground level, is covered with cane poles where the men sleep on sewn *Pandanus* leaf mats. There is no grass on the floor, as in Dani houses. A central fireplace, used for cooking and to heat the house at night, also creates smoke to discourage mosquitoes and the night-time presence of rats. There are two entrances to the house and no second interior level, as is prevalent in Dani and Western Dani houses at higher elevations to the south and southwest.

There are other smaller men's houses throughout the habitation area, each with a scattering of associated family houses. Yeineri informants estimated the current (1991) Yeineri population to be approximately 240 adults plus young infants. The older quarrymen (more than fifty years old) stated that when quarrying operations were at what they called normal capacity, the area population was considerably larger, but none could quantify those statements. Overall, the hamlet architectural style is similar to Yali house clusters. Some wooden fences are present, however, to define space and control pig movement. Outlying tuber (sweet potato, taro, and yam) gardens are not as luxuriant and productive as in the Grand Valley. It also appears that pigs, on a per capita basis, are fewer than within the Dani cultural system, attesting to the lower sweet potato production on the steep hillside slopes versus on broad valley floors or more gentle-sloping valley sides in Dani territory.

Within the Yeineri hamlet and its environs, the population is subdivided into residential kinship segments in much the same fashion as described for communities in the Yali and East region and throughout the Dani, Western Dani, and Damal language groups of the Grand Valley and West region ("Compound and Hamlet" in chapter 3). At Yeineri, it is within these community kinship groups and combinations of them that permanent, but flexible, work groups are formed that independently quarry the stone, own and work it to completion, and control its final distribution. Due to proximity and control of this valuable resource, the focus of function and energy at Yeineri is directed to quarrying rock, manufacturing stone tools and display-exchange stones, and distributing the product.

Although within the Yeineri quarrying system, product ownership is within the kinship residential groups and their leadership; quarry ownership, overall management of the system, and responsibility for security of quarry sites accrue to the most influential leader (big man) living at the Yeineri quarry center and from time to time, to a combination of two or several of the more influential men who reside there or nearby.

The Wano People

The relatively small Wano population (3,000 to 3,500) lives in scattered habitation sites north and northwest of Mulia in rough terrain as far north as down the flank of the central mountain core to its junction with the broad lowlands swamp ("Language Groups and Linguistic Boundaries," chapter 1; figs. 1.3, 2.8, and 5.1). Large areas within the sparsely settled Wano territory are uninhabited and without horticultural gardens. While Hayward (1992:479) was gathering "origin" stories just south of Wano territory at Mulia, indigenous informants told

Fig. 5.2. The Rock River (Ye) runs through the quarry area.

him that their ancestors recognized the Wano "as foragers who cooked leafy plants and the fruit of trees." Today, the Wano supplement a tuber horticultural and pig husbandry subsistence with hunting and gathering. Many of the men, even when going about their business around quarry sites or gardens, routinely carry bows and arrows with which to hunt cassowary birds, marsupials, feral pigs, and tree kangaroos.

The Wano are relatively short in stature. The bare essentials of Wano traditional dress is similar to the Dani and Western Dani: gourd penis sheaths for the men (none of which are ever as long as some of the Dani, Western Dani, and Yali penis sheaths) and, for the females, reed stem skirts and head-back nets. Women do not exchange reed skirts for the Dani-style orchid fiber wedding skirts at marriage. They give birth from the squatting position and rear between two and five children, in comparison to Dani women who usually rear only one to three children (chapter 1).

Lukibut Eber, an indigenous Wano who was medically trained at a Western missionary medical station in Mulia, told me that the number-one killer of the Wano is malaria; number-two, complications from hookworms; and number-three, pneumonia; just another social variant, like the change in house style from a colder climate at higher elevation to a warmer climate at lower elevations. The Wano in this area cremate their dead. Farther north, near their border with the lowland Duvle (estimated population 200, Silzer and Clouse 1991), it is my understanding that in former times some of the Wano placed their dead on stilted platforms, as did the Duvle. Wano informants have told me that when Wano people died while on stone tool trading missions or long hunting trips the bodies were abandoned in caves or rock crevices and not cremated.

Geologic Setting

The primary branch of the Ye River and a subsidiary tributary nearly surround the flat-topped hill on which the Wano operational center for the Yeineri quarry complex is located.

Both branches are crystal clear and full of bright-colored pebbles and cobbles that exhibit combinations of the various minerals and lithologies that make up the desired array of the types of rocks that are quarried (fig. 5.2). It was the full force of the Ye River, both upstream and down from this location, that eroded and exposed a favorable Tertiary sequence of melange shelf strata, ophiolite slices, and metamorphic rocks, including glaucophane-epidote schists, blueschist, greenschist, phillites, amphibolites, slates, and marble. Large boulders and bedrock outcrops along the edges of and within the river bed itself provide most of the available source places for quarrying. Due to the dense vegetative ground cover that is characteristic of the prevailing rain forest climate, few outcrops are visible on adjacent hillsides—even for the discerning eye of a traditional rock-tool prospector. Within the entire rock sequence that is exposed over a distance of some 20 km, different mineralogical mixes, degrees of metamorphism, rock textures, and degrees of stratification afford choices of different kinds of rock that are suitable for a variety of kinds of stone goods and that are amenable to different quarrying techniques. Within the geologic sequence there are no hard sandstones or other suitable kinds of rock locally available for grinding stones. Beds of sandstone that are favorable for the grinding process crop out, however, at scattered locations or are present as exposed large boulder erratics away from the quarry belt outside of Wano territory throughout most of the stone tool use area.

Kinds of Stone Goods Produced and Their Classification

Stone axe and adze blades, knives, chisels, and the profane flat-type je display-exchange stones and puluen are produced and traded outward from the integrated Yeineri quarry complex. According to active Wano quarrymen and their oral history, as related by older Wano males, sacred stones per se were never produced at any of the Yeineri quarries. Also, according to older Wano informants (fifty-five to seventy years old), no perforated disks or other possible shaft

hole implements, hammerstones or pounders, grinding slabs, mortars, or pestles were ever produced anywhere along the Ye River by the Wano or any other language-speaking group of people who might have temporarily made excursions into the area to quarry rock.

The quarrymen at Yeineri recognize and understand my classification of *their* axe and adze blades, which includes the Yeineri-style, Yeineri flat-style, and Yeineri tubular-style axe blades; and the Yeineri-style and Yeineri flat-style adze blades (discussed in chapter 2). The quarrymen's own distinctions of blade types, however, go beyond structure and size (and even disregard structure) to include reference to *specific* quarry source outcrops, with implied degree of hardness, and something that I translate as color-aesthetics (caused by mineralogical content and metamorphic process). With some of the Yeineri-produced tools and both je and puluen display-exchange stones, mineralogical distinctions (which relate to quarry core sources) are apparent and Wano-type categories can easily be understood by outsiders. But for many of the tools, mineralogical identification (indirectly by color) and/or other Wano parameters of tool classification are even argued among the Wano themselves. I suspect that this is for two reasons. At some named quarry sites, a spectrum of related rock types are available, depending on specific location within the named quarry. Also, indistinguishable lithologic types are quarried at more than one named quarry source. Because of these two variables, it is understandable that quarrymen using a quarry site name to identify a specific blade, could be in disagreement as to a "type" distinction for the blade with another quarryman. The Wano quarrymen say that they always look first for the hardest rock, because "the most valuable tools are made from the hardest"; second, for source rock that is amenable to quarrying process; and third, for rock that has, what I feel in an unsure translation is, aesthetic appeal to the user populations. (Any personal "signatures" that might be identified in final flaked axe or adze blades are obliterated by the grinding process.) (For a discussion of the mineralogy of the stone tools produced at

Yeineri refer to chapter 2 and for the je stones, refer to "Sources, Color, and Lithologies" in chapter 3.)

The Manufacturing Process

Seven technological steps are used in the Highlands to produce ground stone tools: (1) locate a suitable quarry rock, (2) break the rock, (3) reduce pieces to manageable sizes, (4) shape preform biface blanks at quarry sites by freehand knapping; and, away from quarry sites, in the final knapping process, intermittently (5) dull biface edges and prepare platforms on individual biface blanks as part of the (6) fine-flaking procedure to produce final bifaces for (7) grinding. Within the Yeineri manufacturing process, sometimes steps two to six are combined into two distinct steps and at other times into three steps.

In addition to the technical steps, Wano work groups at Yeineri reportedly conduct sacred rituals to propitiate a spirit named Elogor relative to quarrying operations. (Similar rituals conducted by the Western Dani at the Tagime quarries and by the Una at the Langda quarrying and manufacturing center are discussed in chapters 6 and 7.) The Wano believe Elogor is a powerful, nonpersonified spirit who lives everywhere and owns all the land. Before departure from Yeineri for a quarry site, upon arrival at the site, and again as a "closing-down" ceremony, tobacco, fruit and tuber (sweet potato, and/or yam, and/or taro) offerings are made to Elogor to ensure successful and safe continuing operations. According to informants, only the elderly Wano, those over sixty years old (author's estimate), may successfully quarry without making offerings to Elogor, an interesting dispensation to the aging. Wano informants say that if offerings are not made, the fires will not break the rock, or, at best, will take a very long time (author's interpretation: one or two days). Although rituals are conducted to propitiate the spiritual owner of the land, including quarry sites, the quarry-men maintain that the sites themselves are not considered to be sacred places. At various times through the later stages of manufacturing,

Elogor and other spirits may also be propitiated with simple acts of ritual to facilitate favorable production and maintain beneficent serenity among the spirits.

Locating favorable specific quarry rock along the "Source of the Axe Rock River" is an ongoing process among the Wano. Unlike the Melanesian Ormu language group (who live north of the Wano across the lowland swamp in a relatively small area along the north coastline of Irian Jaya), where a single individual is assigned and authorized to search for new quarry rock as a full-time occupational specialty, among the Wano no such prospector is identified. Instead, most Wano quarrymen are habitually on the lookout for new rock sources. Some, with a bent for prospecting, range far and wide within the geologically favorable quarry belt of the river drainage. Journeys to quarries of up to two or three days of travel time one way from the Yeineri quarrying center are not considered too far to be within the scope of the integrated operation.

With the diverse kinds of stone goods that are produced, multiple quarry sites that together offer a broad choice of source materials are desired. Rock that is considered to be the most favorable (by hardness) for Yeineri-style adze and axe blades may be different from rock that will quarry-out advantageously along bedding or cleavage planes into thin, tabular pieces from which to shape flat je display-exchange stones, knives, and the Yeineri flat-style adze and axe blades. The Yeineri tubular-style axe blade is made from yet another slightly different kind of rock. Chisels are made from all of the kinds of rock from which the other stone goods are produced, even though hardness is the most sought after rock characteristic, and some chisels that are produced are not as hard as others.

What has evolved through time is a centrally operated quarrying system, within which scattered, individual quarry sites furnish rock of different lithology, hardness, texture, fracture pattern, and color. The quarrymen, working out of Yeineri, know which quarry site will produce the kind of rock that they want from which to make a particular kind of tool (or je display-exchange stone) for local use or need within the Wano population, or to prepare for marketing.

New sites are sought to replace those that have been depleted and to upgrade the efficiency and economics of the system by finding desirable core rock closer to the center of operations. Having a choice of various kinds of desirable rock is always a consideration.

The best times to find new quarry sites are after torrential rains, when erosive flood waters are funneled along the course of the Ye River, exposing previously hidden rock sequences. Newly exposed bedrock outcrops and river-tumbled boulders are found and examined by Wano prospectors. These core rock explorers carefully scrutinize any new exposure they feel might meet their hardness criteria, possess cleavage and/or bedding plane and fracture pattern characteristics that will facilitate quarrying, and where geologically caused fractures are well healed and will not break disadvantageously during either manufacture or tool use. Some newly located bedrock exposures and boulder cores get the approval of head quarrymen for further testing in which rock is quarried to decide the best quarrying technique and to determine if the quarry core can, in fact, be quarried at all. Manageable pieces are flaked to determine how the rock reacts to normal knapping techniques. If deemed to be a commercial find by at least a few of the quarrymen and their quarry leader, then Elogor, the spirit-power owner of all rock, is thanked through ritual at "special places" with vegetable offerings.

The same erosive water power of periodic flooding that exposes new quarry sites also flushes out and carries away debitage accumulations from operational sites, thus destroying the most important artifact of culture that, if preserved in the archaeological record, could serve to not only identify a rock quarry but to furnish valuable information about operations at the site.

From time to time, earthquakes cause landslides within the drainage area of the Ye River and fresh bedrock outcrops and landslide debris are exposed. Although the Wano quarrymen examine such new rock exposures for acceptable core rock, local informants say that seldom has new quarry stone been found in these situations. Individually named quarry sites, which are still in use along the Ye River, and other abandoned sites that are remembered in local oral history, were reportedly all found by "the ancestors." Most of the detail of the original discoveries and early operations has since been forgotten.

Quarrying techniques include the uses of fire; large river-tumbled, rounded hammerstones; and both rock and wooden wedges. Fires are built either on the ground or on wooden platforms against a rock surface that is to be fractured and at other times on top of a large boulder core rock. In addition, sometimes relatively small boulder cores are placed on a fire to be broken apart by the heat. Fire as an engineering technique is used at all named quarry sites throughout the research area.

In addition to heating a core rock to break it, large river-rounded hammerstones are often used to break up core rock without the assistance of fire. The hammerstones are either hurled or handheld and pounded against a rock surface to break off manageable pieces. In some circumstances, rock or wooden wedges are used to break core rock, especially where open fractures or eroded thin crevices are present that allow the use of such a wedge. Tabular slatelike sequences that are quarried in the Yeineri complex for flat-type adze and axe blades, knives, and the flat-type je display-exchange stones are particularly amenable to wedging.

Quarry Ownership

The present owners of the complex of sites that are scattered along the Ye River are Wano. Quarry ownership and control is centralized within the Wano language-speaking group at the Yeineri habitation site, where the group of quarrymen who own and control production apparently include members outside of a single patrilineage. It was tempting for me to identify the controlling group as the Yeineri ("Source of the Axe Rock River") clan, but it seems that some members who have been accepted into the group are not only not consanguineal kinsmen but possibly are not even related as affinal relatives to the leadership. What I observed was unrelated quarrymen who joined the group by consent and who were treated as members, but who, perhaps beyond the scope of my observations, did not play a part in making group decisions relative to ownership and control of the quarries. Ultimately, at any given time within the loosely affiliated sociopolitical organization of the Wano language group, it was the most influential big man at Yeineri, in consensus with the quarrymen around him, who owned and controlled use of individual quarry sites within the entire quarry belt. This is different from two variations for quarry ownership and operation that are contemporaneously in place at Tagime and Langda, the two other major quarrying and manufacturing centers within the research area.

Other Wano, who live at scattered locations far away from Yeineri, reportedly must have permission from the Yeineri quarry owners to quarry stones as individuals or as groups, whether for their own personal uses or for trade. My informants could recall no problem with approvals for people within the Wano language group taking stone, although such individuals or groups are reportedly required to show what they have quarried to Wano quarry leadership. Likewise, I heard no anecdotal stories of intra-Wano group rivalry to control specific quarry sites, although it is difficult to believe that this did not happen. In a future section I discuss incidents of Wano intercession of quarrying operations by people of other language groups within the Wano quarry belt region. Perhaps if the quarry belt were located in a more densely populated environment, local diverse ownership of individual quarry sites by patrilineage groups or clans would prevail.

Quarry Sites within the System

The quarry complex consists of approximately nine specific sites that are strung out along the Ye River drainage, over an estimated horizontal distance of about 15 km. A few of the sites are located on the lower parts of steep hillsides above the very narrow incised Ye River valley floor. Most, however, are at river level. The estimated elevation range of individual sites in the quarry belt is approximately 900 m, from 645 m at Diarindo, the northernmost and lowest site, which is located about halfway between Dagai and Yeineri quarries on figure 5.1, and an estimated 1,500 m at Awigowi, the highest site located south of Mulia and north of Yeineri quarries on figure 5.1. Substantial error (as much as 30 percent) is possible in both the distance and elevation estimates, due to the fact that most of the area was unmapped at the time fieldwork was completed. Relief is substantial (about 3,000 m), and much up-and-down climbing was repeated along often circuitous routes from the MAF (Mission Aviation Fellowship) landing strip at Dagai to various locales within Wano territory. Distances from point to point in the Highlands are not measured in kilometers by indigenous inhabitants but rather by walking time, with significant time differences between dry travel days versus rainy travel days, and for travel by only indigenous inhabitants versus by modern outsiders. The local residents normally travel much faster.

Bagaidewi

Approximately 275 m down the steep, vegetation choked hillside from the men's house at Yeineri, a 3 to 4 m wide horizontal ledge underlies a section of exposed cliff. This quarry floor and cliff are the Bagaidewi rock quarry, pronounced Bagereroit by some Wano (fig. 5.3). At Bagaidewi, pieces of rock for adze and axe blades, knives, chisels, and flat je-type display-exchange stones were, and on a much reduced scale still are, quarried by a fire technique. Probably not more than about 50 m farther down the hillslope below the quarry floor, the Ye River furnishes an ever abundant supply of rounded cobbles from which workers conveniently select hammerstones with which to flake biface blanks while quarrying. According to Wano informants, this quarry was probably the most active of Yeineri individual quarry sites at the time of first contact in the Grand Valley and West region.

The hard, green-blue blueschist rock crops out in a curvilinear quarry face above the

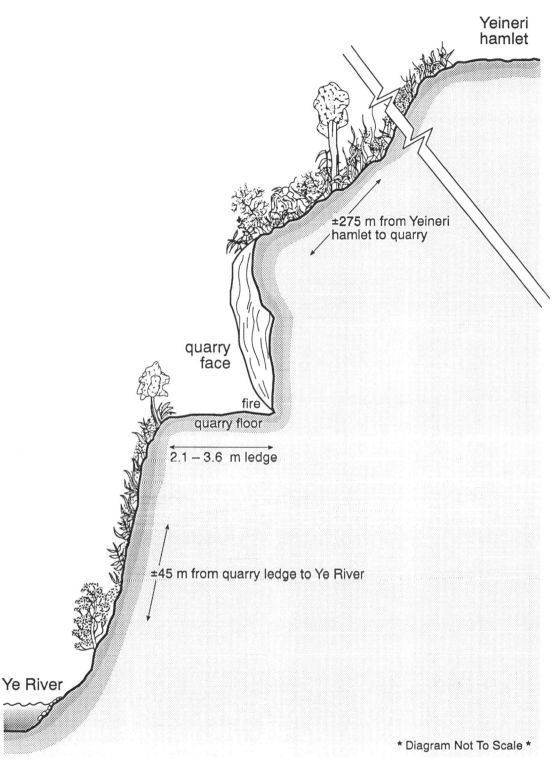

Yeineri hamlet

±275 m from Yeineri hamlet to quarry

quarry face

fire

quarry floor

2.1 – 3.6 m ledge

±45 m from quarry ledge to Ye River

Ye River

* Diagram Not To Scale *

Fig. 5.3. Hillside profile at Bagaidewi quarry

quarry floor. Rock from an active section of the quarry face was identified by the University of Colorado team of mineralogists (chapter 2) to be blueschist. Major minerals are glaucophane (blue) and plagioclase (clear). Minor minerals are chlorite and quartz and accessory minerals are sphene, pyrite, and epidote. The rock texture is schistose, fine-grained. By X-ray analyses the minerals amphibole, albite, and quartz were identified. By the Colorado team's subjective hardness estimates from mineralogical and textural considerations, on a four-part scale of very hard (VH), hard (H), medium (M), and soft (S), the team judged this rock to be "hard (H)." The overall shape of the quarry face is convex outward. Geological folding produced fractures with slick-sided surfaces and lines of weakness in the rock that are approximately parallel to the exposed rock surface, which enhances spheroidal weathering and ultimately breaking off of thin layers during quarry firing. Thus, geological processes enhance the quarrymen's engineering techniques to provide an efficient operation.

Tingen Geri, who first showed me the details of the "Wano bamboo matchbox" fire-starting tool ("Fire-Starting Tools," chapter 1) and three older Wano former quarrymen (estimated age range, fifty-five to seventy years) who had memories of quarrying operations during periods of peak production, told me during nighttime discussions in the Yeineri men's house that quarrying work parties at Bagaidewi consisted of between six and ten men. Another old man (estimated age sixty-five to seventy years) argued in an anecdotal story that one time he was working on the crowded quarry floor when there were about seventeen men, some firing the quarry face and collecting core pieces, while others were off on the ends, shaping biface blanks by freehand flaking.

Some Wano quarrymen told stories of injuries incurred not only at Bagaidewi, but at other sites, by flying spalled hot pieces of rock during the firing process. The fire is hot against the rock as the flames are funneled upward at Bagaidewi from well-engineered fire platforms. Mineralogic alteration by the fires are macroscopically apparent from red-colored surfaces on remainder debris from previous firings.

To heat and fracture the rock, quarrymen first build a wooden platform at heights from 1 to 4 m above the quarry floor and against the quarry face. Thin pieces of rock from former knapping debris and from unwanted quarry core flakes that have accumulated on the quarry floor were selected and arranged as a protective rock hearth on the new firing platform. Small sticks and short sections of larger limbs were arranged on the newly created rock hearth, and a nest of tinder was tucked into the stacked

wood. The day that I was on the quarry floor, a quarryman lit tinder on the ground with the use of a thong-stick fire-starting kit and then lifted that lighted tinder to place it on the platform nested tinder that then set the wood on fire.

Prior to building the new platform from which to fire the rock during the first of my two visits to the quarry floor (May 12, 13, 1991), the work party reviewed the condition of the quarry face; the location of the previously used, still-standing platform; and discussed work objectives. Subtly appearing but significant rock changes are present across the breadth of the quarry face. Whether to tear down the old platform and rebuild a new one at the same spot or to move laterally along the quarry floor and fire another spot was discussed. Finally, the previously used fire platform that was 1.2 m high was torn down before a new platform was built. Previously unworked (not knapped) debris from previous firings had accumulated around the bottom of the old platform. Fire-induced red color was present on some of the previously used fire platform hearth material and some of the rock debris on the quarry floor. Some of this hearth material is debitage from freehand flaking of biface blanks on the quarry floor and not just untouched spall debris. In figure 5.4, the older quarry-floor leader started to knock down the previously used fire platform prior to building the new platform. A fire was started with a thong-stick tool on a large piece of previously spalled core rock next to the remains of the just-demolished old fire platform. After encouraging the flame in a bundle of wood-shaving tinder, the quarryman lifted the burning tinder onto the fire platform hearth to ignite the tinder and wood that had been arranged there. Among the Wano, it was just personal choice whether to use this fire-starting method or the "Wano bamboo matchbox."

As the fire burned, three of the five-man work party sat to one side as the rock face heated. The other two watched the fire and stood by to add logs from time to time to ensure a maximum flow of heat from the fire to the quarry face. After a very hot fire burned for

Fig. 5.4. The platform is knocked down before replacing it.

thirty-five to forty minutes, rock pieces began to spall off from time to time, with a loud "pop" or cracking noise. After fifty minutes, a quarryman took a 3.7 m long pole and rammed the rock wall through the fire. He both rammed and pried heat-loosened pieces of rock off the quarry face, causing them to pile up on the quarry floor. This process of ramming was continued for fifteen to twenty minutes. The

quarrymen advised me that this was a common technique, not only at Bagaidewi but at other quarries where platform fires were used. I named the technique the "fire-pole ram."

A greater quantity of core pieces were accumulated in less time at Bagaidcwi than at other quarry sites where I have observed the use of fire as a primary engineering element in the quarrying process. Here it seemed that both the natural fracturing of the rock and the overhang orientation of the quarry face enhanced the flow of heat against the rock and the spalling of attractively shaped core pieces. Some of the spalled rock, by its natural, almost-tabular shape, was already of a practical structure to be used for flat-type adze or axe blades, for knives, or for flat-type je display-exchange stones. Many of these same naturally shaped tabular pieces were sufficiently thick that with just a little freehand flaking they could be shaped into biface preforms for grinding to finished Yeineri-style adze or Yeineri-style axe blades (described in chapter 2). I estimated that only 30 to 40 percent of core rock bulk that was spalled and/or broken by mechanical device from the quarry face required more than one to three blows from a hammerstone, using the supportive anvil technique, to reduce a core to manageable size for further reduction by freehand flaking.

After heat-spalled core pieces fell or were knocked to the quarry floor, it required thirty-five to sixty minutes before the individual pieces cooled enough for further handling. As soon as core spalls had cooled sufficiently to be worked, three adults selected thin tabular pieces (versus more bulky "chunks") and started to shape biface blanks by freehand flaking. Prior to flaking, the men had each climbed down the slope to the river bank to select their own personal hammerstones and also hammerstones for their sons, who had come along to the quarry to continue their education of how to quarry and knap the rock. I estimated that the ages of the five boys ranged from approximately ten to fourteen years. This is the time-proven system, I was told, by which quarrymen teach their sons to be quarrymen and toolmakers and to follow in their footsteps. Local informants said that in every quarrying group (approximately five to twelve men), however, there were almost always one or more boys who had no interest in quarrying and who did not become adult quarrymen-toolmaker specialists. As the quarry fire continued to burn and be refueled by two attendant quarrymen, the other men and their sons shaped, at their own pace, adze/axe blade biface blanks (color plate 4, fig. 5.5). Due

to the favorable natural tabular shape of the core pieces that were further shaped by knapping at the quarry site, little additional fine-flaking was required back at the habitation site before these pieces were ready to be traded out as blade bifaces ready for grinding or to be ground locally by the Wano.

Igwi

Igwi quarry, now abandoned, is located approximately 200 m upstream and across the river from Bagaidewi. It is a bedrock outcrop that looks like a rounded portion of a very large boulder erratic, about 10 m from the edge of the river and easily within reach of high-water floods. A middle-aged quarryman pointed out a section of the quarry face that his father said produced the "hardest, best" adze/axe blade rock in the entire quarrying system. The rock was sampled and examined by the Colorado team (chapter 2). It was found to be an epidote amphibolite, with the major minerals being epidote, amphibole (interlocking), and minor minerals being plagioclase and chlorite. The rock texture exhibits poorly developed schistocity with a dominant texture that is matted, fine-grained fibrous amphibole with a lesser amount of equant epidote grains. By X-ray analyses, the minerals actinolite, albite, and chlorite were identified. The hardness estimate by the team from mineralogical and textural considerations in their four-part scale is very hard (VH), which does not contradict technically what my informant told me, although it cannot, of course, confirm that this rock is the absolute hardest. (The Colorado team made all of their analyses and hardness estimates without knowing any of the comments about the tools made by either the quarrymen or Highlands users.)

The fire process was reportedly used at Igwi, sometimes being built against the vertical core face and sometimes on top of the sloping face. It would be difficult for an archaeologist without prior knowledge of the use of this outcrop to identify it as a quarry source. To further complicate an archaeological-type identification of the quarry site, there is no remainder debitage from either the quarrying process or

Fig. 5.5. The quarry face is heated.

nearby knapping of quarry-made biface blanks. It has all been washed away by floods. The suspension bridge shown in the upper photograph in figure 5.2 connects the Igwi quarry site and another nearby river bed source to a trail that leads directly into the Yeineri hamlet. While I examined the Igwi quarry rock, a Wano father at the edge of the Ye River decorated the face of his young son with white clay (lower photograph, fig. 5.2).

Diarindo

Diarindo (pronounced Diarendo or Dewirindo by some, means "rock shelter place") is a five- to six-hour walk down river from Yeineri. This is the rock shelter that I used when traveling between Duvle and Wano territory. This is the approximate boundary marker, the river is called the Dagai downriver while here and upriver it is called the Yei. Because of the hardness of the rock at Diarindo, the Wano have considered this to be an especially good quarry source for adze and axe blades. The fire platform technique is used for quarrying.

Abuguruk

Abuguruk is approximately a three-hour walk upriver from Yeineri. The fire method against a river-level quarry face is used to break off manageable pieces for further reduction.

Kudaris Tengganag

Kudaris Tengganag is a short one-day walk upriver from Yeineri. I have little information on this site because I was never able to visit it or speak with contemporary quarrymen about the site.

Nejuwok

Nejuwok is a short one-day walk up river. Fires are not needed to break manageable pieces off the mother core, but are instead broken by the use of large hammerstones.

Wanogome

Wanogome (alt. Wanggokme) is a two-day walk upriver from Yeineri, one if the weather is completely dry. Flat display-exchange stones are quarried here by the fire technique. Quarrymen informants said that rarely is this stone used for percussion blades, although one quarryman showed me a ground, green-colored, 27 cm long blade that I classified as a Yeineri flat-style adze/axe blade and that he classified as a "wanogome." The owner's name is Lukibut Gire. Lukibut recalled that he had quarried this rock while with a seven- or eight-man quarrying group at the Wanogome site approximately one and a half years ago. They had gone to obtain core rock for flat-type je exchange stones. He brought back three je display-exchange stone blanks to Yeineri, of which this blade is a piece of one. The je broke during fine-flaking and since this remaining piece was too short to be of value as a display-exchange stone, he shaped and ground it into a finished "axe" blade. Lukibut says he will trade it to the Dani. He would not put a value on it.

Awigowi

Awigowi (in Wano means "dry season") is a difficult three-day trek upriver from Yeineri. There are steep hillsides to be traversed and several climbs and descents to be made to cross prominent ridges. Awigowi is one of the more important quarry sites within the industrial system by virtue of market demand for the product and relative ease of quarrying core material. The rock at Awigowi is light green, thinly layered slatelike and highly desired by many Dani to be used as profane display-exchange stones and some to be withdrawn from secular use and empowered as sacred ancestor stones. The Wano call the rock from this quarry pibit (or pibit pibit) and many refer to the quarry site as Pibit or Pibit Pibit rather than the place name Awigowi. The Wano name for the rock, pibit, has transferred with the stones outside of Wano territory and both the rock and the quarry site is known by the name pibit (or pibit pibit) throughout the different language groups in the Grand Valley and West region where the rock is traded. Fires are not necessary to quarry the pibit rock as it is quarried from low-lying ledges and broken out with hammerstones and sometimes the use of wedges.

By laboratory analysis of pibit rock samples at the University of Colorado, it was found to be a low- to medium-type metamorphic rock, which the analysts call an epidote chlorite schist. Major mineral constituents are epidote and chlorite. Minor mineral constituents are plagioclase and calcite, with accessory minerals of pyrite and amphibolite. The texture is very fine-grained with slaty cleavage. On the four-part relative hardness scale that was devised for this project, the hardness is rated as medium (M), which is the softest kind of rock analyzed from within the Yeineri quarry system. Even though the rock is relatively soft when compared to the best (hardest, VH) adze and axe blade material, this rock is also sometimes used to make flat-style adze and axe blades, knives, and chisels.

For quarrying trips to Awigowi, Yeineri informants say a work party will vary from as few as five to as many as ten men. Although the quarry is not considered to be a sacred place and women can be present, few ever go there. Women, however, often reportedly accompany the men to the second overnight bivouac spot to carry food that is stashed in caches at two or three locales to be used on the return journey. Travel in this part of Wano territory is through rugged, steep up-and-down uninhabited forest with no habitation sites having tuber gardens as local food supply-points. Hunting and gathering is unsure, and although the quarrymen say that while at the site they can supplement whatever food they are carrying with local, free-growing, red *Pandanus* fruit and *Pandanus* nuts, they like to have dependable food caches that can be used on their return journey to Yeineri.

One Wano quarryman told me that he had been to Awigowi four times to collect stones, each quarrying trip with a work party of approximately seven men. He said that the work parties would stay at the site for three days to procure the stone and that they would return with a total of ten to fifteen large, flat je display-exchange stone blanks. The men would break and pry out flat pieces of the slatelike rock and quickly "size" the pieces with anvil-assisted or freehand percussion knapping for transportation back to Yeineri. Each large blank was suitable to become one je display-exchange stone, or if desired by its owner, one blank would sometimes be purposefully broken to make two flat-type axe blades. If a display-exchange stone blank was broken accidentally during processing, large pieces were made into axe or adze blades and smaller pieces into either stone knives or relatively short adze blades. As percussion tools, Awigowi-sourced blades do not command as high a bartering value as the better quality (harder), dark green and blue blades made from rock that comes from other quarry sites.

Biganme

Biganme quarry is reportedly an approximate seven-day walk from Yeineri. Biganme remains an enigma in my research. I have not yet attempted to locate Biganme on the ground, nor have I ever seen any of the stone goods that would have been produced from Biganme core rock, as it has been described to me. The Wano of Yeineri report that the rock is "crystal, similar but not the same as quartz crystals that the men possess as sacred objects." The description of the rock sounds like obsidian, which I have never seen in any form, in either the Highlands or lowlands of this part of Irian Jaya. Reportedly, Biganme is located outside of the Ye River drainage. It is possible that a local volcanic source is present with obsidian deposits. The Wano who talk about Biganme say that the core rock was used for knives and is not produced today. If there is a quarry source as described, then perhaps a plausible reason for why I have not seen its products is that the rock is of a locally rare lithology, and blades are removed from secular use soon after manufacture and secreted away as sacred objects. Peter Van Arsdale, while reading my manuscript, offered a plausible alternative explanation that the quarry might be quasi-mythical.

Integrated Operation and What Prompts Production

Under the "umbrella" of overall Yeineri big man leadership, site visits to take stone are initiated from within the membership of the individual stone-working groups. Which sites to visit and when, as well as work goals, are determined by consensus of group membership, although the big man leader of each group is often in a state of negotiation with his group to get their consensus to adhere to his personal agenda. These stone manufacturing groups vary in size from as few as approximately five to as many as twelve men with a median work group membership of approximately seven. It is these individual groups, or sometimes combinations of them in unusually numerically large quarrying expeditions, that perform the sacred rituals before taking stone and at the close of each quarry operation.

Women conventionally cook tubers and greens for the men to carry to quarry sites, or sometimes women carry the food themselves to sites and cook it there. They also assist by carrying quarry-made biface blanks and display-exchange stones back to the residences. Rarely do women overnight at the sites, but they are not precluded by custom or taboo from doing so. Women never assist otherwise in quarrying operations, and when at the sites, they stay off to the side, away from the quarry floors and core rock faces.

Permanent shelters are not maintained at any of the quarry sites for overnight work groups. Instead, lean-to shelters are quickly constructed out of tree limbs and branches by each work party to accommodate their needs, although sometimes previously used shelters can be reused.

During each site visit, the initial breaking of the quarry core (Step 2 of the manufacturing process) and reducing pieces to manageable sizes (Step 3 of the manufacturing process) are usually a group cooperative effort. Each team works effectively as a unit until enough manageable pieces have been reduced to a suitable size for reduction by individuals to quarry-made biface blanks. Once the knapping process commences on an individual stone, it is owned by that stone worker until he disposes of it in a manner at his discretion.

All quarry core blanks are carried back to places of residence for further processing and distribution. The number of biface blanks that are removed from a quarry site by a single work party visit is extremely variable, depending on size of the work party, on hardness of the core rock and the ease with which it can be quarried, the type or types of blade blanks and/or display-exchange stones that are being procured, and the vagaries of the quarrying parties' own goals.

Sometimes a single good quality display-exchange stone per man is considered a successful one-day quarrying operation. At other times, two display-exchange stone blanks may be taken. Likewise, a single large axe blade blank per each member of a work party might be considered a meritorious one-day accomplishment; whereas six or seven small adze blade biface blanks might not be considered a "success." At other sites and times, three to eight adze blade biface blanks are considered a worthy daily achievement. I was not able to meaningfully quantify daily production at any hypothetically sustained rate at the Wano Yeineri quarry sites.

The stones brought back from the quarry sites to the specific residences of the men who quarried them are maintained by their owners during final reduction and storaged until distribution. Sometimes the stones are shifted about a bit among the work group that quarried them, during the fine-flaking (Step 6 of the manufacturing process) and grinding (Step 7 of the manufacturing process) processes, but usually a single stone is worked to the stage of distribution by the same man who rough-flaked the biface blank at the quarry site.

There are no sandstone sequences in the geologic column within the area of the quarry belt that could furnish permanently located grinding slabs for the grinding process and only small handheld grindstones can be imported. For this reason, local informants say that during precontact production levels most of the tool goods were traded into user populations as fine-flaked blanks ready for grinding, not as finished tool blades or display-exchange stones. In such cases, the stone goods would receive added value by the labor of whoever ground them en route or at their final user destinations. Some of the grinding slab locations that are present as far away as even the eastern part of Western Dani territory and, possibly even within the geography of the Grand Valley Dani, may have played a role in Step 7 (grinding) of the manufacturing process, in addition to being used to resharpen and shape broken tools once they were in use. (For a discussion and photographs of grinding slabs

that are scattered throughout user areas, refer to "Stationary Grinding Slabs and Mobile Hand Stones" in chapter 2.)

Quarrying and knapping the core rock are the more-efficient labor aspects of the manufacturing process. Grinding is the most labor intensive and time consuming. An example of the size of the handheld grindstones that are used at Yeineri is shown in figure 5.6. In the photograph, a Yeineri toolmaker is shown grinding a Yeineri-style flat axe blade with a grindstone that he says was carried to him through kinship linkage from outside of Wano territory in the Mulia area (fig. 5.1). An old-timer (estimated sixty-five to seventy years of age) at Yeineri who said that he had been to Awigowi quarry three times during his lifetime to procure je exchange pibit pibit core material, related that he ground part-time on a long (60 to 80 cm) display-exchange stone for between one to three years before trading it to users outside of the Yeineri center. Other local informants stated that it takes from approximately eight months to one and a half to three years to grind to completion, using Yeineri grindstones, a good quality (hard) typical Yeineri-style axe blade (25 to 40 cm long). Although I could not measure or make reliable estimates on how many hours are spent actually grinding these large stones, it is acceptable in general terms, that the grinding process is labor intensive.

Contrary to statements by Yeineri informants that most of their stone goods were traded out from the production center as fine flaked biface blanks that were ready for the grinding process, when I examined the "assemblage" of stone goods that were currently present at Yeineri during 1991, I found that most of the "stock" was either completely ground tools and display-exchange stones or were biface cores that were in the process of being ground. In figure 5.7, the tape measure is in inches. Seven flat, completely ground je display-exchange stones are displayed with three Yeineri flat-style axe blades by their proud Yeineri owners. The display-exchange stone above the tape measure in the lower photograph is 63.5 cm long and 8.9 cm wide at its widest point. The unusually long display-

Fig. 5.6. A flat-style axe blade is ground at the habitation site.

exchange stone above it is 76.2 cm long by 11 cm wide. The display-exchange stone along the upper left margin of the photograph is 36.8 cm long by 13.2 cm wide. Next to it is a darker green Yeineri flat-style axe blade that is 43 cm long by 8.9 cm wide at its widest point. All of the stones in the photograph are pibit pibit from the Awigowi quarry except the unusually long (43 cm) darker green flat-style axe blade and the dark green display-exchange stone (63.5 cm long) along the upper edge of the tape measure. The flat-style display-exchange stone displayed by its owner is also a pibit pibit and is approximately 60 cm long. The owner of this stone said that he had been grinding on it for over a one-and-a-half-year period of time. The stones are all being maintained at Yeineri by their makers until hopefully either Dani or Western Dani traders come to Yeineri seeking such stones, or, more likely the Wano will transport the stones for trade to the users. (Trade and the value of stone goods is discussed in chapter 8.) Teniak, the Wano who guided me to Yeineri from Dagai, showed me a valuable pibit pibit display-exchange stone that he acquired during a quarry rock group trip to the Awigowi quarry. Teniak had smoothed the edges and other surfaces of his stone with mini-

mal grinding, which he said took him approximately three months. His stated plans are to carry the stone himself to the Dani to barter for a large pig.

Production is prompted by each quarryman's need and that of nonquarrying relatives for stone goods for their own utilitarian purposes and by the presumed value of "marketplace" demand. The Wano language-group cultural system is pig poor and stone resource rich, compared to their Dani and Western Dani stone goods customers who are, relatively speaking, sweet potato and pig rich and stone poor. Classic marketplace factors are at play between the stone producer and the stone user groups.

Uses of Quarry Sites in Wano Territory by Others than Wano

Information that I acquired independently from both elderly northern Wano and southern Duvle informants (estimated age range fifty-five to sixty-five years) agree that the Duvle controlled and operated a rock quarry just a short distance inside of Wano territory, until as recently as about forty years ago. The time of discovery of the quarry rock by the Duvle is

Fig. 5.7. Exchange stones and axe blade blanks ready for transport

clouded in the oral histories but may have been as recent as only two generations ago. Prior to that time, the Duvle reportedly used river-tumbled stones collected in the Dagai area for trade and local use as percussion tools, supplemented with more assuredly good-quality (hard) blades that were traded from the Wano quarries. The lowland Duvle do not use je (or puluen-type) display-exchange stones that are a fundamental part of Highlands cultural systems.

The abandoned Duvle quarry is known to both local Duvle and Wano as the Faira quarry. The quarry core is a low, flat outcrop of hard metamorphic rock that forms a small island mass in the middle of the Dagai-Ye River. It is located downriver from the Wano Diarindo ("Rock Shelter") quarry and just a few hours walk-climb south, up the Dagai River, from the present-day Dagai Duvle habitation site. The quarry is located in an uninhabited area where Duvle territory merges into Wano-controlled territory. In the memories of the last quarry users, Faira was connected to both river banks by log pole bridges rather than by suspension bridges. The engineering quarry technique was fire, built directly on top of the quarry core surface. Quarried core pieces were carried to either river bank for further reduction to biface blanks and transportation to habitation sites for further processing or trade. Intermittent river floods flushed pieces of quarried core and flaking debitage from the area. It would be extremely difficult, probably impossible, to recognize the site today as a prehistoric quarry without the assistance of knowledgeable local informants.

Informants said that the practice was for Duvle men to go to the site to procure core rock with as few as two men and sometimes as many as eight. The men would go on long, one-day journeys, or at times and depending on distances, stay overnight to procure tool cores. When overnighting, temporary lean-to shelters were built, never permanent shelters. No Duvle informants would discuss the subject of sacredness of the site and the use of ritual to either appease or attempt to propitiate ghosts or spirits that might be associated with the site.

The lowland Duvle belief system regarding ghosts and spirits and the world of the unseen is different from that for the Highlanders.

Duvle women were allowed at the site in the accompaniment of Duvle men. They did not participate directly in quarrying operations, but, at the discretion of a work party leader, were helpful in transporting food and cooking it at the site, as well as helping to transport preform biface blanks back to habitation sites.

One Duvle informant, Buti Tiya who is the second oldest Duvle living at Dagai (age estimate sixty years), remembered that Duvle hunters searching for marsupials, wild pigs, or cassowary birds, might briefly stop by Faira to obtain just a few pieces of adze blade core rock.

The Duvle at Dagai said that in addition to trading adze/axe biface blanks downriver into the Dismal Swamp, they also traded on a rather small scale to Western Dani from the greater Kembu-Manit-Karubaga-Bokondini area (fig. 5.1). Sometimes Western Dani traders would come to them, but the Duvle would rarely go on trading missions into Western Dani territory. They reportedly had no social trade linkages such as those in place between the Yeineri, Tagime, and Langda Sela quarries with their consumers.

At some point in this trading relationship, the Duvle said that they allowed Western Dani to come directly to their Faira quarry source and take stone. That practice built up until the Wano stopped it and shut the quarry down to not only the use of Western Dani outsiders but also to the Duvle. Apparently, when the Wano became targets of the Duvle baby-stealing practice, they retaliated with some baby thefts of their own and in addition, precluded the Duvle passage and the privilege of operating the quarry at Faira (Hampton 1992a, 1992b). At about this same time, the Wano and Duvle concur that a Wano man with a trading mission to the Western Dani Karubaga area was killed by Western Dani, and in retaliation the Wano stopped Western Dani travelers from coming to Faira to take stone. Apparently, the quarry was shut down to use by all outsiders and effectively closed, not to be operated since by either outsiders or the Wano. Both Wano and Duvle informants who were not sure of the time of quarry closure felt confident in their knowledge of the circumstances and guessed that closure was about forty years ago.

Elsewhere, to the south, in the Wano quarry belt, the Wano said the Western Dani, Dani, Damal, or Moni only rarely would come to quarry sites or Wano habitation sites seeking permission to quarry stone. According to the Wano, they would allow these outsiders access for limited use, but the outsiders were required to show quarried rock and blade blanks to Wano before departing Wano territory. Within the sparsely populated quarry belt area, I believe that outside travelers were able to visit certain sites and quarry, from time to time, on their own, or even to locate their own quarry spots, but I have not been able to confirm this idea with informants of the Dani, Western Dani, Nduga, Dem, or Damal language groups. All of this not withstanding, the important link by primary users to stone goods that were sourced in Wano territory was by trade mechanisms, which are discussed in chapter 8.

CHAPTER 6

Tagime Quarries

Whereas the Yeineri quarries and manufacturing center are located in sparsely settled Wano territory (estimated population 3,000 to 3,500) and are separated by one or more language boundaries from the more populated primary market areas for their stone goods, the Tagime quarries and manufacturing center are located in the heartland of the same shared marketing and use areas (fig. 1.3). The Tagime quarries, located within Western Dani territory (estimated population 129,000) but near the language boundary with the Grand Valley Dani (estimated population 100,000), are only a two-hour walk from the relatively concentrated population of the Grand Valley, compared to the Yeineri quarries, which are more than 150 km away from the Grand Valley and separated by rugged terrain that requires arduous travel by circuitous routes.

From Heider's perspective while doing field work with the Dugum Dani in the east-central part of the Grand Valley (Hupainma, fig. 1.21) during the years 1961–63 and 1968, the stones for adze and axe tools that were used in that area were not obtainable locally but were im-

ported. Although Heider recognized that the local inhabitants distinguished between two fundamentally different kinds of adze and axe blade rock, one the black *gu*, and the other the multicolored "green, blue, mottled, streaked, and plain *ebe*," Heider attributed their origin to "apparently only one source" in the Nogolo Basin (author's note: the Yeineri quarries). Heider further stated that, "The *gu* is a dull black stone too soft to hold a good edge for long, and is described as *aik dlek* (*aik*, no tooth; *dlek*, none)" (1970:272–73, 276).

During the early years of my own work, both the Dugum Dani and other Dani apprised me of the fact that although the black gu blades all look the same, some are relatively durable and considered to be valuable tools, while others are softer, will not hold a good edge, and break easily. First one informant and then another told me that there were quarries from which "good quality" black blades were sourced that were different from "the other" (Yeineri-sourced) blades. The best information that I could gather was that such quarries were located somewhere between Pyramid and Kelila, possibly not far outside the northwest end of the Grand Valley (figs. 1.21 and 2.8), and not nearly as far as the Nogolo Basin. The number of rumored locations as sources for the black adze and axe blades increased as word spread among indigenous populations about my quest. In hindsight, after checking numerous locales to no avail, I realized that I was sometimes being led to "sources of opportunity" where an individual had found a single stone or two that he had shaped, by grinding, into an adze or axe blade. Sometimes it was auras of secrecy that made meaningful conversations about such locales difficult—the places had been designated as sacred, wusa, and not to be talked about with the uninitiated. After all, in the minds of local inhabitants, a beneficent spirit had placed the stone where it would be found and/or had guided the finder to it. The geology at these locales was always problematic, and although disappointed that I seemed to be getting no nearer to a discovery of actual quarries, I was accumulating valuable information about "sources of opportunity" (my terminology).

During field research in 1989, while searching for the quarries, my exploration team and I turned northward up a major tributary of the Baliem River. A short distance up the river my assistants found that local inhabitants called the river the "Gume" (*gu*, black or brown-black; *me*, river). As we went upriver in the direction of Kelila, scattered compounds and hamlets with adjoining sweet potato gardens hugged the narrow, but often flat, valley floor. When we came to a fork in the river and to a hamlet called Tagi, we established a base camp, courtesy of the local inhabitants, in the home of a Christian missionary, who was temporarily out of the area. We learned that the name of the left fork of the river, flowing from the west, was known in former times as the Nendagabuk, but today it is known as the Tagime. Tagi is the name of a deceased, locally well-known former leader (big man) in honor of whom his hamlet of residence, the former Nendagabuk River, and the upriver hamlet of Tagineri, were named after Tagi's death. In the Western Dani quarrying area and its environs, "neri" (as in the Wano

language to the west) translates to "where the river begins." The right fork retains the name of the river below the junction, Gume. We explored both forks, searching the rivers and their banks for rocks of just the right lithology and hardness for tool blades. I was especially on the lookout for bedrock exposures or open pits that might either be or have been quarry sites. None were found. However, we were finding black river-tumbled pebbles, cobbles, and boulders that appeared to be a black amorphous argillite.

One day while attending a riverside cremation along the Gu River (Gume), just a short distance up from the river junction, Libarek, a key assistant and the head porter, showed me that in about ten minutes' time he could grind a black Gu River bank pebble, which were abundant, into a typically shaped Dani knife. Finally, several elders (estimated ages fifty-five to sixty years) in the Tagi area agreed that they would take us to the quarry spot and show us how the right kind of harder rock is located and tools are made. The next day, we proceeded directly to the Tagi River just above the river junction and the elders waded around until they had selected several river-tumbled, oblong-shaped, black stones, which averaged approximately 17 cm long. These were then carried uphill on the north side of the river, past riverside habitation sites. After about a ten- to fifteen-minute walk, we arrived at the site of a large boulder that was well known to each of the men but that was buried beneath a covering of organic forest debris. When the matted leaves were cleaned off, a sandstone grinding surface was exposed that had numerous blade grinding marks, some already overgrown with algae. According to the informants, the large sandstone boulder had been, until not long ago, the primary tool grinding slab for the Tagi toolmakers. These retired toolmakers said that the blade blanks they had just selected were so well-sized and -shaped by the spirits of the river that flaking was not necessary. The men also told us that black rock in the Gu River and some in the Tagime that looked similar to the preferred rock they had just collected was too soft to make the best quality hard blades. The men explained that the best tool stone source area is only along the Tagi River and for a short distance downriver from the junction with the Gu River, but not up the Gu River from the river junction. Further, they said that the good quality source core rock can only be successfully selected by local experts.

Although my preconceived idea of one or more bedrock quarry sites appeared to be erroneous, I continued my search for open pits, shafts, or mining drifts up the Tagi River for an estimated distance of 3 to 4 km to the hamlet of Tagineri, at which point the river becomes quite small and enters a dense forest. This is the legendary "point of no return," beyond which local inhabitants did not care to venture. I checked topographic maps of the area and realized that anyone following the steepening drainage could soon work their way up to over 2,750 m of elevation, at which heights hypothermia might become a serious problem for near-naked indigenous travelers. Local residents confirmed what I had already been told at the downriver hamlet of Tagi, that the hamlet of Tagineri is the west end of the Tagi River quarry belt, and that there are no bedrock quarries or mining operations.

Geologic Setting

The lower hillsides of the Tagi Valley between the hamlets of Tagi and Tagineri consist of vegetation covered slopes of the Kembelangan formation, which is Paleocene to Cretaceous in age (chapter 1). The Kembelangan consists of four members, with known lithologies of claystone, shales, argillites, siltstones, and some interbeds of quartzitic sandstones. Due to a combination of the erosional susceptibility of most beds within the Kembelangan and heavy vegetation, visible outcrops of beds of the Kembelangan formation are sparse within the quarrying area, although some few erratic sandstone boulders from the Kembelangan have been converted into permanent grinding slabs by ancestors of the present generation of Tagime toolmakers.

Overlying the Kembelangan and cropping out on upper hillside slopes and forming caprock are limestone beds of the Tertiary and possibly uppermost Cretaceous New Guinea Limestone Group (chapter 1). Large, exposed erratic blocks that have broken away from New Guinea Limestone cliffs have slumped as far downhill as the valley floor. Caves are present within a lower sequence of New Guinea Limestone. Human skeletons are present in some of the caves, which are considered sacred places by the indigenous population.

The Tagime Quarry Area and Local Informants

The Tagime quarry belt, located within Western Dani territory, is a single continuous 3 to 4 km stretch of the Tagi River (Tagime, formerly known as the Nendagabuk) and its river banks. The lower end of the quarrying area is bounded by the hamlet of Tagi, which sprawls across both sides of the river, near its junction with the Gu River (Gume), which in turn is a tributary of the Baliem. The upper end of the quarrying area is bounded by the hamlet of Tagineri, with small compounds adjacent to the river, just before the river disappears into the "forest of no return," the upper reaches of its drainage system. Between the downriver hamlet of Tagi and the upriver hamlet of Tagineri, compounds of different sizes are scattered along the confined valley floor, including the named compounds of Prome, Inluga, and Melebaga. These compounds, as well as those of Tagi and Tagineri, are the scattered loci for what little knapping is done on biface blanks before the grinding process.

A favorite quarrying section of the river is within the sprawling hamlet of Tagi. Small compounds of typical Western Dani and Dani design, with nearby gardens, are located at spots adjacent to the river to facilitate work on core rock that is gathered from the river or along its banks. Today, the manufacture of stone tools along the Tagime quarry belt is a fast disappearing endeavor, perhaps soon to be forgotten except by the older, retired local toolmakers.

At the lower Tagi end of the quarry belt, three local leaders (big men) with varying degrees of influence, Toat Jikwa, Pono Tabuni, and Gimanguk Jikwa, availed themselves in

1992 to numerous conversations and also accompanied me around the Tagi area. Toat is blind in one eye and depends on a walking stick, but he remains "the" quarrying expert who shared a great deal of information about the manufacturing operation in former times. Pono Tabuni is the grandson of the deceased big man Tagi. Reportedly, Gimanguk Jikwa is today on the same high level of influence as Tagi was in the past. Both Toat and Gimanguk are quite elderly (estimated ages seventy years) and are important sources of oral history. At the upriver end of the quarry belt at Tagineri, my local informants in 1992 were Tepinamnip Jikwa, Jirvambo Kogoya, and Pinde Jikwa, who shared information about tool manufacture in that area.

Kinds of Stone Goods Produced and Their Classification

Just as at Yeineri, stone axe and adze blades, knives, chisels, and the profane je flat-type display-exchange stones are produced and traded outward from the tool-making center. The Tagime toolmakers understood my classification of their stone goods (Tagime-style, flat-style, and tubular-style axe blades; Tagime-style and flat-style adze blades; knives and chisels; and flat-type je display-exchange stones [chapters 2 and 3]), but in their own classification the Tagime experts make an extremely important distinction between tool blades, regardless of whether they are axes, adzes, knives, or chisels. That distinction is hardness. Toat Jikwa, with a nodded confirmation from the other Tagi hamlet area informants, explained that it is only the harder, more durable rock that the Tagime experts search for within the confines of the quarrying area. Toat confirmed what I had been told by other informants in 1989: it takes a local expert to recognize the desirable core rock versus the softer rock that is found not only in the Tagi River but that is abundantly available nearby in the Gu River and at other known locales. According to the Tagime informants, it is the softer black rock that is *aik dlek* (too soft and has "no tooth"). Regarding discovery of the hard rock quarry area, my informants said that

they only knew that it was discovered by "the ancestors," and that the location and boundaries of the area had not changed during the lifetimes of the informants. The older, retired Tagime quarrymen maintained that proper Tagime-sourced tools are of a better quality than the jaga (adze) and jaga bilig (axe) green and blue blades that are imported (from Yeineri). To satisfy market demand for tools of lesser value than the good quality Tagime blades, Toat stated that the softer gu blades were sometimes also produced. I observed in both 1989, the year that I located the quarry area, and on a return visit in 1992 that adult males at the Tagi and Tagineri hamlets owned both Tagime- and Yeineri-sourced adze blades, but only Tagime-sourced axe blades. In an informal survey throughout the area, some men agreed with their older leaders that they preferred Tagime-sourced blades versus the green and blue blades that were imported, but other men said they preferred the imported green and blue blades.

The University of Colorado mineralogists identified the Tagime core material and Tagime-style adze blades as being a black meta-argillite (chapter 2). The major mineral components are quartz and siderite, with chlorite being a minor mineral, and muscovite being an accessory mineral. Quartz, chlorite, and muscovite were identified by X-ray analyses. On the Colorado team's four-part hardness scale, based on mineralogical and textural considerations (VH, H, M, S; chapters 2 and 5), the team rated the Tagime rock as "VH." By comparison, the Colorado team rated Yeineri-sourced epidote amphibolite as the "hardest" rock type I had submitted to their scrutiny. The Tagime very fine-grained texture meta-argillite ("very hard"), although possibly not as hard as the Yeineri epidote amphibolite, was interpreted to be harder than the Yeineri blueschist and epidote chlorite schist (chapters 2 and 5).

The Manufacturing Process and Quarry Ownership

Seven technological steps are used in the Highlands to produce ground stone adze and axe blades: (1) locate a suitable quarry rock, (2) break the rock, (3) reduce pieces to manageable sizes, (4) shape preform biface blanks at quarry sites by freehand knapping; and, away from quarry sites, in the final knapping process, intermittently (5) dull biface edges and prepare platforms on individual biface blanks as part of (6) fine-flaking to produce final bifaces for (7) grinding. In the Tagime manufacturing process, some of the seven technological steps of Highlands tool-making (see Yeineri Quarries) are explicitly accounted for while others are combined into separate distinct steps or even omitted. In addition to the technological steps that are used to produce stone goods at Tagime, the toolmakers, within the framework of their own religious ganekhe groups (chapters 1 and 4), conduct rituals at the commencement and closing of quarrying procedures and at appropriate times during the manufacturing process to propitiate landowner spirits to furnish abundant, good quality stones.

According to oral history, the deceased Tagi (grandfather of one of my informants, Pono Tabuni) and several other contemporary big men of the Tagi (precontact) era, controlled the river through the heartland of the tool-making center from about halfway up the Tagi River toward Tagineri (earlier name unknown to me), downriver to a kilometer or so below the junction of the Tagi and Gu Rivers, toward the Grand Valley. The Tagi hamlet informants say that the favorable black rock (meta-argillite) is only present in desirable quantities in the Tagi River, not upriver from the junction with the Gu River. According to informants from both the hamlets of Tagi and Tagineri, the Tagineri people also "quarried" river-transported core rock but on a reduced scale compared to the people of the Tagi hamlet area. There was and is no single centralized quarry ownership and control system as found among the Wano people in the Yeineri quarry belt but two independently operated tool-making areas, which I have named the Tagi hamlet-factory and the Tagineri hamlet-factory. The two factory areas were and are separated by a geographically defined, sociopolitically motivated territorial boundary, about midway between the two

hamlets. I visited the boundary area with local informants from both Tagi and Tagineri to confirm its presence and location.

Reportedly, any of the people within the Tagi hamlet sociopolitical domain could go down to the river and seek river core stones within their territorial area on their own initiative, without specific approval of big men leaders. Similarly, inhabitants of the upriver quarry area could gather stones within their territory. According to my informants, to venture outside of the established sociopolitical boundaries prior to the mid-1960s was to invite ambush and death. The older big men of the Tagi hamlet area said that in former times they were essentially prisoners within their own stone quarrying and tool-making area because until the mid-1960s almost constant ritual wars and conflict kept everyone within their own boundaries. The Tagi informants said that residents of Belokme and beyond toward the Baliem River were their enemies, as were the people up the Tagi River at the hamlet of what is today known as Tagineri. Only the people living along the upper Gu River were friendly. Yet in spite of all these difficulties, a successful tool and je display-exchange stone trade flourished, as is described in chapter 8.

Searching the river and its banks for new core rock by tool-making groups under residential leadership, or now and again, by an individual or two looking for a rock from which to make a tool of expediency, is prompted by flash floods. Engineering techniques to break newly found boulder cores include the use of fire and hurled or hand-held hammerstones, used with or without the assistance of fire. Selected boulders, if not too large, are still usually carried to riverside compounds for further processing. Sometimes such boulders, estimated to range from approximately 11 to 65 kg, are stockpiled along the riverbank or within a riverside compound for future use at a more desirable time. If selected boulder cores are too large to be carried, they are usually broken in place. Informants stated that under some conditions, quarry cores can be fired from the top and broken apart with hammerstones while still in the river.

In 1992, Toat Jikwa and the other Tagi hamlet area elders said that the toolmakers preferred to find stones in the river that were of the right hardness and suitable sizes and shapes that could be ground directly into blades or display-exchange stones without having to further reduce them by knapping. This information corroborated my research data of 1989 when I had first located this tool-making center and had worked with other local informants. Interestingly, the toolmakers of Tagime think of themselves as skilled grinders; they do not think of knapping or flaking as being their primary skill. Informants related that sometimes talented specialists were paid a fee (cowrie shells during precontact times) for custom grinding of tool blade cores that had been found and brought to them by other residents of the quarry area. Some small stones, already reasonably shaped by natural erosion, require at least minor flaking, however, before grinding is commenced. In 1989 and then again in 1992, I observed that flaking, as done by the Tagime toolmakers, even when reducing a larger core, did not require advanced knapping skills; just the holding of a core rock and, with or without anvil assistance, simply knocking off pieces with a convenient hammerstone. During field research in 1992, Toat Jikwa found two naturally shaped, river-tumbled cores that he proclaimed would make excellent jaga bilig (axe blades). One stone was 9.5 cm wide by 31.75 cm long and the other was 11.6 cm wide by 36.8 cm long. Having watched the toolmakers at work at Tagime, I estimated that it would take a maximum of ten minutes to flake each stone into a crude preform blank. Toat estimated it would take approximately five weeks for an individual to grind each stone to completion.

If a large but manageable core boulder is found in the river, it might be carried to the river bank or to a nearby habitation compound and placed on a burning fire to break it. Sometimes larger quarry stones found along the banks of the river are broken apart in-place with fires built on or against the stones. Toat

Fig. 6.1. A selected stone is broken by fire.

Fig. 6.2. Big man Toat is pleased with the results.

said that as soon as a quarry stone is broken, it is known whether or not it will make a good blade. If the color is dark gray to black, it is a good stone. If too brown, it is no good. Sometimes, due to the shape of a boulder that is selected as a core quarry stone, it is broken by hurling hammerstones at it, and a fire is not needed.

In 1992, Toat, with his walking stick in hand and a son by his side, searched the Tagi River near his riverside compound for quarry stones. Finally, Toat found what he was hoping to find and was pleased to tell us that it was a very good stone (fig. 6.1). Two men carried it to shore, then another 50 m to Toat's compound, lifted it over the compound fence, and laid it in the courtyard. A fire was built and the stone was laid directly on top (fig. 6.1). For fifteen minutes it heated and then exploded into three pieces. Toat came from his house to examine the results. The old expert proclaimed that two of the pieces were a good size for grinding.

He selected one piece that he particularly prized (fig. 6.2) and carried it back to his house.

The shape of the second largest piece was then slightly modified at the firing site by minor flaking with the anvil percussion technique, to quickly (approximately ten minutes) create a crude preform that was considered ready for grinding. Toat Jikwa said that the next day he would take me to his favorite grinding slab to show me how the stones are shaped.

I asked Toat about the largest core that he had selected from the fire-broken quarry stone that he intended to make into a large Tagime-style axe blade. He told me that it "would take a long time to grind that stone." Toat said he would invite about ten men to participate, and they would pass the stone from person to person over a period of weeks while the stone was being ground. His wife would furnish food during this time to whomever was grinding the stone. After about two months, the stone would

Fig. 6.3. The grinding commences.

be smooth and ready to put in an axe handle, and then Toat said he would sponsor a ceremony, sacrifice pigs at a ritual feast, and put the stone in a head net to display it.

The next day, on May 15, 1992, Toat Jikwa, Pono Tabuni, Awan Tabuni, and a group of younger local inhabitants led my exploration team and me to the grinding stone that had been revealed to me in 1989. In precontact times Pono Tabuni had used this stone. Before that, he related that he knew that his grandfather, Tagi Tabuni, had also ground stones here.

Near the grinding rock are small rivulets of water trickling down the hillside. A small boy was directed to take bundles of grass, dip them in the water, and carry the bundles back to the grinding stone as the older men began to grind their blades. One was the rough blade blank that had just been processed to the grinding stage the day before, and another was an almost completely finished, medium-sized adze blade. The boy knew exactly what was expected of him. He stood next to the men and dripped water, first from one water-laden bundle of grass and then the other onto the places where the dry meta-argillite tool blades were being ground against the sandstone grinding rock (fig. 6.3).

My informants pointed out that the use of this grinding site by two to six grinders at a time, plus assistants to drip water and to trade off grinding chores, was a common occurrence when the tool-producing center was fully functional. Toat said there were two smaller, permanently located grinding slabs within the Tagi hamlet quarrying area; and the toolmakers at the upper end of the quarry belt (Tagineri) also had their own permanently located large grinding slabs, in addition to portable grindstones.

Stimulation of Production and Distribution of Product

Demand for Tagime products depended on the personal needs of local inhabitants and on the utilitarian and social needs (for je display-exchange stones) throughout the Western Dani, Dani, and other language-speaking groups within the Grand Valley and West region, where all language groups use a mix of Tagime- and Yeineri-derived stone goods (chapter 2). According to Tagime informants, when there were periods of peak demand for tools, they were usually at times of increased timbering or wood chopping activity in the Grand Valley, perhaps related to the alliancewide ebe akho when firewood was stockpiled everywhere, or when large, virgin forest areas were cleared to make new sweet potato gardens. They all concurred, however, that regardless of those times of neighborly peak demand, it was the unpredictable flash floods that caused a spontaneous reaction among the quarrymen. When new core source material was deposited and uncovered after heavy rains, it prompted a flurry of activity along the Tagi River. During this time, fires were built, rocks carried for stockpiling near compounds, and knapping and/or grinding increased dramatically. Overprinting these cyclical fluctuations of tool output, however, was the *grand stimulus* for the need for increased tools that was heralded by the arrival of the sweet potato 1,000 to 300 ya (most likely around 300 ya). A population explosion in the Highlands acted in symbiotic synchrony with rapidly expanding sweet potato production, as the faster-growing, higher-yield per land and labor unit sweet potato replaced the predecessor taro and yam tubers as the primary staple crop. Under this scenario, the virgin forests of vast hillsides and valley floors were cleared probably within the last 250 to 350 years. This does not indicate a slow trickle of tools into the Grand Valley and other Highlands areas over the millennia of horticultural practice but instead a stimulated increase of tool production and dispersion that was related to increased tuber production over a much shorter period of time. Distribution was always by trade (discussed in chapter 7), as outsiders were never allowed to collect their own source core stones from the Tagi River.

Langda-Sela Quarries and Sources of Opportunity

The inhabitants of the Yali and East region use a single, internally produced Langda-Sela-style adze blade and stone knives, but no axe blades or chisels. The majority of these tool blades are produced at a manufacturing center, which consists of a cluster of quarrying and production factories near and including the hamlet of Langda (fig. 7.1), located within Una territory (estimated population 4,600) (fig. 2.1). A significantly lesser number of blades are produced at a functionally similar but much smaller quarrying and production operation at Sela, within the adjacent Kimyal territory (estimated population 6,500). The stone tools are traded outward across language boundaries to all language groups within the Yali and East region. Only a few of these blades trickle across the regional boundary into the Grand Valley and West region where they are never used as profane percussion tools but are sometimes converted into sacred objects. Je-type display-exchange stones, which are so prolifically used in the Grand Valley and West region, are not produced within the Yali and East region but

are imported across the regional boundary from the Dani.

Una Habitat, History of Contact, and Research by Others

The Una habitat is located in a rugged mountainous area of cloud-covered peaks and steep-walled canyons, centered around the Dutch missionary landing strip at Langda (elevation 1,860 m, 139.58° east longitude and 4.39° south latitude). From the Langda ridge, a slope drops precipitously for approximately 800 m to the Ey (Dutch spelling; Yei, English-Indonesian) rock quarry river (fig. 7.2), which tumbles its way southward, joining other fast-flowing rivers, which make their way still farther to the south where they then abruptly spill out from the mountain front into a dense, flat jungle swampland. From here, the rivers that originate in the Highlands meander still farther south to the Arafura Sea. It was from this sea that in 1526 the Portuguese explorer Meneses first reported to the European community his discovery of an

Fig. 7.1. Una house cluster on Langda ridge

Geologic Setting

Little is known about the geology of the greater Langda area. At the time of my field work, there were no published geologic maps, and I had little time to conduct geologic reconnaissance myself. Outcrops are sparse on hill slopes dense with vegetation. Landslide areas and river bottom exposures are difficult to access. A volcanic sequence is known to exist within the area. Based on regional extrapolation from known volcanic rock sequences to the east in Papua New Guinea, these volcanics could be anywhere from Jurassic to Quaternary in age. The stratigraphic relationship of the volcanics to what looks in the field to be outcrops of the Kembelangan formation is unknown. The Kembelangan to the west ranges in age from Paleocene to Cretaceous. I presume that the portable sandstone grinding slabs that have been carried by the Una toolmakers from near Bomela back to the Langda manufacturing area are from sandstone outcrops of the Kembelangan, but I have not visited these locales. Andesite/basaltic rocks from the Langda quarries and from a sampling of Langda-Sela-style adze blades that were collected from throughout the Yali and East region have been identified petrographically (as a part of this project) by Medlin, Munoz, and Swope at the University of Colorado. Metamorphosed volcanic tuffs from samples taken as a part of this project in the Langda area, as well as from Langda-Sela-style knives that were sampled throughout the Yali and East region, have been interpreted by R. N. Guillemette at Texas A&M University.

Langda Manufacturing Center

Within the greater Langda Una residential district there are approximately twenty-six separate house clusters and hamlets. Eleven of these are hamlets associated with quarries, within which the residents manufacture stone tools. Hereafter, I refer to these as hamlet-factories. The eleven hamlet-factories are concentrated along a 17 km stretch of the Ey River and very short stretches of two tributaries near

island of "negroids." Europeans were quick to name this second-largest island in the world New Guinea—after French Guinea in Africa—because of the black-skinned people observed along the coasts. As a backdrop to the north of the Una domain and quarrying area, the Jayawijaya mountains rise to a series of peaks, which vary in elevation from 3,810 m to 4,645 m.

Dick and Margaret Kroneman, missionary linguists with the Summer Institute of Linguistics (SIL), who reside at Langda as guests of the Netherlands Reformation Church while they work on a translation of the Una language, state that the first Dutch explorers came through the Langda area in 1911. According to the Kronemans, other explorers came up from the Asmat lowland area sometime in the 1960s. "A few died and were buried here." In 1971, missionaries from the Netherlands Reformation Church established residence with the Una people at Langda and were supported by helicopter until the present landing strip was officially opened in 1973. The missionaries have hosted foreign visitors since that time, including, in addition to me, researchers Desmond Clark (1991:44–47), Giancarlo Ligabue (1991:36–43), and Nicholas Toth (Schick and Toth 1993:245–51; Toth et al. 1992:88–93).

Fig. 7.2. The Ey (rock quarry river)

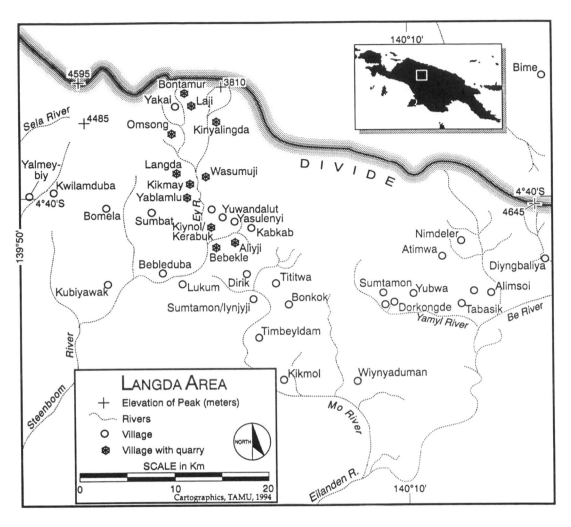

Fig. 7.3. The Una rock quarry
area, centered on Langda

their points of juncture with the Ey (fig. 7.3). Each hamlet-factory group owns the quarrying rights to a section of the river and uses its own labor force for adze blade and knife production. Raw materials for knives and the very few display-exchange and sacred stones that are produced are obtained from hillside outcrops that are located within the geographic boundaries of the area. The hamlet-factories operate within a typical Yali and East region sociopolitical framework of house cluster and hamlet big man leadership (see "Sociopolitical Organization," particularly "Compound and Hamlet," chapter 3). The head quarryman of each hamlet-factory, with the assistance of cooperative work parties, locates within the territorial boundaries of his own river-sourced quarry, boulder cores that are reduced to manageable-sized pieces before being allocated to individual

workers for ownership and further processing. A similarly operated hamlet-factory produces the same kind of stone goods at Sela. I refer to the group of hamlet-factories that are centered around Langda as the Langda manufacturing center and to the quarrying, manufacture, and distribution of products from both Langda and Sela as the Yali and East region stone goods industry. Langda is located approximately 200 km southeast of Wamena in the Grand Valley.

Quarry Ownership

Quarrying rights to adjacent stretches of the river are each owned by a single head quarryman in each of the eleven hamlet-factories. The hamlet-factories are, from north to south: Bontamur, Laji, Kinyalingda, Omsong, Langda, Wasumuji, Kikmay, Yablamula, Kiynol/Kerabuk, Aliyji, and Bebekle. The head quarryman of each hamlet (or in some cases a house cluster) who owns the quarrying rights reportedly inherited the rights from his father, who was the previous head quarryman and who had trained his son or sons to be quarrymen and toolmakers hoping that one son would emerge as the quarry owner at his death. The rights to the quarry area always belong to the head quarryman and not necessarily to the most influential big man of the hamlet, unless they are the same person. Diman Balyo, who was my primary informant at the Langda hamlet, is both the head quarryman and the most influential big man in the hamlet.

Quarry Boundaries

The river itself forms the longitudinal boundary between individually owned, linear shaped quarry sites. Head quarrymen own the rights to take stones out of the river along the shores of their hamlets only. For example, on the north end of the quarry area, near the headwaters of the Ey River, quarrymen from the villages of Bontamur and Laji (alternate spelling Larye) own rights on the east side of the Ey River (fig. 7.3). In former times, quarrymen from Yakai owned the rights to the west side of the river, but the Yakai factory is no longer operational. To the south of Laji, the head quarryman from the hamlet of Kinyalingda (alternate spelling Keynyelengde), owns the rights on the east side of the river below the quarry area that is owned by the head quarryman at Omsong hamlet. Omsong quarrymen also own rights to the river still farther to the south. Diman Balyo at Langda, south of Omsong territory, owns the Langda side of the river, while Kapit (pronounced Kabir) Malyo of the hamlet of Wasumuji (alternate spelling Wasumurji) has the quarry rights on the east side of the river. The quarrymen from Kikmay village, located southwest of Langda, must walk a full day to get to their quarry area on the west side of the river and just downriver from the section controlled by the Langda quarrymen. Kerabuk and Bebekle are two other villages with quarrying rights downstream, but on the east side of the river. Quarry boundaries are not marked, but the quarrymen and others seem to know precisely where the boundaries are located. With permission of the area owners, quarrymen are sometimes allowed to move outside their own areas to search for quality stones in territories owned by others.

Scattered throughout the Ey River quarry area are approximately twenty Una house clusters and hamlets that have no quarrying experts or toolmakers and no head quarrymen who own quarry rights. The residents of Yalar, Yalmebiy, Kwilamduba, Kitikne, Bomela, Sumba, Atala, Sumbat, Yuwandalut, Yasulenyi, Kabkab, Bebleduba, Kubiyalar, Lukum and Dirik trade with qualified quarrymen and toolmakers from active hamlet-factories to fulfill their stone tool needs. My local informants were unable to shed light on how often quarry area boundaries or the number of specifically owned quarries might have changed during recent prehistoric times. Diman Balyo, head quarryman and also hamlet leader at Langda, sadly told me that none of his sons were interested in the quarrying business. He greatly fears that he will have no qualified, father-taught son to whom he can pass quarry ownership.

Leadership within the Quarry Area

According to indigenous informants from Langda, Wasumuji, and Kikmay, there has never been a big man with control over the entire quarrying area and stone tool industry—only big men called *sienye*, with power limited to their own individual hamlets. All of the big men leaders within the greater quarrying area are presently friendly with one another, with the exception of big men from the quarrying hamlets of Laji (alternate spelling Largi), Kikmay (alternate spelling Kiykmay), and the non-quarrying hamlet of Kitikne (near Bomela). Many Una in the greater Langda area bear battle scars from previous wars. Diman has scars on his head, buttocks, and one leg that he attributes to arrow wounds inflicted by people from both the hamlets of Kikmay and Laji. These previously wounded informants said that fighting between hamlets within the rock quarry area and the absence of one big man with influence over the entire area did not seem to hinder the manufacture and trade of stone tools.

Getting around the Quarry Area

Overland travel within the Ey River quarry area is arduous with steep and usually slippery slopes to climb, descend, and traverse; patches of dense jungle growth to pass through; and interesting river crossings to be made. Under good weather conditions, a person might walk from Langda to the village of Lukum at the south end of the quarry area in about two days. At the north end of the quarrying area one could walk from the quarrying village of Laji (pronounced Larye) to the nonquarrying village of Yakai (alternate, Yalar) in an hour or slightly less. To descend from the hamlet-factory of Langda on steep trails through a vertical drop of about 800 m to the quarry area below might take one hour, but to go from the hamlet of Kikmay to the Kikmay quarry area south of the Langda quarrying area, a journey of a full day is required.

Quarrying Methods and Rock Type

Twelve informants from four different hamlet-factories agree on the standard procedures used for quarrying the rock. First, the expert with a helper nearby, searches up and down the targeted area of the river for just the right kind of rock. Kapit Malyo, a quarry owner from Wasumuji, told me that an expert understands the rocks just like a healer (medical doctor) knows a patient. He has a keen sensitivity and knowledge of the rock that allows him to select only the proper stones for quarrying. The search is made amid a conglomeration of boulders of varying sizes and lithologies as the searcher roves up and down the river, looking carefully for newly exposed rock in steep embankments, along the water's edge and out in the shallow clear water. If a top quality, large boulder is identified out in the river, a dam might be built and the water diverted around the stone to dry it and create a working area. Depending on circumstances, a wooden platform might be built next to the stone on which a fire can be introduced to heat the rock. When the rock has been properly heated, large flakes might naturally spall off or be broken off by large boulders hurled against the heated quarry rock. Sometimes a fire might be built against or on top of a desired boulder to assist the spalling/breaking process, without the need for a platform. At other times, large flakes of desired sizes can be broken off from a boulder core by hurling a large, rounded hammerstone, conveniently collected from the river or along its edge, against the boulder core. Often, the naturally rounded hammerstone is simply held and pounded against the boulder core without hurling it. Any of the above procedures can be used to also break off pieces of more normally found boulder quarry stone of "mother rocks" along the edges of the river or protruding from the river's steep banks. Sometimes boulders of just the right quality are found out in the river that are small enough to be hand-carried to the shore where they can then be broken up for further sizing and flaking.

The search is for light-colored gray-green, tan (very light brown), or blue-gray, fine-grained, very hard andesite/basalt and meta-andesite/basalt boulders that exhibit no open fractures or even healed fractures that might break during tool manufacture or tool use. Inherent lines of weakness and healed fractures, too faint to detect with the naked eye, are often present and actually can assist the quarrymen in flaking off desired pieces of rock from larger boulders, but it is always hoped that the presence of these planes of weakness will not cause tool blades to break when they are being shaped or used.

Those Who Quarry

Some of the head quarrymen and stone experts who have the right to quarry and the ability to make stone tools in the Una area are Diman Balyo, Kapit (Kabir) Malyo, Iba Deyal, Kol Balyo, Yibik, Nyonyo Nabyal, Derber Nabyal, Kabin Malyo, Bira Malyo, Kubir Malyo, Eram Tegget, and Ngis Malyo. The head quarrymen, who are also the quarry owners, have authority over who goes to the quarry areas, and they alone may sometimes grant permission for people outside of their hamlet-factory areas to look for rock, under their close supervision. To this extent, the culture seems pragmatic, at least at this time, about quarry use. It is customary for invited assistants who are not quarrymen but who have requested a stone tool and who accompany the quarrymen to the river to furnish food while the quarrymen are at work. Families are welcome to join the quarrymen and may go down to the quarries to prepare and serve food and to help carry stones back to the hamlets for shaping and grinding.

Rituals Associated with Quarrying

There was a time when the Una traditionally placed their dead in trees after wrapping them in *Pandanus* leaves. Ultimately the skulls were removed and placed in the men's house (or sometimes in the family houses). The skulls contained "great spirit power" and had the power to provide good stones for quarrying. The skull has the power: the skull is the stone-giver. In precontact times there was a shaman in each hamlet-factory who was in charge of traditions, and he was the person who would ask permission of the skulls to quarry the stones. Once every five years or so this special shaman big man would call for a major ceremony called *yowali,* when prayers would be offered to the skulls to ask for permission to quarry the stones and for direction to find "many stones." Supposedly, following this big ceremony, massive stone quarrying operations took place, and a major supply of stones would be located and blade blanks stockpiled. Although the missionaries directed burning of skulls and other objects some time ago, reportedly a few skulls are still maintained in hidden places and used in ritual.

Supplications, vegetable offerings, and sometimes a pig were always offered to a female spirit named Alim Yongnum (sometimes called Alim Milmeurum), who owns the land near the river and to Murbilik Kue, the male spirit who owns the stones. While petitioning to these two spirits before a quarrying operation, I was told that prayers were also offered asking for the rains to stop and for the sunshine to appear.

During various sacrificial pig rituals that are held throughout the year, pig fat is sacralized and saved to use at times of quarrying. Boulder cores selected for quarrying are rubbed with the pig fat to make the stones beautiful and to please the spirits that are within the stones.

Sometimes at completion of quarrying operations, remaining quarry core rock was rubbed and "blessed" so that good quality stones would be found on the next visit to the quarry.

Prior to quarrying, large spirit sticks are stuck into the river or into the ground at the edge of the river both to ask the spirits for approval to take stones and to thank the spirits for letting the stones be taken. Such sticks would communicate properly to certain spirits that quarrying operations were in progress. I did not observe personally the use of such sticks while I was at quarry sites.

Factors That Stimulate Quarrying and Prompt Production

Informants say that in precontact times, just as today, stone hunts and quarrying are triggered by almost any large flood, which is thought of as a stone giver. It is recognized that the top quality new core boulders appear after flood waters have receded. In between times of flooding, head quarrymen continue to conduct operations to serve their personal needs as well as to fill requests that have been made by both individuals and groups of people from residential areas that do not have their own quarries and toolmakers.

The Seven-Step Manufacturing Process

Seven distinct technological steps are followed by Una and Kimyal quarrymen-toolmakers in the production of Langda-Sela-style adze blades: (1) Locate a suitable boulder core, (2) break the boulder core, (3) reduce large pieces to manageable sizes, (4) shape preform bifaces, (5) dull edges and grind platforms intermittently with (6) detail fine-flaking, and (7) grind finely flaked bifaces to finished adze blades. All seven steps are meticulously followed by Langda-Sela toolmakers in factory production situations, but some of the steps are usually omitted when adze blades are produced at sources of opportunity, which are discussed at the end of the chapter.

In a well-integrated and predictable work flow pattern, the first three manufacturing steps are carried out at quarry sites, while steps five, six, and seven are followed at scattered places of convenience located within the sprawling habitation sites and gardens of hamlet-factory work groups. A single exception to this is the rare occasion when individual work groups will transport their final-flaked preforms long distances to bedrock outcrops of sandstone for grinding. It is at the quarry sites that the teamwork of work parties are brought to bear, under the leadership of the head quarryman, on the problem of locating suitable boulder cores, breaking them into manageable pieces, and then allocating those pieces to individual ownership of the workers. Individual workers then reduce their allotment of core pieces to biface blanks before departing the quarry work place as a group.

An esoteric formula is used by head quarrymen in the allocation of crude core blanks and the division of flaking labor at each quarrying session. The specific work objectives of each quarry visit varies with the motivating factors for the visit and therefore production goals and individual responsibilities vary from time to time. Often the quarrying sessions are part of the annual routine of acquiring and individually stockpiling biface blanks for future use, but at other times, work party visits are motivated to fill requests that have been relayed to a head quarryman or one of the workers for one or more new tools for an individual or group of individuals. According to the quarrymen, both group and individual production expectations are discussed under the leadership of the quarry owner and understood by the workers before a work party is formed and a visit made to a quarry.

A Typical Workday at a Langda Quarry Site

At about 7:00 A.M. on May 6, 1992, my three assistants and I joined Diman Balyo, the head quarryman and quarry owner at Langda, along the Langda ridge, for what Diman said would be a routine one-day stone-collecting trip to the quarries in the valley below. My arrival at Langda a few days earlier had come at a good time to observe the quarrying operation because Diman said that he had received recent requests from several residents of nearby ham-

lets for adze blades and he wanted to collect stone before the start of the rainy season. Diman said that he would seldom go to the Ey River to quarry during the rainy season—the months of June, July, August, September, and October. The rainy season was just beginning, but on May 6, 1992, we were fortunate. We had sunshine for our descent along a narrow trail, slickened by rains during the previous night, and clear skies prevailed throughout the daylong quarrying operation. As we commenced our climb back up the steep trail at the end of the day, it started to sprinkle, and was pouring rain by the time we crested out on the Langda ridge.

Six quarrying experts, including Nyoyom Napyal, Jiwik Malyo, and Kapit Malyo (who owns the quarry rights across the river from Langda), formed a typical work party under the leadership of Diman Balyo, the head quarryman at Langda. Diman's wife, a teenage daughter, and several children accompanied us to support the quarrymen by providing cooked food at the quarry site. Diman told us that such support by members of the family of each head quarryman was a normal procedure within the Langda manufacturing center. During the hourlong descent, as we slipped and slid down a rain-soaked clayey trail, one of the quarrymen paused long enough in a thick patch of forest to set a small snare trap at the opening of a mouse hole on the forest floor. The quarryman said that he would pick up a mouse that he was sure would be in the trap on our return journey to the Langda hamlet at the end of the day.

Diman and the other quarrymen preceded me, out of sight, over a cliff face just above the river. I could hear the quarrymen break out in a chant, which I recorded and was later to learn was directed to specific spirits, Alim Yongnum (the spirit owner of land) and Murbilik Kue (the spirit owner of the rock), to alert them that we were coming to look for "good stone." Whatever ritual that might have been celebrated was hidden from me as I was still coming down the difficult trail to the river.

When I arrived at the spot, the men were grouped together, among a jumble of crowded

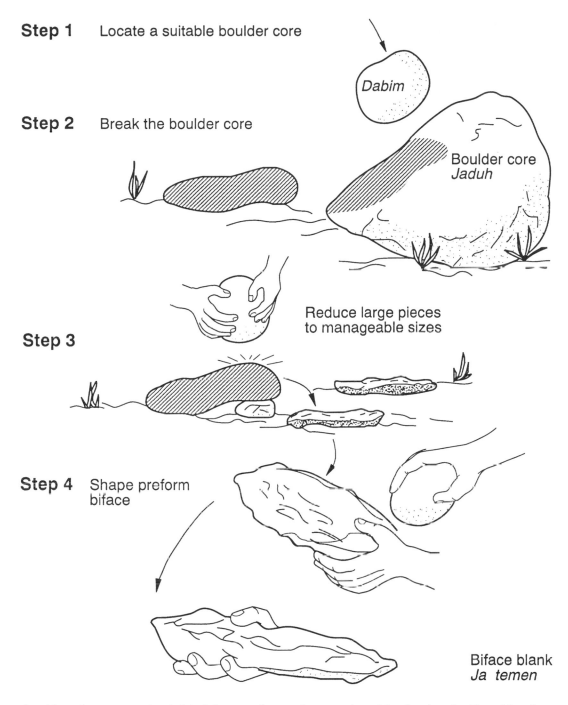

Step 1 Locate a suitable boulder core

Dabim

Step 2 Break the boulder core

Boulder core
Jaduh

Reduce large pieces
to manageable sizes

Step 3

Step 4 Shape preform
biface

Biface blank
Ja temen

Fig. 7.4. Four steps of adze blade manufacture at quarry site

boulders, dense vegetation behind them, and the edge of the river in front. They were looking at a large erratic boulder that rose 6 m out of the water. This, I was advised, was Amalkilkon, a rock of good tool-making quality stone but difficult to access. Thinking this might be a guardian spirit of this part of the river because it had been given a name, I questioned Diman, but he did not want to discuss the subject. The other quarrymen in the party just stared straight ahead and said nothing. It was 9:00 A.M. and work was about to begin.

During the course of the day, I would observe a typical Una quarrying and tool-making crew complete the first four of the seven steps that are sequentially followed to manufacture Langda-Sela-style adze blades (fig. 7.4).

STEPS 1 AND 2: Locating and Breaking Suitable Boulder Cores. During the brief period of rest

Fig. 7.5. A previously worked quarry boulder is selected and tested.

cracks in the rock to facilitate the breaking process, a fire must be used to assist. As soon as wood was gathered, a fire was built on the back, top side of the jaduh. The fire was continuously fueled and allowed to burn for about an hour before Diman selected a heavy, river-rounded hammerstone. He then climbed onto the top of the jaduh, well in front of the heated portion of the rock. A heavy *dabim* (hammerstone) was handed up. Diman carefully positioned himself over the spot he wanted to break, laboriously raised the dabim over his head, and hurled it down onto the jaduh. A few chips flew but nothing else happened. Twice Diman repeated the procedure to no avail. Then he selected another dabim, oblong in shape, and repositioned himself over the place he wanted to strike. Straining every muscle in his body, he raised the dabim, pounded downward, and struck the quarry rock without releasing the dabim (fig. 7.6). A large slab of the quarry rock broke along what appeared to be a fracture plane but did not separate and fall to the ground. Diman and a helper walked around to the side of the jaduh and were able to pull the slab off (fig. 7.7). Pleased with the one slab from jaduh ("mother" boulder core rock), a second quarryman stepped up to the side of the boulder core and, with another large dabim, hammered off a second slab. These two pieces would be further broken down into manageable sizes with handheld (not hurled) hammerstones before the smaller resultant pieces would be shaped by yet smaller hammerstones into rough blade blanks called *ja temen*.

For the moment, the two pieces of rock from the jaduh were abandoned while Diman went off in search of another quarry rock a short distance downstream. A few men followed. Soon a shout of glee went up as Diman found a round boulder out in the river that he judged to be of good tool-making quality and that he therefore called jaduh. With great effort, Diman single-handedly lifted this jaduh and carried it back onto the bank. This boulder core had weathered yellow on the outside but later when broken open was seen to be the usual light gray-green color of tool rocks from this

and contemplation before work began, Diman and another quarryman sat perched atop a large boulder of good-quality quarry stone that they had previously identified and worked (upper photograph in fig. 7.5). This and other large quarry stones—the boulder cores from which the adze blades are made—are called *jaduh* (alternate spelling *jaduk*). In the lower photograph in figure 7.5, another quarryman, under Diman's supervision, examined and tested the top of this jaduh with a handheld hammerstone, but the jaduh did not break. Diman studied the rock carefully, but he already knew it well. Diman explained that on a large jaduh such as this one, if there were no

Fig. 7.6. After the rock is heated a large hammerstone is used.

quarry. Once on shore, Diman and several of his helpers gathered around this particular jaduh and discussed how to break it. Then the jaduh was placed just the way that Diman wanted it, laid over an underlying boulder, before Diman stood on an adjacent, slightly higher boulder with a large dabim in hand (fig. 7.8). Three times he arched up and came down with all of his might, hurling the hammerstone onto the jaduh. After these unsuccessful attempts to break the jaduh in this manner, another quarryman selected yet a third dabim, changed positions relative to the jaduh, and again raised up and came down hard, hurling the dabim against the jaduh. On the second attempt, amid shouts of success, the jaduh split into two pieces. In the upper photograph of color plate 3, the quarryman who broke the stone spontaneously points to the "good break," while Diman Balyo, hunkered in a typical squat position nearby, clapped his hands amid his own shouts of pleasure. For this particular boulder core (jaduh), step 2 of the seven-step manufacturing process had been completed.

STEP 3: REDUCING LARGE PIECES TO MAN-AGEABLE SIZES. Other quarrymen gathered around the two pieces of broken jaduh to help each other break these stones into yet smaller, more manageable pieces with handheld dabim. A team of four worked diligently and rapidly in a small work area of only approximately 4 x 4 m to break up the boulder core. Each member of the team knew his role in the cooperative effort well. Individual training and know-how were obviously important so that the job would be well done, without causing an accident, where one worker could hit another's hand (who would be holding an anvil-supported core while the knapper struck it) or be hit by flying bits of debitage. Diman seemed to be everywhere at one time within the group—simultaneously giving his workers encouragement with complimentary noises of enthusiasm, consulting, giving advice, and at the same time examining the work and identifying rejects.

The small work area was, for the brief time of thirty to forty-five minutes, a beehive of activity where the workmen, with quick, deft strokes of handheld large hammerstones, struck core pieces that were usually braced against anvil supports. Interestingly, one quarryman disappeared into a stand of dense foliage alongside the river to return soon with twigs and leaves. He and another worker fashioned a simple bed of leaves onto which they

Fig. 7.7. A broken slab is removed for further reduction.

spirit of camaraderie as they cooperated amid much friendly advice-giving, shouts of joy at accomplishment, and help to one another. I was impressed by the mobility of the workers as they shifted about in the rather small work area while remaining in a basic squatting position. All the workers used not only their arms and hands but also their legs and feet in a seemingly effortless rhythm to break up the core pieces. At times it seemed as if the workers were using their feet with almost the same dexterity and control of movement as their hands to hold and support core pieces in coordinated efforts with their partners. During all of this activity, Diman Balyo continued to move about the men, encouraging and being helpful.

With an experienced eye, Diman was constantly checking the work. Note in the lower photograph of color plate 3, Diman scrutinizes a piece of core rock to either reject it or approve it as a core piece suitable for the next stage of the reduction process.

While the portable boulder core was reduced by four quarrymen to manageable pieces (step 3) for freehand knapping (step 4), the previously obtained two slablike pieces of core were similarly reduced by the other two quarrymen.

STEP 4: SHAPING PREFORM BIFACE BLANKS. Next, the quarrymen squatted on the ground in a casual manner, not in any particular arrangement, to further shape the crude core blanks by freehand flaking (fig. 7.9). For the process, each toolmaker used two or three hammerstones (called *ja winwin*) that had been selected from an abundance of stones along the edge of the river, plus sometimes a short piece of crude biface *(jauna)*. The description and detail of use of these knapping tools is discussed in the next section, which covers steps 5 and 6 of the tool-making process. For rest breaks from flaking, individuals would often stand up, move about, smoke, visit, eat a refreshing snack of sugar cane and/or a cold steamed potato, and then maybe sit back down at another spot to continue work. The work place was casual and enjoyable. Just as when breaking the original core (jaduh) and its relatively large pieces had

rolled the piece of jaduh they were working on, proceeding to break it up with their dabim. During this part of the process, the workers would sometimes prop an end of a boulder core off the ground by laying it across pieces of wood that had been picked up from the water's edge. Soon the jaduh had been reduced to pieces of suitable size for handheld freehand rough flaking.

The individuals worked together with a

7.8. A hammerstone is hurled to break a selected boulder core.

delighted them, the quarrymen-knappers would shout yips of glee whenever a flake would break off a core in a particularly advantageous way.

During a period of about two hours each quarryman had knapped three to five crude biface blanks that were ready to be transported out of the quarry (fig. 7.10). The longest biface

blank that I was able to measure was 30.5 cm in length, by 10 cm maximum width, by 6.5 cm maximum thickness. The shortest was 14 cm in length, by 5.0 cm maximum width, by 1.3 cm maximum thickness. The mean dimensions of fourteen blades that were measured was 20 cm in length, by 7.3 cm maximum width, by 4.0 cm maximum thickness. The structures of the

Fig. 7.9. Biface blanks are shaped by rough flaking.

rough flaked blanks approached the structures of the finely flaked final blades (steps 5 and 6) before grinding and the ultimate shape of the Langda-Sela-style adze blade (chapter 2). Little waste material was left on most of the crude bifaces for final reduction before grinding.

FOOD PREPARATION AT THE QUARRY SITE. When we first arrived at the quarry site, while the men went to work on the boulder cores (jaduh), the two women and the older children quickly gathered firewood, rocks for heating, and grasses and leaves for a small steam bundle. They had carried sweet potatoes, yams, and greens from their hamlet to cook for the men. One of the quarrymen cut a short limb, stripped the bark from it, and split one end to

create rock tongs with which to move hot rocks from the fire to the steam bundle. A fire was built over the pile of rocks that had been collected and, approximately 3 m from the fire, a mat of grasses and leaves was laid as a ground cover on which to place the vegetables. After they were placed, more grasses and leaves were laid on top and then doused with water from the river. Once the rocks had heated, they were moved with the rock tongs onto the grass bundle (fig. 7.11). About the time all the men had completed their tasks of shaping biface blanks, (approximately 2:00 P.M.), the steam bundle was pulled apart and the men, then the women and children, individually selected food and began to eat (fig. 7.12). A red *Pandanus* fruit had been carried to the quarry, the juices to be used as seasoning for the sweet potatoes.

The men spread out among the riverside rocks to eat, some in quiet individual contemplation, while others visited animatedly with whomever was sitting nearby. Diman's wife and teenage daughter sat and ate together as part of the group and yet in a sense separated from it. The children snacked as they dashed about, ever playful and full of laughter. By the time the men and women had eaten, the biface blanks (ja temen) had been divided among the adults for carrying out of the quarry site.

Before leaving the quarry, Diman Balyo quickly bathed in the Ey River and quietly mumbled some incantations. Upon being questioned about a "closing ritual," he matter-of-factly said that in former times the partially used mother-quarry core rock would have been rubbed with sacred pig grease.

In approximately five hours of work at the quarry, six men had produced twenty-five biface blanks. The head quarryman, Diman Balyo, said that a normal load of stones such as these, to be carried up the steep hillside to Langda, was between three to five blanks per man, but in the cases of stones the size of the largest of these (30.5 cm long, by 10 cm wide) or larger, usually only one to three stones were carried per man. Sometimes one or a few of the men would even stash blanks at a permanent house shelter by the nearest sweet potato garden (about 400 m away) to be fine-flaked at times of leisure when the men might be down at the garden.

During knapping and upon abandonment of the site, no attention was given to waste flakes (jatukul) to be used as small cutting tools (or otherwise), unwanted larger pieces of boulder core rock, or hammerstones that had been selected from along the edges of the river. Intermittent flash floods would eventually wash this material away, leaving only a few flake scars on large boulder cores as artifactual remnants of the quarrying operation. From time to time, each quarryman-toolmaker would carry a hammerstone that he particularly liked from a quarrying operation back to his place of residence to be used there in the fine-flaking process.

Three Manufacturing Steps Undertaken away from Quarry Sites

Three technological steps are performed away from the quarry site to produce a finished ground stone adze blade from a quarry-made biface blank (ja temen) (fig. 7.13). Step 5 (edge dulling and platform grinding) and step 6 (detail fine-flaking), although distinctly performed different mechanical steps, are quickly and intermittently executed as an ongoing mental and technological continuum in the knapping process. A completely flaked blade called a *keilaba* is produced for grinding.

Fig. 7.10. A knapper starts to accumulate quarry-made biface blanks.

Fig. 7.11. A woman prepares to steam vegetables for a midday meal.

KNAPPING TOOLS. The Una and Kimyal tool-makers use three kinds of platform preparation, edge dulling and striking tools in the knapping process. Each knapper, squatting in the traditional position, with buttocks touching the ground, or actually seated on the ground (or on a board) will have two or three naturally rounded hammerstones (called ja winwin) conveniently laying next to him in addition to a rectangular piece of core rock (it can be a discarded broken biface blank) called a *jauna* (edge abrader). One, or in some cases two, of the winwin is a river-tumbled hammerstone of approximately the same hardness as the biface blanks that are being worked. One of the winwin is a softer hammerstone that is, in the

cases I observed, a buff tan-colored, hard argillite or metamorphosed tuff. When the sharp edges of the biface core are rubbed with the softer winwin, a yellowish or gray residue is left on the sharp edges of the core rock.

KNAPPING PROCESS AND TOOL USE. Men knapping adze blades may work alone or in small groups, usually near their houses, but sometimes farther away in a house cluster courtyard, or even away from the hamlet at a house shelter that is located near a sweet potato garden. There is not a specifically designated place for this kind of work. It is simply done at convenient places and times.

When working in groups of two or more,

the men squat or sit casually, in no particularly arranged pattern. There are, however, taboos against passersby walking on the right-hand side of right-handed knappers or on the left-hand side of left-handed knappers. I was told that this practice was to help protect the spiritual peace and skillful work of the toolmaker, not to protect the onlookers or people passing by from flying chips. Right-handed knappers hold the core tool blades in their left hands and work with the knapping tools in their right and vice versa for left-handed knappers.

When commencing a knapping process, a toolmaker first rubs a core blank blade (ja temen) with one of his hard rounded hammerstones (winwin). He says that this is to get a feel of the stone on which he is working, to "feel out" a striking platform, and also to select by feel the precise spot on the rounded hammerstone with which he wants to strike the blade blank on his first downward blow. Two knappers at two different flaking sessions told me they are feeling for a very small, but important flattened spot on the hammerstone (winwin) with which to strike the biface blank (ja temen). When struck with the right spot on the winwin, the winwin will not "slip" at contact and a good flake should be produced. Slightly oblique blows from the winwin near the edge of the ja temen causes flakes to fly off in a manner desired by the toolmaker. When a particularly good blow is struck and a piece flakes off in just the desired fashion, the knapper gives a shout of joy—"arak" or "hayak." Sometimes the others momentarily join in, repeating the same brief shout of glee. The entire operation is quite verbal with communication about the up-to-the-minute results of the work often voiced above the background sounds of the grinding and the click and clack of the blades being flaked and rubbed.

The toolmakers work rapidly, picking up first this hammerstone and then another one. Every so often they pick up a jauna (edge abrader) stone and rub and make dull all of the sharp edges on the ja temen. The toolmakers said that this was a defensive procedure to protect their hands. Holding the ja temen (core tool blade) while knapping causes cuts on both

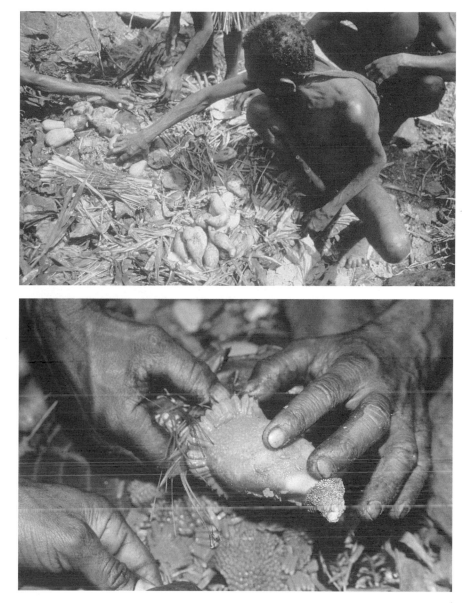

palms and fingers as the ja temen is struck with the hammerstones. Sometimes an argillite or tuffaceous winwin would be quickly picked up to abrade a biface core (ja temen). Residue from the winwin would be rubbed off onto the ja temen. This clay residue seemed to "mark" the ja temen as well as to coat the sharpened edges. After one knapping session the quarrymen showed me their cuts, which were plentiful.

At each of three different tool knapping sessions it became evident that certain toolmakers could knap much faster and better than others; although they were all known in the

Fig. 7.12. The quarrymen eat a midday meal.

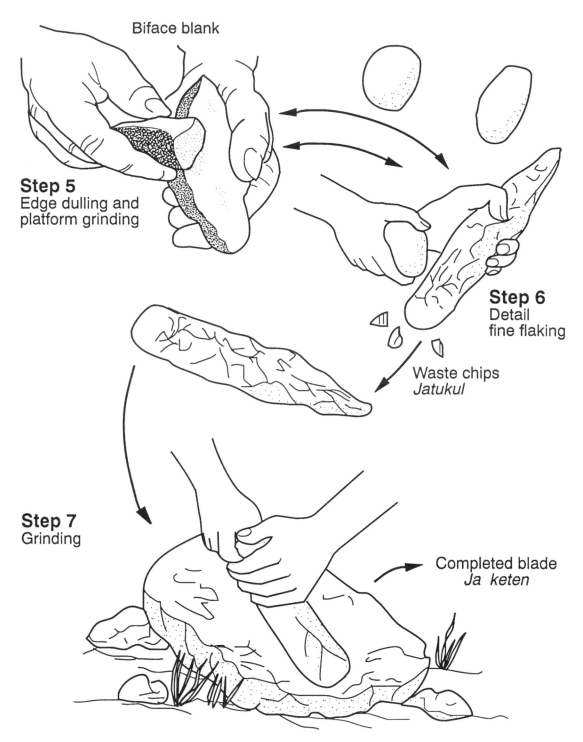

Biface blank

Step 5
Edge dulling and
platform grinding

Step 6
Detail
fine flaking

Waste chips
Jatukul

Step 7
Grinding

Completed blade
Ja keten

Fig. 7.13. Three steps of adze blade manufacture away from quarry site

area as qualified experts. It took one man just thirty minutes to fine-flake a biface blank to finished form, while it took another man forty-two minutes to shape a similar-sized blade, but interruptions due to the knappers visiting among themselves made it difficult to correctly estimate actual knapping time.

As the knapping process progresses on a particular ja temen blank, it is transformed into the finished product called *keilaba*. The keilaba are long, slender blades with parallel sides and one slightly convex-shaped, beveled end for cutting. Although already quite sharp and nicely shaped from just the knapping process, the Una and Kimyal do not consider their blades ready for use until they have been ground, reportedly to make them more durable.

STEPS 5 AND 6: DULLING EDGES, GRINDING PLATFORMS, AND FINE-FLAKING. A pictorial essay of details of the fine-flaking process (steps 5 and 6) is presented in figures 7.14–7.19. In figure 7.14, Diman Balyo strikes a biface blank with a relatively large "hard" river-sourced hammerstone (ja winwin). At his feet, there is a buff-colored "soft" oblong argillite or tuff hammerstone (ja winwin) lying next to an elongate-rectangular andesite/basalt crude biface hammerstone (jauna). Diman uses these three kinds of typical Una and Kimyal hammerstones alternatively in the freehand knapping process. In the upper photograph of figure 7.15, a jauna tool is used to dull sharp edges and grind a platform (step 5, fig. 7.13) before the platform is struck with a hard, rounded hammerstone (winwin, step 6, fig. 7.13). In figure 7.16, a small chip strikes a knapper from his own work. The knapper rubbed his eyes and forehead before going back to work. His knapping partners, including the head quarrymen, paid little attention to the incident as they continued with their own knapping. In figure 7.17, I was concentrating on Diman Balyo, with the camera set on a near-ground-level tripod, when Diman suddenly shouted "Mati" ("dead" in the Indonesian language) and with a look of surprise dropped his hammerstone to the ground, holding two pieces of the blade that had just broken in his hands. Diman said that the stone was sick—it had just died, and there were no bad spirits involved, the stone was just simply sick and died. Diman discarded the smaller of the two pieces and promptly went back to work shaping the other piece.

In the upper and lower photographs of figure 7.18, the typical linear, crestal-positioned flake scar that often extends from the high point of the convex arch on the dorsal side of each blade to the cutting edge, can be seen. This single scar might be thought of as a signature in the stage of process. It identifies a step in fine-flaking, just before final chipping shapes a

blade for grinding. A completely chipped blade that is ready for grinding is called a keilaba. Up to this point in the fine-flaking process (step 6), it has taken a skilled knapper to do the work. All keilaba are shaped so that they will take relatively little grinding (compared to Yeineri-style and Tagime-style blades) to further shape, smooth, and sharpen each blade for utilitarian use and aesthetic perfection.

Fig. 7.14. Diman Balyo shapes a biface for grinding.

Fig. 7.15. An edge-dulling tool and hammerstones are used.

STEP 7: GRINDING. Throughout the Langda manufacturing center, portable, fine-grained sandstone grinding slabs are carried distances of two to four days' walking time (round trip) from sandstone outcrops to the scattered hamlet-factories. Within the Langda hamlet-factory, the toolmakers maintain approximately seven of these portable grindstones.

Sometimes toolmakers from Langda will carry finished flaked stones (keilaba) for a one-day journey over the mountain between Langda and Bomela and remain for several days while the workers grind their stones to the finished ja keten. I could never assess how much actual grinding time it takes to grind the various-sized keilaba to finished products. The

Fig. 7.16. A small chip strikes a knapper from his own work.

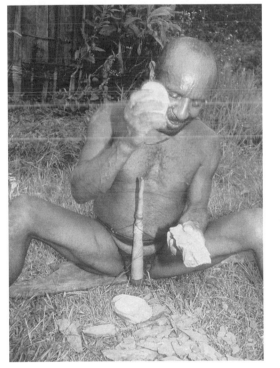

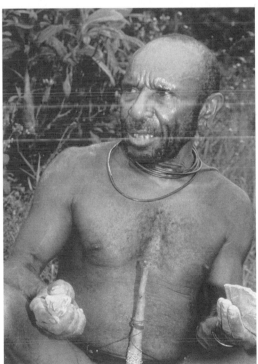

Fig. 7.17. A biface breaks during the knapping process.

head quarryman at Kinyalingda said it took him about five weeks to grind and sharpen a 25 cm long blade. Lamek Napyal, Ngis Malyo, and Yan Molingi Balyo at Langda agreed that it took about ten days to grind to completion a big (25 cm) blade. Kabit Balyo says that he can grind the short blades, 7.5 to 18 cm long, to a finished state in one to three hours of continuous work. The toolmakers all agreed that there was quite a variance in grinding time depending on just how much grinding was done per blade other than just sharpening the beveled, cutting edge of each tool.

For the grinding process the toolmakers like to be near water, but on some occasions they set their grinding stones down by the front of their houses and add water to a surface as they grind from water gourds. At other times, several men will carry their grinding stones out to a marshy area, squat down with water puddles all around them, and go to work while enjoying a continuous chatter of conversation (fig. 7.19).

Fig. 7.18. After fine-flaking, bifaces are ready for grinding.

Fig. 7.19. Finished, chipped bifaces are ground on portable slabs.

A to-and-fro motion is used to sharpen the beveled cutting edge of a tool blade and a sideways motion to smooth sharp side edges and to polish the stone to an appealing functional and aesthetic value (fig. 7.20). Once the grinding commences, a beneficial slime paste soon develops containing microparticles from the core stone, sand grains from the grinding rock, and water. In the Una process, the blades are rarely ground to remove all flake scars, as is done in the Grand Valley and West region.

STONE KNIVES. According to Langda informants, although a small percentage of total knife production is sourced from the same quarries as the Langda-Sela-style andesite/basalt and meta-andesite/basalt adze blades, most of the knives produced at Langda come from what is described as thin layers of rock found within the volcanic sequence at various locales uphill, away from the river-centered adze blade quarries. As discussed in chapter 2 ("Yali and East," Knives), the mineralogy of knives collected throughout the Yali and East region, including one in a grinding stage of production at Langda, is compatible with the possible volcanic tuff sources for knives as described by informants.

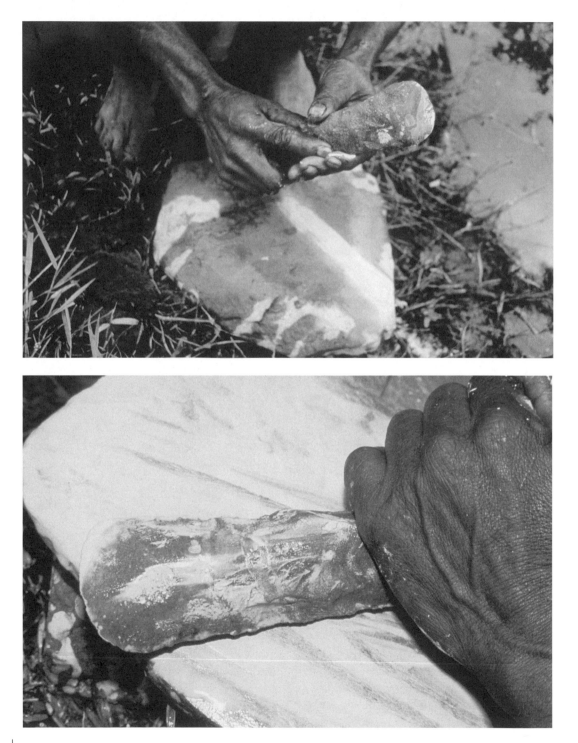

Fig. 7.20. Water is used in the grinding process.

CHAPTER 8

Trade

To understand the movement of goods and the associated transactions of trade, archaeologists, other anthropologist specialists, prehistorians, and economists continue to study the related substantive issues of value-setting, geographic trade networks, and trading mechanisms.

For my discussion of these issues in the Highlands of Irian Jaya (fig. 8.1), I will differentiate between the terms trade and exchange. I use the term "trade" to refer to all movements of an individual product and interpersonal transfers of manufactured products and raw materials that are unaccompanied by ceremony. Trade is private and without ceremony where traders stress material benefit rather than sociopolitical gain. Although trade is an underpinning of social ritual and economic aspects of the cultural systems within the Highlands of Irian Jaya, I do not consider trade to be a system unto itself, as has been interpreted for coastal trade in eastern Papua New Guinea, especially the Kula trade ring, as presented by Malinowsky (1922) in his classical work *Argonauts of the Western Pacific*. Trade in the High-

lands is an open-ended affair for which there is no closure. The term "exchange" is used as an abbreviation for "ceremonial exchange." Exchange transactions stress sociopolitical benefit more than material gain and involve prestige and status. Such transfers of material goods are usually between relatives, are often channeled by or through a leader, and are public and ceremonial. Big men leaders instigate the exchange ceremonies at which they then redistribute the exchange goods (chapter 3). The term "barter," which is the payment of specific goods, one for the other, excluding the use of money, in this case is not used because cowrie shells were used as money in at least some parts of the Highlands, and by using my definition of trade, this term becomes unnecessary.

In the Highlands of Irian Jaya, stone goods from manufacturing centers, other kinds of finished products (such as salt, fiber nets, and shell necklaces), and raw materials moved at precontact times along a vast trading network from points of origin to user areas. Within use areas, goods continued to trade from owner to

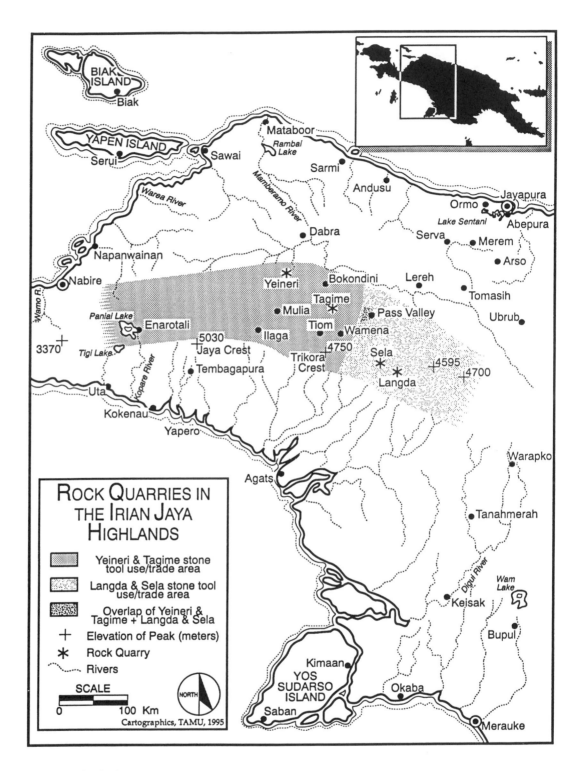

Fig. 8.1. The quarries in their regional setting in Irian Jaya

owner, and valuables were kept in a constant state of recirculation by exchange. The patterns of trade (and exchange at rites of passage and other ceremonials, chapter 3) account for the distribution of material goods while the mechanisms of trade (which are discussed in this chapter) and exchange account for the behavior

that moved the material goods (raw materials and manufactured objects) from points of origin to and within use areas. Both the geographic patterns of trade and exchange and the mechanisms of the related processes are important from ethnographical and ethnogenesis perspectives.

The Traders

In the Highlands of Irian Jaya, men dominated the production, transfer (between individuals and between groups), and consumption of trade goods; although women were strongly involved in production. Men manufactured the stone goods; harvested forest products, which, in addition to wood and bamboo, included whole birds and bird plumage, cassowary bone, and marsupial furs. Women played a supportive role in furnishing food for these endeavors, produced most of the salt that was traded, played a major role in raising the pigs, manufactured nets and skirts (that were traded locally), and collected medicinal plants, some of which were traded. Sea shells were traded into the Highlands from the lowland coasts, used mostly by men to sew onto ornamental necklaces and bibs, in addition to which cowrie shells, sewn onto fiber string exchange bands and also maintained loosely, were used as money.

The trading networks along which goods flowed were made up of social linkages of male members within primarily single patrilineages, with a fewer number of trading partnerships extended by distance or maintained in the entirety among social male friends outside of kinship. Within the study area there were no professional traders like Pospisil (1956:224–26) described among the Kapauku to the west, although men traded goods locally on their own account when opportunities presented themselves. Women also traded locally for and with foodstuffs, medicinal plants, fibers for string, orchid and palm fibers, skirts, and nets, but they were not part of trading networks that moved goods over longer distances.

Using ground checks, I was able to confirm a Wilil mid–Grand Valley Dani dialect patrilineage linkage over a distance of approximately 35 km from the mid–Grand Valley language group across a major language change to the northern Yali dialect of the Yali language group, in the Pass Valley–Landikma area (figs. 2.1 and 8.2). The principal obstacle to individual movement within a trade linkage did not seem to be physical distance or language barrier but the presence of enemies: the more densely settled an area, the more restricted the movement of an individual or group carrying trade goods because of the presence of more enemies.

Trade goods moved in a series of chainlike steps from producers to the consumers. The goods followed routes of social linkages to move into, through, and around enemy territories, rather than by the most direct physical routes. Any given user-area might actually be the territory of an enemy group of the originator of the goods or of the last member of the trade link that was moving the item (or items). At various points within a trading linkage there were intermediaries who usually used the durable goods while they had them. Often such items (stone goods and shells primarily) continued to circulate within local groups before being moved on, along a regional gradient. Some goods moved rapidly through intermediaries, such as perishables and special bow staves and spear woods, fiber products, coloring pigments, and sometimes salt. (Even coloring pigments, chiefly red ochres, and salt were often stored in the houses of intermediaries for varying periods of time, while part was traded for local use before the remainder was traded on.)

Risk of injury, loss of life, and the expenditure of time for the trader traveling often arduous routes did not seem to be reflected in any measurable way in the trade rates of goods that were transported. The energy of labor in such endeavors was cheap, with little differentiation in value of goods relative to distance from points of origin.

Trade Routes and Flow of Goods

An overprint of trails and routes, some well traveled and easy to follow and others less used and often difficult to discern even for indigenous local inhabitants, connected the habitation areas of the Irian Jaya Highlands one to the other, regardless of intervening language boundaries and different sociopolitical affiliations. Within this web of trails and routes that had been built up through millennia, the people were connected to the origins of raw

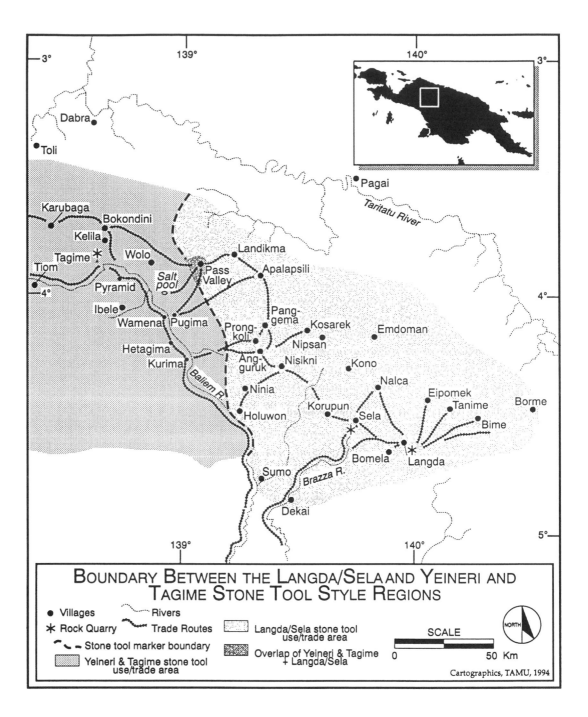

BOUNDARY BETWEEN THE LANGDA/SELA AND YEINERI AND
TAGIME STONE TOOL STYLE REGIONS

*Fig. 8.2. Trade routes in the
west and east use-regions*

materials as well as to the manufacturing centers for stone goods. As would be expected, there was a radically reduced number of routes to both the north and south lowlands from the central mountain core and across aprons of lowland swamps to both ocean coasts due to the difficult terrain.

By the time of first-contact with modern outsiders, at least five trade routes existed between the north and south coastlines and the central Highlands of Irian Jaya, any of which might have been routes for the migrants who first entered the central mountain core. It was along these routes that sea shells were traded from their points of origin into the interior: (1) Nabire to Enarotali, (2) Uta and the Kokenau-Mimika area to Enarotali, (3) Agats area through the Baliem Gorge to south of Wamena, (4) Agats area up the Brazza River to Sela, and (5) Mataboor (mouth of Mamberano River) to

Dabra area and by a western fork to the Yeineri area and by an eastern fork to the Bokondini area (figs. P.1 and 1.31; and Hampton 1997:24–25). Routes up the Fly River from the south coast and the Sepik River on the north coast probably also furnished trade linkages from the oceans to the central mountain core near the Irian Jaya–Papua New Guinea boundary, but these routes have not been confirmed by research. By all routes, points of ingress from the coastlines were at the mouths of rivers (except at Nabire) connected to arduous overland routes at the base of the central mountain core. In addition, an interregional trail that follows a series of topographic lows connects Enarotali on the west with the Ilaga-Mulia area on the east and hence from the Mulia area by dividing routes into Western Dani territory and ultimately the Grand Valley (fig. 1.21).

Within the Highlands and on the flanks of the central mountain core, physiographic barriers to trail and route networks were high elevation (cold temperature), steep relief, and/or rivers. These natural features were also constraints to the development of population centers. In the flat lowlands, the rivers were the arteries for travel and therefore trade, and they often became the loci for habitation sites along their banks.

Although the flows of raw materials and manufactured goods were initially *away* from points of origin, once goods reached population centers, the flows became the sum effects of countless transfers of goods that took place in all directions. Local trade transactions occurred virtually everywhere. Redistribution within sociopolitical groups by rites of passage and other ceremonial exchanges fueled continual circulation of valuables (chapter 3). Flows tended to funnel into population centers before moving outward again. The preponderance of goods in use at any given time in the Highlands was in the population centers. The majority of recipients and ultimate users of durable manufactured goods who were located two or more trading links away from a point of origin rarely knew either the point of origin or how the goods had gotten to them; they generally only knew their own source.

Trading activity, like accumulations of material objects, was centered within concentrations of population, rather than at stone goods or salt manufacturing centers per se. Where more people were concentrated, more trading transactions occurred. Although the incidence of economic trade transactions increased at times and places of large pig-killing ceremonies (rites of passage rituals and other sociopolitical ceremonials), it would be incorrect to classify these occasions as proto-markets. In addition to the ceremonial exchanges that were the business of the gatherings, dyadic trade transactions occurred both before and after the primary business of "exchange," but routine continual trading activity in the hamlets, which was not associated with special group events, accounted for the trade of more items.

Trade Goods

The simple classificatory lists that follow are meant to serve the purpose of this analysis of the trade of stone goods by broadly aggregating.

Durables

STONE GOODS. The following kinds of stone goods were traded in the Irian Jaya Highlands at the times of first-contact: axe blade blanks and finished axe blades, adze blade blanks and finished adze blades, manufactured display-exchange stones, knives, chisels, chert nodules, portable grindstones, and red ochres and pigments. For detailed discussions of the quarrying, manufacture, typologies, and uses of these kinds of stone goods, as well as of some natural stone objects that may have been traded, refer to chapters 2–7.

SHELLS. At the time of first-contact, three kinds of sea shells were considered as valuables and used principally as money or ornaments across the Irian Jaya Highlands: primarily one species of cowrie shell (*Cypea moneta*), the bailer shell (*Melo hunteri Perry*), and the nassa shell (*Nassarius* sp.) (for detail, see Hampton 1997: 156–66). It was the cowrie that was used as currency and that, as a durable, probably had a stabilizing effect on trade when other valuables or perishables were in short supply. In addition to its use as money in the form of loose shells, the cowrie shells were used as valuables and sewn onto narrow fiber exchange bands (jerak, mid–Grand Valley Dani dialect, chapter 3). The relatively large bailer shell was cut into sections and used for necklaces. Gardner said that the bailer was "an object prized above almost all others by the Dani, who cut them into irregular saucers to wear as necklaces and exchange for pigs or other wealth" (Gardner and Heider 1968:5). The small nassa snail shells were sewn onto fiber string chest bibs and worn as ornaments, and, like the bailer shell necklaces *(mikak)*, also used as valuables and presented sometimes at ceremonials as items of exchange.

From his early work (1941 and 1942) with the Kapauku at Enarotali (fig. P.1) and from an exploratory trip to the Moni in the extreme western part of the study area, Christian missionary explorer E. H. Mickelson said that "the cowrie shell has an important place in the economy of these mountain people" and that, when discovered, the "Kapauku were using cowrie shells as the medium of exchange" (1966:31–33). In a photograph, Mickelson (1966: 299) demonstrated that the dorsal side of a Kapauku cowrie shell had been cut off and ground in the same fashion as all the cowrie shells in use that I observed during my research in the Highlands east of Enarotali (1982–93). In a Kafiavana rock shelter, located eastward, nearly the entire length of the central mountain cordillera of the island of New Guinea from Enarotali, to not far from Kuk Yuku (fig. 1.2) in the Central Highlands of Papua New Guinea, White (1967a:279–80) found four "money" cowries that were some 9,000 years old, three with their dorsal sides also ground off, as they are today across the entire New Guinea Highlands. Pospisil, doing his doctoral studies in the Enarotali area, stated that the Kapauku economy was a money economy and that cowries provided the standard currency. Pospisil found that the "old" Kapauku cowries differed according to shape and size, and that there were six uniquely described cowries, each having

their own value. Pospisil added that intertribal trade was made possible by the universal acceptance of cowries as currency (1956:206, 207, 226). (Their value, however, varied from area to area.)

To the east of Enarotali within my study area, O'Brien, working with the Western Dani in the Konda Valley (near Bokondini, fig. 1.1), noted that "Cowries form the basic Dani currency, either singly or sewn onto braided string bands, and they may also be worn as ornaments" (1969:42). Heider (1970:289), working southeast of O'Brien's area, at a location northeast of Wamena (fig. 1.21), noted that the cowrie shells used by the Dani reached the Highlands in precontact times by an intricate trade network, and that although the Dani differentiated colors and shapes of shells, they did not have an intricate system of classification like that used by the Kapauku, located 500 km to the west at Enarotali.

SALT. Sodium chloride salt was a luxury for the indigenous inhabitants of the Irian Jaya Highlands and was highly valued as a trade commodity. Processed salt was in the form of manufactured cakes (or balls) that were hardened like rock salt, which when wrapped with banana leaves and tied tightly with strips of rattan could be stored as a durable for future use or trade (fig. 8.3). From interviews of older informants (sixty to eighty years old) throughout the central Highlands research area, at select possible points of origin on both the north and south coasts of Irian Jaya, and also from a literature search, I have concluded that no salt was traded up into the Highlands from the coastlines as were sea shells. Instead, the points of origin for the salt cakes or salt "balls" that were traded extensively in the Highlands were from manufacturing centers at brine pools (discussed previously in "Brine Pools (Salt)," chapter 1).

RED OCHRE AND HEMATITE. Red pigment was a significant trade item in both the Grand Valley and West, and the Yali and East regions. Although an orange-red clay that was used for body-mudding throughout the research area

Fig. 8.3. The salt cake, a prized commodity for domestic use and trade

was available in both regions, indigenous informants reported that the origin for the highly regarded red pigment that was used for sacred purposes was located within Yali territory ("Passive and Performing Arts," chapter 1; "Painted Display-Exchange-Type Stones and Sacred Boards in the Yali and East Region," chapter 4). Although I have not precisely located the Yali point or points of origin for the "sacred red," I was told by indigenous inhabitants, while near the Yali hamlet of Ninia in 1987, that the source was one to two days walking time from Ninia (fig. 2.8). Even though lacking more definitive evidence at this time, I utilize such a location for trade analyses.

Archaeological excavations in Papua New Guinea have shown that red pigment has been used in the greater New Guinea Highlands for more than 6,000 years. Level seven, which contained red pigment and red-stained grindstones at Kiowa rock shelter east of Mt. Hagen (Bulmer 1966:97–98, 108a), has been dated to older than 4,150±140 B.C. (Y-1370) (Bulmer 1966:108b). Red pigment has also been found to be present in level three at Yuku rock shelter, which yielded a radiocarbon date of 4,760±265 B.C. (GX-3111A) (Bulmer 1974:32) (fig. 1.2).

Nondurables

Finished Products. The following list is not meant to be all-inclusive, but to highlight those items that my indigenous informants felt were significant to the continual flow of goods by trade mechanisms within their cultural systems at contact time. By quantity, fiber nets that were manufactured by different people, with different net-making skills and using different techniques for decoration, were the single most traded nondurable, finished product (chapter 1). Different styles of women's reed and fiber string skirts were traded locally among the women (chapter 1). Hardwood arrowheads, sometimes bone tipped, were traded by men interregionally as well as penis gourds from local gourd arbors that were traded intraregionally.

RAW MATERIALS. The trade of raw materials was a significant factor in the maintenance of lifestyle strategies of different sociopolitical groups. Forest products moved from areas of relatively sparse population (usually located in landscapes of rugged terrain) to areas of dense population where nearby forests had been largely exploited. In general, the people who controlled the forest sources for raw materials practiced extensive horticultural subsistence versus the prime user populations who practiced a more intensive form of horticulture and were relatively "pig wealthy." Raw materials that were traded from the forests included: special woods for spears and bow staves; bark and bark fibers for string; rattan; certain live birds (especially cassowaries); cassowary feathers and plumes; birds of paradise plumes and feathers; parrot, cockatoo, egret, and miscellaneous feathers; dead birds; bat wing bones and cassowary femurs; marsupial and rodent fur; seeds; orchid and palm fibers; and certain medicinal plants.

PIGS. Pigs are the primary wealth item in the Highlands of Irian Jaya. Domestic pigs are the nexus of Highlands subsistence, wealth, and lifestyles and are a principal factor in trade and exchange.

Value-Setting

If there was a common denominator for the value of stone goods across the research area at the time of first-contact, it would have been pigs and cowrie shells. Since pig breeding constituted the primary way to generate wealth, it is understandable that pigs would not only be the most-traded commodity in the Highlands, but also the item against which the value of all other material goods would be measured. Every adult male who had been involved with trade and exchange could have related, by quick mental calculations, the value of his material goods to pigs and cowrie shells, relative to his particular area. As Pospisil, in his study of the Kapauku people in the Kamu Valley near Enarotali (fig. P.1), so succinctly stated:

All articles of trade have a customary price from which the actual price may differ due to the factors given. A moral value is attached to the customary price. It is regarded as a fair price and the man demanding it is considered honest. . . . The fluctuation of price because of temporary imbalance of the supply-demand level is rather

infrequent. . . . The factor of kin and friendship ties between the parties tends to lower the price. . . . Competition between two sellers has a lowering effect on the price, and . . . a political leader often is given a commodity for a lower price than normal because the seller expects future favors from such a man. (1956:214)

During the course of my field research, I found no contradictions while among the people of either the Grand Valley and West or the Yali and East regions to any of the principles of pricing as stated by Pospisil.

While visiting the widely separated Yeineri, Tagime, and Langda stone goods manufacturing centers, I found that each toolmaker set the "customary price" that he anticipated receiving from a local trade or that he perceived he might receive by an ultimate trade to a user who was living at a distant location. At the stone goods factories, it was explained to me that it was only the expert quarryman-toolmaker who understood the details of the quality of the rock and the workmanship done on a stone at that point in the process when the stone was to be first traded. During the course of my research, I found, in general terms, little discrepancy in the "customary prices" quoted to me by elder quarrymen (fifty-five to seventy-five years old) at the stone factories and "customary prices" quoted to me by elder users (fifty-five to seventy-five years old) at diverse locations and different distances from quarry sites. In all cases, I asked my informants to tell me the value of different kinds of stone goods when traditional trade was still a routine part of each informant's life. It was never difficult to get a consensus among informants at either factory or use sites regarding the value of large axe and adze blades and display-exchange stones, but it seemed that in practice small adze blades, knives, and chisels traded for so many different kinds of objects that a concensus of value relative to pigs or cowrie shells could never be reached.

As a reasonable value throughout the Grand Valley and West region, whether at the Tagime or Yeineri manufacturing center or a considerable distance away in user-areas, one "good quality" large axe blade generally equated in value with one large pig. Both manufacturers and users also placed a customary value for a "good quality" je display-exchange stone as one large pig. Within the range of subjective variances of "long" cowrie shell bands (approximately 5.0 m to 7.5 m), "good quality" bailer shell neck pieces, and "large" nassa shell chest bibs, these objects also individually equated in value to one "large" pig. To esoteric traders there were, of course, significant variances in the absolute value of both medium- and large-sized pigs that were based on absolute size, the general health of the pig, the age of the pig, the sex of the pig, and whether the pig was pregnant.

Perhaps the most meaningful relationship of stone goods and other valuables to the value of cowrie shells relative to pigs, comes from Archbold. When he first entered the Grand Valley in 1938, Archbold found that he could purchase 10 kg of sweet potatoes for one "average" cowrie shell, and "6–10 good ones would purchase an ordinary pig" (Archbold et al. 1942:253).

In the Yali and East region, the indigenous inhabitants similarly equated the value of a quality, large Langda-Sela-style adze blade (approximately 24–28 cm long) and a quality sie (or siengga) display-exchange stone to one "big" pig.

Movement of Goods

Trading patterns in the Highlands were complex. To analyze the movements of stone objects within overall patterns that accounted for the distribution of stone goods as they might be found in the archaeological record, summary statements from indigenous inhabitants and modern researchers at fourteen scattered control points of information are presented. Perspectives from the manufacturers of stone goods at points of origin and from traders and users scattered throughout the area are included. The data are presented from control points from west to east across the Highlands area. (figs. 1.31, 2.8, 8.1, and 8.2 serve as map references.)

Enarotali Area

In the Enarotali area, Pospisil (1956:222–23) reported that intraregional trade between different sociopolitical groups consisted of net bags decorated with boar tusks and orchid fiber wrappings and pigs from the Kamu Valley traded in exchange for "charm stones," bright-colored feathers, cassowary feathers and femurs, bundles of inner bark for string manufacture, resin, and carcasses of marsupials and rats from other areas. For those areas that did not have desirable local products, the only intensive trade with the Kamu Valley was the transfer of pigs.

Regarding intertribal trade, Pospisil (1956:224–25) reported that the Kamu Valley near Enarotali is a segment in a chain of trade that starts in the Uta-Mimika-Kokenau coastal area to the south and ends some place in the interior of the mountainous valleys northeast of Kapauku territory. According to Pospisil:

> The inter-tribal trade can be compared to a chain reaction. It starts at the coast and follows the road north and east. It involves many regions and tribes whose traders exchange commodities, carry them a relatively short distance, then trade them with their colleagues from the north, receiving goods which thus go in the reverse direction.... Shells move along the trade route by pulsation of the chain reaction from the coast to the interior. From the interior comes red ochre, palm wood, and stone axes and knives. The stone tools are said to be produced in "Kajaa country," located some place near the Baliem Valley. [I assume this to be Yeineri.] (1956:224–25)

Ilaga

Although Larson (1987:17–18) made few comments about trade, he did point out that the main trade route (on which Ilaga was located) that connected the Grand Valley with the south coast via the Enarotali area went through the southern half of the "Dani tribe." Large bailer shells, small nassa shells, and salt were traded from the west into the "North Baliem" (west of the Grand Valley) in exchange for Dani pigs and cowries. The salt cakes were made at the Homeyo salt springs, located not far from Ilaga. Larson states that, "Western Dani parties . . . worked their way west on the same trails carrying small pigs and highly valued cowrie shells traded from farther east, and even herding large pigs over the trail, some as far as Ilaga; others on to one of the Moni salt springs farther west" (1987:18).

Mulia

At contact time, the Mulia area was an important locus for trade in the western Irian Jaya Highlands. It was located along the same east-west trade artery as Ilaga and due south of the Yeineri stone goods manufacturing center. Mulia was the southern connection for dispersal of stone goods coming out of Yeineri and moving onward via kinship linkages, eastward into the North Baliem region to trade for pigs and westward toward Enarotali to trade for shells. The Mulia area possessed sandstone grindstones and, in a sense, was a grinding center for biface blanks that were traded from the Yeineri quarries and ground in the Mulia area before being traded onward to users in both the east and west. Informants at both the Yeineri manufacturing center and within the Mulia area stated there was a brisk movement from Yeineri to the Mulia area of both ground finished blades and flaked but not ground, biface adze and axe blade blanks, as well as je-type flat display-exchange stones, knives and chisels. Some men in the Mulia area who were known as "grinders" said that occasionally they would travel to Yeineri not to trade for finished blades or flaked bifaces but to quarry their own biface blanks. During that time, they reported trading pigs, cowrie shells, and salt to the Wano for stone goods. They considered most of the stone goods to be in-transit to Western Dani and Dani user populations to the east and to Damal, Moni, and Kapauku to the west. In this instance, the Mulia area grinder-traders could be considered true middlemen in the in-transit flow of stone goods.

Yeineri Stone Goods Manufacturing Center

At Yeineri, the Wano quarrymen-toolmakers

stated that they often traded both finished, ground stone axe and adze blades, knives, chisels, and flat je-type display-exchange stones, as well as larger numbers of not-ground, flaked biface axe and adze blades outward in all directions except due west into sparsely settled Wano territory. Stone goods, they said, moved southward into the Mulia area, eastward toward the Bokondini area, and occasionally to the lowlands to the north in the Dabra area. Yeineri quarrymen-toolmakers traded primarily for pigs and cowries to the south and east. When they wanted salt, they reportedly made combined trading missions and salt-making journeys to the Homeyo salt pool, not far from Ilaga, rather than trade their stone goods to residents of the Mulia-Ilaga area for salt. Although on at least rare occasions Mulia area people came to the Yeineri area to quarry their own stone, the Yeineri Wano disagreed with Hayward's comment that, "parties of Dani men from Mulia regularly travelled to the area to quarry stone axe blades" (1992:16).

In all Highlands cases (trade to the south, east, or west), the quarrymen toolmakers said that trade was initiated from time to time by traders at either end of a particular kinship (or trading friend) linkage. Rarely did quarrymen-toolmakers set out to travel past the first two links of a trading network, but most quarrymen specialists had been on one to three such missions during their lifetimes. The presence of enemies was the primary reason given for the restricted movement of traders into other territories, not language boundaries or geographic distance.

Konda Valley–Bokondini Area

O'Brien, working in the Konda Valley west of Bokondini, stated that:

> The stones used for tools and for *jao* (exchange stones) have a single center of origin, a quarry located on the Kembe River [Yeineri quarries] approximately 50 miles west of Karubaga. No Dani in the Konda Valley has visited the quarry site. . . . The Konda Valley Dani receive stone blanks as well as finished celts and *jao* stones from

people living closer to the Kembe Quarry in valleys to the west and northwest to whom they trade pigs and cowrie shells. (1969:43–46)

O'Brien further stated, relative probably to tool stones moving to the south to the Mulia area that, "The rocks are roughly shaped by men living at the quarry but the final grinding, polishing, and shaping into artifacts is usually done by Dani living in valleys south of the quarry who import stones from the Kembe Valley" (1969:44). She also pointed out that via a trade network, stone goods were traded to the Konda Valley for pigs and cowries; pigs and stone goods were traded onward from the Konda Valley to Bokondini for cowries; pigs, shells, and stone goods were traded via linkages to the Grand Valley for cowries; and the Konda Valley Dani received bailer, nassa shells, some cowries, and salt from an Ilaga source for pigs and cowries (1969:44–46). The Konda Dani regarded Ilaga as the western terminus of their trade routes and were unaware of the network stretching on through the Enarotali area to the ultimate source of sea shells. Even Konda myths failed to reveal knowledge of the ocean.

Since Tagime stone goods were known to be present on all sides of the Konda Valley (Karubaga, compounds to the north, Bokondini, and Kelila), I presume that they were also used by the Konda Valley Western Dani, even though it was not mentioned by O'Brien (1969) (fig. 1.31).

Tagime Quarries

From the Tagime manufacturing center, stone goods were distributed by trade directly into densely populated user populations of Western Dani in the greater Karubaga-Bokondini area to the north and northwest, and southeastward to the Dani in the Grand Valley. Axe blades, large adze blades, and je flat-type display-exchange stones were traded for pigs and other items of wealth including bailer shell necklaces (mikak), nassa shell bibs (walimo), cowrie shell exchange bands (jerak), and head-back nets (nogen). Small adze blades, knives, and chisels were traded for an assortment of lesser valued items. Quarrymen informants in both 1989 and 1992 stated that most of the stone goods traded outward from the manufacturing center via trade linkages were to users who were often separated from the quarrying center by warring factions. The quarrymen-toolmakers said that rarely did any of them leave Tagime territory to trade their goods because they were surrounded by enemies. Much of their trade was custom-ordered by people who sent in messages through nearby enemy territories for what they wanted produced. These messages were sent through families from hamlet to hamlet until the last member of a trade linkage would get the order to Tagime. Finished products moved outward along the trading linkages to buyers who received their products and sent back payments to the toolmakers. Ownership of an artifact did not transfer to a buyer until the toolmaker had received payment. Informants at the manufacturing center said there rarely was much bargaining, and usually both parties to a transaction were satisfied with a trade. It was said to not be unusual for live pigs to be moved through enemy territory in order to make a payment.

During times of intermittent peace, the quarrymen could recall when men came directly to the quarrying center from habitation compounds and hamlets such as Wolo, Muliana, Magi, Pyramid, Kelila, Bokondini, and Karubaga to order tools and make trades. Headmen Weak at Mebagaima and Silimeke at Pokhe on Sekan Ridge told me that when representing their people they both sent orders via kinship linkages to Tagime. They also said that most of the men in the Sekan Ridge area (along the east margin of the Grand Valley, southeast of Aikima, fig. 1.21) had never been to Tagime, but all of them had tools from Tagime quarries and knew with certainty the difference between Tagime- and Yeineri-sourced blades.

Wamena–Grand Valley

At Hupainma, north of Sekan Ridge (fig. 1.21), Wali recalled that he often initiated trades for his constituents through linkages with Tagime, but during the period of incessant ritual and revenge warfare up into the mid- and late

1960s, single traders could never, without the assistance of trading networks, consummate trading transactions with Tagime toolmakers. Wali recounted that large axe blades and "good" je stones usually traded for a "big pig."

Yeineri stone goods traded from their point of origin into the Grand Valley by short-distance trading mechanisms via kinship linkages along two primary routes: (1) the northern route from Yeineri to the Karubaga area into the Bokondini area and hence south and south-eastward into the Grand Valley and (2) by a southern route from Yeineri to Mulia and hence east and southeastward via the Tiom area into the Grand Valley (figs. 1.31 and 8.2). North-south trade from numerous points along these two east-west trending lines of direction supplied all inhabitants from Yeineri eastward into the Grand Valley with Yeineri-sourced stone goods.

As discussed in the previous section, Tagime stone goods often moved in response to buyers' requests from many parts of the Grand Valley (fig. 1.21). Once in the Grand Valley, both Tagime and Yeineri products recirculated locally, while more of those same products continued to accumulate. I saw mixes of the two tool types and of display-exchange stones that originated at both Tagime and Yeineri in habitation sites all the way from the Baliem Gorge at the south end of the Grand Valley to Pyramid and Belokme located at the north end of the Grand Valley (fig. 1.21). Even the Tagime toolmakers owned Yeineri-sourced blades, in addition to their own Tagime adze and axe blades, knives, and chisels.

The two most valuable trade commodities that were produced within the Grand Valley were pigs and salt. At the root of successful pig production, relative to other less-densely settled areas within more rugged terrain, was the abundance of sweet potatoes the horticulturists fed their pigs. Indigenous informants, who lived great distances both east and west of the Grand Valley and who had never been there, said that to many people the Grand Valley was a place of almost mythical proportions for its abundance of pigs. Pigs circulated within the Grand Valley as both valuable trade and exchange items and also were exported as items of trade to people outside the Grand Valley. It was because of the Grand Valley production of salt and pigs, primarily pigs, that it became the center for the largest accumulation of durable valuables in the entire study area.

Within the Grand Valley, all members of the Gutelu alliance, especially those people who lived within the Gutelu Dloko–Mabel confederacy, enjoyed a trade advantage because the source for salt from the Ileukaima salt pool was located in the hills east of Jiwika (fig. 1.21). The area around the Ileukaima salt pool was a manufacturing center for producing durable salt cakes (see "Brine Pools (Salt)," chapter 1). Two other known brine pools in the Grand Valley were of little consequence as producers of salt for trade purposes because of their small size.

From his work among the Mugogo sociopolitical group between Wamena and the Baliem River and with the Siep-Gosi and Itlai-Hadluk groups north of Wamena and the Baliem River (figs. 1.21 and 1.31), Peters (1975: 1, 70–74) made important observations regarding the movement of material goods. He stated that pigs, shell strings (jerak), long flat stones (je), nets (su), cowrie shells (jetakegen), bailer shells (mikak), and nassa shells (walimoegen) were traded among the Dani within the Grand Valley, and that pigs, salt, and tobacco were traded by the Mugugo southward and then to the west interregionally for stone axes ("probably from a stone pit near Mulia"), salt cakes, nassa shells, orchid fibers, nets, and cassowary feathers. Peters (1975:72–73) further stated that the Mugugo, the Siep-Gosi, and the Itlai-Hadluk had trade relationships with the Yali to the east and primarily traded pigs and tobacco to the Yali "[f]or bows of dark coulored wood; very fine nets and cords for women's skirts; little bamboo knives; cassowary feathers; feathers from the bird of paradise; *heisan,* a kind of tree fiber from which the Dani make *dibat; gamy,* corky wood which is used for magical purposes; sago; and *hedaly,* a type of resin, also used for magical purposes."

Heider (1970:27–28) pointed out that the flanking forests of the Grand Valley had been regularly searched and hunted for many years and were no longer productive for the large population, consequently, raw materials of the forest were mainly imported from Yali territory. These imports included fibers from bushes; a thick bark cloth; bamboo (especially for knives and containers); a laurel *(Lauracea actinodaphne)* for light-colored fighting spears; feathers from cassowary birds; birds of paradise, cockatoos, parrots, and others; femurs from cassowary birds that are used for knives to split the red *Pandanus* fruit; and red mineral pigments. In addition to forest products, Heider (1970:29) concluded that cowrie and nassa shells were imported into the Grand Valley from the Yali, as well as "it being conceivable" that at least some bailer shells also entered the Grand Valley from the Yali. Yali-made fine nets and elaborately barbed and decorated arrow points were also imported.

Since there was significantly less continuous warfare between Dani and Yali factions than between groups on either side of the Dani-Yali language border, and because people on both sides of this language boundary desired goods the other had to offer, it is understandable that brisk, continuous trade existed between the two language groups.

Boundary between Grand Valley and West Region and Yali and East Region

Although most kinds of material objects moved by trade mechanisms across *all* language boundaries in the Highlands study area, certain kinds of finished stone goods (and a few other objects) circulated only in clearly defined areas and did not trade in large numbers across the Grand Valley and West and the Yali and East regional boundary. Relative to this boundary, Yeineri and Tagime-style and flat-style axe and adze blades, knives, and chisels required for utilitarian purposes were used only in the Grand Valley and West region. As commodity counterparts and relative to the same Highlands' boundary, Langda-Sela-style adzes and knives traded and were used as utilitarian tools

only in the Yali and East region (figs. 2.1 and 8.2), although some traded southward from the Una and Kimyal down the Brazza River drainage into the Asmat. From both the archaeological and the ethnogenesis perspectives, the cultural behavior associated with this boundary has important implications. Indigenous elderly informants (fifty-five to seventy years) living on both sides of the boundary present insights helpful to these perspectives.

DUGUM DANI NEIGHBORHOOD AND GUTELU SALT POOL. At Hupainma, Wali Wilil and other elders stated there had always been considerable trade between Dani of the Dugum Dani neighborhood and Yali in the Pass Valley, Landikma, and Apalapsali areas. This trade was along a kinship network of Wilils that extended from the Grand Valley to Apalapsali (fig. 8.2). As "big man," Wali said that he initiated most of the trades for the Dugum Dani, and during his lifetime he had gone on several trading missions, visiting and staying with relatives as far away as Apalapsali. While visiting the Pass Valley area, I confirmed there were people with the name Wilil living in the northern Yali territory who *spoke the Yali language.*

Wali and other Dugum Dani elders concurred that the Dani traded pigs, salt (from Gutelu-controlled Ilcukaima salt pool), and tobacco to the Yali for string nets, rattan, bamboo, gami (special medicinal and magical bark), red mineral pigment, birds of paradise and cassowary bird feathers, cassowary leg bones, wood (probably laurel) for long spears, both hardwood and bamboo arrow tips, and cowrie shells. On the few trips he made, Wali said that because the trail was difficult, his party took only small pigs, never large pigs, because the men had to carry the pigs in headback nets. Often, women made these trading trips with the men, but only the younger women went, the older women were considered too weak to travel such a long and arduous distance. The women did not carry pigs, but were responsible to carry food for the journey and to prepare it.

Wali said he never initiated trades to the Yali

with Dani stone goods because he did not want to give up his je display-exchange stones or puluen when the Yali would take pigs and salt in trade instead. As far as he knew, the Yali did not want Dani axe or adze blades, but they liked je and puluen for uses as exchange and religious stones. Likewise, Wali and other Dani men never used Yali-sourced stone tools. When asked about this, Wali, after much thought and discussion with several advisors, replied that Yali adze blades were more difficult to haft than Dani blades. Since this is mechanically not true (possibly the converse), I concluded that it was probably a case of having ancestors who never used Yali stone tools. In response to the same question, other Dani and Western Dani scattered throughout the Grand Valley and West region replied that either they just continued to use the tools that they had inherited because they liked them, or that they did not know about the Yali kind of tools.

Wali and other Dugum Dani said Yali men would come to their area when they wanted salt, but the only ones who came to trade had local relatives there. According to Wali, traders on either side of the boundary always had relatives or trading friends who lived across the boundary with whom they could stay.

Daoke Mabel (oldest son of deceased Gutelu Mabel) told me that his father initiated many trades with the Yali, for the same kinds of raw materials and manufactured goods for which Wali and other Dani traded. Gutelu often traded both pigs and salt to the Yali, and on rare occasions, he was known to have traded je-type display-exchange stones. When asked, Daoke did not know why his father in particular, and Dani in general, did not use Yali-sourced stone tools, or perhaps he was not inclined to share this information with me.

PUGIMA AND KURIMA. In a similar fashion, I found that the older informants in the Pugima and Kurima areas had enjoyed trade relations with Yali as did the Dugum Dani and the Gutelu Mabels (fig. 8.2), but these older residents (fifty-five to sixty-five years) also did not have an answer as to why Dani did not use Yali

adze blades or knives. Some people replied that they guessed they only used Dani-type tools because that is the way it had always been. It is reasonable that a people would not want to give up a satisfactory technology with which they were familiar.

PASS VALLEY. At Pass Valley there was a mix of Yeineri, Tagime, and Langda-Sela types of tools, as well as Yeineri and Tagime-sourced je-type display-exchange stones and puluen (fig. 8.2). Stone goods flowed into the area via different trade networks ending at a physiographical regional funneling of communication routes between the Highlands on the south and the lowlands to the northeast. Trade kinship linkages were identified that extended to the northwest, west, and southwest to Walak and Dani territories and to the east and southeast farther into Yali territory (figs. 2.8 and 8.2). Determining whether this is an area with vigorous trade caused by physiographic circumstances in conjunction with being located along a dividing line of regions with great product contrast is problematic without additional research. Farther east, at Apalapsali, only Langda-Sela-type stone goods were used.

ANGGURUK AREA. The flow of Langda-Sela-style adze blades and knives was, from their points of origin at Langda and Sela into the central part of Yali territory in the Angguruk area, primarily along two connecting sets of trade networks (fig. 8.2). Stone goods moved from the manufacturing centers via kinship linkages into the Korupun area and from the Korupun area along other trading linkages to the Angguruk area. Petrus Sama and seven other elderly informants (fifty-five to seventy years) at Angguruk and nearby Pasikni stated that many people in the Angguruk territory had kinship roots in the Korupun area. Their trade for Langda-Sela-type adzes and knives and for cowrie shells was primarily along kinship linkages to Korupun, some bypassing Nisikni and others passing through Nisikni. The Angguruk Yali traded pigs primarily, less often Dani-sourced salt, and sometimes Dani-sourced je-type flat display-exchange stones (sie in Yali language). These items were traded eastward for the Langda-Sela-style adze blades, knives, and cowrie shells.

Two Yali men at Pasikni told me that they thought cowrie shells were some kind of a nut that came from a tree. They did not know that their cowrie shells, obtained from the Korupun area, or their nassa and bailer shells, traded from the Dani at Kurima, were products from an ocean, about which they knew nothing.

The elderly informants of the Angguruk-Prongkoli-Pasikni area stated that on occasions during their lifetimes they had traveled to the Korupun area and stayed with relatives while they were on missions farther south at lower elevations into the Seng to gather rattan for skirting material. They said that most trading of Langda-Sela-style adze blades and knives into their area was initiated from the Korupun end of the trading linkage.

In the Angguruk-Prongkoli-Panggema triangle, Langda-Sela adze blades and knives traded from Angguruk, via relatives, to Panggema for pigs and Dani salt, which the Panggema men reportedly traded in addition to nassa shells, bailer shells, and Dani display-exchange stones from Pugima. Angguruk, also traded Langda-Sela originated tools eastward to Kosarek for specialty forest products and nets that they moved along in trade to the Dani at Kurima. During at least one long period of time there was reportedly no trading activity because of war between the people of Angguruk and Prongkoli, although Panggema and Prongkoli continued to trade. Angguruk, Prongkoli, and Panggema all had trade relations with the Dani with whom they exchanged forest products for pigs, "Gutelu salt," shells, and je-type Dani display-exchange stones and puluen, which they called sie.

Although Koch's research in the Angguruk area was entitled *Conflict and Its Management Among the Jale People of West New Guinea*, Koch made several important statements in his dissertation relative to the movement of goods and trade among the Yali.

Polished, flat, oblongated stones, known as *sie* and traded from Hóvólama [Dani], have no utilitarian use but rather represent valuables chiefly transferred as marriage and death considerations. . . . Unlike in other parts of New Guinea, trade in Jalémó [Yali territory] is not a commercial enterprise pursued to gain wealth. While most intra-regional trade follows lines of kinship, trading partnerships connecting two persons of different, especially distant regions are usually based on friendship ties created by a mutual interest in exchanging goods. Trade relationships are often perpetuated by the children of original partners. The use of kinship terms between family members of trading partners is indicative of the permanency of these arrangements. (1967:115–16, 125)

LANGDA AND SELA MANUFACTURING CENTERS. Diman Balyo and the other head quarrymen at quarry-factories within the Langda manufacturing center said that in addition to direct trade of their stone goods to people at nearby habitation sites who did not have quarrying operations of their own (fig. 7.3 and "Quarry Boundaries," chapter 7), they also traded by kinship linkages and "trading friends" to Bime, Tanime, Eipomek, Nalca, and Bomela and by kinship linkages past Bomela into the Sela-Nalca-Korupun-Dekai trading networks (fig. 8.2). These quarrymen knew that their stone goods were sometimes traded outward from the ends of these networks, but they had no knowledge of details. The informants agreed that usually trades were initiated by people who wanted the tools and came directly to the manufacturing center, but trades were also initiated through their trading networks by people at more remote locations. In exchange for their stone goods, the quarrymen-toolmakers said they usually received pigs, shells, fine nets, and arrows. On rare occasions women were traded. In such instances, they stated it took five or six "good" stone axes, plus an undefined number of nets and arrows, to trade for one woman. Such trading was distinct from presentation of bridewealth at times of marriages.

The Langda area manufacturing center trade network connected into trade networks that were channeled down the Brazza River to the Dekai area and on southward into the northern Asmat of the lowlands (fig. 8.2). Langda-Sela-style adze blades have been identified at Dekai as well as at other points farther south along the Brazza River by my colleagues. I suspect, but have not confirmed, that some sea shell exotics that I observed in the Langda and Sela areas were traded up the Brazza River, along with cowrie shells from the south.

Concluding Comments

Methodology

One antecedently supposed theory ("holism") and one-time-proven premise for archaeological work ("context") were combined to provide the underpinnings for a defined methodological approach to the Highlands' field work.

I continue to agree with the importance of "context" for anthropologic and archaeological work and with Malinowski (1922:xvi), who early on advocated "holism," and James Peacock (1986) that an adequate understanding of culture may be hoped for only if we take a holistic approach. That is, we must be aware that any cultural system, however complex and whether historic or prehistoric, is so internally interconnected that if we pull out any of its components, including its *material supports,* and disregard that element's imbeddedness in the whole, we will fail to understand it.

Further, to derive the most benefit from an ethnography at a material goods-behavioral systems level of contribution for both archaeological practical applications and theoretical research, the *contexts* (note: *plural*) in which the artifacts occur must be established from evolutionary, various cultural, and natural environmental perspectives.

Cultural Stage

The Highlands people lived as "segmentary societies" with traditional goods in their unique cultural phase or variation (including, but not limited to, technology, subsistence, economics, politics, and belief system) of a worldwide evolutionary Neolithic stage. They had evolved in their Highlands environment from earlier-arriving mobile hunter-gatherers and were in transition to becoming chiefdoms with central accumulations and redistribution. Already the Highlanders were involved in an early stage of craft specialization in their tool-making industries. The raw materials they employed in their technology included rock, wood, bamboo, bone, rattan, vegetal fiber, bark, grass, gourds, banana trunk, banana and *Pandanus* leaves, reeds, orchid and palm fibers, shell, seeds, cocoons, and feathers. The people had never developed basketry nor pottery (a hallmark constituent of the Neolithic in many parts of the world). They did know how to plait plant fibers into armbands and to weave, but without fixed looms. The Highlanders' ground stone adze and axe blades are characteristic of those found in the archaeological record worldwide, concentrations of which are considered to be signatures of the Neolithic.

Relationship of the Highlanders' Seen and Unseen Worlds

The Highlanders' world consisted of the seen and the unseen. In day-to-day cultural intercourse the Highlanders accounted by both routine and not-so-routine activities for both the seen and unseen inhabitants. Unseen life entities (ghosts and spirits) derived from the world of the seen. The population of unseen entities just increased in number with correlative increasing cumulative supernatural power as humans in the seen world died and their edai egen soul matter entered the world of the unseen as ghost entities that later evolved into spirits. Ghosts and spirits abounded everywhere in the landscape and nearly always had to be placated. It took the leadership and shamanic abilities of the big men, with their in-depth knowledge of the unseen living entities and of ways to harness and channel their supernatural power back into the world of the seen through tangible power stones, to protect the people from malevolent actions and to keep Highlander societies from falling into states of chaos.

The Highlander mechanism of using material supports for the personification of their "god-power" by an intimate relationship between the seen and the living "unseen" impacts not only our theoretical understanding of the evolution of religious thought but also of the manifestation of a belief system by the material supports in a culture.

In the sense that any profane appearing objects and places either are, or at any time could become, hierophanies, the entire landscape in the Highlands of Irian Jaya must be treated with due respect. The archetypal paradigm here to help us interpret the archaeological record of the Stone Age is that the entire cosmos can be a hierophany and that all prehistoric archaeological objects and places should be scrutinized, as difficult as the job may be, from such a perspective.

Stone Goods in the Cultural System

Profane Stone Tools and Profane Symbolic Stones

Within the study area seven kinds of profane ground stone tools were used—adzes, axes, knives, chisels, permanently fixed grinding slabs (bedrock and large erratic boulders), portable grinding slabs, and handheld grindstones—in addition to small unground chert flakes (most 1.5–2.5 cm long), naturally shaped hammerstones and anvils, and the culturally important profane display-exchange symbolic stones. All of the tools and symbolic stones were manufactured at four quarrying-manufacturing centers within the area of use with no outside long-distance trade for either raw materials or finished stone products. Within one language group (Wano) an unusual stone-striker bamboo fire-starting kit is present.

Within the entire research area, eleven mutually exclusive different styles of axe and adze blades, three styles of knives, and two styles of chisels (in addition to display-exchange stones that were sourced at the Yeineri and Tagime quarry systems) were defined. The axe and adze blades, knives, chisels, and display-exchange stones produced within the Yeineri manufacturing system are all made from metamorphic rock: blue schist, epidote amphibolite, and epidote chlorite schist. The stone goods produced at Tagime are metamorphosed argillite. Langda- and Sela-produced adze blades are andesite/basalt, hydrothermally altered andesite/basalt, and slightly metamorphosed andesite/basalt. Langda-Sela-style knives are produced from metamorphosed volcanic tuffs from within the same volcanic sequence as the andesite/basalts. The Yeineri-, Tagime-, and Langda-Sela-produced lithic types are each distinctly different from the other by lithology and color. The Tagime and Yeineri outputs are distinctly different lithologically, but alike structurally and, in both respects different from Langda- and Sela-produced lithics, which are both the same, lithologically and structurally.

These tools were used in two adjacent ground stone tool manufacturing, trade, and use regions that are geographically separated by the distribution and uses of mutually exclusive styles of profane stone tool blades (fig. 2.1). In the Grand Valley and West region, ground stone axe and adze blades, knives, and chisels were manufactured and traded outward from the Yeineri and Tagime quarries for profane uses, to the exclusion of adze blades and knives of distinctly different styles that are manufactured and traded within the Yali and East region from the Langda-Sela quarry belt (fig. 2.1). With the exception of the Pass Valley area in Yali territory, where there is a tool-type mix, the profane ground stone tool types of the two regions conform with language boundaries to form a regional border; although other kinds of goods trade across this boundary, including the culturally important profane display-exchange-type stones that are manufactured at both the Yeineri and Tagime quarries but not at Langda or Sela. Ground stone tool blades and profane symbolic stones that are sourced at the Yeineri and Tagime quarries trade freely across language boundaries within the Grand Valley and West region. Similarly, Langda-Sela adze blades and knives trade across language boundaries in the Yali and East region. Axes are not used in the Yali and East region; hence, neither axe blades nor the chisels that are used in the Grand Valley and West to drill seating-holes in axe handles are produced within the Langda-Sela manufacturing systems. The very few profane tool blades that trade across the regional boundary are never seen being used for their original profane purposes in the "region" in which the artifacts did not originate but are secreted away from public view to be ritually converted to sacred stones.

Both the sympatric, synchronic (same region in the same time) different adze/axe blade styles (by lithologic, structural, and blade size variations) in the Grand Valley and West region and the synchronic, allopatric (same time, different regions) distinct structural (also blade lithology and degree of grinding) differences that exist between the Langda and Sela adze blades of the Yali and East region and the Yeineri- and Tagime-produced blades in the Grand Valley and West region reflect the manufacturers-users technological responses to the available kinds of raw materials. The perceived functional (activity) needs for the Langda-Sela-style adze blades were the same as the *combined* perceived functional needs of the Yeineri *and* Tagime styles of adze and axe blades. In response to the materials available, it is seen that a rather wide range of forms and degrees of grinding will fulfill the culturally desired functions for the tools equally well.

Archaeological research has identified numerous sets of assemblages that vary significantly, but "for which the spectrum of variation may not be clearly associated with geography or time" (Isaac 1977). One possible solution to the problem is for a researcher in such a dilemma to develop a model involving co-existent traditions living in interpenetrating territories (Bordes 1961; Leakey 1971). Another solution has been the "activity differentiation model" made famous by Binford and Binford (1966). The synchronic data of my research would be beneficial to the fine-turning (or rethinking) of either approach for application to specific research problems. Neither of the two aforementioned models would lead to a correct interpretation of the tool mix in the Grand Valley and West region.

In addition to pigs, the profane display-exchange stones are economic and social binders of the cultural systems, without which the systems would cease to exist in their present form. The Highlanders' sociopolitical organization (alliance, confederation, hamlet, and compound in the Grand Valley and West and the district, village [hamlet], and house cluster in the Yali and East) provides the hierarchy and framework within which the stones move. Within most, if not all, of the different language-speaking groups within the study area, the display-exchange stones are necessities for marriage and funeral presentations and important as usual parts of war indemnity payments. In the Grand Valley, indigenous informants say that a war cannot be stopped without the payment of large numbers of the stones. The exchange of ownership by public display and presentation of the display-exchange stones not only fuels the economy by the repayment of debts and the establishment of new obligations, but it appeases the ghosts and ancestral and other spirits of the unseen world that are observing and listening to the proceedings. The many formal displays of these stone items of wealth before distribution also establish social prestige and indirectly political power—when both humans and ghosts/spirits are alerted to the donor's identification by loud pronouncements by ceremonial leaders. It is the presentation of sacrificial pigs and the exchange of display-exchange stones at marriage and funeral rites and for indemnity payments that mark the continual circulation of wealth items. The *longest,* and therefore most valuable, display-exchange stones are owned and circulated by the wealthiest and most influential men in the community.

The display-exchange stones are symbols of wealth that are evolved mixed-media expressions of three-dimensional art. These sculptured art pieces consist of both the flat and the tubular types of display-exchange stones. Initially the stones are selected by quarrymen and shaped and usually ground at quarries, before being traded into the use-areas where some are further ground and most are decorated with small, natural materials. The fundamental aesthetic qualities of the display-exchange stones derive from their simple form and natural colors—stones of certain structures and colors being more desirable to individuals in one area, and stones of slightly different structures and colors being sought by individuals in other areas.

Once acquired, the owners of display-exchange stones usually decorate the midparts with bits of fur, one or a few feathers (even dried whole skins and heads of small birds), one or several kinds of miniature symbolic female skirts, and other small objects. All of the objects used to decorate the stones are individually symbolic in themselves and, taken in entirety as a decoration bundle, the items are representative of many facets of the Highlanders' way of life. The items of decoration, taken individually, or in their normal decorative group associations, do not, however, identify the stones as being male or female. From the people's viewpoint, the stones are not anthropomorphic with gender identification as suggested by Heider (1970:289). Perhaps this is as good an example as any as to how a researcher's ethnocentrism might lead down a path to erroneous inferences about artifacts found in the archaeological record.

These works of art, that serve as symbols of wealth and are meticulously laid out in conformance with rigorous culturally approved patterns on display "bundles" for viewing before presentation, make powerful social statements to the indigenous users and furnish outside researchers with insights to the peoples' motivation and response to aesthetics. The articles themselves are static mixed-media (when decorated) works of art, but their use in a display-exchange presentation is nothing less than a primary prop in participation of the performing arts.

I posit that the profane display-exchange stone evolved in the Grand Valley and West region in former times from both the Yeineri and Tagime flat and tubular styles of axe blades. The degree of grinding and the structure of many of the flat-style je are quite similar to the flat-style axe blade, even to the detail that one end of the je is often sharpened like the bit end of an axe blade. The je puluen is structurally like the tubular-style axe blade in all respects. There is even a size range overlap in which some of the flat je and puluen je have the same dimensions as the corresponding larger axe blade types. What appears to have happened through time is that to introduce valuable display-exchange stones into a changing economy, the lengths of certain types of utilitarian stone tools (axes) were simply increased to create through quarrying and manufacturing processes another product. If the premise is correct, a rather revealing interpretation is available from the stone goods, not only about the manufacturing process but about an evolving, more complex Highlands' cultural system.

In addition to a need for more valuable durable items of wealth than the less valuable cowrie shell for trade and exchange, a valuable and durable item was needed to be able to *accumulate* wealth—both sweet potatoes and pigs are nondurables and could not be stored.

Profane Tool Uses

Percussion tools (in this case adzes and axes) were designed—had evolved—as two tool types, each type to be task specific. The ground stone adze, not the larger axe, was the all-purpose chopping and adzing tool of the Irian Jaya Highlands, used for a variety of tasks such as the heavy work of chopping down trees (except the largest in the forest, where ring-barking was thought to have been used) and splitting wood; to fine-finish work on bows and spears, cutting banana bunches and *Pandanus* fruits from trees, and within a segment of the population in the Grand Valley and West region, for amputating finger joints in ritual procedures. Tool size (both the adze blade and the overall adze tool) did not always appear (etically) to be commensurate with the task for which it was used. Shape and flexibility of the shaft, as well as other mechanical attributes, were intuitively known by the users.

An adult male usually owned only one hafted adze blade tool at a time, but each adult male owned one to three adze blades that he could haft at any given time. Since any one adze blade was used for multiple kinds of tasks, I am not optimistic about use-wear analyses to determine accurate uses of any single blade. To my knowledge such analyses has never been undertaken on traditionally sourced adze blades from the Highlands of Irian Jaya.

An ethnographic insight that bears on interpretational problems with *both* hand axe and hafted stone blade chopping tools in the archaeological record is the mechanics of use. Reiterating, it was the ground stone smaller adze that was the workhorse tool of the Irian Jaya Highlands and *the* tool that was used to down timber, not the larger axe. Why not the larger and heavier axe that is similar in shape to a modern steel axe? In the Grand Valley and West region, once felled, the tall timber was split with the longer and heavier axe as the next step in the lumbering practice to produce rough planks to then be adzed as finished boards for both fence and house construction. Both the adze and the axe were designed to obtain optimum cutting efficiency for their different uses. When using the axe in the Grand Valley and West to split logs that are lying on the ground, an overhead, straight-down motion is used. But to use an axe to cut down a vertically standing tree, a side-on motion is necessary. The users recognized the disadvantages of this side-angle motion with an axe, which for them did not overcome its theoretical advantages of a longer handle and a heavier blade. All language groups opted for the adze for cutting down vertical-standing trees and parts of trees and other objects that presented themselves at various angles, where smaller, more manageable tools than axes were necessary to be able to use overhand, vertical-down strokes. Both mechanical advantage and a controlled blade strike angle with a forceful swing of the tool are enhanced by such a direct overhead-down motion.

When chopping down a tree with an adze, the hands are held touching each other on the haft to be able to obtain full momentum on the downward stroke by creating a comfortable pivot point at the wrists. By forward-flexing the wrists just before the blade strikes the tree, both blade strike angle is controlled and mechanical advantage gained. At times, a woodchopper may work while holding the haft with only one hand. The pivot point principle is still in effect.

PERCUSSION: CHOPPING AND ADZING. When chopping a tree down, the worker chops higher as his blade bites deeper. He wastes no energy chopping away the frayed material at the base of each cut, as is done by axe cutters when cutting down trees as they change the angles and strike points of their blows. A neat pile of chips accumulates at the base of the tree. I hypothesize that the spring effect of the adze at the end of each stroke assists the woodcutter in flicking chips away from the cut. At the moment of blade impact, the haft of the shaft bends backward and then rebounds as the tool is pulled away from the cut. The Irianese lumberjacks work with the finesse of a professional golfer, striking each blow with a carefully designed bit morphology at just the right angle to create the optimum effect. Baseball pitchers and tennis professionals (when serving the ball) understand the principles of the overhand-down motion well. When working in tree tops cutting wood or from scaffolding in a forest to fell a large tree above buttressed roots, it is understandable that the overhead-and-down chopping stroke of an adze is more manageable than a similar stroke with a heavy axe.

Technically the adze (not the axe) is related to the hand-chopper, which when felling a tree, the "cutter uses his forearm as a kind of helve and stands face-on to the tree he is felling" (Steensberg 1980: 40,41). The woodcutter holds the stone with both hands and uses a straight forward and down motion.

Less than one-third to less than one-half of the length of adze blades (regardless of style, size, or bulk of the blades and the overall tools) is bound to the socket. When properly used by the people with their intuitive overhand stroke, they do not suffer the consequences of blades being pulled or knocked from the hafts, even when forceful, full-overhead swings of the tool are employed. This observation has significant application to inferences that might be made by researchers when searching for or evaluating possible haft wear marks on archaeologically generated tool blades. Without this sort of grounded truth I can imagine that it would be difficult to conclude with confidence that possible use wear, only about 4 cm from the proximal end of a normal 12 cm long blade, was in fact haft wear at all. What might be hinging on a correct inference could be, for example, something as important as whether or not a blade found in the Upper Paleolithic or Mesolithic context had been hafted.

SLICING AND CUTTING. An important lesson learned from observations of the uses of High-lander ground stone knives was their perfunctory replacement with an organic tool for several critical functions. Neither the stone knives produced in the Grand Valley and West nor those produced in the Yali and East regions were adequate. The Highlanders needed a surgically sharp knife. The people had no obsidian, which is superior in almost every way to modern surgical scalpels (Haviland 1993:79), chert in large enough pieces, or orthoquartzite from which knives were made and are found in abundance in the archaeological record in other parts of the world, and which are often interpreted as having been used for surgical and/or animal disarticulation, skinning, and butchering procedures. The people added the bamboo knife to their tool kit of ground stone and bone knives. The surgical sharpness of the bamboo knives was advantageous, if not essential, for the castration, disarticulation, butchering, and skinning of pigs as the Highlanders animal husbandry practices became a featured aspect of their newly developed way of life.

Just as killed-animals can be processed with bamboo knives and without the need of stone, so can animals *be killed* with bamboo projectile points and spears. The impact of these possible uses of bamboo (and then loss from the archaeological record through natural decay processes) for the killing, disarticulation, skinning, and butchering of medium- and large-sized animals, as well as for surgical procedures on both animals and humans must impact our analysis of certain archaeological sites.

STATIONARY GRINDING SLABS. The largest ground stone tools that are present in the High-lands are permanently located sandstone grinding slabs (select spots on bedrock outcrops and large erractics) and smaller portable but stationary grinding slabs. Both play a key role as tools of abrasion in lithic reduction. Most are also used to shape, smooth, and sharpen bone knives, bone and wooden awls and needles, and certain hardwood and bone arrow tips. Learning to recognize and interpret the use-wear linear grooves (and sometimes cupulelike indentations) that were the result of these latter uses is extremely important because use-wear marks such as these are often the only archaeological remainders left to tell us of the presence of other-than-stone kinds of tools. The use-wear marks on some large grinding slabs are books of information for the discerning and knowledgeable archaeologist.

By way of a cautionary tale it is pointed out that the concave grinding surfaces on many of the Highlanders' portable grinding slabs, formed only by grinding adze and axe blades, are similar in shape to some surfaces that are formed, for example, on the common "metates" found in the southwestern United States and Mexico, from the prehistoric Levant (Wright 1992:64), and for that matter, worldwide, by food processing.

CHERT (FLINT) FLAKES. Small chert nodules are broken into small flakes using the bipolar reduction technique. The sharp, unretouched, edges of individual flakes (1.5 to 3.5 cm long dimension) are used for numerous tasks: cutting and shaping, incising, boring, splitting and drilling bamboo, wood, bone, reed, and shell tools and adornments. Because no large chert nodules are available, small flakes must suffice. The cultural significance of this tiny tool is out of proportion to the very small size of the cutting flakes. No Highlander adult male is without one or several of these tools in his tool kit. Put into archaeological context, this is a point to be remembered. How many millions of tiny razor-sharp chert flakes are scattered unnoticed throughout the archaeological record? Might this small type of simple tool be an important adjunct to the bamboo technology (to cut and shape the bamboo) mentioned above and that Geoffrey Pope (1994) proposed was important in interpreting the archaeological record in an easterly direction from the Movius Line and corresponding to the natural range of bamboo in Asia?

Quarrying and Manufacturing

Almost all manufactured ground stone profane tools and symbolic stones originated at four quarrying-manufacturing centers: Yeineri, Tagime, Langda, and Sela (fig. 2.1). The quarrymen and tool shapers were basically the same people. Craft specialization had not evolved to the point where the two functions were separated as individual specialties.

Principles for quarrying and the stages of manufacturing are established for both flake and ground stone reduction industries. Although my manufacturing model was built from observations of people traditionally quarrying rock for the manufacturing of ground stone tools, steps 1 through 6 deal consecutively with quarrying and knapping techniques that could end up in step 6 with a finished flake chipped tool.

The Manufacturing Centers

Relative to the kinds and distribution of suitable raw materials, four widely scattered production centers furnished the stone goods for the area. The quarrymen-owners-manufacturers were from four distinctly different language groups who furnished their products across a broad area to at least eighteen different language groups. Products varied due to raw material variance.

Yeineri, a single, integrated quarrying and manufacturing center included at least nine named quarries that are scattered over a distance of about 15 km along the Ye River. The quarries were owned and operated from a single, advantageously located within the quarry belt, manufacturing center of Wano people. A variety of axe and adze blades, knives, chisels, and flat-style exchange stones were manufactured from rock quarried at different locations within the system to take advantage of those rock characteristics (hardness, ease of quarrying and manufacture, and aesthetics) most suitable for the products desired. The products were marketed by trade across language boundaries to users who lived in other more populated language-speaking groups. Because of the absence in the quarry belt of sandstone for grinding tools, many of the manufactured goods were traded as finished flaked biface blades, ready to be ground, rather than as finished ground stone tools. Raw core materials were quarried from surface bedrock exposures and large boulder erratics. No pit quarries, mining shafts, or drifts were used in the quarrying process. Engineering techniques for quarrying consisted of the uses of fire, large hammerstones, and wood and rock wedges.

Unwanted quarry core waste and flaking debitage were (and no doubt still are) periodically washed away from steep hillside and river bottom quarries by torrential rains and flooding. It would be difficult to identify the Yeineri quarries in an archaeological context, and it would take unusual preservation to be able to identify the Yeineri hamlet as a large operation center for a regionally important industry, since large accumulations of fine-flaking debitage were not concentrated.

Although overall leadership and responsibility for the Yeineri quarries was assumed by a single big man or a combination of a few such men at Yeineri, ownership of the products of production—the individual stones—was with the individual workers who helped in cooperative efforts to quarry the raw materials, took a share of the raw core rock, and individually worked it through to tool completion for local use or trade. Production was stimulated by the needs of individual quarrymen and their kinfolk for tools and exchange stones for personal utilitarian purposes and by a perceived demand of the marketplace.

Whereas the Yeineri quarries and manufacturing center were located in sparsely settled Wano territory and were separated by one or more language boundaries from the more populated primary markets for their stone goods, the Tagime quarries and manufacturing center were located along the banks of the Tagi River in the heartland of the same marketing area. The Tagime toolmakers were able to supplement the highly desirable blueschist, epidote amphibolite, and epidote chlorite schist stone products from the Yeineri manufacturing center with custom-made meta-argillite and, to accommodate certain marketing demands, an inferior, softer (and less expensive) less-metamorphosed argillite. Tagime output traded across language boundaries within the Grand Valley and West marketing area.

It is unlikely that the Tagime stone goods manufacturing center, with its two, side-by-side "quarrying" areas could be recognized in archaeological context. There were no exposed bedrock quarry sites, open pits, or mines. Also, no centralized large accumulations of either

quarrying or knapping debitage would be found. Along the river bottoms and banks, flash floods would have washed away all quarrying waste material. A small amount of flake waste prevailed in a process where the ratio of waste-flake volume to preform-core volume was low. This is due to the fact that the toolmakers ground crudely shaped bulky preforms to completion, rather than first knapping them to approximate final shape. The Tagime toolmakers might be characterized as "grinders, not knappers." Perhaps this was due to easy local access to quality sandstone grinding slabs. Most blades left the manufacturing area as completely ground objects, versus those from Yeineri, many of which were ground a distance away from the manufacturing center by other than the toolmakers themselves.

The inhabitants of the Yali and East region used a single, internally produced–style adze blade, which I defined as the Langda-Sela style, and also stone knives, but no axe blades or chisels, as were used in the adjoining Grand Valley and West region. The majority of these tool blades were produced at an industrial center that consisted of separate quarrying-production factories, each separately owned, near and including the hamlet of Langda, located within Una territory. A significantly lesser number of blades were produced at a functionally similar but small quarrying and production operation at Sela, within adjacent Kimyal territory.

Within the greater Langda Una residential district there were approximately twenty-six separate house clusters and hamlets. Eleven of these were hamlets with associated quarries, within which the residents manufactured stone tools. The eleven hamlet-factories were concentrated along an approximate 17 km stretch of the Ey River and very short stretches of two tributaries near their points of junction with the Ey. By erosional and transport processes, the rivers concentrated the raw materials for adze blade production. The one religious and the seven explicit technological steps of my Highlands tool reduction model were followed to produce adze blades of the same structural style, from the same kind of core rock, by each of the eleven independently operated hamlet-factories within the manufacturing area. Each factory produced the same kinds of products, which included the Langda-Sela-style adze blades, knives and minor nonutilitarian objects. Whether the original discovery of the favorable concentration of raw materials for tools was made by migrants and then the area settled, or whether the original settlers were in the area for other reasons and then discovered and developed the use of the raw materials is problematic.

Each hamlet-factory was an integrated operation in which a skilled labor force lived within the confines of a sometimes-sprawling hamlet, in addition to one head quarryman who *owned* and *operated* the nearby riverside quarry, which was the source of raw materials for the adze blade production of that particular factory group. There were no bedrock cliff face or open pit quarries, or shaft or drift mining operations from which raw materials were procured for the production of adze blades. The head quarryman (who was also the owner of the quarry) was not necessarily the overall most influential leader in the hamlet. The head quarryman supervised all quarrying operations within his quarry area and had authority to allow people outside of his hamlet-factory group to accompany him to the quarry to collect core rock. Cooperative work parties, under the leadership of the head quarryman, located boulder cores within the territorial boundaries of their own river-sourced quarry, which they reduced to manageable-sized pieces before being allocated pieces by the head quarryman for ownership and further processing.

Few knives were produced from the andesite/basalt and meta-andesite/basalt boulders of the riverside quarries, which were the single source of raw materials for Langda-Sela-style adze blades. Instead, the quarry sources for knives and "other objects" were reportedly away from the river bottom quarries and located at special places along sparse hillside exposures of lamellar tuff sequences. I have concluded that the raw materials for all of the stone products of the Langda manufacturing center were sourced from within the same geological volcanic sequence.

Engineering techniques to break the large volcanic boulder cores at the quarry sites into manageable-sized pieces for further reduction included the uses of fire and both hurled and handheld hammerstones. Biface blanks were always produced at the quarry sites and then carried to the hamlet-factories for fine-flaking and grinding. There were no permanently located sandstone grinding slabs within the factory areas as there were at the Tagime factories in the Grand Valley and West region. Portable, but stationary grinding slabs were carried to factory sites from sandstone outcrops of the Kembelangan (?) formation, which was located a two- to four-day round-trip journey away from the different Langda-centered hamlet-factories, but within territory that was controlled by Una language-speaking people.

The Una and Kimyal were excellent knappers, who through two phases of freehand knapping, first the creation of biface blanks at the quarry sites and then final shaping before grinding by fine knapping, created knapped blades of uniform structure before the grinding phase was commenced. Less grinding was required among the Una and Kimyal to produce finished ground stone adze blades than among any of the toolmakers in the Grand Valley and West region. This was because the knappers shaped their blades to a structure in detail almost like that of the finished products, and because they did not smooth all of the flake scar marks by grinding. The ability of each toolmaker to create a seemingly cloned structure in finished adze blades, regardless of their length, may be a stage in the evolutionary process of improving technology. By having the skill and paying attention to careful knapping, the Langda-Sela toolmakers saved significant time and energy in the manufacturing process. This knapping-grinding strategy may have actually been caused by the cultural stress of the absence of grindstones within the factory areas.

Role of Women
Women conventionally cooked tubers and greens for the men to carry to quarry sites, or sometimes women carried the food themselves to sites and cooked it there. They also assisted

by carrying quarry-made biface blanks and display-exchange stones back to the residences. Rarely did women overnight at the sites. Women never assisted otherwise in quarrying operations, and when at the sites, they stayed off to the side, away from the quarry floors and core rock faces.

Permanent shelters were not maintained at any of the quarry sites for overnight work groups. Instead, lean-to shelters were quickly constructed out of tree limbs and branches by each work party to accommodate their needs. Sometimes previously used shelters could be reused.

Price Setting

All articles of trade had a "customary" price, to which an esoteric moral value was attached, although actual trade prices usually differed slightly from the "customary" price that was initially assigned by a product's originator. At all of the stone goods manufacturing centers, it was the toolmakers who set the "customary" price that they anticipated receiving for a product. If there was a common denominator for the value of stone goods across the research area at the time of first-contact, it would have been pigs and cowrie shells. In general terms, the value of one large, good-quality adze/axe blade and je display-exchange stone in the Grand Valley and West region related to one large pig. Similarly, in the Yali and East region, one large Langda-Sela-style adze blade related in value to one large pig.

Trade and Exchange

At first-contact the study area was covered by a network of trade routes that extended from coast to coast. An overprint of trails and routes, some well traveled and easy to follow and others less used and often difficult to discern, connected the habitation sites of the Irian Jaya Highlands, regardless of intervening language boundaries and different sociopolitical affiliations. Within this web of trails and routes that had been built up through the millennia, the people were connected to the origins of organic raw materials as well as to the manufacturing

centers for stone goods. As would be expected, there were radically fewer routes to both the north and south sea coasts from the central mountain core than within the Highlands itself. Although the flows of raw materials and manufactured goods were initially away from points of origin, once goods reached population centers, the flows became the sum effects of countless trades that took place in all directions. Local transactions occurred everywhere. Redistribution within sociopolitical groups by rites of passage, other ceremonial exchanges, and war indemnity payments fueled the continual circulation of valuables. Although the incidence of economic trade increased at times and places of large pig-killing ceremonies (rites of passage and other sociopolitical ceremonials), I do not interpret these occasions as proto-markets.

The trading network consisted of a web of overlapping personal connections, each of which were created by individual men of patrilineage membership and occasionally extended to nonrelated trading friends. There were no professional traders as such. Routes of movement of goods followed the networking of kinship-social linkages rather than necessarily the shortest overland routes between different points of trade. Each personal network was an open system. Within the overall pattern of the flow of goods, individual items were traded beyond the limits of individual traders. The goods most commonly traded were pigs; stone goods; shells; salt; red ochre and hematite; finished products such as fiber nets, string bags, and hardwood arrowheads; plus all manner of raw material products from the forest.

Social linkages (kinship and trading friends), which comprised the trading networks for the flow of goods that moved through them, extended across physiographic, ecological, sociopolitical (even in wartime), and language boundaries. The trade of goods across political boundaries of warring factions shows the importance of economics, even in a horticultural stone-based cultural system. When certain kinds of material goods, such as the Langda-Sela-sourced stone tools of the Yali and East region and the Tagime- and Yeineri-sourced stone tools of the Grand Valley and

West region stopped moving at the East-West regional boundary, it was not because one type of tool or entire tool kit was technologically superior, but for what I call "cultural habit." Indigenous inhabitants who lived on each side of the boundary used the types of tools their ancestors had used. They were comfortable with the stone tool technology they had inherited. Distance from points of origin, physiographic obstacles, and language boundaries did not directly determine the boundaries that stopped the flow of profane stone tools from different points of origin and that forms the boundary between the two stone tool use regions. Trade networks were in place across the same regional boundary line, and stone commodities, other than tools (je-type display-exchange stones and puluen from the Grand Valley and West to the Yali and East), as well as numerous other kinds of items readily traded across the boundary. Since there is a significant difference in the structure of the Langda-Sela adze blades and the Tagime and Yeineri axe and adze blades, the reason for choice on each side of the boundary becomes more understandable to an outsider. The relative value of the large Langda-Sela adze blade and the Tagime and Yeineri axe blades was apparently approximately equal to all users. I posit that the reason the je-type display-exchange stones traded across the regional boundary from the Grand Valley and West to the Yali and East was that there were just no sources of the right kinds of rock within the Yali and East region.

Creation and Uses of Sacred Symbolic Stones and Sacred Stone Tools

Need for Supernaturally Powerful Stones

The broad range of sacred ancestral stones, stone tools, and natural stones, empowered with supernatural power, in all of their functional simplicity and complexities, are the tangible objects that the Highlanders used to harness the power of the unseen supernatural world and direct it beneficially for their social uses. The Highlanders knew that most personal and socially adverse conditions were caused by ghosts and spirits from the unseen world of the

supernatural. They needed to combat supernatural power with supernatural power. They adopted a strategy of channeling power from the world of the unseen into the controllable world of the seen. Tactically the men developed a ritual mechanism for removing god-power from the world of the unseen and installing that god-power into tangible ancestor stones and, in a like manner, for "charging" other profane stones with supernatural power to create sacred power stone tools (chapter 4). The ancestor stones (ganekhe), ganekhe packets, and ganekhe cabinet became not only the focal point of worship but also the power generators and power box used to charge and recharge other stone tools with supernatural power. The ganekhe cabinet was awesome with its contained cumulative supernatural power.

Belief System

Within Highlander belief systems, the people traditionally worship ancestor spirits; in at least most of the Grand Valley and West region (I suspect over a broader area), they worship the sun (to a lesser degree the moon); and throughout the entire area they live in perpetual fear of ghosts and a multitude of spirits that inhabit the landscape. The practice of ancestor worship, from which females are precluded, is the core of this complex belief system. The theoretical issue of whether the conception of ancestors is influenced by a belief in other ghosts and spirits (or the converse) is not herein addressed. It is pointed out, however, that some theorists have claimed to find the origin of religion in ancestor worship (Hinnells 1984:39). As early as 1877, Herbert Spencer wrote in *Principles of Society* that "ancestor worship is the root of every religion" (Eliade 1987b:264). Spencer's theory rested on an idea in the scholarship of his day that religion as a whole had a common origin from which its many forms derived.

As far as the Highlands are concerned, it is problematic whether ancestor worship preceded sun worship or vice versa. What we do know is that the Highlander details of ancestor worship with the ritual use of material props was the people's intellectual response to be able to understand, worship, propitiate, and manipulate the supernatural power of select personified male ancestors, as well as the cumulative spiritual power of the selected male ancestors as a group, at the same time that the sun spirit was worshiped as the single most powerful spirit entity of all. Whereas the worshiped ancestor spirits were all male, the sun spirit was female and thought of as mother sun. Perhaps the powerful female sun spirit is the archetypal goddess figure that eludes us both in the archaeological record and in our theoretical constructs of the evolution of religion. The rather complex form of sun cult leadership and organization makes a rather profound statement about the evolutionary stage of sun worship in the Highlanders' belief system.

Like the personified human ancestor spirits with their "spirit bones" bodies, the sun spirit was not to be denied her stone body. At each of the three sacred sun houses at the sun center (lower Pass Valley), the sun stone "spirit bones" were many sparkling quartz crystals covering a somewhat circular, flat natural rock. These special sun stones were unique objects of the sun cult's ganekhe. It is professed by members of the sun cult that the sun-spirit departs her stone body in the sun house each morning to travel across the sky by day as that visible ball of blinding bright light that we know as the sun, and to return to her stone body each night. Of reference importance is the belief that when the sky is dark at night, the sun stone, with its included spirit, *is* the sun, not just a symbol *of* the sun. It is before this sun-stone spirit entity that live pig sacrifices and vegetable offerings are made in ways quite similar to the sacred rituals that are celebrated before the ancestor stones.

When the female sun spirit is contained within her stone body and at rest, she can be looked at, but when the same spirit is free of her body and traversing the sky, she is emanating tremendous heat and life-giving supernatural energy and cannot be directly looked at for long. The interpretation by the Highlanders, at their stage of cultural evolution, of this blinding white light as *being* their most powerful spirit power impacts not only our theoretical understanding of the evolution of the multiple uses of bright light as symbolic references for god-power and sacredness, but to the evolution of religious practice itself.

A Sacred Place for the Ancestor Stones

Pertinent to archaeological considerations, compelling analogies exist between the organization, contents, and uses of sacred space by the indigenous Highlanders to places of worship in most historically known religions, regardless of the supernatural entities that are being worshiped and the ways those religions are defined. In the Highlanders architectural plan of sacred space, "a place for the people" (outdoor courtyard with sacrificial ground altars, fig. 4.20), a "place for the religious leaders and practicing members of each ganekhe group" (the men's house or pilamo wusa, figs. 4.19 and 4.20), a place for "religious relics" (fig. 4.19), and a place for the "most sacred and powerful religious objects" (the ganekhe cabinet) is defined. I submit that the ganekhe cabinet with its contained power is the Highlander evolutionary predecessor and analogue of the Ark of the Covenant of the Judeo-Christian tradition. The Highlander organization and use of sacred space, as well as its detailed uses of certain material objects, furnishes a template for archeological applications, as well as for comparative religious studies and an understanding of the evolution of religious practice.

Supernaturally Empowered Stone Tools

In addition to the ganekhe packets, with their personified ancestral spirit stones and accompanying objects, which are worshiped and utilized within the sanctity of the men's house, there are a vast array of other kinds of power packets and power stones that are used away from sacred space to help solve all kinds of social problems. Power packets, each with one or more power stones, were composed into what might be thought of as sacred tool kits, with their supernaturally empowered tools; to be used to handle the kinds of personal, social, political, and natural problems with which the people in any cultural system must contend, but for which there are no profane tools in the technological tool kits that can be helpful.

The supernaturally empowered tools and tool kits are arguably just as important for the maintenance of cultural stability as the profane technological tools and tool kits. The number of sacred ancestor stones and supernaturally empowered stone tools within the cultural systems are approximately the same as the number of profane stone tools.

The power packets, and their removable power objects, can be found scattered throughout the cultural system. Some are at points of temporary storage, some are at places of permanent installation, such as the ganekhe packets inside of the ganekhe cabinets, and others are found being used by their owners at diverse activities to help keep life in order and to promote community success. A war chief might be using a power packet with its power stone out near the field of battle to prepare his warriors for success; a big man of a surgical team at a pig castration might have a power packet (or individual stone) lying nearby to protect the area from marauding ghosts; the groundskeeper for a ghost bundle memorial site (wagun ai) might carry a power packet to the site from a nearby compound while he is preparing it for a memorial service; a group of horticulturists with a wusahun in charge might carry one of several supernaturally charged adze blades to plant with sweet potatoes in a new field to act as a "fertilizer" and ensure good potato growth; and a woman might be putting an empowered ball-stone in the corner of a pig sty to ensure the health of a pregnant pig. Many other women would be carrying one or two empowered stone balls in the bottoms of their head-back nets both to protect babies inside from ants that are attracted when the babies urinate and as protective devices against marauding ghosts. Probably the second most important and widely used power packet, after the ancestral ganekhe stone and packet, is the religio-medical kit with its power stone/stones and other variable material tools/objects. Theoretically the widespread use of such a kit is understandable when we consider that an individual's good health is basic to a viable life. The number and variance of specific "medical" tools in a kit and from kit to kit indicate quite a range in the details of specific medical treatment methods.

Power packets, including ancestor (ganekhe), religio-medical, and all other, range in size from as small as about 7 cm in length to as long as about 40 cm. Their outer covering is usually banana trunk bark (gisakpel), *Pandanus* bark, heisan bark, cocoon "cloth," a tightly folded small carrying net (nogen), or, in still rarer instances, a relatively small, purselike, woven fiber string bag.

Spirit Installation and a Dichotomy

In Highlander constructions of sacred stones that to the people *are* living personified ancestral spirit entities and that to outside researchers are *symbolic stones,* as well as in the people's constructions of supernaturally powered tools to deal with the unknown, indestructible stones are the principle empowered objects but they are almost always intimately combined in a functional relationship with a varying combination of destructible pieces of string, grass, leaves, and wood. Herein is the dichotomy that furnishes us with a possible Rosetta stone to be applied to archaeological interpretations.

The ancestral spirit stones and the supernaturally empowered *tool* stones are more often than not, in their profane context, common tool blades: adze, axe, knife, or chisel. Through spirit installation and empowerment the profane stone tools (and, in lesser numbers, display-exchange stones and other kinds of objects) become hierophanies (things wholly different from what they appear to be) and are henceforth classified, thought about, and used by their owners in radically different ways than for the purposes for which they were originally manufactured.

A typical ganekhe packet, for example, might consist of an inner ancestor stone object or objects wrapped with a cocoon cloth, then two or more wrapping cloths of tree bark, all enclosed in a banana trunk (gisakpel) or *Pandanus* leaf outer wrapper and tightly tied with narrow bands of gisakpel, rattan, or fiber string cording. The symbolic ancestor stone or stones (as well as "power stone tools" in the contexts of their own functions and wrapped in their own packets) would have been wrapped with a single or multiple tied-off loops of strands of grass or fiber string. One or more small leaves might (or might not) be bound against the stone with the string and/or grass loops. The stone/s would be nested within a cocoon cloth wrapper on a few slender special leaves (jiwi and wolo by mid–Grand Valley terminology) and perhaps (but not always) with a small stick of aromatic vine root and, perhaps, a piece of aromatic bark (gami). The wolo leaves on which the ancestor stone/s lay are a bit of an enigma to the living population. The leaves smell slightly aromatic and are thought of as being in some way medicinal and spiritually powerful. This kind of leaf, as well as jiwi leaves, is included with the sacred stones in all kinds of power packets as well as with the ancestral spirit stones in the ganekhe packets. Informants say that the leaves have been so-used since the times of "the ancestors." Some say that just as babies are laid on soft leaves in carrying nets, so are spirit stones cushioned with wusa leaves in their carrying packets. I have observed freshly cut wolo and jiwi leaves laid out on ground altars before the ganekhe cabinet to receive supernatural emanations before their inclusion with religio-medical power stones in religio-medical power kits. I have not yet confirmed the scientific identifications or chemical analyses of these leaves.

At the first-time installation of an ancestral spirit into a "spirit bones" stone or other object, it is the tying of the knot of the fiber string or grass dibat that is the symbolic moment when the previously inanimate object is joined with the life of an ancestor spirit. This is when the object becomes a tangible "living" entity with supernatural power, instead of an artifact that is profane and dead, or, at best an object that inherently contains some sort of unidentified supernatural power that cannot be beneficially controlled. Just as the presence of a dibat on a human being signifies that there is life (edai egen) within the body, a dibat on a nonhuman material object signifies that there is spirit life within that object. Without the dibat, a ganekhe object has either not yet been empowered with an ancestral spirit or for whatever reason has been desacralized and can again be treated as a profane artifact—dead,

without spirit and not to be worshiped or feared. By the repeated rejuvenation of personalized ancestral spiritual power within a ganekhe (or of the rejuvenation of spirit power in the sacred power tools) through numerous dibat installation procedures, a bundle of knotted grass stems or loops of fiber string builds up on the spirit-stone entity. The knotted side of a grass bundle or fiber string loops identifies the front side of any spirit stone or other object. At the same time that a tied-on dibat signals the installation of spirit power within a stone, it also commences to act with its own previously installed power to protect the spirit dwelling within the object the dibat is wrapped around.

Rather private sacred dibat isin procedures are sometimes officiated by big men shamans (wusahun) with an accompanying pig sacrifice to fix power renewal and protective dibat onto both power stone tools, as well as around the necks of human individuals.

The well-known dichotomy of opposites, in this case indestructible rocks and stones and destructible organic materials of grass stems, fiber, string, leaves, and pieces of wood, are combined in a theoretically provocative scenario that tangibly defines esoterically manageable spirit-power. In Chinese cosmology the principle of Yin and Yang combines opposites to produce all that comes to be. A psychological principle is at play in the human psyche, which manifests itself universally. Be that as it may, applicable theory is not reviewed within the scope of this book but merely pointed out to alert other interested researchers. I conclude that the behavior associated with the details of the creation and uses of material objects with contained spirit-power by the Highlanders furnishes us with an archetypal Rosetta stone that can at least furnish boundaries of understanding to be applied to our interpretations of similar stones and other objects found in the archaeological record. There are at least hundreds, possibly thousands, of stone tools, projectile points, rodent mandibles, shell goods, and short sticks that are curated worldwide in museums that are looped with one or more strands of grass and/or fiber string, with and without leaves bound to the primary object. Through my own research at the Texas Archaeological Research Laboratory, Austin, and courtesy of Ms. Roberta McGregor, Witte Museum, San Antonio, Texas, numerous such objects have been identified just in Texas alone (ongoing personal project). Other examples worldwide are being brought to my attention for use in a manuscript that is being prepared on the subject.

Human Mandibles as Religious Relics

Stored as a religious relic to the right side of his relatively large ganekhe cabinet, Gutelu maintained a special ganekhe packet that contains seven pig-fat anointed, soot-browned and blackened human jawbones, each wrapped with many individual loops of grass that were put on the jawbones at spirit installation and rejuvenation rituals. The jawbones lay nested inside each other. These seven jawbones, according to their owners, are from seven male ancestors, each from *the* big man of seven contiguous generations, genealogically flowing and contemporaneously touching in the packet to form an unbroken chain of patrilineage descent from the *first* human from which *all* succeeding humans descended. By the Mabel patrilineage origin myth, Gutelu is in the ninth generation from the first human in the Grand Valley. The seven touching jawbones, each with its collected bundle of empowering loops of grass stems, represent a continuous flowering chain of immense supernatural power that has been building from the time of creation until just two generations ago. Three of the Mabel informants said that the three short bones alongside the jawbones in the ganekhe bundle are human collar bones (clavicles) that were from people eaten by the ancestors.

The maintenance of human bones as religious relics in places of worship are well known in later-evolved historical religions. Accepting the premise that the Grand Valley Dani were living in their variance of a Neolithic cultural stage of evolution, these jawbones may be the culturally earliest example of human bones as religious relics for which we have behavioral documentation.

The Power Circle

During certain rituals in the sacred space of the "men's house" and adjoining courtyard, supernatural power that effervesces from the individual ancestral stones (the ganekhe) and that also combines to form an aura of immense unified power within the ganekhe cabinet is transferred from object to object, object to person, person to person, and object to object to sacred pig. To the people involved, the power is awesome. For an outside researcher it is difficult to know where to enter this never-ending flow of power to analyze and describe it from a nonparticipating secular viewpoint. It seems that this supernatural power, of and from the unseen world, just *is*. It does not seem to have beginning or an end, but just *is*.

To further our understanding of the boundaries of behavior that might be associated with interpretative sacred stones found in the archaeological record, it behooves us to increase our knowledge of such complex behavior. It is doubtful that the *details* of such behavior could be explicitly applied to artifacts found in the archaeological record, although when studying both the theory and practical aspects of the evolution of belief systems and religion, this kind of detail might prove invaluable.

Cultural Flow of Stones from the Profane to the Sacred

The flow of manufactured stone goods is initially outward, away from quarry-factories toward trade-targeted user populations along the social trading linkages that comprise the Highlands trade networks. Once within local use areas, the stones are further circulated about by trade, exchange, gifting, inheritance, and according to other social mores of the people. All stone tools (adze and axe blades, knives, and chisels) and display-exchange stones (that together comprise the totality of quarry-factory output) are manufactured and traded to their users as profane objects. No sacred objects are produced as such at the quarry-manufacturing sites or are traded as such. It is within the use-areas that profane stone artifacts are withdrawn from the secular from time to time and converted to sacred objects with supernatural power. The temporally consecutive four steps in the creation of sacred ancestor stones and supernaturally empowered tool stones in the Irian Jaya Highlands are: (1) manufacture of profane stone tools and profane display-exchange stones at quarry-factory sites, (2) trade outward from points of origin of profane objects to use areas, (3) individual selection of profane object and withdrawal from profane use for conversion to ancestor stone or supernaturally empowered tool, and (4) ritual conversion from the profane to the sacred.

I have concluded that there are approximately as many sacred symbolic stones and supernaturally empowered stone tools (including ritually empowered natural stones)—hierophanies—being used within the Highlands cultural systems as profane tool stones and display-exchange stones. Supernaturally empowered small adze blades were a particularly favored item with which to fertilize sweet potato crops.

The relatively few Yeineri- and Tagime-sourced adze/axe blades that trickled eastward across the regional boundary, and similarly the relatively few Langda-Sela-style adze blades that trickled westward into the Grand Valley and West region, were not hafted and used in adzes as utilitarian tools but were traded about and ultimately empowered and used as sacred stones. During the fieldwork I observed a few Yeineri and Tagime adze blades used as sacred stones as far eastward as the Una-speaking people in the Langda area. If there is a model here for consideration when making inferences about the uses of apparent utilitarian stone tool blades found in the archaeological record, it is that on the outer fringes of a tool-type distribution, other than profane utilitarian uses might be suspected for the artifacts.

It became apparent during the course of the study that to improve our archaeological identifications of seemingly profane tool stones that are found in the archaeological record and our inferences of associated behavior, we must advance measurably our understanding of the sacred stone—the hierophanies—that are cre-

ated from the profane and may be present in the same record. The missing link that prompts error in some of our interpretations is our incomplete understanding of the magnitude of hierophanies that are present in nonliterate cultural systems.

Areal Distribution of Stone Tools and Symbolic Stones

Outward from points of origin within the two stone tool trade and use regions, the distribution and accumulation of tools related directly to the distribution of population, rather than to distance from manufacturing centers. This is contrary to Colin Renfrew's "Law of Monotonic decrement," where archaeological "finds are abundant near the source, and there is a fall-off in frequency or abundance with distance from the source" (1977:72).

Stone Tools as Language Boundaries and Cultural Markers

Stone tools and symbolic display-exchange stones traded regularly across language boundaries in the Irian Jaya Highlands, within each of two adjacent stone tool use regions. Economic (to include subsistence) needs in the Highlands area, with the availability of only a limited number of scattered locations with suitable raw materials, overcame any problems associated with language boundaries as effective barriers to trade. I conclude that the distribution of stone tool types (or styles) and symbolic stones in the archaeological record are not reliable markers of inferred language boundaries.

In the Highlands it was always possible to observe a cultural system with its component integrating parts at work at any given geographic point, but it was not possible to assign a single geographic boundary that would define an integrated cultural system (traits: economic, to include subsistence; political; religious; language; material, to include technology, of course; and art-aesthetic). Interpenetrating individual "traits" into (and across) adjacent language groups obscured any distinct geographic definition of individual cultural systems for archaeological applications. I doubt one would argue that we derive the most value from our interpretations of stone goods found in the archaeological record when we are able to include such interpretations into a systemic cultural framework. At the nexus of the problem is the absence of an archaeologically workable definition of a cultural system. With foreknowledge of risk of burning up my computer with angry e-mail responses, I posit that we still do not have "culture" or "cultural system" most advantageously (and correctly) defined to be able to effectively communicate on the subject of material goods as cultural markers.

I conclude that the distribution of profane stone tools in the Highlands of Irian Jaya are great harbingers of technological (and cognitive) information, valid markers for subsistence, and, on a more inclusive broader scale, of economic systems, but until we have a more unified agreement on a scientific definition of "cultural system," the distribution of stone tools should not be considered a valid cultural marker. As Glynn Isaac (1977:5) might have put it, we would be trying to squeeze too much blood from stones.

Why No Pottery, Chiefs, or a Civilization?

As a concluding statement I would like to account for the absence of pottery and basketry in the baggage of the Highlanders. In the New Guinea Highlands, horticulture, including systems of water control, developed just as early as in Europe, both the Near and Far East, and the Americas. But, in most of those other areas, pottery appeared in the archaeological record as a signature of the Neolithic (Service 1971). In Highlands New Guinea none of the available seed plants were suitable for domestication as was grain (barley, wheat, rice, maize) in other parts of the world. None of the plants that were

domesticated (tubers: taro, yams, and later sweet potatoes; bananas; and sugar cane) needed to be stored. They could be harvested at any time throughout the year. The Highlanders just had no need for pottery for food storage, or baskets with which to winnow, carry, or store seeds, in their ecological environment. In the Melanesian lowlands around the perimeter of New Guinea, pottery did, however, appear. It was needed at lower elevations to store sago flour.

Following a thought trajectory of Axel Steensberg (1986:20, 32–34), not only did the Highlanders have no need to store food plants, they could not. The plants would rot. Since none of the domesticated plants could be stored, no concentration of inheritable wealth developed. Big men could accumulate wives, gardens, pigs, and durable valuables that would allow them to participate in, *or control,* exchange relationships, but they could not maintain an important position into very old age, nor could their sons simply take over (inherit) their positions (Brown 1978:93, 94). Because food could not be stored for many days in the humid tropical climate and grain was not present as a cultivar, no central administration, no system of accounting and labeling evolved as was necessary in a grain subsistence society. No cities and no divisions of labor developed. The New Guinea Highlanders did not evolve out of a late Neolithic stage with segmentary societies and develop full-fledged chiefdoms or states within a "civilization" because of the environment in which they lived. Stated as a more general principle, the cultural stage to which any given people evolved—from band hunter-gatherers to modern state civilizations—relates directly to the environmental "contexts" of the place in which the people adapted, not to inherent cognitive or physical advantages of one group of people versus another.

In figure A.1, in the packet on the left, the outer covering consists of a single piece of cocoon cloth tied with a fiber string. The power stone (wamaket) is a gray-weathered, black naturally shaped stone that is rectangular in plan view and quite arcuate in cross section. It is 11.8 cm long by 5.2 cm wide, and 1.3 cm thick. On its visible, concave side a wide red stripe has been painted longitudinally after a double looped fiber string dibat and a band of braided yellow orchid cording were tied around the upper midsection of the stone. On the reverse convex side of the stone, eleven nassa shells are tied along the lower side of the orchid fiber cording. The nassa shell-decorated side of the stone rests in the cocoon cloth wrapping on a stick (piece of jiwi root that is 9 cm long), a piece of gami wood that is 4.8 cm long, a *nalelen* nut, assorted linear sali leaves (or possible jiwi), and about eight wolo leaves. The wolo leaf is called *woloka* in some areas. It is slightly aromatic. This is the only painted healer's power stone that I have observed in the Highlands. The outer covering of the packet on the right is bark cloth. This packet, when tightly secured with its fiber string, is 6 by 22 cm. Two power stones with two dried wolo leaves are included. The power stone on the left is an important device used for magical purposes. It is an *imak,* used for witchcraft. This particular imak is a black mudstone ammonite fossil that protrudes slightly from a woven handle. The fossil protrudes 1.5 cm from a 18.5 cm long fiber string woven handle. The power is a special kind of spirit that resides inside the fossil and can be directed out of the object only by the specialist wusahun who is a sorcerer. Alula, for example, is not a specialist sorcerer who handles these kinds of powers and would not have a use for this particular symbolic object. Alula reportedly has, however, the ability to counteract sorcery- (imak) induced illness. The power stone to the right of the imak is, in its present symbolic power stone context, a *uken* that was transformed by the introduction of supernatural power into a former Yeineri flat-style adze blade, 10.5 cm long by 3.3 cm wide by 1.9 cm thick.

In figure A.2, in the upper photograph, the outer covering of the religio-medical kit is a beautifully handwoven, yellow and brown-colored, orchid fiber cord purse with a long trailing loop of a tightly woven string band that is looped several times around the packet to secure it. Within the outer covering of the yellow purse is a multifolded piece of dark red-brown bark cloth into which the contents of the healing kit are wrapped. The power stone is a uken, which in this instance was, in its former profane tool context, a small green-colored Yeineri-style adze blade. Four boar tusks accompany the power stone as the other contents of the healing kit that are wrapped inside the bark cloth after each use. A string of pig-grease-rubbed, aged, brown-colored marsupial mandibles is tied to one corner of the yellow purse. Its mandible attachments are slipped inside the purse when not in use. By exposing the mandibles outside the healing kit during times of use of the power stone, a healer is putting the ghosts and spirits on visual notice that the healer is following their edict. The emptied outer banana bark covering of another healing kit is shown at the top of the lower photograph in figure A.2. The inner contents include a reddish brown–colored cocoon cloth wrapped power stone with several accompanying small pig tails, wolo and jiwi leaves, and a stick of gami wood. The power stone (wamaket) is a river-tumbled, round, black mudstone or meta-argillite sphere, which is wrapped with two turns of yellow orchid fiber braided cording and four fiber string dibat. This black stone ball is typical of stone balls that are used throughout the Highlands. Women often carry one

Fig. A.1. Two religio-medical healing kits.

such ball, usually smaller, in the bottom of a carrying net, to protect a human baby or pig that is within the net, but separated from the power stone by a soft layer of leaves. A more common use of these stone balls is to set them inside a corner of a pig sty of a female pig to encourage the birth of many healthy piglets. Sometimes such small power stones are even fed to female pigs inside a potato to hopefully ingest the pig with fertility promoting spirit power. A pig will usually spit the stone out, but it is hoped that the fertility spirit power has already been transmitted. The gami stick, such as the one within the packet, is even more pervasively used throughout the Highlands. Almost everyone owns one or more. They are aromatic bark from the gami (alt. kami) tree, which I suspect might be a cinnamon. People eat the wood to cure minor ailments by nibbling off bits from the end of a stick and spitting it in a rapid succession. Sometimes this efficacious practice is a procedure of a healer, directed at the sick or hurt part of a patient to drive out the illness or pain-causing spirit(s).

Pieces of gami are also worn as amulets from strings around the neck and hung from the walls or ceilings inside huts. Gami sticks are placed beside sick people in their houses. Pieces of the gami bark or short sticks broken from small limbs of the gami tree are thought to possess inherent supernatural qualities and, with further empowerment through ritual, are thought to become even more powerful.

To the right of the cocoon cloth wrapped power stone is a stick (piece of an aerial root or liana) that is included with the power stone in the outer banana trunk wrapping to make up the entire contents of this religio-medical kit. These special sticks are called vines, sometimes roots, by the indigenous people. They too, are slightly, but only slightly, aromatic. The inner wood of the aerial root (or liana) is subtly yellow in color. It may have been this aspect of the wood that led the people to believe that it possessed inherent power or at least was favorably inclined to accept power and be a transmitter.

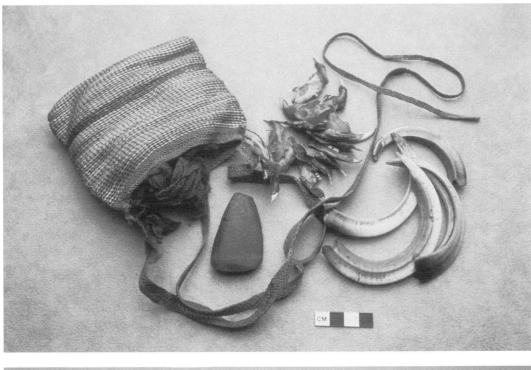

Fig. A.2. Two kits: adze blade and the rock sphere power stones

Adams, R. McC. 1953. Anthropological Perspectives on Ancient Trade. *Current Anthropology* 15:239–58.

Alland, A. 1977. *The Artistic Animal: An Inquiry into the Biological Roots of Art.* Garden City, N.Y.: Anchor Books.

Allbrook, D., and L. Freedman. 1977. Evolution of the Hominid Tool-Making Hand and Forearm. In *Stone Tools as Cultural Markers: Change, Evolution and Complexity,* edited by R.V.S. Wright. Atlantic Highlands, N.J.: Humanities Press.

Allen, J. 1972. The First Decade in New Guinea Archaeology. *Antiquity* 46(183):180–90.

Allen, J.; J. Golson; and R. Jones, eds. 1977. *Sunda and Sahul, Prehistoric Studies in Southeast Asia, Melanesia and Australia.* New York: Academic Press.

Ammerman, A. J., and L. L. Cavalli-Sforza. 1984. *The Neolithic Transition and the Genetics of Populations in Europe.* Princeton, N.J.: Princeton University Press.

Archbold, R. 1941. Unknown New Guinea. *National Geographic* 79(3):315–44.

Archbold, R.; A. L. Rand; and L. J. Brass. 1942. Results of the Archbold Expeditions, No. 41. Summary of the 1938–1939 New Guinea Expedition. *Bulletin of the American Museum of Natural History* 79(3):197–288.

Arriaza, B., and E. Ferorelli. 1955. Chile's Chinchorro Mummies. *National Geographic* 187(3):68–69.

Aufenanger, H., and G. Holtker. 1940. *Die Gende in Zentralneuguinea: Vom Leben und Denken eines Papua-Stammes in Bismark-Gebirge.* Missiondruckerei St.

Bailey, B. C.; G. Head; M. Jenike; B. Owen; R. Rechtman; and E. Zechenter. 1989. Hunting and Gathering in Tropical Rain Forest: Is It Possible? *American Anthropologist* 91:59–82.

Balter, M. 1993. New Look at Neolithic Sites Reveals Complex Societies. *Science* 262:179, 180.

Berndt, R. M. 1964. Warfare in the New Guinea Highlands. *American Anthropologist* 66(4): 183–203.

Bernier, R. M. 1991. Body Art and the Maasai. Unpublished paper, Fine Arts Department, University of Colorado, Boulder.

Bijlmer, H. J. T. 1923. Anthropological Results of the Dutch Scientific Central New Guinea Expedition A° 1920, Followed by an Essay on the Anthropology of the Papuans. *Nova Guinea* 7:355–448.

Binford, L. R. 1968. Archaeological Perspectives. In *New Perspectives in Archaeology,* edited by S. R. Binford and L. R. Binford, pp. 5–32 Chicago: Aldine.

———. 1978. *Nunamiut Ethnoarchaeology.* New York: Academic Press.

———. 1981. *Bones: Ancient Men and Modern Myths.* New York: Academic Press.

———. 1983. *In Pursuit of the Past.* New York: Thames and Hudson.

———. 1989. *Debating Archaeology.* New York: Academic Press.

———. 1991. A Corporate Caribou Hunt: Documenting the Archaeology of Past Lifeways. In *Expedition: Ethnoarchaeology* (Special Issue) 30(1):33–43.

Binford, L. R., and S. R. Binford. 1966. A Preliminary Analysis of Functional Variability in the Mousterian of Levallois Facies. In *Recent Studies in Palaeoanthropology,* edited by J. D. Clark and F. C. Howell, pp. 238–95. *American Anthropologist* (Special Publication) 68(2):2.

Binns, R. A., and I. McBryde. 1972. *A Petrological Analysis of Ground-Edge Artefacts from Northern New South Wales.* Canberra: Australian Institute of Aboriginal Studies.

Birdsell, J. B. 1977. The Recalibration of a

Paradigm for the First Peopling of Greater Australia. In *Sunda and Sahul, Prehistoric Studies in Southeast Asia, Melanesia, and Australia,* edited by J. Allen, J. Golson, and R. Jones, pp. 113–67. New York: Academic Press.

Blackwood, B. 1939. Folk-stories of a Stone Age People in New Guinea. *Folk-Lore* 50(3):209–42.

———. 1964. The Technology of a Modern Stone Age People in New Guinea. In *Occasional Papers on Technology,* 3, edited by T. K. Penniman and R. M. Blackwood, pp. 1–76. Oxford: Oxford University Press.

Bordes, F. 1961. Mousterian Cultures in France. *Science* 134(3482):803–10.

Bradley, R., and M. Edmonds. 1993. *Interpreting the Axe Trade: Production and Exchange in Neolithic Britain.* Cambridge: Cambridge University Press.

Brain, P. 1986. *Galen on Bloodletting.* Cambridge: Cambridge University Press.

Brass, L. J. 1941. The 1938–39 Expedition to the Snow Mountains, Netherlands, New Guinea. *Journal of the Arnold Arboretum* 22:272–342.

Broekhuijse, J. T. 1967. *De Wiligiman-Dani Een cultureel-anthropologishe studie over religie en oorlogvoering in de Baliem-vallei.* The Netherlands: H. Gianotten N.V., Tillburg.

Bromley, M. H. 1960. A Preliminary Report on Law among the Grand Valley Dani of Netherlands New Guinea. *Nieuw-Guinea Studien,* 4(3):235–59.

———. 1962. The Function of Fighting in Grand Valley Dani Society. *Ethnology* No. 1, Hollandia, West Irian: Bureau of Native Affairs.

———. 1967. The Linguistic Relationships of Grand Valley Dani: A Lexico-Statistical Classification. *Oceania* 37(4):286–308.

———. 1972. The Grammar of Lower Grand Valley Dani in Discourse Perspective. Ph.D. diss., Yale University, New Haven.

———. 1981. *A Grammar of Lower Grand Valley Dani.* Canberra: Australian National University Press.

Brown, P. 1978. *Highland Peoples of New Guinea.* Cambridge: Cambridge University Press.

Bulmer, S. 1966. The Prehistory of the Australian New Guinea Highlands. M.A. thesis, University of Auckland, Auckland, New Zealand.

———. 1974. Settlement and Economy in Prehistoric Papua New Guinea. *Working Papers in Archaeology* No. 30, Department of Anthropology, University of Auckland, Auckland, New Zealand.

———. 1976. *The Prehistory of the New Guinea Highlands.* Auckland, New Zealand: University of Auckland Archaeological Society.

Burch, E. S., Jr. 1971. The Nonempirical Environment of the Arctic Alaskan Eskimos. *Southwestern Journal of Anthropology* 27(2):148–65.

Burton, J. 1984. Quarrying in a Tribal Society. *World Archaeology* 16(2):234–47.

Cavalli-Sforza, L. L.; P. Menozzi; and A. Piazza. 1994. *The History and Geography of Human Genes.* Princeton, N.J.: Princeton University Press.

Chappell, J. 1966. Stone Axe Factories in the Highlands of East New Guinea. *Proceedings of the Prehistoric Society* 32:96–121.

———. 1976. Aspects of Late Quaternary Paleogeography of the Australian-East Indonesian Region. In *Origins of the Australians,* edited by R. L. Kirk and A. G. Thorne, pp. 11–22. Canberra: Australian Institute of Aboriginal Studies.

Childe, G. V. 1963. *Man Makes Himself.* New York: Mentor Books.

———. 1969. *What Happened in History.* Middlesex, Eng.: Penguin Books.

Clark, D. 1991. How to Make a Neolithic Axe. *Ligabue Magazine* 18:44–47.

Clements, F. E. 1932. Primitive Concepts of Disease. *American Archaeology and Ethnology* 32:185–252.

Crosby, E. 1977. An Archaeologically Oriented Classification of Ethnographic Material Culture. In *Stone Tools as Cultural Markers: Change, Evolution, and Complexity,* edited by R. V. S. Wright, pp. 83–96. Atlantic Highlands, N.J.: Humanities Press.

Davies, H. L. 1971. Periodotite-Gabbro-Basalt Complex of Eastern Papua—An Overthrust Plate of Oceanic Mantle and Crust. *Bureau of Mineral Resources Australian Bulletin* 128, Sydney.

Diamond, J. 1997. *Guns, Germs, and Steel*. New York: W. W. Norton & Company.

Dixon, J. E. 1993. *Quest for the Origins of the First Americans*. Albuquerque: University of New Mexico Press.

Dow, D. B., and H. Hartono. 1984. The Mechanism of Pleistocene Plate Convergence along Northeastern Irian Jaya. Indonesian Petroleum Association, Proceedings of the Thirteenth Annual Convention, pp. 144–50. Jakarta, Indonesia.

Dozy, J. J. 1939. Geological Results of the Carstenz Expedition, 1936. *Leidse Geol. Mededelingen*, 11:68–131.

Eliade, M. 1958. *Patterns in Comparative Religion*. New York: New American Library.

———. 1974. *The Myth of the Eternal Return, or Cosmos and History*. Princeton, N.J.: Princeton University Press.

———. 1987a. *The Sacred and the Profane: The Nature of Religion*. New York: Harcourt Brace.

———. 1987b. *The Encyclopedia of Religion*, vol. 2. New York: Macmillan.

Ellenberger, J. D. 1962. On Economic Development amongst the Damals (Uhundunis) North of the Carstensz Mountain Range. *Working Papers in Dani Ethnology*. No. 1, UNTEA in West New Guinea, West Irian, pp. 70–79. Hollandia, West Irian.

Ellsmore, R. T. 1945. New Guinea's Mountain and Swampland Dwellers. *National Geographic Magazine* 88(6):671–94.

Frazer, J. G. 1968. *The Belief in Immortality, the Belief among the Polynesians*, vol. 2. London: Dawsons of Pall Mall.

Freud, S. 1913. *Totem and Taboo*.

Furst, P. T. 1976. *Hallucinogens and Culture*. Novato, Calif.: Chandler Sharp.

Gardner, R. G. 1963. *Dead Birds*. A film produced by the Film Study Center, Peabody Museum, Harvard University. New York: Contemporary Films.

———. 1972. A Chronicle of the Human Experience: Dead Birds. In *The Documentary Experience: From Nanook to Woodstock*, edited by L. Jacobs, pp. 430–36. New York: Hopkinson and Blake.

Gardner, R. G., and K. G. Heider. 1968. *Gardens of War: Life and Death in New Guinea Stone Age*. New York: Random House.

Gibson, K. R., and T. Ingold, eds. 1993. *Tools, Language and Cognition in Human Evolution*. Cambridge: Cambridge University Press.

Golson, J. 1989. The Origins and Development of New Guinea Agriculture. In *Foraging and Farming*, edited by D. C. Harris and G. C. Hillman, pp. 678–87. London: Institute of Archaeology, University College.

Gould, R. A. 1978. Beyond Analogy in Ethnoarchaeology. In *Explorations in Ethnoarchaeology*, edited by R. A. Gould. Albuquerque: University of New Mexico Press.

———. 1980. *Living Archaeology*. Cambridge: Cambridge University Press.

———. 1990. *Recovering the Past*. Albuquerque: University of New Mexico Press.

Gould, R. E., ed. 1978. *Explorations in Ethnoarchaeology*. Albuquerque: University of New Mexico Press.

Groube, L. 1989. The Taming of the Rain Forests: A Model for Late Pleistocene Forest Exploitation in New Guinea. In *Foraging and Farming*, edited by D. R. Harris and G. C. Hillman, pp. 292–303. London: Institute of Archaeology, University College.

Groube, L.; J. Chappell; and D. Price. 1986. A 40,000 Year Old Human Occupation Site at Huon Peninsula, Papua New Guinea. *Nature* 324: 453–55.

Hadingham, E., and J. Newbury. 1994. The Mummies of Xinjiang. *Discovery* (April): 69–77.

Hamilton, W. 1979. Tectonics of the Indonesian Region. *USGS Professional Paper 1078*. Washington, D.C.: U.S. Government Printing Office.

Hampton, O. W. 1987. Anthropological Explorations in the Highlands of Irian Jaya, Indonesia. Unpublished Explorers Club Flag Report. New York: Explorers Club.

———. 1988. Anthropological Explorations in the Highlands of Irian Jaya, Indonesia. Unpublished Explorers Club Flag Report. New York: Explorers Club.

———. 1989. Anthropological Explorations in

the Highlands of Irian Jaya, Indonesia, vol. 3. Unpublished Explorers Club Flag Report. New York: Explorers Club.

———. 1992a. Anthropological Explorations in the Highlands of Irian Jaya, Indonesia, vol. 5. Unpublished Explorers Club Flag Report. New York: Explorers Club.

———. 1992b. Stone Age Mysteries in Irian Jaya, Indonesia. Part I—Journey to a Remote Stone Age Rock Quarry Center and Discovery of a Unique Fire Starting Tool. *The Explorer's Journal* 70(3):89–96.

———. 1992c. Stone Age Mysteries in Irian Jaya, Part II—The Yeineri Rock Quarries. *The Explorer's Journal* 70(4):133–40.

———. 1993. Anthropological Explorations in the Highlands of Irian Jaya, Indonesia, vol. 6. Unpublished Explorers Club Flag Report, New York: Explorers Club.

———. 1997. The Quarrying, Manufacture, Trade, and Uses of Profane and Sacred Stone Tools and Symbolic Stones in the Highlands of Irian Jaya, Indonesia. Vols. 1, 2, and 3. Ph.D. diss., Texas A&M University. Ann Arbor, Mich.: University Microfilms, 1999.

Harrar, H. 1965. *I Come from the Stone Age.* Translated from the German by Edward Fitzgerald. New York: E. P. Dutton.

Harris, M. 1980. *Culture, People, Nature.* New York: Harper and Row.

Hastings, M. 1945. A WAC in Shangrila. *Reader's Digest* 47:1–13.

Haviland, W. A. 1993. *Cultural Anthropology.* New York: Harcourt Brace.

Hawkes, C. 1954. Archaeological Theory and Method: Some Suggestions From the Old World. *American Anthropologist* 56 (1): 155–68.

Hayden, B., ed. 1987. *Lithic Studies Among the Contemporary Highland Maya.* Tucson: University of Arizona Press.

Hayward, D. J. 1992. Christianity and the Traditional Beliefs of the Mulia Dani: An Ethnography of Religious Belief among the Western Dani of Irian Jaya, Indonesia. Ph.D. diss., University of California, Santa Barbara.

Heider, K. G. 1970. *The Dugum Dani. A Papuan Culture in the Highlands of West New Guinea.*

New York: Wenner-Gren Foundation for Anthropological Research.

Hester, T. R., ed. 1991. *The Burned Middens of Texas: An Archaeological Symposium, Studies in Archaeology* 13. Austin: Texas Archaeological Research Laboratory, University of Texas.

Highlands, D. 1990. What's Indigenous? An Essay on Building. In *Vernacular Architecture: Paradigms of Environmental Response,* edited by M. Turin, pp. 101–14. Aldershot, Eng.: Avebury.

Hinnells, J. R., ed. 1984. *The Facts on File Dictionary of Religions.* New York: Facts on File.

Hiroa, T. R. 1930. Samoan Material Culture. *Bernice P. Bishop Museum Bulletin* 75, Honolulu.

Hirsch, E., and M. O'Hanlon, eds. 1996. *The Anthropology of Landscape, Perspectives on Place and Space.* Oxford and New York: Oxford University Press.

Hitt, R. T. 1962. *Cannibal Valley.* Grand Rapids, Mich.: Zondervan Publishing House.

Hodder, I. 1982a. *Symbols in Action: Ethnoarchaeological Studies of Material Culture.* Cambridge: Cambridge University Press.

———. 1982b. *The Present Past: An Introduction to Anthropology for Archaeologists.* New York: Pica Press.

———. 1986. *Reading the Past.* Cambridge: Cambridge University Press.

Hope, G. S. 1977. Observations on the History of Human Usage of Subalpine Areas near Mt. Jaya. *Irian, Bulletin of West Irian Development* 1(241). Jayapura, Indonesia: University of Cenderawasih Printshop.

———. 1982. Pollen from Archaeological Sites at Kosipe Mission, Papua New Guinea. In *Archeometry: An Australian Perspective,* edited by W. A. Ambrose and P. Duerden, pp. 211–19. Canberra: Australian National University.

Hope, G. S., and J. H. Hope. 1976. Man on Mt. Jaya. In *The Equatorial Glaciers of New Guinea,* edited by G. S. Hope, J. A. Peterson, U. Radok, and I. Allison, pp. 225–41. Rotterdam, Eng.: A. A. Baldema.

Hope, J. H., and G. S. Hope. 1976.

Paleoenvironments of Man in New Guinea. In *The Origin of Australians,* edited by R. L. Thorne and A. G. Thorne, pp. 29–53. Canberra: Australian Institute of Aboriginal Studies.

Isaac, G. 1977. Squeezing Blood from Stones. In *Stone Tools as Cultural Markers: Change, Evolution and Complexity,* edited by R.V.S. Wright. Atlantic Highlands, N.J.: Humanities Press.

John-Steiner, V. 1985. *Notebooks of the Mind.* Albuquerque: University of New Mexico Press.

Jones, R. 1977. Introduction. In *Sunda and Sahul: Prehistoric Studies in Southeast Asia, Melanesia and Australia,* edited by J. Allen, J. Golson, and R. Jones, pp. 1–9. New York: Academic Press.

———. 1989. *New Guinea Stone Age Trade.* Terra Australis 3. Department of Prehistory, Research School of Pacific Studies. Canberra: Australian National University,.

Kaeppler, A. 1978. Dance in Anthropological Perspective. *Annual Review of Anthropology* 7:31–49.

Klein, R. G. 1989. *The Human Career.* Chicago. University of Chicago Press.

Kirch, P. V. 1978. Ethnoarchaeology and the Study of Agricultural Adaptation in the Humid Tropics. In *Explorations in Ethnoarchaeology,* edited by R. A. Gould. Albuquerque: University of New Mexico Press.

Koch, K. F. 1967. Conflict and Its Management among the Jale People of West Guinea. Ph.D. diss., University of California, Berkeley. University Microfilm, Ann Arbor.

———. 1970. Cannibalistic Revenge in Jale Warfare. *Natural History* 79(2):40–51.

Kottak, C. P. 1991. *Anthropology, The Exploration of Human Diversity.* New York: McGraw-Hill.

Kramer, C., ed. 1979. *Ethnoarchaeology.* New York: Columbia University Press.

Lambert, R. J. 1972. *Hagen Axes: A Pilot Study of Axe Typology in the Central Highlands of New Guinea.* Australian Department of Prehistory, Canberra.

Larson, G. F. 1962. Warfare and Feuding in the Ilaga Valley. *Working Papers in Dani Ethnology* No. 1, pp. 32–39. Hollandia: Bureau of Native Affairs.

———. 1970. *Linguistic Research in Western Dani and Migani (East Central Mountains).* International Committee on Urgent Anthropological Research in New Guinea, Amsterdam.

———. 1987. The Structure and Demography of the Cycle of Warfare among the Ilaga Dani of Irian Jaya. Vols. 1 and 2. Ph.D. diss., University of Michigan, Ann Arbor. University Microfilm, Ann Arbor.

Leakey, M. D. 1971. *Olduvai Gorge,* vol. 3. Cambridge: Cambridge University Press.

Leroi-Gourhan, A. 1975. The Flowers Found with Shanidar IV, a Neanderthal Burial in Iraq. *Science* 190:562–64.

Le Roux, C. C. F. M. 1948. *De Gergpapoa's van Nieuw-Guinea en hun Woongebied,* Vol. 1–3. The Netherlands: Brill, Leiden.

Ligabue, G. 1991. A White Man among Cannibals. *Ligabue Magazine* 18:36–43.

Lomax, A. 1968. Folk Song Style and Culture. *American Association for the Advancement of Sciences Publication* No. 88, Washington, D.C.

Lomax, A., and C. Arensberg. 1977. A Worldwide Evolutionary Classification of Cultures by Subsistence Systems. *Current Anthropology* 18:659–708.

Lowendorf, L., and D. L. Carmichael. 1994. Personal communications with Lowendorf and review of unpublished report by L. Lowendorf and D. L. Carmichael. Flagstaff, Arizona. July 1994.

Madge, J. 1962. *The Origins of Scientific Sociology.* Glencoe, N.Y.: Free Press.

Malinowski, B. 1922. *Argonauts of The Western Pacific.* Paperback edition 1962. New York: Dutton.

———. 1954. *Myth in Primitive Psychology. Magic, Science, and Religion and Other Essays.* Garden City, Iowa: Doubleday Anchor Books.

Matthiessen, P. 1962 *Under the Mountain Wall.* New York: Viking Press.

McElroy, A., and P. K. Townsend. 1989. *Medical Anthropology in Ecological Perspective.* Boulder, Colo.: Westview Press.

Mead, M. 1940. The Mountain Arapesh, Supernaturalism. *Anthropological Papers of the American Museum of Natural History* 37(3), New York.

Medway, L. 1972. The Quaternary Mammals of Malesian: A Review. In *The Quaternary Era in Malesian,* edited by P. Ashton and M. Ashton, pp. 63–72. Aberdeen, Scotland: Hull.

Mellaart, J. 1975 *The Neolithic of the Near East.* New York: Charles Scribner and Sons.

Mickelson, E. H. 1966. *God Can.* Jayapura, Indonesia: Christian Missionary Fellowships.

Mitton, R. D. 1972. Stone as a Cultural Factor in the Central and Eastern Highlands. In *Irian: Bulletin of Irian Jaya* 1(3):4–11. Jayapura, Indonesia: University of Cenderawasih Printshop.

Money-Kyrle, R. E. 1965. *The Meaning of Sacrifice.* New York: Johnson Reprint Corp.

Moore, J. H. 1994. Ethnogenetic Theories of Human Evolution. *National Geographic Research & Exploration* 10(1):10–37.

Moore, L. G.; P. W. Van Arsdale; J. E. Glittenberg; and R. A. Aldrich. 1980. *The Biocultural Basis of Health.* Prospect Heights, Ill.: Waveland Press.

Nelson, H., and R. Jurmain. 1991. *Introduction to Physical Anthropology.* St. Paul: West Publishing.

Nelson, S. M. 1990. The Neolithic of Northeastern China and Korea. *Antiquity* 64:234–48.

Neufeldt, V., and D. B. Guralnik, eds. 1988. *Webster's New World Dictionary of American English.* New York: Simon and Schuster.

O'Brien, D. 1966. Twentieth-Century Stone-Age Culture. *Discovery* 1(2):31–37.

———. 1969. The Economics of Dani Marriage. Parts 1 and 2. Ph.D. diss., Yale University, New Haven. University Microfilms, Ann Arbor.

Olausson, D. S. 1982. Lithic Technological Analysis of the Thin-Butted Flint Axe. *Acta Archaeologica,* edited by C. J. Becker, 53:48–57. Copenhagen, Denmark.

Peacock, J. L. 1986. *The Anthropological Lens: Harsh Light, Soft Focus.* Cambridge: Cambridge University Press.

Pearsall, D. M., and D. R. Piperno. 1995. *The Silica Bodies of Tropical American Grasses: Morphology, Taxonomy and Implications for Grass Systematics and Fossil Phytolits Identification* (manuscript in review by Smithsonian Tropical Research Institute, Washington, D.C.).

Pearson, M. P., and C. Richards. 1994. *Architecture and Order.* London: Routledge.

Petrequin, A. M., and P. Petrequin. 1988. *Le NeoLithique Des Lacs, Prehistoire des lacs de Chalain et de Clairvaux* (4000–2000 av. J.-C.). Paris: Editions Errance.

Peters, H. L. 1975. Some Observations on the Social and Religious Life of a Dani Group. *Irian, Bulletin for Irian Jaya Development* 4(2):1–197. Jayapura, Indonesia: University of Cenderawasih Printshop.

Phillips, P. 1955. American Archaeology and General Anthropological Theory. *Southwestern Journal of Anthropology* 11:246–50.

Ploeg, A. 1966. Some Comparative Remarks about the Dani of the Baliem Valley and the Dani at Bokondini-Bijdragen tot de Taal-, Land-. *Vokenkunde* 122(2):254–73.

Pope, G. G. 1994. Bamboo and Human Evolution. In *Physical Anthropology 93/94,* edited by E. Angeloni, pp. 162–66. Guilford, Conn.: Dushkin Publishing Group.

Pospisil, L. J. 1956. Law among the Kapauku of Netherlands New Guinea. Ph.D. diss., Yale University, New Haven. University Microfilms, Ann Arbor.

Powell, J. M. 1982. Plant Resources and Paleobotanical Evidence for Plant Use in the Papua New Guinea Highlands. *Archaeology in Oceania* 17:28–37.

Price, B. J. 1982. Cultural Materialism: A Theoretical Review. *American Antiquity* 47:709–41.

Preucel, R. W., ed. 1991. *Processual and Postprocessual Archaeologies, Multiple Ways of Knowing the Past.* Carbondale: Center for Archaeological Investigations, Southern Illinois University.

Raglan, A. 1964. *The Temple and the House.* London: Routledge and Kegan Paul.

Rapoport, A. 1969. *House Form and Culture.* Englewood Cliffs, N.J.: Prentice-Hall.

Rappaport, R. A. 1984. *Pigs for the Ancestors, Ritual in the Ecology of a New Guinea People.* New Haven, Conn.: Yale University Press.

Reay, M. 1959. *The Kuma: Freedom and Conformity in the New Guinea Highlands.* Melbourne: Melbourne University Press.

Renfrew, C. 1977. Alternative Models for Exchange and Spatial Distribution. In *Exchange Systems in Prehistory,* edited by T. K. Earle and J. E. Ericson, pp. 71–90. New York: Academic Press.

——. 1987. *Archaeology and Language: The Puzzle of Indo-European Origins.* Cambridge: Cambridge University Press.

Richardson, D. 1977. *Lords of the Earth.* Ventura, Calif.: Regal Books.

Roberts, L. 1992. Anthropologists Climb (Gingerly) on Board. *Science* 258:1300–1301.

Rogers, S. L. 1976. *The Shaman's Healing Way.* Ramona, Calif.: Acoma Books.

Sahlins, M. 1963. Poor Man, Rich Man, Big Man, Chief: Political Types in Melanesia and Polynesia. *Comparative Studies in Society and History* 53:285–303.

Sargent, W. 1974. *People of the Valley.* New York: Random House.

Sauer, C. O. 1952. *Agriculture Origins and Dispersals.* New York: American Geographical Society.

Schick, K. D., and N. Toth. 1993. *Making Silent Stones Speak: Human Evolution and the Dawn of Technology.* New York: Simon and Schuster.

Schiffer, M. B. 1987. *Formation Processes of the Archaeological Record.* Albuquerque: University of New Mexico Press.

Semenov, S. A. 1964. *Prehistoric Technology.* London: Cory, Adams, and Mackay.

——. 1975. Model Stone Axes. In *Soviet Union* (7:304):39–41.

Semyonov, S. A. See Semenov.

Service, E. 1971. *Primitive Social Organization. An Evolutionary Perspective.* 2nd ed. New York: Random House.

Shih, X. 1992. The Discovery of the Pre-Yangshao Culture and Its Significance. In *Pacific Northeast Asia in Prehistory; Hunter-Fisher-Gatherers-Farmers, and Sociopolitical Elites,* edited by C. M. Aikens and S. N. Rhee, pp. 125–32. Pullman, Wash.: Washington State University Press.

Sillitoe, P. 1988. *Made in Niugini: Technology in the Highlands of Papua New Guinea.* London: British Museum Publications.

Silzer, J., and H. H. Clouse. 1991. Index of Irian Jaya Languages. *Irian: Bulletin of Irian Jaya.* Jayapura. Indonesia: University of Cenderawasih and the Summer Institute of Linguistics.

Snell, L. A. 1913. Eenige Gegevens Betreffende de Kennis der zeden, Gewoonten en taal der Pesechem van Centraal-Nieuw-Guinea. *Bull. 68 der Maatschappij ter Bevord. V.H. Natuwrk. Onderz. der Ned. Kolomien,* pp. 57–86, The Hague.

Sokal, R. R.; N. L. Oden; and C. Wilson. 1991. Genetic Evidence for the Spread of Agriculture in Europe by Demic Diffusion. *Nature* 351:143–45.

Solecki, R. S. 1971. *Shanidar, the First Flower People.* New York: Alfred A. Knopf.

Spindler, K. 1994. *The Man in the Ice.* New York: Harmony Books.

Spriggs, M. 1984. The Lapite Cultural Complex: Origins, Distribution, Contemporaries, and Successors. In *Out of Asia: Peopling the Americas and the Pacific,* edited by R. Kirk and E. Szathmary, pp. 202–23. Canberra: Journal of Pacific History.

Steensberg, A. 1980. *New Guinea Gardens.* New York: Academic Press.

——. 1986. *Man the Manipulator.* Copenhagen: National Museum of Denmark.

Stringer, C. B., and C. Gamble. 1993. *In Search of the Neanderthals: Solving the Puzzle of Human Origins.* New York: Thames and Hudson.

Thomas, J. 1991. *Rethinking the Neolithic.* Cambridge: Cambridge University Press.

Tilley, C. 1996. *An Ethnography of the Neolithic.* Cambridge: Cambridge University Press.

Torrence, R. 1986. *Production and Exchange of Stone Tools.* Cambridge: Cambridge University Press.

Toth, N.; D. Clark; and G. Ligabue. 1992. The Last Stone Ax Makers. *Scientific American* 267(1):88–93.

Troels-Smith, J. 1937. Beile aus dem Mesolithicum Danemarks. Ein Einteilungsversuch. *Acta Archaeologica* 8: 278–94.

Van Arsdale, P. W. 1993. *The Asmat, An Ethnography and Film Guide.* Englewood, Colo.: Center for Cultural Dynamics.

Van Gennep, A. 1960[1908]. *The Rites of Passage.* Chicago: University of Chicago Press.

Visser, W. A., and Hermes, J. J. 1962. *Geological Results of the Exploration for Oil in Netherlands New Guinea.* K. Ned. Geol. Mynbouwk. Genoot. Geol. Sr. 20, The Hague.

Von Staden, H. 1989. *Herophelus: The Art of Medicine in Early Alexandria.* Cambridge: Cambridge University Press.

Wa, Y. 1992. Neolithic Tradition in Northeast China. In *Pacific Northeast Asia in Prehistory; Hunter-Fisher-Gatherers-Farmers, and Sociopolitical Elites,* edited by C. M. Aikens and S. N. Rhee, pp. 139–56. Pullman, Wash.: Washington State University Press.

Wagner, R. 1967. *The Curse of Souw: Principles of Daribi Clan Definition and Alliance.* Chicago: University of Chicago Press.

Watson, J. B. 1967. Horticultural Tradition of the Eastern New Guinea Highlands. *Oceania* 38(2):81–98.

Watson, P. J. 1995. Archaeology, Anthropology, and the Culture Concept. *American Anthropologist* 97(4):683–94.

Welsch, R. L.; J. Terrell; and J. A. Nadolski. 1992. Language and Culture on the North Coast of New Guinea. *American Anthropologist* 94:568–99.

Welton, J. E. 1984. *SEM Petrology Atlas.* Tulsa, Okla.: American Association of Petroleum Geologists.

White, J. P. 1967a. Taim Bilong Bipo: Investigations Towards a Prehistory of the Papua–New Guinea Highlands. Ph.D. diss., Australian National University, Canberra.

———. 1967b. Ethno-Archaeology in New Guinea: Two Examples. *Mankind* 6(9): 409–14.

White, J. P., and J. F. O'Connell. 1982. *A Prehistory of Australia, New Guinea, and Sahul.* Sydney: Academic Press.

White, J. P., and D. H. Thomas. 1972. What Mean These Stones? Ethno-Toponomic Models Archaeological Interpretations New Guinea Highlands. In *Models in Archaeology,* edited by D. T. Clarke, pp. 275–308. London: Methuen.

White, J. P.; K. A. W. Crook; and B. P. Buxton. 1970. Kosipe: A Late Pleistocene Site in the Papuan Highlands. *Proceedings of the Prehistoric Society* 36:152–70.

Whittle, A. 1985. *Neolithic Europe: A Survey.* Cambridge: Cambridge University Press.

Wilk, R., and M. B. Schiffer. 1981. The Modern Material Culture Field School. In *Modern Material Culture: The Archaeology of Us,* edited by R. A. Gould and M. B. Schiffer, pp. 21–23. New York: Academic Press.

Wilson, F. 1981. *The Conquest of Copper Mountain.* New York: Atheneum.

Wilson, F. W. 1981. *Art as Revelation.* New York: Universe Books.

Wirz, P. 1924. Anthropologische and Ethnologische Ergebuisse der Central New-Guinea Expedition 1921–1922. *Nova Guinea* 14(1):148.

———. 1925. *In Herzen von New-Guinea Tagebuck einer Reise ins Innere von Hollandisch New-Guinea.* Zurich.

Wright, K. 1992. A Classification System for Ground Stone Tools from the Prehistoric Levant. *Paleorient* 18/2:53–81.

Yan, W. 1992. Origins of Agriculture and Animal Husbandry in China. In *Pacific Northeast Asia In Prehistory; Hunter-Fisher-Gatherers-Farmers, and Sociopolitical Elites,* edited by C. M. Aikens and S. N. Rhee, pp. 113–24. Pullman, Wash.: Washington State University Press.

Yellen, J. E. 1977. *Archaeological Approaches to the Present.* New York: Academic Press.

Pages containing illustrations appear in italics.

128; and personal items, 135; and power of spirit, 156–60; profane vs. sacred use of space, 131; rites of passage, 18–19; summary of, 291–92; and surrounding environment, 42–49. *See also* sociopolitical structures; spiritual beliefs/practices

cutting tools, adze vs. other tools, 53, 68, 295–96. *See also* knives

Dagai hamlet, 221–22

Dagai River, 221–22

Damal language group, 9

dancing, 32

Dani language groups: control of Tagime quarry, 243; dress and adornment of, *12, 14, 16*; housing design, 131, 133; resources of, 237; and string necklaces, 41; summary of, 9–10; trade network role, 287–88; as warriors, 29–30; weaving technique, 40; and Yali, 287

death: causes of, 130, 224; rituals surrounding, 18–21, 114–21, plate 2. *See also* ghosts and spirits

decoration: adze blades, 87; display-exchange stones, *107, 108,* 109–13, *114,* 212–15, *217,* 294; for sacred bands, 115, 116, 196; sacred stones, *126,* 152. *See also* dress and adornment

Diamond, Jared, 8

Diarindo quarry, 233

dibat (string necklaces), 41, 42, 179–80, 198

digging sticks, importance of, 33

display-exchange bands, 40, *105,* 141, 280

display-exchange stones: cultural system role, 292, 293–94; decoration of, *107, 108,* 109–13, *114,* 212–15, *217, 294*; as durable symbols of wealth, 104, 294–95; funeral display and distribution, 18, 114–21; manufacture of, 236–37, *238*; quarry sources, 233, 234; as sculpted art, 31; as source for sacred stones, 125; structure and nomenclature, 104–106, *107, 109*; uses, 114; valuation, 113–14; as war indemnity payments, 102, 104, 121–22, 293

district, 293

division of labor by gender, 40–41

dogs, societal role of, 26–27

Dow, D. B., 46

dress and adornment: arm bands, 31; dog products as, 27; male and female, 10–16, *17*, plate 2; necklaces, 41, 42, 45, 179–80, 198; Wali's, 139; of Wano people, 224

Dugum Dani neighborhood, 30, 287–88

Duvle language group, 9, 35, 223, 237, 239–40

ear excision, 21

earthquakes, 47, 227

East and Yali region. *See* Yali and East region

ebe akho ceremony, 101–102, 115, 121

ecology, and pressure to develop manipulative skills, 307

economic system, importance in stone tool culture, 300–301. *See also* trading network

edai-egen (soul matter), 14–15, 48, 158–59. *See also* spiritual beliefs/practices

Edmonds, M., 7

elevation, geographical, 5, 10

Eliade, Mircea, 21, 47–48

Elogor (spirit of quarry), 226

emotions, need for expression during sacred rituals, 167–68

empowerment of stones/stone tools, 41, 80–81, 126, 177–84, 212–14

Enarotali area, 42, 283

engineering activities, 5–6, 28–29, 245, 297–98

environment: overview of, 42–49; reaction vs. management response to, 7–8. *See also* contexts

etani (decoration). *See* decoration

ethnoarcheological approach, xvii–xviii

ethnography of Highlanders, xx

evil spirits, 48–49

evolutionary considerations, 4, 33

exchange transactions, 275–76. *See also* display-exchange stones; trading network

Ey River, 251, *253*

Faira quarry, 239–40

Faris, James, 31

farming, 7–8, 26–28, 307. *See also* horticulture

father's payment at marriage, 122–23

fauna of study area, 26–27, 44–45. *See also* pigs

feathers, sacred uses of, 144, 180, 198, 211

feet, agility of, 10

females: dress and adornment, 11, 14, *15–16, 17*, 40, plate 2; gardening role, 26; ghosts/spirits of, 48, 130; as healers, 193–98; quarrying support role, 234, 235, 264–65; religious role of, 21, 139, 168; restriction on ritual participation, 22, 128, 139, 156, 301; role in stone tool manufacture, 299–300; sacred objects

Gutelu Mabel, 145–46
Gutelu salt pool, 287–88

haft of adzes, 53–54, 72–76, 88
Hallowell, Irving, 48
Hamilton, Warren, 46
hamlets and compounds. *See* compounds and hamlets
hammerstones: and food preparation, 135; profane uses of, 81, 93, 292; and tool manufacturing process, 227, 228, 233, 234, 260–63, 266–67, 269
hand-foot loom technique, 40
handles, power stones with, 200–12
handstones, mobile grinding, 93, 95, 97
hardness, as major distinction in quarrying stone, 244
harp, reed mouth, 32, *33*, 79, *81*
Harrar, Heinrich, 221
Harris, Marvin, 30
Hartono, H., 46
Haviland, W. A., 18
Hawkes, Christopher, xviii
Hayward, D. J., 224, 284
head-back carrying nets, 11, 14, 40, 202, *208*
headhunting, 21
health and healing: causes of death for Wano people, 224; healers, 17, 185; medical kits, 186–98, 303; practices/beliefs, 14–15, *16*, 17; and string necklaces, 41
heat and fracture technique for quarrying, 227, 228, 229–30, 232
heavenly bodies, beliefs about, 49, 203, 206, 208–12, 301–302
Heider, Karl G.: axe uses, 60; cowrie shell uses, 280; Dani warriors, 30; forest depletion, 286; and gender identification of stones, 294; on health beliefs of Dugum Dani, 14–15; pulu blades, 77; rites of passage, 119, 120; social significance of stones, 105; sociopolitical framework, 100, 101, 102; stone qualities, 241; sun worship, 203, 206, 209
hematite, as trade good, 280–81
Hermes, J. J., 46
hierophanies, 47–48, 292
Highlands, New Guinea: and horticulture developments, 5; isolation of people, xx; language groupings, 8–10; summary of culture, 291–92

Hiroa, T. R., 54
holism, importance in ethnographic work, 291
holy water, 141
Hope, J. H. and G. S., 3
horticulture: archeological evidence for, 26, *27*; developments in, 4–5; garden work, *13*, *24*; overview of, 24, 25, 26–27, *28, 29*; stone tools for, 26
hosting of spirits, 48
house clusters, 28, 103, 293. *See also* compounds and hamlets
houses, organization and construction of, 28–29, 101, 103–104, 128, 252, 254, 293. *See also* compounds and hamlets; sacred houses
human relics. *See* relics, human
hunter-gatherer society, 3, 8
hunting, dogs in, 27
Huon, 4
Hupla language group, 9

Igwi quarry, 232–33
Ilaga, and trading network, 283–84
incense and healing rituals, 194
indemnity payments, sacred stones as, 102, 104, 121–22, 293
Indonesia, and study area, 5
initiation ceremonies, boys, 41, 115, 128
injuries, quarrying, 230
insects, 45
Interpreting the Axe Trade: Production and Exchange in Neolithic Britain (Bradley and Edmonds), 7
Irian Jaya Highlands: as segmentary society, 8; tool uses, 295
Irian Jaya Province, 5

jawbones. *See* mandibles
Jaya Crest, 42
je/jao (display-exchange stones). *See* display-exchange stones
Jiwiki, sacred compound at, 146–60

Kaeppler, A., 32
Kamu Valley, 42
Kapauku people, 42
Kembelangan formation, 46
kembu (evil spirits), 48–49
Kimyal language group, 9, 198–99
kinship ties, 100

Klein, R., 6
knapping of stone tools: process of, 235; skills
    in, 68, 262–63, *265, 266–69, 270–72,* 299
knives: bamboo, 33, 296; bone, 36, 76–77, 296;
    raw material sources for, 299; sacred uses of,
    141, 170; stone, 34, 55, *79,* 88–92, 273–74; types
    of, 292
Koch, K. F., 101, 103, 128, 137, 289
Konda Valley–Bokondini Area, and trading
    network, 284–85
Kosipe, 4
Kroneman, Dick and Margaret, 252
Kudaris Tengganag quarry, 233
Kuk, 4
Kula trade ring, 275
Kurima area, trading network in, 288

labor force for manufacture of stone tools,
    230–32, 256–57, 258–65, 299
ladder of reliability, xviii
lakes and rivers, 45, 221–22, *224,* 251, *253*
landscape. *See* geographic setting
Langda-Sela area quarries: adze blades/tools of,
    63, *72–76,* 83–87; as center for quarrying, 297,
    298–99; geographic setting, 251–52, *253, 254, 255,*
    256; geologic setting, 252; leadership of, 255–56;
    and lithology of tool sources, 55–59, 292–93;
    manufacturing process, 257–74; market for, 257;
    methods and rock type, 256; ownership issue,
    254–55; rituals at, 257; skilled workers of, 256–
    57; trading network in, 251, 289–90
language boundaries/cultural markers, *52,* 293,
    306–307
language groups: Duvle, 9, 35, 223, 237, 239–40;
    Kimyal, 9, 198–99; sharing of stone tool
    manufacturing production, 297; structure
    and distribution of, 8–10; Wano, 35, 222, 224,
    297. *See also* Dani language groups; Una
    language group; Yali language group
Larson, G. F., 9, 30, 48, 102, 121–22, 123, 283–84
Law of Monotonic decrement, 306
leadership, societal: male dominance of, 22, 24;
    quarrying operations, 235, 254–56; and
    warfare, 101, 185–86. *See also* big men
life expectancy, 10
Ligabue, Giancarlo, 252
limestone, 45–46
linguistic boundaries/cultural markers, *52,* 293,
    306–307. *See also* language groups

liru (string-handled power stones), 200–12
lithology of stones: display-exchange stones,
    106, 108–109; and profane uses of stone
    tools, 51–52, 55–59, 292–93; and Yeineri
    quarry, 225–26
loft-style sleeping quarters, 133–34
Lomax, A., 32
looms: lack of, 33; weaving and braiding, 10, 31,
    38–42, 215, *217*
Lowendorf, Larry, 48
Lukuluku sun house, 208, 211–12

McGregor, Roberta, 305
males: dress and adornment, 10–11, *12–13;*
    handling of sacred stones, 127–28; as societal
    leaders, 22, 24; weaving by, 40. *See also* big
    men
Malinowski, B., 275, 291
mandibles: human, 153–54, 305, plate 8; pig, 143,
    147–48, plate 7
manipulation of spirits/ghosts. *See* ghosts and
    spirits
Man Makes Himself (Childe), 7
Man the Manipulator (Steensberg), 54
manufacture of tools: and hammerstones, 227,
    228, 233, 234, 260–63, 266–67, 269; labor
    force, 230–32, 256–57, 258–65, 299; overview
    of techniques, 297–300; quarrying opera-
    tions, 59, 106, 226–27, 235–37, *238,* 244–49,
    257–74, 292
marriage: bride's skirt, *16;* and decoration of
    display-exchange stones, 111–13; and *ebe
    akho* ceremony, 121; importance of, 18;
    wealth transfer in, 122–23; weddings, 41
marsupials, 45
"mass killings" of pigs, 28
material supports for religious belief, 292
Matthiesson, P., xix
Mead, Margaret, xx
medical practices. *See* health and healing
medicinal plants, 17
Medlin, Elizabeth A., 57, 252
Mellaart, James, 7
men. *See* males
Meneses, 251
"men's house," 128
Mesolithic. *See* Neolithic era
metamorphic rock, as tool source, 292
methodology, xx–xxi, 55–59

role, 100, 129, 161, 185, 209, 211; boards, 213, *216;* circular ground stone disks, 215, 217, *218–19;* empowerment of, 41, 42, 80–81, 126, 170, 177–84, 212–14; feathers, 144, 180, 198, 211; ferns, 143, 169, 179, plate 7; flow to profane use, 305–306; foods as, 162, 165–67, 173–77; introduction, 123–27; knives as, 141, 170; meaning and usage, 301–305; ownership issues, 127–28; personal power uses for, 198–212; *puluen* stone, 105–106, 140, 148, 160–61, 184–85, plate 7; and quarrying sources, 225; ritual uses of, 18; social uses of, 185–215; sociopolitical factors in storage of, 128–29; and stone trade, 293; string necklaces, 41, 42, 179–80, 198; as war indemnity payments, 102, 104, 121–22, 293. *See also ganekhe* cabinet; *ganekhe* objects; pigs

sacrificial rituals: ancestor worship, 20–22, 159; finger/joint amputation, 6, 21, 22, 23, plate 2; pigs, 21–22, 162, 166, 167–70, 211, 257

Sahlins, 24

Sahul continent, 3, 44

sali (girl's skirt), 111–13

sali-wood amulets, 203

salt resources: brine pools, 47, 146, 211; as trade good, 280, *281,* 284, 286

sandstone grinding slabs, techniques for using, 296–97

sea shells, 115, 116, 196, 278–80, 282

secret rituals, 100

seen and unseen worlds, 19–21, 125, 292, 294, 301. *See also* spiritual beliefs/practices

segmentary (farmers/herders) society, 8, 291

Sela area. *See* Langda-Sela area

Service, Elman, 8

shamans: big men as, 24; dancing as entrance to trance, 32; empowerment of objects by, 41, 212; as healers, 17; *puluen* stone ritual, 148–49; role of, 292; and symbolic stone usage, 100

shells, 115, 116, 196, 278–80, 282

shelters: at quarry sites, 235, 300. *See also* houses

sie/siengga (display-exchange stones). *See* display-exchange stones

Silimo language group, 9

Silzer, J., 8

singing, 31–32

size of tools, and uses, 295

Sjam, Sjamsuarni, xix

skirts, *16,* 110–13

skulls as relics of power, 257

sleeping quarters, loft-style, 133–34

slicing and cutting tools, adzes as, 53, 68, 295–96. *See also* knives

smoke inhalation, and housing design, 133

snakes, healing uses of, 192

societies, classification system for, 8

sociopolitical structures: Grand Valley and West region, 28–29, 101, 102, 128, 293; overview, 100–104, 293; and polygyny, 17; power stones' role in, 185–215; storage of profane and sacred objects, 128–29; trading network, 275–76, 300–301; warrior culture, 5, 29–30; Yali and East region, 101, 128, 293. *See also* big men; cultural system; gender dichotomies; warfare

sorcery, and death, 130

soul, beliefs about, 14–16, 48, 158–59. *See also* spiritual beliefs/practices

space, profane and sacred. *See* houses

spalling of rock, 232

spears, 30

Spencer, Herbert, 301

spiders, 45

"spirit bones," 21

spirit enclosure, and healing rituals, 186

spirit installation, 303–305

spirits and ghosts. *See* ghosts and spirits

spirit sticks, 257

spiritual beliefs/practices: adornment as expression of, 11, 14; and artistic work, 30–31; belief system overview, 19–21; cosmology, 49, 203, 206, 208–12, 301–302; death, 18–21, 20, 114–21, 130, 224, plate 2; healing beliefs/practices, 14–15; men's responsibilities, 100–101; and quarrying operation, 226, 257; sacredness of environment, 48–49; soul beliefs, 14–16, 48, 158–59; and unseen world, 19–21, 125, 292, 294, 301. *See also* ancestor worship; ghosts and spirits; rituals; sacred houses; sacred objects

stars, significance of, 49

state society, 8

stationary grinding slabs, 93–97, 296–97

stature of study group, 10

steam bundles, building of, 165–66, 174

Steele, D. Gentry, 105

warfare: Dani reputation for, 29–30; and political leadership, 101, 185–86; and quarrying operations, 245; rituals surrounding, 18, 162–63, 183–84; "ritual warfare" as variation on human sacrifice, 21; sacred stones' role in, 102, 104, 121–22, 293; and trade disruption, 287; trophies from, 135–36, 142

waro leget (ghost-spirit enclosures), 19

warriors. *See* warfare

watchtowers, 29

water, and grinding process, 93–94

water control ditches, 4

watercraft, and migrations to Southeast Asian islands, 3

water snakes, healing uses of, 192

wealth: display-exchange stones as symbols of, 104, 294–95; importance in societal leadership, 22; pigs as symbols of, 17, 286, 294; transfer during marriage ceremonies, 122–23

weapons, 12, 30, 33, 142, 145

weather and climate, 42–44, 227

weaving and braiding, 10, 31, 33, 38–42, 215, 217

weddings. *See* marriage

wedges, and quarrying process, 234

Western Dani language group, 9. *See also* Dani language groups

West region. *See* Grand Valley and West region

What Happened in History (Childe), 7

White, J. P., 280

witchcraft, 48

women. *See* females

wooden objects, 26, 33–34, 203

work parties for tool manufacture, 230–32, 256–57, 258–65

woven string handles, power stones with, 200–212

Yali and East region: decoration of display-exchange stones, 109; housing, 29, 101, 136–37; red ochre deposits in, 281; social structures, 101, 128, 293; stone tools of, 56, 82–93; trading network, 287–90

Yali language group: and Dani, 287; dress and adornment, 11, 13, 14, 17; overview, 9; stone vs. bone tools, 36, 38; weaving techniques, 40

Yalogon compound, 137–45

Yan, Wen-ming, 7

Yeineri: adze blades of, 63, 64, 66–72; adze tools of, 72–76; axes of, 62–63; and lithology of tool sources, 292–93; quality of blades vs. Tagime, 244; as quarrying-manufacture center, 59, 106, 297; and trading network, 284

Yeineri quarries: geographic setting, 221–23; geologic setting, 224–25; manufacturing process, 226–27, 235–37; ownership issue, 227–28, 237, 239–40; site descriptions, 228–35; stone tools types, 225–26; Wano people, 224

Ye River, 221–22, 224

Yuku, 4